PRAISE FOR AMERICAN TROJAN

"In this gripping memoir, American Trojan, former USC President Max Nikias charts his remarkable odyssey from a small village in Cyprus to the presidency of the University of Southern California, when the campus rose to be ranked among the nation's top universities. He has lived through the British occupation of Cyprus, the Turkish invasion of the island, the various Greek coups of the 1970s, his own near penniless arrival in America, a meteoric rise as a newly hired engineering professor to the president of the university—all culminating in a fascinating final dissection of the woke hysterias of recent years that have done so much damage to higher education, and to those few who sought so bravely to resist the madness."

VICTOR DAVIS HANSON
The Hoover Institution, Stanford University;
Author, The Dying Citizen

"A tremendous read! An inspiring account of how a brilliant young engineer from Cyprus came to embody the American dream. Max Nikias's journey from immigrant scholar to president of the University of Southern California is a testament to his extraordinary vision, unshakable character, and exceptional leadership. American Trojan captures his infectious enthusiasm, his transformative impact on higher education, and his enduring devotion to the Trojan Family. A remarkable life, told with clarity, conviction, and heart."

GENERAL DAVID PETRAEUS
US Army (Ret.); former Commander of the Surge in Iraq, US Central Command, and Coalition Forces in Afghanistan; former Director of the CIA; co-author of the New York Times bestseller
Conflict: The Evolution of Warfare from 1945 to Gaza.

"Max Nikias is a fantastic leader and a great friend. His story is the embodiment of the American Dream. He came from Cyprus with nothing but a brilliant mind and a strong work ethic, and used both to build a life of purpose, vision, and results. At USC, he didn't just lead, he transformed the place. The rankings, the endowment, the reputation of the entire university skyrocketed under his watch. In American Trojan, Max shows what real leadership looks like. These are lessons anyone can use if they want to be useful and make a difference."

ARNOLD SCHWARZENEGGER
38th Governor of California

PRAISE FOR AMERICAN TROJAN

"This memoir is the story of the American dream. Max Nikias arrived here with nothing but smarts and charm from his old world, home country, which was in the midst of a terrible war. Here, he raised a beautiful family, contributed to our national security through his scientific research, and achieved the pinnacle of academic success as president of USC. Max's story is an inspiring read."

Robert C. O'Brien
27th US National Security Advisor

"From humble beginnings in war-ravaged Cyprus, to the leadership helm of USC, American Trojan is Max Nikias' odyssey of resilience, vision, and discovery. A disciple of leadership, Max navigates through the shoals of challenge with courage, intellect, and unshakable optimism. This compelling memoir is more than Max's story—it is a testament to the power of education, the fiery immigrant spirit, and the pursuit of excellence."

Arthur Dimopoulos
Executive Director of the National Hellenic Society

"American Trojan is a powerful and inspiring story of loss, perseverance, and leadership. As a fellow Cypriot, I was deeply moved by Max Nikias's journey—from the tragedy of losing everything during the invasion of Cyprus to rising as a transformative figure in American higher education. His story is not only a testament to the strength of the immigrant spirit but also a blueprint for bold and principled leadership in challenging times. This book offers not only a personal story of resilience but also important insights into the challenges and possibilities facing universities today."

Kyriacos Papastylianou
President, Federation of Cypriot American Organizations

"The pantheon of Greek epics has a new entry—American Trojan. Max Nikias' journey begins in the unlikeliest of places, a small mountainous village on the island of Cyprus and becomes a hero's journey in short order. In part a story of immigrant success, in part of first-hand account of events and trends that shaped America, this book is an invaluable guide during this tipping point in American history."

Endy Zemenides
Executive Director, Hellenic American Leadership Council

AMERICAN TROJAN

AMERICAN TROJAN

LEADERSHIP, RESILIENCE, AND THE RENEWAL OF HIGHER EDUCATION

C. L. Max Nikias

New York • London

First American edition published in 2026 by Encounter Books, an activity of Encounter for Culture and Education, Inc., a nonprofit, tax exempt corporation.
Encounter Books website address: www.encounterbooks.com

Manufactured in Canada and printed on acid-free paper. The paper used in this publication meets the minimum requirements of ANSI/NISO Z39.48–1992 (R 1997) (*Permanence of Paper*).

FIRST AMERICAN EDITION

LIBRARY OF CONGRESS CATALOGING-IN-PUBLICATION DATA IS AVAILABLE

Information for this title can be found at the Library of Congress website under the following ISBN 978-1-64177-493-2.

Table of Contents

Prologue *page* 1

PART ONE
CYPRUS AND GREECE YEARS

1. The Troubled Island *page* 7
2. Beach Town *page* 23
3. Coming of Age *page* 35
4. Army Training *page* 45
5. Refugees *page* 57

PART TWO
IMMIGRATING TO THE UNITED STATES

6. America America *page* 75
7. Perseverance *page* 89
8. Through the Wilderness *page* 99

PART THREE
EARLY ACADEMIC CAREER

9. Second Homecoming *page* 111
10. The Fall and the Rise *page* 121
11. The Human Element in Tech Progress *page* 135
12. Back to the Roots *page* 147

PART FOUR
THE RISE OF USC

13. Act With Intention *page* 163
14. Seize the Moment *page* 179
15. Sea of Change *page* 193
16. Being Tested *page* 207

17. In the Eye of the Storm *page* 219

18. Catalysts of Change *page* 235

19. Pinnacle of Leadership *page* 249

20. Successes and Embarrassment *page* 265

21. Learner Centric *page* 281

22. Confronting Tragedy *page* 291

23. The Gothic Revival *page* 301

24. The Rise of Hecuba *page* 317

25. Invaluable Asset *page* 325

26. Relentless Planning *page* 335

27. The Campaign *page* 353

Part Five

THE FUTURE OF HIGHER EDUCATION

28. Enduring Harsh NCAA Penalties *page* 371

29. Endless Adventures *page* 385

30. In the Spotlight *page* 401

31. Stormy Waters *page* 417

32. Gradually, Then Suddenly *page* 429

33. Is There Any Hope? *page* 443

Epilogue *page* 463

Acknowledgements *page* 469

Awards and Honors *page* 471

National Academies 471

Awards 471

Honorary Degrees 472

Technical Awards & Recognitions 472

Undergraduate Scholarship 473

Presidential Accomplishments (2009–2018) 473

About the Author *page* 475

Endnotes *page* 477

Index *page* 529

«ἐὰν μὴ ἔλπηται ἀνέλπιστον οὐκ ἐξευρήσει,
ἀνεξερεύνητον ἐὸν καὶ ἄπορον»

ΉΡΆΚΛΕΙΤΟΣ, «Ό ΛΌΓΟΣ ΚΑΊ ΤΌ ΈΝ», ΆΠΌΣΠΑΣΜΑ 18

"If you do not expect the unexpected, you will not find it, for it is hard to be sought out and difficult."

HERACLITUS, FRAGMENT 18

For Niki

Ἐπεὶ περίεσσι γυναικῶν εἶδός τε μέγεθός τε ἰδὲ φρένας ἔνδον ἐΐσας

Epei periessi gynaikon eidos te megethos te ide phrenas endon eisas

Prologue

As I looked out at the crowd gathered for my inauguration as the 11th President of the University of Southern California, I reflected on the long journey that had led me to this moment.

Decades after my wife and I arrived in the United States, it seemed that our American Dream had come true. Observing the joyous faces of more than 10,000 people, this assembly dwarfed the tiny village of fewer than 1,000 residents where I'd been born.

A wave of joy and gratitude rose up in me as I thought of my parents and the many teachers and mentors whose support and encouragement had shaped and inspired me along the way.

On that day, I carried their hopes and dreams, along with the weight of the expectations and responsibilities that come from being an immigrant who has made the great voyage to pursue a new life in America.

I always admired this country's enduring values and principles, which were built on the democratic ideals of Western Civilization and my own Greek heritage—freedom, equality, and justice. And I still believe in American exceptionalism, the idea that this country has a unique role to play as a shining example for the rest of the world.

As the platform party processed into Alumni Park, I thought of my personal family, who had suffered greatly when we lost our home and became refugees during the Turkish invasion of 1974. I remembered the sadness and anger my wife and daughters felt when we were finally allowed back into the village in 2003. There we saw the crumbled cross that marked my grandfather's grave, a historical remnant of the looting and the vandalism from nearly three decades earlier.

I looked out with gratitude at my beautiful wife, Niki, the proud mother of our wonderful daughters, Georgiana and Maria, who ensured that our family would be part of the Trojan Family.

And I thought that my family is no different from the families of tens of millions of immigrants and refugees around the world, whose lives have been permanently uprooted by the tumultuous tides of history. For those who share our story, we all understand what it is like to be the underdog, to start with nothing, to lose everything, and then rebuild it all again.

My life is part of that great symphony, and my fate is interconnected with all those who have shared the voyage. It has taken me from that small island to the far reaches of the world, through times of tragedy and triumph, through pioneering periods of science and technology, discovering extraordinary new territory in the field of engineering, and through exciting and turbulent periods of academic leadership.

I am humbled by the many people who worked tirelessly to create supportive environments for the creation of new knowledge and to provide greater educational opportunities for students from all walks of life. All of these efforts added to the nation's economic and technological achievements, strengthening our commitment to American competitiveness.

As I walked to the podium to deliver my inaugural address, I wondered why I had been so fortunate.

At that moment, I couldn't have known how rapidly we would elevate USC, leading it to become one of the most selective and competitive research universities in the nation. I couldn't have imagined how quickly we would physically transform the entire university, the amount of work required in the ever-changing landscape of collegiate athletics, or that we would conduct one of the most successful fundraising campaigns in the history of higher education.

And yet, along with all of our accomplishments, I also couldn't have predicted the road ahead. I couldn't comprehend the challenges or the headlines that would emerge from the actions of a dean of the medical school, or a gynecologist in the student health center who had been hired by USC before I arrived at the university.

I wouldn't have believed that in the court of public opinion so-called "justice" would all too often be determined by the media and social media, which, in my opinion, reflected the views of those who rushed to judgment and refused to accept any evidence that didn't fit into their personal or activist agendas.

I also couldn't have foreseen the undercurrent of microaggressions, trigger warnings, safe spaces, cancel culture, and the mob mentality that would increase the divisions and shake the foundation of higher education.

And I couldn't have predicted that after I stepped down as president, these forces would suddenly explode in the chaos we have seen on college campuses across the nation.

Higher education has reached a crossroads. The nation's most prestigious, elite universities have lost their luster, facing charges of antisemitism and dealing with pro-Palestinian and pro-Hamas protests, encampments, and activist faculty and students who are aligned against their own institutions.

The question is, "Can universities save themselves and, therefore, save American exceptionalism?"

* * *

From the day we landed in the U.S., and for the 46 years that have passed since that time, I have dedicated my life and career to American higher education.

In every position I held—from faculty member to center director to dean to provost to president—I always looked after the highest interests of the university's students, staff, and faculty.

Through my research and academic leadership, I also looked after the highest interests of this nation via projects that have advanced national defense and technological competitiveness.

Although it breaks my heart to see the state of higher education today, I still believe in the American Dream. And I still want to believe that there are ways and means built into American society to overcome the lapses.

For me and my family, and our American experience, I am eternally grateful for the entire voyage. To convey why, I need to start the story at the very beginning.

PART ONE

CYPRUS AND GREECE YEARS

CHAPTER 1

The Troubled Island

«ὅπη νεὼς στείλαιμ' ἂν οὔριον πτερὸν
εἰς γῆν ἐναλίαν Κύπρον, οὗ μ' ἐθέσπισεν
οἰκεῖν 'Απόλλων, ὄνομα νησιωτικὸν
Σαλαμῖνα θέμενον τῆς ἐκεῖ χάριν πάτρας.»

ΈΎΡΙΠΊΔΟΥ ΈΛΈΝΗ, 147–150

"Whereby to steer my galley's prosperous wing
To sea-girt Cyprus, where Apollo bade
That I should dwell, and, for the homeland's sake,
Give it the island-name of Salamis."[1]

EURIPIDES, *HELEN*, LINES 147–150

I was five the night British soldiers came to our house unannounced, demanding to enter our bedrooms to find out what we were learning in class.

I hadn't started school yet, but my sister, Maroula, who was three years older, was in elementary school. I remember sitting on the bed watching the British soldier take all of the notebooks out of my sister's briefcase, looking for anything "Greek."

It was a tense moment because our next-door neighbors had experienced the same treatment. When a solider discovered the daughter had drawn an image of the Greek flag in her notebook, the father was arrested and sent to jail for six months. Fortunately, for us, the soldiers didn't find anything and for at least one night we could collectively breathe a sigh of relief.

Throughout my life, I have always believed that to understand a person's complete journey, you must understand the context and culture that shaped their early experiences.

Although I later traveled to distant regions of the globe, collaborating with some of the world's most brilliant minds and leading one of America's most prestigious academic institutions, in many ways I am still the boy who grew up on the island of Cyprus—filled with optimism and bursting with curiosity.

I entered the world on a warm fall afternoon in 1952 in the picturesque village of Komi Kebir on the Karpas Peninsula of Cyprus, a small island country in the Eastern Mediterranean. Dating back to classical antiquity, Cyprus was internationally renowned for the rich deposits that emerged from its copper mines.

According to mythology, after the Trojan War, the Greek hero Teucer settled down in Cyprus and called his city Salamis in memory of his old island home.

The village where I grew up was only about 20 miles from the ancient ruins of Salamis, and I always felt that there were thousands of years of history all around me.

❊ ❊ ❊

I have often said that the island some call "the unsinkable aircraft carrier in the Eastern Mediterranean" has had many landlords.[2] Because of its prime location on the global map, the island spent hundreds of years as a pawn in a game of global domination, changing hands from the Greeks, Phoenicians, Assyrians, Persians, Romans, Byzantines, Crusaders, Venetians, and many others. For example, Richard the Lionheart conquered the island on his way to the Holy Land, and then sold it to the Franks. [3]

By the time I was born, the latest landlord was the British. The crown had been handed to Cyprus as part of a deal in 1878 during the decline of the Turkish Ottoman Empire. In 1925, the island was recognized as a crown colony.

I was too young to know it at the time, but the deal which was sealed nearly 75 years before my birth would have a dramatic impact on my life and my family.

When I was growing up, the population was nearly 80 percent Greek Cypriots, 18 percent Turkish Cypriots, with around 2 percent Armenians and Maronites.

Over the centuries, the Church of Cyprus, founded by Apostles Paul and Barnabas, had become very wealthy thanks to the generosity of faithful philanthropists. When the British took over the island, it was the Church that primarily invested in education as a way to pass Hellenic values and traditions on to future generations.

The Church created the Gymnasia, a set of specialized schools in each town in Cyprus and recruited the best teachers from Greece. On March 25th—which is the equivalent of July 4th in America—the teachers would tell Greek Cypriot students, "This is a national holiday, you should go home." When the British were celebrating a national holiday, the teachers would say, "You're Greeks. This is not your holiday. You're not British."

As you can imagine, this didn't go over very well. At one point, the tensions escalated to the point that the British rounded up all of the Church's chosen teachers and shipped them back to Greece.[4]

The Colonial Government "was seeing the educational problem from the viewpoint that the schools should help create the Cyprus nation and drop anything that would link the people emotionally to foreign countries."[5] The constant tension over preserving Hellenic identity and culture placed the Orthodox Church and the British Colonial government on a collision course.

In 1950, two years before I was born, the Church organized a referendum for the people of Cyprus to vote on *enosis*, a union with Greece. It was approved overwhelmingly, with 96 percent of the population voting in favor of it.[6]

To gain greater control, in 1954, Britain announced plans to move its Middle East military headquarters to Cyprus.[7] At one point, anyone who published what the colonial government considered "seditious literature" faced the extreme penalty of up to two years in prison.[8]

Seeing no other alternative to protect their heritage and tradition, the Church worked with the Greek government to fund a military organization called Ethniki Organosis Kyprion Agoniston (EOKA), which translates to the National Organization of Cypriot Fighters.

To evict the British from the island, the EOKA attacked police stations, military outposts, and even the homes of colonial officials.[9] However, the British were equally determined to crush the EOKA movement, creating detention camps to hold those they believed were involved.[10]

This led to a four-year struggle, with tremendous violence taking place on both sides.

Although times have changed dramatically since the 1950s, it was in the tense environment of the anti-colonial struggle that I would spend the first eight years of my life.

* * *

I was only eight years old when the first winds of change began to blow.

One night a strange man knocked on our front door. He wanted to talk to my father right away, insisting they speak privately at the local coffee shop. I didn't know it then, but that conversation would be the first domino in a series of events that would change the course of my entire life.

The man turned out to be a real estate developer from Famagusta, a beach city that served as the main port for the island of Cyprus. He had heard that my father was a skilled carpenter. And he spun a story about the endless opportunities awaiting my dad, telling him this was the perfect moment to get in on the ground floor of gorgeous new hotels, apartments, and condos that would soon put the beach city on the global map.

They talked about prospects and possibilities for two hours. When my father returned home, he had a smile on his face and a vision forming in his mind.

To my father, the vibrant life of the city must have stood in sharp contrast to the sleepy village of Komi Kebir. He imagined a new world where jobs were plentiful and business was booming. He could also imagine finally having freedom from the shadow of his prominent and successful father-in-law.

But for now, the village was his life. And the tensions of the anti-colonial struggle were all around us. Throughout my childhood, British soldiers were a persistent presence in my village. I was accustomed to seeing them in their tan uniforms and black berets, but because of EOKA they had taken on a more antagonistic approach.

On the road to Famagusta and other nearby villages, they now manned roadblocks, checkpoints, and bus stops, where they would make people line up so they could search their pockets for guns, bombs, or whatever. There were curfews in the village almost every evening.

Most of the soldiers were generally polite. One evening, they even provided my father with a personal escort when he needed to deliver medicine to a relative.

But other memories linger in my mind of the apprehension and uncertainty of growing up. I remember being with my father in his workshop when a British soldier punched my dad in the stomach for no reason. To this day, I don't know why he did it, but I can still feel the anger, humiliation, and the helplessness.

I recall the fear too. When I was only four years old, I remember approaching a checkpoint with my father, seeing the imposing soldiers who noticed I was literally shaking. They may have thought I was afraid of them, but I truly feared them finding the tiny water pistol hidden in my pocket. I believed that if they found it, both my father and I could have been in serious trouble. Fortunately, they let us through the checkpoint without a thorough search and I stopped trembling.

A year later, when I was five, our family had another close call. The British colonial government issued an executive decree that schools on Cyprus were no longer allowed to teach anything about EOKA or Greece. That's when British soldiers showed up to our house, searching for anything "Greek."

❋ ❋ ❋

As was common in a tiny village of barely a thousand people with only one doctor, I was delivered by a mid-wife in our family home. Growing up, I heard the story of my older sister, Maroula, who developed an infection as a baby and the family feared she may not live.

Fortunately, my arrival into the world was much smoother, and I joined a bustling household that consisted of my older sister, my parents—Loizos and Georgoula—along with my maternal grandfather.

We didn't have many of the modern conveniences that most families take for granted today. Forget about a car or TV. We didn't have electricity, a phone, or even running water.

In fact, if we needed water, we had to draw it from a local fountain. Several times a week, we would walk to the local square and wait in line with the other villagers.

Nevertheless, by village standards, we were considered upper-middle class. We had a battery-charged radio, a clay oven, and a two-story house!

❋ ❋ ❋

As a kid, I was inquisitive and had a natural sense of adventure. I was also fearless (except when it came to snakes. I was terrified of them, which was unfortunate because they seemed to be everywhere).

In those days I used to call the neighborhood kids together to play soccer—making a few mistakes in judgement along the way. One day after my father saw me play, he pulled me aside and scolded me, "I noticed you made the rules, and then changed them in the middle of the game to your advantage." It was an important lesson: *You always play by the rules.*

One day my heightened sense of self met a strong wave of humility when I thought I could beat-up a boy three years older than me. Big mistake. Our Turkish Cypriot barber ran out of his shop to save me and took me home. It might have been exactly what was needed to soften any illusions of heightened self-importance.

But looking back, it was also a significant act of kindness from a man who didn't share my Greek heritage. It was a reminder that we all have a shared humanity, and I'm grateful that he helped save me from myself.

My pride took another hit when it came to a rather awkward problem. I may have been fast at learning arithmetic, but I was slow at potty training. Even in first grade, I had embarrassing "wet" accidents.

* * *

I was fortunate to grow up in a family that consisted of a long line of leaders.

My mother's father, Loizos Habeshi, served as the "common leader," the equivalent of the mayor of the village. In fact, my mother's side of the family was renowned throughout the Karpas Peninsula because my grandfather, great grandfather, and great-great-grandfather had all been "common leaders."

My grandfather from my father's side was a man of many talents. He worked as an elementary school teacher, a public works supervisor, and even ran some coffee shops. He lived to the ripe old age of 90—quite an accomplishment in a village with no medical facilities!

I'm proud to carry his first name "Chrysostomos" for something else he passed on to me—a lifelong love of history.

When I later graduated from high school, I quietly thanked my grandfather when I received an award as the "best student" in history class.

Despite the positive impact he had on many people, Chrysostomos had one significant personality flaw. He couldn't hold a job very long because he often quarreled with his supervisors. My dad constantly reminded me that there was a lesson to be learned there: show self-restraint and don't let anger blind your decisions.

* * *

Thankfully, I also grew up in a home that was a laboratory for my inquisitive mind, and I quickly became a virtual sponge. Since my grandfather was the village mayor, visitors were a constant presence in our home, turning it into a hub of intellectual discourse which I found intoxicating.

Every Sunday he hosted VIPs from the cities of Famagusta and Nicosia for lunch and conversation about everything from current events to politics to business. Since we had no refrigeration for food, everything had to be cooked in our primitive clay oven the same day. So, my mother, with help from relatives and neighbors, had to get up at 4:00 a.m. to bake bread, cake, slow-cooked meat, potatoes, and whatever else was needed.

Grandfather always wanted extra food for his guests to take home, so my mother would account for that as well. I couldn't help but notice how he always went the extra mile with others. For instance, when it came time to harvest our olive and carob trees, he insisted on feeding dozens of workers dinner before they went home. The extra work drove my mother crazy, but he did it for two reasons: first, he was by nature a generous man who instinctively knew the importance of gratitude. And second, he was a master at public relations. There's a reason he was mayor for 26 years—he knew how to please and respect the people. I didn't realize it at the time, but my grandfather was providing me an early lesson in leadership.

Although both of my parents' formal education ended after sixth grade, they were determined that the greatest honor their only son could bring to the family was to excel academically.

My elementary school wasn't exactly an ideal learning environment. Long before laptop computers or the immersive classrooms of today, we were squeezed into two cramped rooms.

As if teaching wasn't difficult enough already, we only had two instructors for all of the students in first through sixth grade, meaning they each had to teach *three* grades.

However, the multi-age classroom taught me how to interact with older students. This trained me to compete and negotiate with those who had more knowledge and experience.

* * *

Although both of my parents left school early, they were determined that education held all of the answers.

For my mother, her greatest desire, her greatest hope, and the thing that would bring greatest honor to our family would be for me to become a high school teacher.

I can still hear her voice saying, "Δεν πρέπει να φέρνεις ντροπή στην οικογένεια!", which means, "You must not bring shame to the family!" Her words became ingrained in my soul and I did my best to not let her down.

She also spent every waking moment by constantly testing my arithmetic skills.

At the dinner table, or strolling around the house, my mother was relentless, training me to be a human calculator, quizzing me in addition, subtraction, or multiplication.

At the time, it was a lot of pressure, and I'm sure there were moments I would have rather been playing soccer with my friends, but looking back I am extremely grateful for the incredible gift she gave me. I can't help but think that her constant quizzing formed the foundation for my later interest in mathematics and perhaps even engineering.

* * *

In his own way, my father was also playing a part in ensuring my future in higher education. He didn't confess it to me until I applied to college, but he harbored hopes of me becoming a doctor.

Although my father lacked a formal education, he was an excellent student, who had the gift of writing beautiful letters that eloquently expressed his ideas.

He also knew the importance of staying informed. I distinctly remember the day in second grade when he waved a newspaper in front of me, saying, "You must read this every day!"

I don't know how many other kids at that age who were going from room to room in their house, with their mother quizzing them in arithmetic and their father insisting on a daily reading habit.

In fact, I don't know how many households even had the daily paper. Most of the men in the village went to the coffee shop and read the paper there, so they didn't have to pay for it.

But my father brought the paper home every day and made a big production of fanning it out, rustling the pages, and viewing it as a window into the world beyond our small village.

I took my father's insistence seriously, and at a very young age I started to carefully study the newspaper headlines and look at the photos and cartoons. I'll be honest that my favorite section was Sports, where I could see the latest exploits of my favorite soccer stars.

I soon found myself applying what I learned from my family

with others and utilized my mathematics skills to tutor my older sister and cousins. At the time, I didn't realize they were only asking me questions because they were trying to get out of doing their homework.

Through all of these experiences, the real lesson that has stuck with me has been the importance of a daily reading habit, and then teaching what I learned to others.

❋ ❋ ❋

My parents weren't the only ones who were searching for signs of an intellect that would bring honor to our family.

In addition to being mayor of our village, my grandfather owned a grocery store, with a large coffee shop. For the men of the village, this was a popular place to hang out and relax after work every afternoon. It was like a social club for the working classes, a welcoming space where they could read the newspaper, listen to the radio, and hear the latest gossip. And, for them, the time was sacrosanct.

The one thing the men didn't want was some little kid interrupting their relaxation, even if it was the mayor's grandson. However, my grandfather was on a quest to confirm a hint of higher intelligence inside of me.

So while the men were engaged in the serious discussions that are conducted in local coffee shops, my grandfather designed a game he called, "Find the song."

One of the perks of his shop was a stack of at least 100 music records that he provided to customers for their entertainment.

As a child, my favorite song was a catchy Greek tune called "*Po Po Po Maria*." Every time I came in, my grandfather would mix up this giant stack of records, making sure my favorite was hidden like a needle in a haystack.

Time and again, no matter where he hid it, I always found it because I recognized the label on the cover of the record.

It was an ingenious strategy and my grandfather Habeshi joyfully boasted, "My little two-year old grandson has a photographic memory!"

It became my first claim to fame and the recognition from the men throughout the village boosted my self-esteem considerably.

* * *

In another way, I was deeply influenced by my godparents, who lived 30 miles away in a larger village.

My godfather had moved to America as young man and, like many Greek Americans, entered the restaurant business. During WWII, he was drafted into the U.S. Army and did his duty by serving the country. He would tell tales about his military service, and his wife would laugh. He wasn't exactly serving on the front lines, but rather serving soldiers in the mess hall. But he later used his talents to become very successful in the restaurant business in New Jersey.

He was so successful that he retired at 50, married my mother's cousin from the village, and moved to Cyprus.

Proud of his military service and the U.S. as a country, every month he would dress up, get in the car, and drive to the capital of Nicosia. There he would go to the American Embassy and pick up his pension check. He lived to 90 and he did this every month.

To me, my godfather wasn't just someone who had lived in America, he embodied America. A place where it was always summer, where people dressed fancier, and everyone lived in big, beautiful houses.

In his early retirement, he had reimagined himself as somewhat of a movie mogul, operating a local theater. Each week during the summer, my godfather would take me down to the movie distributor in Nicosia to pick the movies for the week.

I would look at the colorful posters that had come all of the way from Hollywood and my godfather would say, “So what do you think, should we get this one with Victor Mature or this Western with John Wayne?”

I was a kid, of course. I didn’t know anything about the quality of the movies.

Like many pre-teen boys, I loved the Westerns—*High Noon* being a particular favorite and just about anything starring Victor Mature, such as *Sampson and Delilah* and *The Big Circus*.

I didn’t know it then, but more than 50 years later, I would tour the beautiful new facility for USC’s top-ranked School of Cinematic Arts. Throughout the building, in all of the hallways, are the original framed posters of some of those Hollywood classics I saw in Cyprus as a child.

* * *

My godparents also introduced me to the magical world of live theater. I specifically remember going to Salamis to see the classic tragedy, *Oedipus the King* by Sophocles. This was to be my very first time to see real actors in an open, ancient Greek theater.

On the way, my godfather told me, “When you go to see a Greek tragedy, you should know the story up front. You’re not going there to be surprised. You’re going there to see the acting.”

When we arrived, he made sure we sat in the front row near the orchestra, so I could clearly see every actors’ expression.

When it was over, I remember being most affected by a scene where a messenger tells the story of the future king who is taken as an infant to the mountains to be abandoned and die. I was filled with relief when a shepherd saved his life. That day solidified my love for Greek tragedies and live theater in general.

Thanks to my godparents, I gained a true appreciation for cinema and theater. Also, thanks to them, I learned to never buy the “cheap seats” for a live performance. It’s well worth the extra money to see the actors up close.

* * *

I didn't know it then, but my father had been planning on making his own move for independence.

A year after the real estate developer knocked on our door, the one who talked about the gorgeous new hotels, apartments, and condos that would soon put the beach city on the global map, my father announced that our family was moving to Famagusta. In truth, he had already made the move in his mind.

Shortly after the conversation in the coffee shop, he had purchased a lot on the outskirts of Famagusta, an area surrounded by orange and lemon orchards. His plan was to build a complex with four apartments, one in which we would live and the others we would rent to pay the mortgage.

It was only about 25 miles away from our village but worlds apart.

My father told us it was because there were better schools for me and my sister. He also said there were more opportunities for his carpentry and construction business because of an anticipated economic boom. He was excited to help build hotels and apartments to attract tourists.

But today, looking back, I suspect there was a third reason—he was establishing his independence from my mother's father. The two got along, but it was probably difficult for my father to be "man of the house" while living with the village mayor.

Both my mother and her father were strongly against the move to Famagusta. My mom was very close to her dad because she lost her own mother when she was only six years old. But my father was very decisive and determined, and he wasn't about to change his mind. So the plan went forward.

Just before Christmas in 1961, we packed our belongings and said our goodbyes. For my entire extended family, it was a moment of heightened and mixed emotions.

My mother and grandfather were in tears as we left the village. It was also traumatic for me and my sister as we bid farewell to our friends.

Yes, a new birth is painful, but as I was about to learn it also means an exciting new beginning.

* * *

As I got older, all of my experiences would create a longing for independence—for me, for my family, and for my beloved island of Cyprus.

In 1960, I was eight years old when the United Kingdom finally granted the island independence, and the Republic of Cyprus was born. I remember how intently my father and I listened to the radio when our leader Archbishop Makarios shouted, "Νενικηκαμεν" "Νενικηκαμεν"—"We are victorious!"

But the expression on my father's face told me he wasn't so sure. He turned to me and said, "We are not victorious, this is the beginning of more trouble."

Recent years have proven him correct. The region has been restless ever since.

CHAPTER 2

Beach Town

«Τή γλώσσα μοῦ ἔδωσαν ἑλληνική·
τό σπίτι φτωχικό στίς ἀμμουδιές τοῦ Ὁμήρου.»
ΌΔΥΣΣΈΑΣ ΈΛΎΤΗΣ, «ΤΌ ἌΞΙΟΝ ἘΣΤΊ» ΤΌ ΠΆΘΟΣ, ΨΑΛΜΌΣ II

"The language of the Hellenes was given to me,
My house poor on Homer's shores."[1]
ODYSSEUS ELYTIS, "WORTHY IT IS" THE PASSION, PSALM II

We left the comfort of our small village for the uncertainty of the "big city." Komi Kebir had fewer than 1,000 people. Famagusta was nearly 40 times larger, with a population of 39,000. During the boom years, a decade later, in the summer, the population more than doubled to 90,000, drawing tourists from across Europe and around the world.[2]

Our living arrangements also changed dramatically. We couldn't afford a car, so my father wisely rented an old house in the center of the city. The great thing was that it was within walking distance of my elementary school, my sister's middle school, and my dad's workshop.

But there were downsides too. Overnight we had gone from owning an upper-middle-class house to renting a small place in a crowded and noisy urban environment at the heart of the industrial district. Gone were the calm and quiet of the village, which were now replaced by the congested streets and the constant noise of a booming and bustling city at all hours of the day and night.

Even my favorite pastime wasn't the same. In the village, we played soccer in the streets. But in the city, we had to dodge traffic every time we tried to play.

I also felt a surge of insecurity when I realized that all of the other families seemed wealthier than us. The city kids seemed more sophisticated, more talkative, and more aggressive.

Change is never easy at any age, but for a socially shy nine-year-old, it can be traumatic. Looking back, that was a major turning point in my life. I worried that I might get lost in the shuffle, and that I might not live up to my family's expectations of becoming a teacher.

⁂ ⁂ ⁂

A loud knock came at 4:00 a.m. In the pale moonlight, several men were engaged in a hushed and somber conversation with my parents at the entrance of our house.

For my mother, the news was devastating. Back in the village, her father had suffered a heart attack and passed away. Convinced that his death was caused by the stress of us leaving the village, my mother was shattered by her sadness. Unfortunately, she would carry the heavy weight of blame and guilt for a long time.

As our family mourned a great loss, I also learned a dark lesson about people. When my grandfather served as mayor of the village, his life was filled with friends and he was always treated with the highest respect. But as soon as the funeral was finished, it seemed like his legacy was quickly wiped from their memories. My parents later told me that my grandfather's so-called "friends" turned away from the family after he died, almost as if he never existed.

⁂ ⁂ ⁂

As my family was trying to find its footing in Famagusta, my challenges in school were also just beginning. My world had been turned completely upside down and I was struggling to find my identity.

In the classroom, I found the city kids to be more confident and more assertive. Every time the teacher asked a question, their hands shot into the air, eagerly shouting, "Me, me, me!"

I had never experienced anything like it. As a shy kid, if I didn't adapt quickly, I was in serious peril of being overlooked and left behind.

* * *

But beyond school, there were other challenges that taught me about life outside the classroom.

During the summer, I worked in my father's workshop. I learned a lot about the world of carpentry and construction sites, as well as the difficulties of running a small business.

I saw that it was a constant struggle for my father to make payroll because his customers didn't always pay him on time. To his credit, he always paid his employees before he paid himself.

The experience provided me with an important education about how finances actually worked. Back in those days, most transactions were strictly cash. The first time I saw a signed check, I was in fifth grade.

* * *

There were moments when I felt like I was finally fitting in.

I proudly joined the Boy Scouts, which led to the greatest honor of my life, up to that point. I was chosen to be the flag bearer for a national holiday parade.

To this day, I don't know why I was chosen. I suppose they

picked me because, despite being shy, I was a diligent student who followed the rules. But when I was selected over dozens of others who were born and raised in Famagusta, I was frankly shocked.

It was wonderful to see my mother, who had such a hard time adjusting to her new environment, rediscover one of her great passions: celebrating her children's accomplishments.

She made a huge deal out of me being the flag bearer and quickly shared the exciting news with her cousins and everyone she met.

While I was glad that everyone was proud of me, there was something that I didn't share with anyone. I was terrified. For a shy kid, who didn't like being the center of attention, being in a parade created serious anxiety. I kept imagining hundreds of people lined up along the streets, all of their eyes staring directly at me.

On the day of the parade, I did my best to hide my insecurities. But I could feel my heart pounding and my hands sweating as I marched down Famagusta's main street, proudly displaying the Boy Scouts' flag.

When we finally reached the end of the route, I breathed a huge sigh of relief that it had ended without incident.

However, it was quickly clear that I had made a serious mistake. Over the entire route, instead of staring straight ahead, I looked down at the street the whole time. I really don't remember why, but my best guess is I was afraid of making eye contact with the crowd or losing my footing on the road. Probably both.

In any case, the experience turned out to be bittersweet. It was another lesson learned—when you are carrying the flag and the hopes of others, even if you don't feel confident inside, keep your head up and your eyes on the goal ahead.

❊ ❊ ❊

In those days, no matter where you lived on Cyprus, or what nationality you were, everyone had one thing in common: fear.

Although we lived in a city with the world's most beautiful beach, the clouds of international conflict were always swirling overhead.

But by the mid-1960s during the intercommunal conflict, the situation was much more serious than British soldiers making sweeps to search houses and belongings.

When Cyprus became an independent republic in 1960, Turkey never gave up its ambition to control part of the island. Neither side was satisfied with the newly established constitution, which attempted a compromise of shared governance.

While Greek Cypriots welcomed *enosis*, a union with Greece, Turkish Cypriots were fighting for *taksim*, the idea of dividing the nation into a portion that was completely controlled by the Turks.

In December 1963, a month after JFK's assassination and days before Christmas, thousands of years of troubled history boiled over when the political disagreement exploded into violence.[3]

More than 500 Greek and Turkish Cypriots were killed.[4] Turkish planes buzzed overhead, and we were told to dig trenches in our neighborhoods to avoid being hit by bombs. I remember my father nervously pacing the house, telling my mother that if there was going to be an invasion that evening, we should be prepared to leave.

Fortunately for us, most of the violence and destruction was about 50 miles away in the capital of Nicosia and other parts of the island. After several months of intercommunal violence, Turkish planes dropped napalm bombs on the island.[5]

The fear did not abate at school. I'll never forget one afternoon when I was in sixth grade. A rumor spread quickly that the Turkish militia was attacking Famagusta.

Our principal raced into our classroom and announced to the students, "Go home and run as fast as you can!" Within seconds, a panic enveloped the entire city. I remember everyone running and screaming, sprinting into the streets and racing for home.

Luckily, I lived nearby and got home quickly, where I found my mother breathlessly waiting for me at our front door. She pulled me inside, closed the door, and hugged me harder than ever before.

After I caught my breath, I looked outside. It was a scene of eerie calm.

After a moment, I heard an adult outside saying, "Wait a minute, has anybody heard any gunshots? Has anyone seen any soldiers?"

That's when reality set in. We weren't under attack. There was never any danger. It was all a hoax.

* * *

But there were other times when the fear was justified.

In the industrial zone of Famagusta, there was a small clinic where babies were delivered.

One Sunday morning, a bus from a faraway village, which was bringing a woman to the clinic to give birth, was ambushed by the Turkish Cypriot militias, who were organized by Turkish military officers. Soldiers were shooting at the bus as it bounced along the road to Famagusta.

From the window in our house, my father and I could see people gathering outside the clinic, so we went to see what was happening.

As we approached, I could see the shattered bus windows. It was the first time I had witnessed so many bullet holes.

Then our attention turned to the baby. I remember the doctor in charge of the clinic, stumbling out into the street to address the crowd. He announced that they had just delivered the baby and no one was injured.

The parents were happy, of course. But it was a miracle no one got killed.

❊ ❊ ❊

With all of the uncertainty around me, I had my own brush with mortality in 1964. I suddenly developed a fever, cough, and had trouble breathing. My parents rushed me to the hospital where they took X-rays and discovered I had a serious case of pneumonia. One look at my parents' grim faces told me it could be deadly.

The doctor prescribed antibiotics and ordered me to stay in bed for a month. He also made house calls nearly every day, something that never would have happened if we still lived back in the village. I sometimes wonder if I would have survived had it happened in Komi Kebir.

Fortunately, my teachers assigned homework, so I didn't fall behind in my studies. I diligently followed orders and, after several long weeks, I made a full recovery.

❊ ❊ ❊

Around this time, our lives changed again when we moved into a new home. My father finally completed the construction of the four-apartment complex he had dreamed about for so long.

Shortly after the move, I had to make more adjustments when I began the Cypriot version of middle school. I wasn't the best student in any particular subject, but thanks to my inherited work ethic, I managed to get above-average grades and enjoyed my classes.

Although our new home moved us far away from the noise of the industrial center of town, it also created other challenges. Because we didn't have a car, our main mode of transportation was still two wheels instead of four. Even if it was pouring rain, my father and I rarely took the bus and often had to pedal our bikes long distances. But I never complained. I've always loved bicycles, and to this day I still prefer them to cars. These days my weekend is not complete unless I get in some quality bike riding time.

* * *

Just as I was beginning to explore and enjoy new experiences, conflict emerged on the island once again.

In April of 1967, Greece's democratic government was overthrown by a military junta.[6] A few months after the coup, responding to the new intercommunal conflict, Turkey bombed the island and appeared to be getting ready to invade us again.

In the end, the colonels of the military junta gave major concessions to Turkey and even withdrew the large Greek army division protecting the island. Further bloodshed was temporarily avoided, but it was the beginning of the end of Greece being able to stop a Turkish invasion.

* * *

Despite the seeds of division and conflict being sown throughout Cyprus, Famagusta was sailing full steam ahead into what has come to be known as the "Golden Years."

Cyprus became an independent republic at the perfect moment. Around the world, two industries were taking off: plane travel and the Madison Avenue marketing machine.

One glance at an image of the beautiful beaches of Famagusta and people were ready to head for the airport in search of the perfect paradise.

Seemingly overnight, the economy boomed as contractors raced to meet the demand for luxury hotels, upscale restaurants, and chic stores. Famagusta was becoming the glamorous beach resort of the island and celebrities such as Elizabeth Taylor, Richard Burton, Brigitte Bardot, Raquel Welch, Sophia Loren, and Paul Newman began to flock to our once quaint little city on the Eastern Mediterranean.[7]

Of course, no one was happier about the changing image of Famagusta than my dad. It turned out he was right when he predicted there would eventually be a thriving economy for his carpentry business.

He quadrupled his employees from four to sixteen and he accelerated our mortgage payments. It took six long years for it to happen, but we were finally in the black.

It really hit me that we had "made it" when we bought our first TV. Most importantly, my mother stopped complaining about moving to Famagusta. She finally embraced our new life in the city with optimism.

* * *

We all have certain years that mark major turning points in our lives. For me, one of them was 1967. In addition to my family's financial good fortune, it was the year I hit my stride in school.

My self-confidence blossomed in ninth grade when I fell in love with algebra and geometry. Of course, my parents first sparked my interest in mathematics back in the village, but I credit my ninth-grade math teacher, Mr. Poullis, for re-igniting the fire and taking it to a new level.

I became one of those students who loved to learn. It's hard to say which I enjoyed more during my free time, studying or watching our new TV. Thankfully, I found a happy medium.

One morning as I sat in my English class, I learned I was Mr. Poullis's star pupil. Out of the blue, an eleventh grader came into our room and whispered something to the teacher. The instructor turned to me and said, "Hey, Nikias, Mr. Poullis wants to see you right now in his eleventh-grade math class."

"For what? What did I do?"

"I don't know," the student replied as he took me to the classroom.

As I walked into the class, about 40 kids eyed me suspiciously. Two of them stood in front of a nonlinear equation on the blackboard.

Mr. Poullis tried to make me feel comfortable and said, "Oh, Nikias. Come on in. Come on in. You're probably wondering why I invited a ninth grader into the eleventh-grade class."

"Yeah," I replied shyly.

"Do you see this equation on the blackboard?"

I looked at it and nervously nodded, yes.

"Okay, why don't you solve it for them?"

Obviously, no one in the class could do it and now he wanted me, a lowly ninth grader, to embarrass them. I couldn't look at the other faces as I picked up the chalk. My hand shook as I tackled the problem. Moments later I said, "That's it."

The smile on Mr. Poullis's face told me I nailed it. But I could tell most of the students in the class felt both angry and humiliated. How dare this young know-it-all show them up? For a few days, it was the talk of the school. Even though I felt pride in my accomplishment, I wished I had done it in private and not in front of the older kids. I was happy when the talk died down and I was no longer the center of attention.

* * *

At the end of the school year, my father attended a meeting that had the potential to set the stage for the rest of my life.

He met with my teachers to determine which public high school—or "gymnasium" as we called them—I would attend for the tenth through twelfth grades. This was a monumental decision, since some were considered more elite than others. More than most other countries, the type of school you attended in Cyprus could directly impact your entire future.

I wanted to go to the "First Gymnasium" because it was considered the finest school in the area and they concentrated on my favorite subjects—mathematics, the sciences, and classic Greek literature. If I got accepted, it would be a dream come true for my parents, who never made it past sixth grade and desperately wanted a better education for their son.

I'll never forget that rainy Sunday afternoon when dad came home to tell me the results of the meeting. He entered my bedroom and quietly sat down next to me. His heavy breathing told me his heart was pounding.

His voice trembled as he spoke, "I don't want you to spend any more summers helping me in my workshop. Your days of manual labor are over."

I wasn't sure how to react until he told me this was a reward for all my hard work in school.

"Your teachers are going to recommend you to the First Gymnasium of Famagusta. And they're convinced you're the caliber of student who can later attend a university abroad."

Cyprus didn't have its own university until 1990.

I was thrilled, but dad was on cloud nine. I'm sure he silently reflected on everything the family went through to get to that point. From the difficult decision to move us from the village to the tough economic times the family endured—it was finally all worth it.

My mother recognized it too. She was in tears from happiness. Their son was going to get the education they always wanted, but couldn't have.

It was a sign that more changes were on the horizon, not only in my academic life but in my personal life as well.

CHAPTER 3

Coming of Age

« Ἔρως ἀνίκατε μάχαν,
Ἔρως, ὃς ἐν κτήμασι πίπτεις.»
ΣΟΦΟΚΛΈΟΥΣ ἈΝΤΙΓΌΝΗ, 781–82

"Love, invisible in battle,
Love, plunderer of wealth."[1]
SOPHOCLES, *ANTIGONE*, LINES 781–82

In the fall of 1967, my future started coming into focus. I was finally entering the most prestigious school in Famagusta, but I was also fully aware that I carried the hopes and ambitions of so many others—my family, my friends, and my former teachers.

As I walked the hallways on the first day of school, I felt the pride of my own accomplishments, but also the pressure of entering a new environment where I would be facing new challenges and new competition. It was time to seize the moment, to discover what I could really do, and to prove that I could move to the next level academically and socially.

For the first few months, the biggest obstacles to my success were internal. I was nervous and insecure, and I missed my old friends and my favorite teachers, like Mr. Poullis. However, I dealt with my doubts by putting up a confident front, projecting composure and self-assurance in all of my interactions.

Up to that point, I had never worked so hard for anything in my life. I'd get to class by 7:30 a.m., rush home for lunch about 1:00 p.m. where I also read the newspaper, and then race back to school for extra lessons into the late afternoon. I spent most of my evenings hitting the books again.

During the week, I spent very little time hanging out with friends or watching TV. There was only one mantra constantly running through my mind—*study, study, study*.

I also experienced the positive peer pressure of being at a prestigious school. We knew we were part of a privileged group, and we were all looking for every advantage to prepare for the challenging college entrance exams.

The key was extra tutoring. Even the very best students were paying for these services, which went far beyond what we were learning in high school. We were working with top teachers, taking special classes in math, physics, chemistry, and other subjects. To us, it wasn't work. It was like someone had hit the "fast-forward" button on my life. Everything was accelerated and to this day it's amazing how much we learned in such a short period of time.

All of that hard work paid off in more ways than just on my report card. Thanks to my success in algebra, trigonometry, and geometry, my self-confidence increased dramatically by the second semester and I really started to hit my stride.

* * *

During my first year at the First Gymnasium of Famagusta, I matured a lot and fell in love with my new school. But by summer break, I was ready to spread my wings.

One afternoon as I was riding my bike through the center of town, I came across a casual friend who invited me to a party.

On Saturday night, I put on my favorite shirt, checked myself out in the mirror, and tried to contain my excitement. Little did I know, my life was about to change forever.

Soon after I walked through the door, I spotted a gorgeous, long-haired girl who looked vaguely familiar. Suddenly, I remembered her. She was my friend's younger sister and a year behind me in middle school.

At school she wore glasses and more casual clothes. But on the night of the party, she looked like a supermodel. I was captivated. To me, she was not just another teenager. She was the most beautiful girl I had ever seen. I asked around and learned that her name was Niki.

When I finally found the courage to strike up a conversation, I discovered she was just as smart as she was beautiful. She didn't like to brag, but she had been selected to attend the First Gymnasium because she was an excellent student in mathematics. I would later learn that not only had she skipped a grade, but she was also tutoring her older siblings at home.

We also shared other similarities. Even though she had just finished middle school, we were both on the same track for students who excelled in the sciences, mathematics, and the Greek classics.

If I could have dreamed up the ideal girl, Niki checked all the boxes. Beautiful. Intelligent. Common interests. It seemed like fate had brought us both together that night.

With infatuation in the air, I spent the rest of the evening trying to impress her. We danced to Charles Aznavour, the Beatles, and Tom Jones. To this day, when I hear the song *Delilah*, I still remember the electricity of that night.

As the party came to a close, I displayed my dancing skills by doing the *sirtáki*, a folkdance that features both slow and fast rhythms, made famous in the movie *Zorba the Greek*. Admittedly, I was showing off for Niki.

In any case, I must have done something right. After that night, Niki and I started finding excuses to get together as often as possible. It was a magical summer.

Our friends knew we were "an item," of course. But we had to keep our budding relationship a secret from Niki's parents, especially her father. Her dad believed his talented daughter was too young to be dating, especially an older boy.

But young love always finds a way. So, we spent that summer finding reasons to meet up for Sunday movie matinees, days on the beach and afternoons in the park, wherever and whenever we could find a way to spend time together.

* * *

After an amazing summer, I was brimming with optimism and confidence when classes resumed in the fall. Not only did I have a steady girlfriend, but I was excelling academically in more than just mathematics. It was also easier to see Niki since we now attended the same school, although we didn't have any classes together.

When my mind wasn't focused on schoolwork, it drifted to daydreams about my new love. It was especially persistent when I was reading verses of poetry from Lipertis, Seferis, Elytis, and especially Kavafi.

* * *

As much as I loved that school year, I couldn't wait for summer break. One of the perks of attending the Gymnasium in Famagusta was an annual excursion to Greece, following the second year of high school. The summer of 1969 was my turn and I wanted to make the most of it.

There was only one problem. I would have to be away from Niki for three weeks. In those days, teenagers had no way of keeping in contact through text messages or social media. Although we would miss each other dearly, Niki understood and was excited for me.

She was enthusiastic because her boyfriend was about to leave the island of Cyprus for the first time in his life to visit a place he'd only dreamed about.

On the big day, we embarked for the port city of Piraeus, Greece, via the island of Rhodes. During the 36-hour journey, I barely slept a wink, my mind filled with anticipation about all of the places I wanted to see.

The entire country of Greece is about the size of the state of Florida. In less than three weeks, we were scheduled to visit nearly every major historical and archaeological site, with the exception of a few islands. Considering that Greece is comprised of 227 islands, that's an extremely ambitious travel itinerary.

All of these years later, much of the trip feels like a blur, but it was a whirlwind tour of some of the most renowned landmarks of all time. We visited the Acropolis, Epidaurus and Olympia, Mycenae and Marathon, Thermopylae, Delphi, Vergina, Salonika, and a host of other sites. I was in heaven.

The highlight of the trip was Athens itself, the birthplace of democracy. It was the first time I had seen an actual big city. I was awestruck, captivated by its beauty, fascinated by its history, enticed by its possibilities.

* * *

One area that made a major impression on me also introduced us to the social side of Athens. We explored many of the hidden wonders of the city, especially the oldest neighborhood, known as the Plaka.

Distinguished as the "neighborhood of the Gods"[2] because it is in the shadow of the Acropolis, I felt an immediate kinship with the Plaka. With its street closed off to most automobile traffic, it's like a village within the city. To this day, I still love going to this section of Athens.

Plaka was also the epicenter of the city's culture and entertainment. In the 1960s and 1970s, this neighborhood was the pulse of the new wave, where all of the emerging artists, singers, and composers came together in one place, like Greenwich

Village in New York.

Even though we were in our teens, we learned that the Athenians knew how to party! Music blared everywhere. It occurred to me that if you lived there, every evening must feel like Saturday night.

❋ ❋ ❋

When I wasn't spending time with my classmates on the tour, I was making other social connections that would be important for my future.

My father had a cousin from the village, who was now a doctor with his own practice in Athens. I met him and his wife and their three children when they had me over for dinner one night. Over time, I became very close with their family, especially their oldest daughter, Effie, who is the godmother of our daughter, Maria.

But it was one conversation we had that would inspire a new vision in my mind. During dinner, I mentioned that my dream was to attend the National Technical University of Athens, commonly known as Metsovion Polytechnic. At the time I didn't think much of my academic ambitions, but I remembered how impressed they were because it was incredibly difficult to get into that university.

After dinner, on the ride back to my hotel, my father's cousin drove me by the campus. As we drove by Patission Avenue, he casually said, "Oh, by the way, there's Metsovion Polytechnic."

And there it was, the equivalent of the MIT or the Caltech of Greece. A place that accepts only the best of the best.

I looked out at the large gates surrounding the beautiful campus and—boom—my photographic memory took a picture. Over several decades, that image has stayed with me as clear as ever.

The first time I saw that campus, I could feel that it was part of my destiny.

⁂ ⁂ ⁂

After nearly three weeks, the trip of a lifetime was coming to a close. I was sad to leave Greece behind, but I would be returning to Niki and my senior year of high school.

As we left, I knew I was saying "goodbye," but not "farewell." I hoped I would return, possibly even to live there one day.

⁂ ⁂ ⁂

When I arrived back in Famagusta, I knew that my senior year would be a pivotal moment in my life. I had my heart set on attending the Metsovion Polytechnic. But I also knew that to get there, I would have to excel in every subject and ace the entrance exams later in the year.

I had to be prepared in a variety of disciplines, including trigonometry, algebra, geometry, physics, and chemistry.

Each exam was scheduled to last two hours and were to be administered in the capital city of Nicosia over several days. Yes, they were a big deal!

But as I was spending most of my time studying for the most important exams of my life, a seemingly insignificant event changed the course of my life forever.

In mathematics we call it a "perturbation"—a minor occurrence that changes the trajectory in an unpredictable way.

Near the end of my senior year, that's exactly what happened when I filled out a form to designate my decision about my academic major in college.

I listed chemical engineering as my first choice, electrical engineering as my second, and civil engineering as my third. For most college students today, the selection of a major may seem like an arbitrary choice that can be easily changed multiple times. However, at the time, this was a critical decision. In Cyprus, the choice of a college major affected the types of questions you would be asked on the entrance exams, ultimately impacting my entire future.

On my way to the headmaster's office to turn in the form, I ran into my chemistry teacher. It was just a coincidence.

He looked at my choices and shook his head. "Chemical engineering is your first choice? Blegh!"

Now keep in mind, this was my chemistry teacher.

"Nikias, I know you love mathematics," he said. "Chemical engineering doesn't have much math. Electrical engineering is the discipline that has a lot of mathematics. Why not go with what you love?"

Maybe it was the fact that my chemistry teacher was telling me not to choose chemistry as a major, or maybe it was that I sensed he was right, but whatever the reason, I immediately got a new form and made electrical engineering my first choice.

This may appear to be a minor event, but in hindsight it had a major impact on my life. Who knows where I would be today, or how my life would be different, if I had chosen chemical engineering.

In any case, I'm forever grateful that I happened to run into my chemistry teacher at that moment on that day.

* * *

After a year of extraordinary experiences and great progress, graduation day was finally on the horizon. By any measure, my high school years were an enormous success. I learned, I matured, and thanks to Niki—I fell in love. Who could ask for more?

To make it even better, I was honored with the "Leadership Award" and "Best History Student Award." The only people prouder than me were my parents, who saw my accomplishments as a result of years of patience, sacrifice, and loving support. They were overjoyed that their only son was on the path to a successful future. But first, I had to pass the entrance exams.

* * *

A few weeks after graduation, I headed to the capital city of Nicosia. While I was cautiously optimistic that I was prepared to do well, I could feel the tension from the other students around me.

I took a deep breath, said a silent prayer, and started the test.

To my relief, I sailed through the exams. On the trigonometry test, we were given two hours. It took me only 20 minutes.

Surprised, I quickly looked over the material to make sure I wasn't missing something.

Then I said to myself, "I learned this all before, I'm finished."

I turned in my work and promptly headed to the cafeteria to get a coffee.

My trigonometry teacher from Famagusta was there that day. He checked his watch, and rushed up to me in a panic.

"Oh, my God, you just arrived!" he shouted. "You missed the exam. You have to run!"

"No, no, no, I finished," I said calmly.

"What do you mean, you finished?" he asked skeptically. "How did you solve the problems?"

After walking him through the answers, he calmed down a little. But then he blasted me.

"You never finish early," he said. "Even if you're 100 percent certain that your answers are correct, you never leave an exam early. You look at your answers again and again until the instructor tells you to stop!"

In the end, not only was I fortunate enough to pass all the exams, I ranked among the very top students in all of Cyprus. And best of all, thanks to my test scores, I received a five-year scholarship covering all my educational and living expenses at my dream university.

But before I could head off to my dream school, there was a little matter I had to take care of first. It would take up the next two years of my life.

CHAPTER 4

Army Training

«Αὕτη ἡ μελέτη τῶν πρός τὸν πόλεμον.
καὶ γὰρ πρῴ ἀνίστασθαι ἐθίζει καὶ ψύχη καὶ θάλπη ἀνέχεσθαι,
γυμνάζει δὲ καὶ ὁδοιπορίαις καὶ δρόμοις.»

ΞΕΝΟΦΏΝΤΟΣ ΚΎΡΟΥ ΠΑΙΔΕΊΑΣ, Α 2.10

"The exercise itself is the best possible training for the needs of war.
It accustoms them to early rising; it hardens them to endure heat and cold;
it teaches them to march and to run at the top of their speed."[1]

XENOPHON, *CYROPAEDIA*, BOOK I, 2.10

If you have never experienced military training, the circumstances are extreme and every element is designed to break down your will so that your psyche will be more susceptible to new ideas.

For the next two years, my formal education would be placed on hold while I received special training through mandatory military service.

The humiliations began right away when they shaved our precious hair as close as the razor could get to the skin. We engaged in endless drills from morning to night and were frequently placed in situations that were designed to embarrass or ridicule, testing our wills and our temperaments.

Sergeants screamed in our faces during the day and shouted in the middle of the night, shaking us from the depths of sleep, sending us running outside for more exercises.

The sergeants also devised some imaginative ways to test the strength and endurance of the human body. The most popular—and also the most painful—was a drill affectionately known as "bunnies" where we were forced to hold our hands at our necks, and then crouch down like we were sitting on a chair while simultaneously jumping and turning.

Even if you're in great shape, it takes only a few minutes for the pain to begin creeping through your body, attacking one muscle and then the next.

It was a frequent and painful reminder that we were not in control, and that leadership is sometimes about learning how to endure the pain until you can find the relief on the other side.

When I arrived for my first 40 days of training at the military camp in Karaolos, which was a few miles north of Famagusta, I knew that the camp held its own history. After World War II, it housed more than 50,000 European Jews immigrating to Palestine searching for a new life in what was to become the State of Israel.[2]

During their migration from 1946 to 1949, a conflict with the British led them to this camp.[3] While they were delayed on the way to the final destination of their promised land, Greek Cypriots from Famagusta regularly provided food and clothing to the many refugees.

Although nearly a quarter century had passed, my fellow rookie soldiers and I slept in the same stark chambers where those refugees had likely spent several sleepless nights.

However, for us there would be no exodus beyond the camp for the first 40 days. Like the Biblical concept of 40 days and 40 nights, our confinement seemed to last for an eternity.

Although I would miss going to study in Athens, my friends, and especially Niki, these brutal months proved to be another major turning point in my life.

Throughout my military service, I was learning, observing, and applying timeless principles and lessons of leadership.

But looking back, I was also cultivating fellowship, exercising humility, leading from the front, and learning to stay calm in times of great stress.

❊ ❊ ❊

In spring of 1970, I had been chosen by the headmaster of the Gymnasium to deliver a speech on behalf of the students, celebrating Greek Independence Day. It's the equivalent of the Fourth of July for Americans, a revolution against the Ottomans that eventually helped Greece become independent in 1829.

Although I was nervous when I gave that speech, a captain in the Cyprus National Guard had been very impressed with my inspirational tone.

It was one of many instances in my life in which I learned the lesson that even if you are anxious about the outcome, if you prepare well, put yourself out there, and project confidence, unpredictable and sometimes life-changing things can happen.

Four months later, that same captain was stationed in the Karaolos military camp. During one inspection in our barracks chamber, he asked each of us questions to learn more about us. When he saw me, he suddenly stopped, recognizing me from my speech at the Gymnasium. Because of that connection, he started a longer conversation with me.

I must confess that I sensed an expression of admiration from this captain—and all of my superiors—when they were told that I passed the entrance examinations and planned to study at Metsovion Polytechnic. I detected a level of respect that wasn't always given to the other soldiers.

After that initial interaction, the captain asked me to come to his office a few afternoons per week and work as a clerk. We were still "rookies" engaged in intense training, so simply having the opportunity to work in his officc was a big deal.

Early one morning in August 1970, as we were coming to the end of our 40-day training, he came to my barracks during inspection and said, "You are going on a trip!"

"A trip? To where?" I asked hesitantly.

"If you don't know already, maybe you're not as smart as I thought," he said.

At only 18, I was selected by the Cyprus Government Defense Department as one of 40 Greek Cypriots to go on leave abroad for special training. There I had the opportunity to become a second lieutenant of the Cyprus National Guard at a school of Greek army officers on the Island of Crete. For the next six months, the experience would be intense, but transformative.

Unfortunately, I was never able to thank this captain for his confidence in me. He loved sports cars, especially racing convertibles. Four years after he recommended me for special training, I read in a newspaper that he had been killed during a car crash on the main highway between Athens and Thessaloniki.

❊ ❊ ❊

Although it has been many years since I first set foot on the Island of Crete for special training, in my mind the memories are still as vivid as if they happened yesterday.

The voyage to the island was the type ancient sailors might have written about in their journals. During the evening, strong winds and stormy weather tossed and turned the ship, which was at the whim of mother nature in that tumultuous Aegean Sea. We had little time to enjoy the journey because even the strongest among us spent most of the trip vomiting.

But on the final leg of the journey, the island unveiled its true beauty, as our ship sailed into the harbor of Heraklion.

During those winter months, I grew to love the green colors, the cool rain, and the white snow on the peaks of Mount Psiloritis, where the final two weeks of our training was held.

It was on Crete that I learned to make sound decisions and to take full responsibility. Throughout my life and career, those lessons have served me well and taught me how to serve others.

❊ ❊ ❊

When we finally arrived at the port of Heraklion, the storms had receded and everything was incredibly calm. To make it even better, the people on Crete were so polite and welcoming, a refreshing change from the exhausting expedition.

However, as soon as we entered the school camp, things quickly changed again. The friendly smiles and the warm greetings faded fast.

One superior shouted, “How dare you show up in this sacred school in civilian clothes!”

Immediately, we had to drop all of our supplies and run up a steep hill in the casual clothes we were wearing.

It was a wake-up call, a shock to the system, to prepare us for the tough tasks ahead.

We were trained to respond with mottos that represented an important mindset for a leader.

If a superior greeted you by saying, “Morning, soldier,” you didn't say, “Good morning,” in return. Instead, we responded with the lessons they wanted to be ever-present in our minds. We would say, “Always take responsibility. No excuses. There are no obstacles.”

After being forced to say this several times per day, it begins to become a natural part of your mentality. When a challenge arises, you actually begin to think those mottos because they have flashed through your mind thousands of times, like a muscle that gets stronger from being triggered over and over.

* * *

The complexity of the camp was made even clearer by a variety of drills we endured, which challenged our rationality and our resolve. We were now engrossed in a world in which there was no personality, no opinion, and no ego. The only duty we had was to obey every order, no matter how outrageous it sounded.

A typical day began at 4:00 a.m., when we were awakened by

the sharp sound of a loud trumpet. Immediately, without thinking, we were all out of bed like missiles lifting off. We shook away the fog of sleep, slipped on our shoes, and got dressed in an instant.

As we were racing to get ready, our sergeants were stalking the barracks, shouting, "Oh, my God! You are *so* slow. Not yet out, out . . . out!"

We hustled out of the chambers and darted into the darkness for grueling morning exercises and exhausting runs.

At the heart of our campus was the "holy square," a hallowed area where you were never allowed to walk. You always had to be running. If you entered the square, everyone was in constant motion, always racing from place to place.

After morning exercises, we ran to the cafeteria, where our meager breakfast often consisted of only a hot drink, bread and butter, and marmalade.

Following breakfast, we hit the ground running again, heading to the classroom, where we were drilled in an array of topics focused around building our leadership skills.

Depending on the day, we had classroom courses on strategy, tactics, discipline, and the importance of equipment and supplies. We studied endless examples of battles by the Greek army throughout history, with a special emphasis on World War II.

When we weren't in the classroom, we were out in the field, observing our officers and applying the lessons we were learning in our daily lectures.

As officers in training, our education was, by necessity, extensive. In the classroom, we had many hours of intense leadership lessons, absorbing lectures, photos, and short movies focused on military tactics, simulating different theatres of battle. We also studied the historical importance of supply chains and logistics in winning a war.[4]

In other lessons, we were taught topography and how to read detailed maps, especially in the evening when you may need special instruments like altimeters to understand how to navigate by using the evening stars.

In the field, we would engage in real-life simulations, learning about different weapons and military equipment, studying the importance of engineering in the building of bridges, using boats in rivers, and even the intricate details of how a car engine works in case we needed to make sudden repairs.

We were also trained to use a variety of weapons—pistols, rifles, machine guns, mortars, and heavy infantry artillery. It was common to find us on the shooting range, where we would be graded on our accuracy and ability to hit a target.

A favorite training for many soldiers was hand-to-hand combat, especially the spear fights, where you could take out your frustrations on a dummy.

Late in the day, after a large lunch and dinner, we again engaged in feats of physical endurance designed to keep us in peak condition and withstand every circumstance. In the evening, we were always cleaning our chambers, oiling our guns, or polishing our boots.

On Saturday morning, we were awakened early for the most intrusive inspection, which we called the "real Golgotha of the crucifixion." It was a nerve-wracking time when we had to demonstrate that our weapons were perfectly clean. We held our breaths as officers squinted an eye to look down the barrel of our guns.

At night, if we were really unfortunate, we had to guard one of the camp's watchtowers. The worst was what we called the "Germanic" hour, a terrible time between 2:00 and 4:00 a.m. that also meant we got no sleep.

While guarding the watchtower and fighting fatigue, the Germanic hour emphasized our own insignificance as we contemplated the incomprehensibility of our universe.

On other nights over those six months, I kept focused and connected to the outside world by writing frequent letters to Niki.

* * *

Toward the end of our six-month training, we made another trip. For two weeks, we camped out in tents on the Mountain of Psiloritis. In the middle of winter, enduring the rain and the snow, we braved the cold and harsh conditions as we conducted military exercises to capture the mountain.

As the sun sank along the horizon, we engaged in evening patrols and learned deception tactics. As we made our way to the top of the mountain, I'll admit I did run out of breath at the end. But once we got there, the scenery was stunning. I'll never forget how green and beautiful the view was from the mountaintop.

The extreme conditions were withering, but I realized this was a turning point. Our days were filled with difficult training, classes on strategy and tactics, and military exercises on the mountain.

I loved every minute of it.

* * *

On the weekends, we could find rest and relaxation in the city of Heraklion. At the military school, there was no hot water. Even in the middle of winter, it was like the water for our showers was being pumped in straight from an iceberg. Each morning we would shiver and shudder, enduring the streams of freezing water.

In Heraklion, we had one thing on our minds. Before we went to the tavernas or the movies, many of us—including myself—would rent a room by the hour at a small hotel or inn. Then we would take turns immersing ourselves in the pleasure of a hot shower. After an entire week of freezing cold, it was worth every penny!

* * *

After the graduation ceremony in Crete, I returned to Cyprus as a second lieutenant, where I was appointed to the 201st Infantry Battalion on the outskirts of Famagusta.

During this time, I was practicing leadership not just by learning in the classroom or by taking orders from my commanding officers, but also by doing leadership. The experience wasn't perfect, but it was an excellent and invaluable training ground.

In the evening, I stayed at home with my family. Very early each morning, a driver in a military jeep would pick me up from home and deliver me to the camp, where I was in charge of running the infantry battalion's office of supply and transport. It was a major responsibility, monitoring a lot of logistics and coordinating everything with central command.

At night, sometimes I would be assigned to conduct weekend patrols with the military police, keeping soldiers out of trouble in bars and other places.

One Saturday evening, I joined a group of other officers for a night on the town. We went to a tavern and got drunk with Greek ouzo. I was literally sick for a week, and I never did it again.

It was a difficult lesson to learn, but an important one to remember.

* * *

There were many other experiences that taught me valuable lessons. One evening when I was an officer on duty and working in the office, I saw a note on the calendar. It said that we were supposed to have an off-camp exercise with central command.

No one had mentioned this to us, and no one in our cohort was prepared. I could have simply ignored the note, later blaming the group's poor performance on the fact that we were surprised. Instead, I took action.

I went back to our quarters and told my fellow soldiers. For most of evening, I worked with them to prepare for the exercise.

Early in the morning, our captain came rushing into our chambers. His face was pale and he was clearly panicking. Breathlessly, he explained that he had missed the exercise on the calendar and we needed to prepare right away.

You should have seen the relief on his face when I calmly told him that I'd already taken care of it. Fortunately, he praised me in front of everyone for being proactive.

❊ ❊ ❊

In the summer of 1971, an unexpected opportunity arose. All male Greek Cypriots were required to complete two years of mandatory military service as soon as they graduated from high school. But one morning the commander of my battalion said, "Congratulations, you are being released from the army to pursue your Metsovion Polytechnic studies because you already have a scholarship from the Greek Scholarship Foundation!"

I was stunned. And elated. I could join Niki when she went to college in Athens—an entire year earlier than I'd expected. It was a miracle.

But as he read the requirements, it became apparent that you had to be born in 1951. Since I was born in 1952, I wasn't eligible.

It turns out that the law had been written very specifically, probably as a favor to the families of one elite private school in the capital of Nicosia.

While I was fine with doing my duty, the Chief Administrator of the district of Famagusta summed up his feelings in a conversation with my father.

He said, "The rich always get what they want . . . the rest of us what we deserve."

❊ ❊ ❊

Today when I look back at those years, they make me realize that I had learned many important lessons from my commanding officers and my fellow soldiers.

Cyprus wouldn't be invaded by Turkey until 1974, but for two years the island would experience "the winds of Civil War." During those two years, there was a palpable tension among the Greek Cypriots on the island, which would later trigger the invasion by Turkey. But for me, being in Athens was a blessing because I was focusing on my studies.

After I finished my military service and was released from the army in July 1972, I went to Athens and reunited with Niki in August.

As I made the trip to rejoin my great loves, I ran my fingers through my closely-cropped hair. After two years of restrictions, I knew I was going to have to make a change.

The first thing I did when arriving at college—I grew out my hair and a beard.

CHAPTER 5

Refugees

"ὦ τέκν', ἔοιγμεν ναυτίλοισιν οἵτινες
χειμῶνος ἐκφυγόντες ἄγριον μένος
ἐς χεῖρα γῆι συνῆψαν, εἶτα χερσόθεν
πνοαῖσιν ἠλάθησαν ἐς πόντον πάλιν."

ΕΥΡΙΠΙΔΟΥ ΗΡΑΚΛΕΙΔΑΙ, 427–430

"My children, we are like sailors
who have escaped the wild blast of the storm and
have the dry land in their grasp,
then are driven by winds into the deep again."[1]

EURIPIDES, *CHILDREN OF HERACLES*, LINES 427–430

While Athens represented a new stage of life for me and for Niki, it also helped us clarify our shared vision for the future. After spending so much time apart, we knew exactly what we wanted.

For the next few years, we would enjoy college in one of the world's great cities. We planned to earn our degrees and then return to Famagusta, where I would work as an engineer and she would become an accountant. We anticipated a quiet and comfortable life, returning to that beautiful beach town to be with our families.

We didn't know it then, but we would soon learn that even the best plans can be changed by circumstances beyond your control. In his classic book *Poetics*, Aristotle describes the term "peripeteia" as the "most powerful part of the plot," especially in a tragedy.[2]

Niki and I couldn't have imagined that the incidents of history would introduce us to the true meaning of "peripeteia." We couldn't have foreseen the larger events written into our destinies, events that would act as a major destructive force in our lives and those of our families.

And yet, when we look back on those times, our memories of Athens still fill us with gratitude and happiness. We still consider our time in Athens the very best years of our lives.

We were excited to be living in a place whose star shines brightly throughout history. For both of us, Athens would be a place of growth and exploration, a space where we would encounter a "new wave" of ideas and philosophies that would alter our lives and our shared destiny.

While I immersed myself in the challenging studies at the Metsovion Polytechnic, Niki engaged her intellect at the Athens University of Economics and Business.

For the next few years, our horizons would be greatly expanded despite the fact that our lives were often contained in only a few city blocks.

After several long months apart, we were together at last. Both of our campuses were on Patision Avenue, within a short walking distance of each other.

I had arrived in Athens ahead of Niki, so I had already scouted out our living options. We soon found an apartment off Leoforos Alexandras, very close to both of our universities.

For the first two years, we kept it a secret from our parents that we were sharing an apartment. Niki even had her mail sent to the address of a friend, and when our relatives visited she went to stay in that apartment. It took a lot of effort to keep up that ruse, but I suspect our parents knew we were living together.

Because of the location of our apartment, the heart of Athens was literally our campus life. Everywhere we went we were surrounded by beauty and history, in addition to all of the benefits that a great city offers the mind and the soul.

The Polytechnic campus was next to the National Archeological Museum of Athens, a short distance from the Acropolis, where we frequently spent weekends surrounded by ancient architecture as we watched modern Athens bustling below us.

During the week, we were learning the virtue of intense effort, relentlessly studying and preparing for extremely difficult exams. Unlike virtually every other university, the Polytechnic was—and still is—an institution with a five-year curriculum.

In that time, students worked toward a diploma that is equivalent to both a bachelor's and a master's degree, what many universities now call a "progressive degree program."

The challenge for me was amplified by the fact that I wasn't taking just any college curriculum. I was studying highly advanced electrical and mechanical engineering. The sheer volume of difficult material, and the long hours spent studying, meant that I had to learn how to prioritize and absorb information very quickly and effectively.

My first two years were intense. During the first year, we took an incredible 12 courses. Imagine immersing yourself in very advanced mathematics, physics, chemistry, mechanics, descriptive and differential geometry, metallurgy, computer programming, and engineering design and practice—all at the same time!

Clearly, I didn't have a lot of free time like many college students, and the courses were so demanding that you couldn't hold down even a part-time job.

As a student from outside of Greece, I was very fortunate to have an academic scholarship. The Greek State Scholarship was essential to our survival and what little enjoyment we could afford. It gave me the financial support to make the transition to living in an expensive city, a passport to new worlds of possibility and opportunity.

❋ ❋ ❋

To keep up with the pace of my classes and to maintain my scholarship, I had to work very hard and study endlessly.

My classmates and I spent most of our days moving from one class to another. On weekday evenings, we held marathon study sessions at each other's apartments. On weekends, we caught up on sleep and with our studies.

Weekends were also for hanging out. Friday and Saturday evenings were usually for entertainment, with some Sunday afternoons spent watching soccer games.

During our undergraduate years, Niki and I loved getting away to the nearby islands, especially Ayia Marina on the island of Aegina. However, most weekends were spent with our friends who were primarily our classmates.

The youth of the time, especially the college students, created special places to express their ideals and aspirations. These were called "boite de nuit," a French term that loosely translates to "nightclub," but they were considered "music synagogues." Every Friday or Saturday night, Niki and I gathered together with our friends to watch the most famous artists and singers of the time experiment with new styles, break new ground, and write their own histories.

For someone who had grown up in a small village, this exposure to such a wide array of intellectual and artistic ideas was a revelation. I was like a sponge, soaking up all of these new perspectives and experiences.

* * *

Before I could continue my exploration of Athens, the winds of change would begin blowing once again.

From 1972 to 1977, those were extremely turbulent times for Greece, for Cyprus, and for my family.

After the 1967 military junta, when Niki and I went to college, we had to be very careful as Greek Cypriots. We were officially citizens of the Republic of Cyprus, not Greece. In order to live in the country and to stay in Athens, we had to get permits from Greek immigration.

As students, we were always aware of the many restrictions. For instance, you could not sing songs by Mikis Theodorakis in the tavernas because all artists who openly opposed the government in the foreign press were censored by the dictatorship.

But in November 1973, the fall of my sophomore year, everything changed. The seismic shifts caused by the strain of suppression intensified, and the epicenter of the coming upheaval centered on the Polytechnic campus.

The students who had been protesting and striking against the military junta took over all of the buildings on campus. They began broadcasting from a radio station, calling themselves the "Free Besieged," which was a reference to a Dionysios Solomos poem about the siege of the Greek city of Mesolonghi by the Ottomans.[3]

Three days later, on a Friday evening, we were at a peaceful gathering on Patision Avenue in front of the main entrance to the Polytechnic.

Students were singing Dionysis Savvopoulos' song, *When will it be Starry Again*, a metaphor for the light of democracy being obscured by the dark clouds of dictatorship.

Everyone was singing and dancing, and you could feel a sense of togetherness that comes from being part of something larger than yourself.

Then we heard the first gun shots.

Up until that point, the police and the military had remained in the background. What we didn't know was that Brigadier General Ioannides, the leader of the extreme faction of the military junta, had taken power. Determined to crush the student uprising at the Polytechnic, he unleashed tanks on the city of Athens.

It was a prelude to what he would do a few months later on July 15, 1974. In the heart of summer, he would be the instigator of a military coup against President Makarios in Cyprus.

But on that Friday night, we couldn't see that far into the future. Niki and I looked down Leoforos Alexandras, the main avenue which ended near the Polytechnic campus. We could see the tanks coming. Then they started shooting. They weren't shooting directly at people but firing into the air to scare us.

Then it was chaos. Everyone running and shouting. You could feel the tanks vibrating on the streets.

We ran into Pedion Areos park, which was filled with trees and bushes. Out of breath, our hearts racing, we could hear the heavy footsteps of the police chasing us.

Somehow we managed to camouflage ourselves. Then we heard the tanks barreling down Leoforos Alexandras, rolling toward the Polytechnic. One crashed into the university's main gate and tore its way onto the campus.

In the darkness, we realized that our apartment which had been so ideally located between our campuses, was now too dangerous for us to return to for the evening.

When the police dispersed, we slipped into the darkness and made our way to a friend's apartment, where we stayed the night.

I don't think we slept at all. We were all too filled with adrenaline, anger, and anxiety.

But when you're young and stupid, you also do crazy things. In those days, you couldn't just turn on the television or look at social media to get the latest information. On Sunday at noon, Niki and I decided to see the aftermath for ourselves. So we walked down to the Polytechnic campus.

We were stunned. The military tanks had shredded the campus gates. It looked like the scene of a looting. There was a major police presence, officers still swirling around.

One bad-tempered policeman was holding a large nightstick. He saw me and Niki holding hands, and then shouted, "What are you doing here?"

"We just came to see what's going on," I said.

He raised the nightstick and came running toward us. We ran for our lives. Thank goodness we were younger and in better shape. But it was another moment that highlighted how tensions make people do strange things.

⁂ ⁂ ⁂

We didn't know it then, but we had witnessed a major moment in the history of Greece. To this day, every year on November 17th, the President of Greece visits the campus of the Polytechnic, placing flowers and a wreath where the tank demolished the main gate.

Nearly 50 years after those dark days, thousands of people still gather outside the gates of the Polytechnic, marking the symbolic stand of democracy against dictatorship.

The events at the Polytechnic would trigger a series of major geopolitical moves in the Eastern Mediterranean. The next 12 months would change our lives forever.

⁂ ⁂ ⁂

As the summer of 1974 approached, Niki and I were relieved that we'd finished our final exams in June. In July, we spent time together relaxing in Ayia Marina, and we were excited about returning home to Famagusta for the rest of the summer.

However, because we were still hiding the fact that we were living together, we didn't want to raise any suspicions. Although our families knew each other, we decided to travel separately to avoid having them meet us at the airport.

Niki flew to Cyprus on Sunday, and I was scheduled to depart for the island the next morning. As it turned out, that simple decision may have saved my life.

At 8:30 a.m. on Monday, July 15, 1974, the military junta of Greece launched a coup against President Makarios in Cyprus. President Makarios escaped the assault of tanks at the presidential palace in Nicosia and, with the help of the British, he escaped the island.

Unaware of the coup, I woke up on July 15 in a great mood, dreaming of spending the rest of the summer with Niki and our families in Famagusta.

I ran down to get a taxi to the airport and the kiosk worker frowned at me and said, "What the hell are you doing? There's a rumor that they killed President Makarios in Cyprus. There's a coup."

Then I remembered. At every rank, the Cyprus National Guard was primarily staffed by Greek military officers. Thus, the Greek military junta had direct control over them.

I was stunned. All of the excitement drained out of me.

"Are you kidding me?" I said.

"You can't go to the airport."

The next few days were hell. At that time, there weren't news outlets or social media like we have today. And during a coup, they always want to control communications, so there was no way to get information.

I went to stay with the Karavi family who had welcomed me with open arms when I'd visited Athens for the first time. On Saturday morning, July 20, Dr. Karavi woke me up to tell me that Turkey had invaded the island. It was the worst-case scenario. My dreams turned into a nightmare.

But three days after the Turkish invasion of Cyprus, the military junta that had held power in Greece since 1967 collapsed. As quickly as Cyprus had been overtaken, democracy was restored to Greece.

For me, this was a very emotional and bittersweet time. In Athens, people were swarming the streets, celebrating their newfound freedom from the junta. At the same time, Greek Cypriot students were demonstrating in front of the tomb of the Unknown Soldier in Syntagma Square, with a hunger strike and a large sign that read: "Do not celebrate. Cyprus is burning."

It seemed only a coincidence that Niki and I had chosen to

travel separately. But looking back, my battalion—the 201st battalion—was the first to be drafted when the Turkish invasion arrived. They were sent straight to the front lines and were quickly decimated.

Many members of my battalion are still missing, and they have never been able to find their bodies. No one knows what happened to them. Several of them were taken as prisoners in Turkey.

⁂ ⁂ ⁂

While I was still trying to get information about our families, one day I returned to the building where Niki and I shared an apartment. The penthouse was owned by a woman who knew we were from Cyprus. She asked about my family.

"I have no news," I said. "I really don't know what's going on."

She hesitated, looked around, and then spoke softly. "I can listen to a secret Greek station from Germany. I don't want you to tell anybody."

I could see the fear on her face. Although democracy had been restored in Greece, people were still afraid the military might stage another coup. So they were very cautious.

"You're welcome to come to my apartment in the afternoons to listen . . . as long as you keep the volume low."

I nodded, grateful that someone was willing to take a personal risk to help me.

For the next few days, I went to her apartment and listened to Deutsche Welle, an international news program out of Germany.

That's the only way I was getting any news about what was happening in Cyprus. Then, after the military junta fell in Greece, everything opened up.

One night, at the Karavi family home, the phone rang and Dr. Karavi answered. He talked for a short time, and then called to me.

He said, "Your dad is on the phone. He's okay. They're all okay."

I could finally breathe again. I fought back tears as I heard my father's voice. I asked about Niki, but he said he hadn't seen her family. I don't remember everything he said, but I will never forget the end of the conversation. He said, "Stay away. We've been destroyed. And don't you dare come back to Cyprus anytime soon."

* * *

The next day Niki called. She and her family were okay, but along with my relatives, they were now part of a caravan of refugees who would leave the towns and villages of the north to move to the southern part of the island.

The Turkish invasion of Cyprus was the plan all along, of course. Turkey had long had its eyes on the crown jewel of Cyprus and the military junta had handed them the keys to the island.

In the summer of 1974, a Greek poet named Yannis Ritsos wrote about Cyprus: "Keep faith, little daughter of ours, who has become our mother . . ."

By August 14, 1974, the Turkish army occupied 40 percent of the northern part of the island of Cyprus, including our hometown of Famagusta.[4]

In less than a month, our families had gone from living happy and successful lives to losing everything. To escape the deadly bombs being dropped by Turkish aircraft, they left overnight without any of their possessions, believing they would be able to return once the bombing stopped.

But they soon realized they were now refugees. Over a period of six months, the Turkish soldiers ran rampant through my homeland, looting the businesses and homes of the northern part of Cyprus, where nearly one-third of the island nation's population had once lived.

They took everything, including artwork from the churches,

which ended up scattered in places around the world, including as part of collections in the United States.

***

In America, President Johnson's promise to protect Cyprus was not kept. President Nixon was preoccupied with the Watergate Scandal and many foreign policy decisions had been delegated to Henry Kissinger. Many Greek Cypriots have never forgiven Kissinger for turning a blind eye to the Turkish invasion.

For me and for Niki, it was a life-changing moment. Once you lose everything—your property and your possessions, the businesses you've built, and photo albums that collect your memories—there is no going back. It is then that you understand the true meaning of *apatris*, which is the Greek word for "stateless." In many ways, it is a scar that always stays with you, a wound that never heals, a trauma that stains the soul.

And yet, in the midst of tragedy, being stateless also contains the hope for its opposite—a chance to find a new home, which we would later do in the United States.

The evening Famagusta fell to the Turks, I walked the streets of Athens alone. After countless blocks, I sat down at an outdoor café, feeling like life was empty and meaningless. This is what it feels like to be a refugee, I thought.

In that moment, if you allow yourself to fully feel the pain, you learn one big lesson. For me, the lesson was that—in all of our lives—evil days always arrive. You can't prevent them or control them, but you can take steps to cushion yourself against the impact. This is the survival instinct that kicks in when you lose everything.

Sitting alone at that outdoor café in Athens, I felt a surge of anger and power that I had never felt before. I made a vow to never be a refugee again. No matter what happened, never again would I become a casualty of circumstance. Instead, I would immediately take action to move toward a better future.

The night Famagusta fell, I realized that my family and Niki's would be in financial ruin. I also wasn't sure that I could rely on my academic stipend, which was supporting us while we were in school.

The next morning, I started looking for a job. I frantically searched through the newspapers, skimming the job announcements.

Meeting with a woman about a job in Omonoia Square, I was taken aback when she learned that I was a Greek Cypriot from Famagusta, which had fallen to the Turks only the day before. Her face transformed and she broke down in tears.

"No, no, this job is not for you," she said.

Before I could protest, she went on.

"You are a student of the Metsovion Polytechnic. I have a close friend at the National Bank of Greece. He's a manager of the engineering division. I'm going to give him a call right now and I'm going to send you over there, and they have to give you a job."

This woman had no reason to help me, and I never met her again, but I will always be grateful that she did me a major favor with a single phone call.

* * *

The National Bank of Greece in Klafthmonos Square welcomed me with open arms and gave me the job right away. Many of the employees in the engineering division were Polytechnic graduates, and it was a great experience while I worked with them for about a year.

With my intense class schedule, I had to miss some classes, but I had no choice because I needed the money. Fortunately, they provided me with some flexibility that allowed me to work and stay in school. But that was a very challenging year for me.

* * *

The devastation in Cyprus in the summer of 1974 proved to me that after a terrible tragedy there is also opportunity for a new beginning.

During my second phone call with Niki, I told her that I wanted to get engaged.

"Are you crazy?" she said. "We don't even know where we are going to sleep tomorrow night!"

Looking back, she was dealing with the grief of losing her home and surviving a humanitarian disaster. But for me, the physical distance between Cyprus and Athens gave me the psychological space to think beyond those terrible days and to imagine a better future.

When Niki eventually returned to Athens, we discussed it again and agreed it was the right decision. I sent a letter to my father, asking him to speak to Niki's dad.

After that horrible summer, during the Christmas break in 1974, Niki and I returned to Cyprus by ship to get engaged.

Only then did I truly understand the terrible trauma Niki and our families had been living.

This was the first time I had seen the tragedy with my own eyes. The once beautiful landscape was littered with refugee camps. One-third of the refugees were sleeping in tents in these camps. The rest "were jammed into overcrowded houses and apartments."[5]

It was also the first moment that I saw the sadness in my father's eyes. Six months before the invasion, he had paid off the mortgage on the four-apartment complex that had been his dream. Now he had lost everything, including the business he had built from scratch. My parents were living in a one-bedroom apartment next to a small workshop which he was now leasing.

For the next five years, he did public works projects, building apartments to house refugees. But he and his business would never be the same.

Even when others held out hope for a settlement for Greek Cypriots, and for a return of refugees to their homes, he remained pessimistic and became very risk averse.

He once told me, "Only a seismic event will get the Turks off of the island."

As I write this more than fifty years later in 2025, the Turks are still there and no settlement has been achieved.

⁂ ⁂ ⁂

Christmas of 1974 was a very traumatic experience for me. Seeing the devastation firsthand, combined with the cold and rainy winter, literally made me sick. I caught a virus and spent the next three days in bed with a high fever.

However, I couldn't stay under the weather for long. To get married in the Cyprus Orthodox Church, the engagement must happen in front of the entire community, and you must sign an "ecclesiastical contract," which cannot be broken without the permission of a metropolitan judge, who will then rule if the engagement can be broken.

There was only one problem. You first needed to get a "certificate of freedom" from the congregation to which you currently belonged. And you needed the priest of your neighborhood to certify that you had not been engaged before.

Normally, this wouldn't be a problem. But because of the invasion, Famagusta's priests were scattered throughout the southern part of the island.

We had to trek to the town of Larnaca and then to a village near the Troodos Mountains, looking for the priests from our neighborhoods.

Niki and I had been living in Athens. How in the world did our local priests know if we had been engaged to someone else? Just in case, and for insurance, I took my father on that journey, and Niki took her mother, because they knew the priests.

Back then it was very serious. Looking at it now, the whole expedition seems comical. In the midst of all of this tragedy, we were spending countless hours searching for priests in refugee camps who had no idea if we had already been engaged or not.

To make it even more absurd, when we finally found the priest from my neighborhood, he couldn't stop cursing Henry Kissinger who hadn't stopped the Turks, unlike LBJ who did.

At the end of that trip, with so many things weighing on my mind, my father said something that altered the trajectory of my life.

"You should pursue graduate studies abroad," he said.

It was a sad moment. But I knew he was right. I had never really considered studying abroad, but his suggestion provided me with a sudden flash of inspiration.

As with my entire journey, the road ahead would not be easy. I would have to close a chapter of my life, turn my back on tragedy, and trust that a better future awaited.

For the moment, that meant returning to Athens with Niki.

PART TWO

IMMIGRATING TO THE UNITED STATES

CHAPTER 6

America America

«Σὰ βγεῖς στὸν πηγαιμὸ γιὰ τὴν Ἰθάκη,
νὰ εὔχεσαι νἆναι μακρὺς ὁ δρόμος,
γεμάτος περιπέτειες, γεμάτος γνώσεις.»

Κ. Π. ΚΑΒΆΦΗΣ, ἸΘΆΚΗ

"As you set out for Ithaka,
hope your road is a long one,
full of adventure, full of discovery." [1]

C. P. CAVAFY, "ITHAKA"

As I entered my third year at the Polytechnic in the fall of 1974, I was in the middle of a personal crisis. Niki and I were surviving thanks to "tickets" provided by the government to Greek Cypriot refugees studying in Athens. These tickets allowed us to eat lunch for free not only at our own college campus, but at any university campus.

I was working at the National Bank of Greece and going to school. More importantly, I had lost faith in my academic pursuits. I felt disoriented and was asking, "What is engineering all about?"

After two years of taking around 20 courses in mathematics, physics, and the sciences, I was lost in the intellectual wilderness searching for meaning and purpose. Then, just at the moment I needed it, I stepped into the classroom of a man who would change my life.

In his very first presentation, Professor Diamesis said, "Let me tell you what an engineering system is all about." He started with the sonar system, then a radar system, and then a communications system. One by one, he broke them down, using the mathematics of signal processing to model each of these distinct systems.

At the time, he also had oversight of the sonar and radar systems for the Greek Navy, so he wasn't just pulling problems from books. He was bringing real-life examples into the classroom, information that was always changing and evolving.

It was a revelation. For the first time in my life, I saw engineering systems and mathematics coming together in a new way that rekindled my interest and ignited my curiosity. I enjoyed his lectures so much that I took all of his classes after that. In my fifth year at the Polytechnic, I did a research project with his group. His influence was the reason I pursued systems and signal processing for my graduate studies, following that same direction for research with my own graduate students.

In a poetic coincidence, many years later his youngest son became a Ph.D. student at USC when I was dean of engineering.

⁂ ⁂ ⁂

I was thinking about my aspirations to pursue graduate studies abroad. I started taking tutoring lessons in English and making sure that all of my engineering books were also in English, so that I would learn all of the proper terminology.

I was concerned that learning a new language might be difficult, but I found out that I was very fortunate. Like medicine, engineering terminology is filled with Greek and Latin words. It was very easy for me to learn and I rarely had to search through a dictionary to find a definition.

In June 1977, I took my final undergraduate exams. The test for each subject lasted eight hours—non-stop. You couldn't speak to any of the other students. You could bring water and a sandwich into the exam room, but you could only leave briefly to go to the bathroom.

The first day I spent eight hours on "electrical machine designs." The second day was devoted to "power systems and transmission lines." And the third was "electrical circuits and electronics designs." Fortunately, I survived and passed with flying colors.

Later, I officially became a professional engineer, getting my license to practice through the Technical Chamber of Greece. Niki had graduated with a bachelor's degree in accounting in 1975 and began working full-time as an accountant for a real estate development company in Athens.

Although Athens had provided us with many wonderful memories, other adventures were calling to us.

* * *

One month after graduating from the Polytechnic, Niki and I returned to Cyprus to get married. At that time, Cyprus remained a divided island trying to recover economically from the Turkish invasion and the immense challenges of housing one-third of its citizens who were refugees.

Normally, starting a new life together is a happy time. But for us, that long, hot summer did not provide us with good memories. Instead, I remember visiting our relatives, who were still living in refugee camps, so that we could give them invitations to our wedding.

In my mind, this visit only reinforced the catastrophe that had hit the island three years earlier. I was bothered by the fact that there were no street names or numbers on the refugee camps, just people forced to live anonymous lives in these terrible conditions. It was tragic.

Three days after our wedding, the beloved Archbishop Makarios died and Cyprus went into national mourning for 40 days. We were extremely fortunate. If he had died three days earlier, no church could have had any weddings for 40 days.

For me and Niki, it was a sign that we needed space from Cyprus.

* * *

In September 1977, we decided to move to England. We chose the most affordable option, traveling 72 hours by bus from Athens to London. However, by the time we reached Calais, France, we discovered that the bus company had filed for bankruptcy, stranding us at the port for the entire evening.

The next morning, we spent our limited savings, buying new tickets for the ferry to Dover, and then a train to London. By the time we arrived, we were exhausted. In many ways, this would be an omen for the next year of our lives.

Niki and I rented a two-room apartment in a house in North London near Alexandra Park. If you wanted to use the electricity and gas, you had to insert coins in a machine.

I bought a used Austin Morris car for only £200 which looked nice on the outside, although the driver's side had a piece of carpet covering a hole in the floor.

Niki had received a transfer and worked full-time at her company's offices near Oxford Square which provided the majority of our income throughout our time in London.

I had been accepted by two universities: Imperial College London for a master's degree in electrical engineering and Queen Mary University of London, where I could get my Ph.D. directly.

I chose Queen Mary University for two reasons. One, it gave me the opportunity to start a Ph.D. research program right away. And two, my advisor-to-be and I were already exchanging a large volume of letters, where he was explaining the parameters of the project.

Later I discovered that he belonged to the Philatelic Society of London and gave many presentations. I began to suspect the exchange of letters was less about his enthusiasm for the research project and more about collecting Greek stamps from me! I would also learn that it was a big mistake to attend Queen Mary University, my first major misstep when it came to my education.

I shared a large office with six other international graduate students who were all shocked to find out that I didn't attend Imperial College. One of them went as far as to tell me that I should revisit the offer if it was still available.

After one semester, I realized they were right. I didn't like my advisor, had concerns about the topic of my research, and had borrowed money to pay the tuition at Queen Mary College. I did end up publishing a few papers with my advisor, but nevertheless I was very depressed.

To make ends meet, a few nights a week, I began working as a receptionist at the Edwards Hotel in Hyde Park. Although London is a beautiful, vibrant city, at that point in our lives we didn't have the money to really enjoy it. Our big night was often going to McDonald's on Piccadilly Square for a hamburger!

* * *

Despite some great times in London, I felt like I was at a crossroads, possibly a dead end. I couldn't see myself finishing my thesis and it was impossible to make the leap in the United Kingdom unless you were married to a British citizen.

My friend Andreas Polydoros stayed with us for a few days on his way back to the United States. He was doing his graduate studies in electrical engineering at the State University of New York at Buffalo, where Polytechnic graduates had an excellent academic reputation among the faculty.

He offered to recommend me to one of the professors and encouraged me to apply to the university for graduate studies.

I was accepted for an M.S. and a Ph.D. in electrical engineering, with Peter Scott as my thesis advisor. He had a joint NIH grant with Dr. John Siegel, Chief of the Department of Surgery at Buffalo General Hospital (BGH).

I was offered a full research assistantship and a tuition waiver to start in January, 1979. So, it is fair to say that an NIH grant made it possible for us to come to America.

One night when I was working at the Edwards Hotel, a group of American tourists were in the lobby. One of them was chatting with me and bragged about going to America for graduate studies. When I mentioned that I had been accepted at SUNY Buffalo, he said, "Oh, my God, that's a lot of snow."

Then he proceeded to tell me: "To succeed as an immigrant in America, you have a very small margin of error."

I took his advice to heart. And it would shape my attitude throughout my graduate studies and into my career.

Sadly, I had to sell my beloved Austin Morris car at auction in London before we left for America. But that was soon replaced by one of my happiest moments in London when I went to the U.S. Embassy to receive our F-1 Visas to travel to America.

And things were about to change for the better.

* * *

Our journey to America began with a red-eye flight from Heathrow to JFK.

We were traveling to the "land of opportunity," and yet this was truly the first time in my life that I truly felt like an immigrant.

During the nearly eight-hour trip on the plane, I wanted to be happy and optimistic, but my mind was filled with memories of the time I had lost in London and the many questions I had about the future.

Niki and I were not only coming to America, but I felt we needed to do our best to stay in America. I recalled my father's advice to never return to Cyprus. But then I wondered where would we settle, where would we find a home?

And what did we really know about America?

In Greece and Cyprus, anti-American sentiments were running high, especially in the media. In 1974, the U.S. had failed to stop the Turkish invasion, although Greece was a fellow member of NATO and the guarantor powers of the Republic of Cyprus were three NATO members: the U.K, Greece and Turkey. (Turkey had also used NATO weapons to divide the island, causing so much destruction and loss of life.)

Most of what we knew about American culture came from books, newspapers, magazines, television, and movies. But from our friends who had studied in the U.S. and our professors who had taught there, we heard that America had the best system of universities in the world, especially in engineering and the sciences. They praised the "freedom of speech" and "freedom of expression" on their campuses.

I remember that the original *Rocky* movie was playing, starring Sylvester Stallone. There's a scene where a fight promoter calls Rocky in for a meeting.

"Rocky, do you believe that America is the land of opportunity?" the promoter says.

"Yeah," says Rocky unenthusiastically.

At that moment, with all the doubts swirling in my head, it was so inspiring. And I had to ask myself, "Did I believe America was the land of opportunity?

As we flew with all of our worldly possessions packed in a few suitcases, we had only $2,500 to our names. Niki and I were thinking of receiving our degrees, and then moving back to Greece. But had I been able to see the future, I would have definitely said, "Yes! I believe America is the land of opportunity!"

I couldn't have known that 33 years later I would get to know the actual Rocky, when Sylvester Stallone and his wife, Jennifer, became USC parents who we hosted at football games.

On Friday, January 12, 1979, we landed at JFK. The tourists at the Edwards Hotel in London were right, it was cold. Buffalo would be even colder.

But Niki and I didn't care about the cold or the snow. We were in America!

* * *

It wasn't long before we realized how far Buffalo was from New York. At that time, there was no way to search the internet or your phone to find the distance from city to city. We were surprised we would need another flight to get to our final destination, and shocked that there was only one option at 7:00 p.m.

During our first day in America, we waited in JFK for more than 12 hours. But the long delay also led to our second surprise. We discovered that, unlike in Europe, coffee refills were free!

We finally arrived in Buffalo around 8:00 p.m. Through the windows, we could see a thick blanket of snow covering the entire city. Our friend Andreas was waiting for us, his warm breath forming small clouds as he happily welcomed us to America.

As we drove, we were amazed that the snow was piled up several feet above the car. We had never seen so much snow in our lives, and the entire city was dark and cold.

It was a sign that even in the land of opportunity we needed time to adapt to our new environment.

* * *

While we were looking for a permanent place to live, we stayed with Andreas in the Princeton Apartments, which were right across the street from the main campus of the university.

When we first saw the apartment complex, my first thought was that it looked like the military barracks in Crete.

Niki took a long look around and instantly broke into tears.

"Is this where we're going to live?" she asked.

But for the next three years, it would not only be where we

lived, but also where we would learn to love America.

⁂ ⁂ ⁂

The next day we enjoyed the luxury of fine dining, with our first American meal at Denny's. I tried to order dessert, but my British and Greek Cypriot accents made it difficult for the waitress to understand me.

"Carrot cake," I said.

"What?" she asked.

"Carrot cake," I tried again.

She looked at me blankly, my order lost in translation. Then Andreas pronounced it with his American accent.

"Carrot cake," he said with a smile.

"Oh, okay. Carrot cake," said the waitress.

America was clearly going to be an adjustment.

⁂ ⁂ ⁂

Soon, we would be introduced to other amazing aspects of American culture. The first time we experienced what President Reagan called "the charm of the American supermarket," we were impressed by the spaciousness and abundance available to everyone.

Nearly 40 years later, when I asked Niki what she remembers most about Buffalo she immediately replied, "The supermarkets!"

⁂ ⁂ ⁂

Over the next three years, I would be so busy with research, studying, and preparing my thesis that I had little free time to explore many interests outside of the academic environment.

I also had to figure out options for transportation because I would be attending classes and also working at Buffalo General Hospital (BGH). For $250, I bought a car that had no heating system.

On some mornings, during my drive downtown to BGH, I would have to open the window slightly to keep it from fogging over. At stoplights, I chipped away at the frozen crystals forming on the windshield with an ice scraper.

Looking back, I don't know how I survived Buffalo winters without a heater in my car. But when you're determined to reach a goal, you can make anything happen.

* * *

In Buffalo, there were also other changes coming that would alter my career path and even my personal identity.

When I started my Ph.D. program, I met my thesis advisor, Professor Peter Scott. We were having a great conversation and everything was going along well, but there was only one problem. He couldn't pronounce my first name, Chrysostomos.

I told Dr. Scott that growing up people had called me "Makis."

He said, "No, no, that's not right. How about Max? It has 'punch' to it. Besides, it was my father's name."

From that moment on, I would be known personally and professionally as "Max Nikias."

* * *

In addition to getting a new nickname, I would gain many things from two very important mentors in Buffalo, Dr. Peter Scott and Dr. John Siegal.

These two extraordinary men were co-investigators on an

NIH grant. During the academic year, I worked two days a week at BGH and my graduate research stipend was $600 per month. During the summer, I worked full time at BGH for three months for $1,200 per month, plus tuition remission.

Dr. Scott was a good man and a great teacher, with the ability to explain incredibly complex subjects in very simple terms. He was much more than just a professor. He was also a great performer. Unlike many academics, his lectures were filled with interesting stories and dramatic details. It was like theatre. Needless to say, I was extremely impressed and tried to model my teaching after his style.

Dr. John Siegel, the chief of surgery at BGH, was a great researcher and a great surgeon. He taught me how to run a research group, how to treat your research collaborators, and how to always be kind, supportive, and willing to give advice. He was a true gentleman, and even after he left Buffalo, we would collaborate for another 10 years, publishing many papers and securing two patents.

There is a very important story that reveals the character of Dr. John Siegel. Niki and I had arrived in Buffalo in January. By March, I was beginning to find my way around, but I had only interacted with Dr. Siegel two or three times.

One night, we were out with another couple at a restaurant when Niki started to have severe pain on her lower right side. My friend said, "We have to take her to the emergency room at BGH. It's not far from here. And it could be appendicitis."

We rushed Niki to the emergency room. As they took her away for observation, the on-call doctor asked, "Who's her doctor?"

We'd only been in Buffalo for two months and hadn't even been to the student health center. I'm not sure why I said what I did next. I suppose I was thinking Niki might get better treatment if she wasn't just a random international student who walked into the emergency room.

"I know Dr. John Siegel," I said.

"How do you know Dr. Siegel?" he asked.

"I work with him in his research laboratory."

"Okay," he said, and then headed off to do a series of exams on Niki.

After about three hours, he emerged. By this time, it's 3:00 a.m.

"The good news is it doesn't appear to be appendicitis, but we still need to verify that," the doctor said.

I was relieved and thanked him for his help. Then he said something that terrified me.

"Now I just need to call Dr. Siegel," he said.

In a moment, my heartrate raced from calm to panic.

"Oh, no. Please don't do that," I begged.

"No, you don't understand," he said. "As chief of the Department of Surgery, Dr. Siegel has a very strict protocol. Anyone who registers as his patient, after we collect all the data in the emergency room, we must call him with all of the results."

It's 3:00 a.m. I'm exhausted and still concerned about Niki. If they'd done tests on me, they would have realized I was practically having a panic attack.

"But please, can't you just wait until morning to call him?" I pleaded.

"No, I'm sorry. We have to follow the protocol."

And then he left. I'm sitting there in the waiting area, my head in my hands, afraid of what I'd done. A few moments later, the on-call doctor returns.

"Dr. Siegel is on the phone. He wants to talk to you," he said.

I was crushed. The walk to the phone was one of the longest in my life. I felt terrible that I'd used Dr. Siegel's name and he barely even knew me.

Clearly, Dr. Siegel had been asleep and I was the reason he'd been awakened.

"I'm really sorry, Dr. Siegel," I said.

He spoke in a very low, soft voice.

"No, no, Max, it's fine," he whispered. "I just want you to know that Niki is fine. There is nothing to worry about it. It was an ovulation pain midway through her cycle. It's very common, especially for young women. All the results verify that. It's not appendicitis. There's nothing to worry about. And they should be finishing soon. Take her home, take Sunday off, and relax."

The next time I saw him in the laboratory, he immediately asked how Niki was doing. That story tells you all you need to know about Dr. John Siegel. He was not only a great surgeon and researcher, he was also a true gentleman.

The way he treated everyone with care and respect was a great lesson for me in learning how to treat my own graduate students later. And for that, I am forever grateful.

* * *

Niki recovered quickly. After one semester, she entered the university's School of Management to earn her M.B.A. in finance.

In three years, I completed both my master's of science degree and my Ph.D., which required me to take four courses per semester instead of two. At the same time, I was working at BGH, finishing my thesis, and teaching undergraduate courses.

We were constantly working so hard, attending classes, studying and conducting research in the lab. Our lives were consumed by work 24/7, it seemed.

And yet, although it was cold and snowing most of the winter, and even in the spring, we didn't care. We were in America and we loved it.

We will never forget our very first Thanksgiving in America. We hadn't had time to absorb and adjust to the culture. On Thanksgiving, we didn't have money for a big dinner, so we thought we would go out to eat.

We soon learned that everything was closed. It was cold and dark and very lonely.

When I became president at USC, we remembered how lonely that holiday can be for students who are not with their families.

It was Niki's idea to host Thanksgiving dinners at the president's home in San Marino for students who didn't go home for the holidays.

❊ ❊ ❊

Soon I would be entering an environment that would introduce me to important colleagues and mentors, who were working in a revolutionary area of advanced technology.

Fortunately, once again, I would find myself in the right place at the right time.

CHAPTER 7

Perseverance

« τῷ λόγῳ ὃς καρτερεῖν κελεύει.
εἰ οὖν βούλει, καὶ ἡμεῖς ἐπὶ τῇ ζητήσει ἐπιμείνωμέν τε καὶ καρτερήσωμεν,
ἵνα καὶ μὴ ἡμῶν αὐτὴ ἡ ἀνδρεία καταγελάσῃ,
ὅτι οὐκ ἀνδρείως αὐτὴν ζητοῦμεν,
εἰ ἄρα πολλάκις αὐτὴ ἡ καρτέρησίς ἐστιν ἀνδρεία.»

ΠΛΆΤΩΝΟΣ ΛΆΧΗΣ, 194A

"That which enjoins endurance.
And, if you please, let us too be steadfast and enduring in our inquiry,
so as not to be ridiculed by courage herself
for failing to be courageous in our search for her,
when we might perchance find after all that this very endurance is courage."[1]

PLATO, *LACHES*, 194A

It was an exciting time to work at Buffalo General Hospital, where major innovations were happening in the area of coronary artery bypass surgery. But on the academic front I faced a major setback on my quest for an original topic for my Ph.D. dissertation.

I had several ideas for new signal processing methodologies, but they all led down dead ends.

One day, while meeting with my advisor, he said, "You need to seriously think about what you want to do for your thesis."

I had exhausted all of my ideas and was starting to feel depressed. After wasting precious time in London pursuing the wrong program, I feared that I was making another mistake.

To make it worse, in the summer of 1979, Niki and I returned to Cyprus for a short visit with our families. When we arrived at the airport, my father-in-law pulled me aside and said, "How long are you going to be studying at the university? When are you going to get a real job?"

It seemed that everyone was questioning my future, including myself.

This was all weighing on my mind when I returned for the fall semester. I was taking an advanced course in detection and estimation theory for sonar, radar, and communications from Dr. Jim Caprio.

He was a very tough teacher, who ran his classes on an almost military schedule. His class was on Monday morning at 8:00 a.m. He chose that time on purpose, probably as a way to weed out those who weren't dedicated enough. One day, during a break, he started talking to me about exciting new areas of advanced signal processing, modern techniques in spectral analysis.

He described its potential for the future of digital signal processing and recommended a new book on the subject, which was really a recently published collection of papers. It was just a simple, innocent conversation. But for me, it was a "light bulb" moment. As soon as class ended, I ran to find the book he recommended.

And that did it for me! After all of the searching and the anxiety, suddenly the answer just appeared. Soon I was on the path to an exciting Ph.D. thesis topic that would not only have application to biomedicine—and my current work at BGH—but also in groundbreaking areas of sonar, radar, and communications.

Things were beginning to change for the better.

* * *

Once again, the old adage "timing is everything" proved true. My thesis would introduce me to exciting new areas of research that were just taking off. Over the next few decades, virtually every system in technology would make the transition from "analog" to "digital."

Major fields like sonar, radar, communications, seismic exploration, biomedical signal analysis and audio-video processing, all underwent the transition from analog to digital at the same time.

In January 1980, when President Reagan was inaugurated, the United States began a major defense build-up during the heart of the Cold War. There was a massive increase in funding for research in these areas, and to upgrade all of these military and civilian systems for the coming digital world.

It just happened that Dr. Caprio also did work for Carlsbad, an aerospace company in Buffalo, so he knew this area was going to become important and very exciting for research and new digital systems development.

* * *

In addition to my mentors Dr. Scott and Dr. Siegel, there was another professor who played a very important role in my life at SUNY Buffalo. This was the very confident Greek-American Professor Dimitri Lainiotis, who was also the former chairman of the electrical engineering department.

Everything he did was bigger than life. He was very smart and everything he was doing was the very best research in the world. During my first semester, I took two important graduate courses with him.

At a time of great uncertainty, he filled me with confidence, saying, "You are going to excel in America because you are technically competent and willing to work hard."

With his strong personality, he also had opinions about others in the department. There was one particular faculty member that, for some reason, he didn't really like. At one point, I think we were eating lunch in the cafeteria and the faculty member walked past our table.

He said, "It won't be too long after you start your academic career that he will be asking you to write recommendation letters for him. And that's because you are going to be more successful and more famous than him."

I laughed. The idea was absurd. I hadn't even established myself in my Ph.D. program, and here was Professor Lainiotis predicting my success. I wrote off his comments as eccentricity.

And yet, looking back, he was right. That particular professor did ask me to support him many times over the course of his career.

* * *

In Buffalo we got our first glimpse of serious crime in the United States, as well as how the media can sensationalize a tragic event.

As we adjusted to our new life in America, we were very fortunate to be immediately and warmly welcomed by the Greek student community.

When we first arrived in Buffalo, we connected with the local church. The priest and his wife had three little children, and they hosted us at their house for lunch one Sunday.

He wanted us to work with him to organize an event called "Cyprus Awareness Week," and he even planned to invite the Consul General of Cyprus in New York City to come to Buffalo.

We were happy to help organize the event, providing some film we had received from the Consulate of Cyprus, as well as our personal experiences about the invasion, the refugees, and other things.

But one Sunday evening, a few weeks before Cyprus Awareness Week, the priest was shot and killed in the church.

If it wasn't tragic enough, the media made it worse. It was our first experience with local radio, newspapers, and television sensationalizing an event with misinformation. They were making all of these wild speculations, wondering if the priest led a double life, or if he was doing drugs, or if he was spending evenings at a cabaret with women, or even if he'd had an affair and was killed by the husband.

Just one story after another, none of them true.

It turns out there were two young burglars, who had spent much of the afternoon drinking beer and taking LSD.[2] The priest was shot once in the wrist and four times in the torso.

On the following Sunday after the incident, Niki and I were leaving church when we were approached by the FBI. They flashed their badges and cornered us, pulling us aside to ask us questions.

Although they were very polite, we were scared to death. We had only been in the country for a few months and here we were being questioned by the FBI. There was more misinformation that the killing could have been connected to Cyprus Awareness Week, which we were helping organize.

Someone suggested to the FBI that Turkish agents may have killed the priest because the event was only a couple of weeks away. It didn't make any sense to me.

Of course, we had no details that could help the FBI, but it was really frightening. We were just sad for the priest, his family, and the other church members.

On top of the tragedy, his family had to endure all of these terrible stories that questioned his character. But we were introduced to the dark side of democracy, when "freedom of speech" is sometimes confused with saying anything you want, even if it's not true.

❊ ❊ ❊

By October 1981, after years of intense effort and deep study, I was ready to defend my Ph.D. thesis.

And yet, what should have been a culmination of all of those years of learning and hard work was filled with more uncertainty because of external circumstances.

Dr. John Siegel had accepted a new appointment as Deputy Director of the Maryland Institute for Emergency Medical Services Systems (MIEMSS), known as the Shock and Trauma Center of the University of Maryland Hospital in Baltimore. For him, this was a great career opportunity. But for me, his departure renewed anxiety about the future.

Because financial support for my studies was tied to Dr. Siegel's research grant, I worried that his leaving might affect our already tenuous economic situation. At the same time, my thesis advisor Peter Scott wasn't thrilled when I told him that I wanted to move up the date of my graduation and defend my thesis earlier because we were publishing papers together.

Looking back, knowing what I know today, I wish I would have been able to better control my fears about the future.

But, at that time, my reasoning was overridden by impatience and my ambition was to start my academic career as soon as possible.

* * *

After defending my thesis successfully, I presented my first professional research paper in Canada at a workshop in Hamilton, Ontario.

Soon after, I had interviews at the University of Ohio and the University of Connecticut. Throughout the process, there were many signs Connecticut might be the right place for me. When they made me an offer, I accepted because I thought it was a better electrical engineering group.

However, before I could officially accept the job at the University of Connecticut and begin my academic career, there was one small issue.

I needed an H-1B Visa, which would allow me to get on the university's payroll as a person from another country who can perform services of an "exceptional nature."

At that time, the exceptional nature was a shortage of engineers, especially highly-skilled electrical engineers with a Ph.D. degree, so I wasn't displacing an American worker. There simply weren't enough people with that specific skill-set in the entire country at the time.

I signed all of the paperwork, and the international office at the University of Connecticut filed it with the Hartford immigration office.

I was planning to start my position at the university on January 1, 1982. So, in November, I drove from Buffalo to Connecticut to stay for a week to get everything settled.

I went to the immigration office in Hartford and I will never forget how rude they were. First of all, you wait in this enormous line, and then you sit forever until they call your number.

When I finally got to the counter, I politely explained my situation.

Without even looking at any of my paperwork, the woman practically shouted, "The earliest is going to be April or May of next year. There's a backlog."

"But I can't do that. I have to start my job," I pleaded.

"Go. We're done here," she said. "That's the earliest we can do it."

She was so rude. The entire experience left a bad taste in my mouth.

And then my mind began spinning. I thought, "Oh, my God. What do I do? I'm in limbo. I won't have a job. I won't have a paycheck. Just when I thought my career was about to take off, I'm stalled once again."

So, I drive all the way back to Buffalo, and I'm depressed. There was nothing I could do but wait. I was still fuming when I shared the incident with one of my assistant professors.

That's when I learned about Mr. Berger.

This assistant professor said, "Listen, you need a lawyer. There's a guy here in Buffalo, Mr. Berger. He helped me get my H-1B Visa when I started here. I think you should go and see him. Let me call him."

So he calls Mr. Berger and makes me an appointment. I go to his office and there's this big guy sitting behind a little desk.

He says, "First of all, I need a retainer—$2,000 cash."

If you've seen the television show *Better Call Saul*, I started getting suspicions that he might be that type of lawyer.

To get my H-1B Visa—in order to get paid at my job—I had to borrow $2,000 from my cousin, who I had helped come to the United States to study.

I give Mr. Berger his $2,000 cash retainer and I'm expecting real results from this guy.

As soon as I hand over the money, he calls the Hartford Immigration Office and puts them on speakerphone.

For 40 minutes, we're sitting together in this little room, listening to elevator music. Mr. Berger is sitting back in his chair waiting.

After a while, the wait became unbearable. I felt like I should have brought a book, or something to do.

Finally, a voice comes on the speakerphone. Mr. Berger immediately launched into a tirade.

"Lady, I am an attorney, Mr. Berger blah, blah, blah, and I represent so and so. And let me tell you something. Next time I call, you don't put me on hold that long. I prefer the music of my radio to your music."

I'm sitting there thinking, "Wow, he talks to an immigration officer like that? And I just gave him $2,000 cash."

The immigration lady explained the backlog, as well as the impossibility of my request.

But then she used the "magic" words. "Unless there are extenuating circumstances."

And then Mr. Berger hangs up! I'm thinking, "For $2,000, this is what I get?"

He leans forward and says, "The only way we can get it through is extenuating circumstances, so what are you going to teach? Why are they hiring you at UConn?"

I explain that I am the first professor ever hired by the University of Connecticut in the area of digital signal processing. I'm going to introduce a new curriculum, including undergraduate and graduate courses they have never had before. And that's why they hired me.

Mr. Berger looked unimpressed.

"Okay, what else?"

Then I remembered that the chairman of the department had already told me what I was going to teach in the spring semester.

I said, "UConn has a contract with a Naval base in New London, Connecticut. A submarine base. And one of the courses I'm going to teach at the master's degree level twice a week is in advanced digital signal processing methods with applications to sonar. That's one of the reasons they hired me."

"That's it!" said Mr. Berger. "You go back and tell your department chairman I want a letter from him addressed to Hartford immigration, and you get me the original copy of the documents that explain what you just told me. Tell him to use the expression 'and it is of national security interest, according to the New London naval base.'"

So, I talked to my chairman and he said, "Of course, Max. That's why we got this big contract from the Navy. It's the new digital technologies. It is of national security interest."

And that was it. After all of that drama, I got the letter and drove it to Mr. Berger's office. Ten days later, my H-1B Visa was in my mailbox in Buffalo.

I learned two important lessons from that experience. First of all, it helps to do work of national security interest for the U.S. government. And second, it always pays to have a good lawyer. The money is worth it, even if you have to borrow it!

* * *

As we ended our time in Buffalo, Niki and I felt like we had grown dramatically as people and in our knowledge of America.

She had been working very hard to complete a very demanding M.B.A. program in finance and I had finally completed my Ph.D.

As we graduated from SUNY Buffalo, both of our diplomas were signed by a young university president named Steven B. Sample.

Years later, of course, we would once again cross paths at the University of Southern California, where we would both serve as president.

But before that, I had to celebrate a milestone in my own life. After all of the years of being a student, I was finally going to be a professor with a real job.

I was about to begin my most productive years of engineering research before I accepted leadership roles.

Thanks to much perseverance, my career was about to take off.

CHAPTER 8

Through the Wilderness

«ἀλλ' ἐπεὶ οὐδ' ὄπιθεν κακὸς ἔσσεαι οὐδ' ἀνοήμων,
οὐδέ σε πάγχυ γε μῆτις 'Οδυσσῆος προλέλοιπεν,
ἐλπωρή τοι ἔπειτα τελευτῆσαι τάδε ἔργα.»

ΌΜΉΡΟΥ ΌΔΎΣΣΕΙΑ, Β 278–280

"You'll be neither a coward nor a dolt hereafter
If your father's spirit is well instilled in you,
Such a man was he in fulfilling word and deed,
Then your journey will be neither in vain nor without result."[1]

HOMER, *ODYSSEY*, BOOK II, 278–280

I began my academic career in the 1980s, when the transformation from analog to digital engineering systems was as disruptive and exciting as artificial intelligence is today. Analog systems were slow, inaccurate and inflexible. Thanks to the microelectronics revolution, digital systems were leading to the rise of faster and smaller computers. Digital signal processing powered the transition to faster and more flexible radar, sonar, and telecommunications systems and so many other applications.

Many considered this time a "renaissance" in engineering and the sciences, fueled by massive defense funding from the Reagan administration's Strategic Defense Initiative (SDI).

For me and Niki, this time would be a continuation of our journey together, exploring our new life in America, starting our own family, and buying our first house.

For me personally, there would be many changes in roles and

responsibilities, becoming a father for the first time, and dealing with the declining health of my own father, which would cause me to face my own mortality.

Professionally, I was also going through a tremendous transformation. I'm not sure why, but for most researchers, their 30s are the most productive and filled with the most original ideas. And that was certainly the case for me.

Everything really began to blossom a few years later in Boston, but the seeds of success were planted in Storrs, Connecticut.

* * *

If Buffalo seemed like a major departure from Cyprus, or Athens, or London, Connecticut was a different world entirely.

To travel from Buffalo to Connecticut, once again I had to borrow money to buy a more reliable car that would deliver us safely to our destination.

When we arrived in Storrs, Niki and I were in for another shock. Culture shock. First of all, Storrs isn't really a city. It's a town of just over 15,000 people with a university campus.

Gone were the dark Buffalo winters, but also missing were the massive supermarkets that had reminded us of America's extraordinary abundance. The University of Connecticut was rural and isolated, surrounded by woods and lakes, with mosquitoes in the summer. The major city skyline and traffic jams were replaced by the sight of cows wandering in fields!

At UConn, once again, we would have to make major adjustments. But how could I pass up this opportunity? As an assistant professor of electrical engineering, my nine-month salary would be $23,000. It doesn't sound like much today, but when I left SUNY Buffalo my advisor was a little upset because I would be making more than him.

Adapting to our new environment was a challenge. This time there were no tears when we were looking for a place to live, but

I knew Niki's heart longed for life in a large city.

Niki would stay in Buffalo for the first semester to finish her MBA and later work at the UConn Foundation as a member of their financial investment team.

For the first six months, I saved money by renting a room in a house close to campus. The family was very nice. He was a pharmacist and she was a teacher, and politically they were very liberal. One night I heard the woman crying hysterically, and I couldn't understand what was so upsetting to her. Then I heard her shouting, "Reagan is going to get us into nuclear war with the Soviets!"

Little did any of us know that only five years later, President Reagan would stand in front of the Brandenberg Gate in Berlin and utter the words, "Mr. Gorbachev, tear down this wall!," a line that several of his top advisors insisted he remove from his speech.[2]

⁂

Once at Storrs, I immediately threw myself into preparing proposals for the new courses I wanted to teach in digital signal processing.

I didn't just want a job, I wanted to be known as an innovator. And I was willing to put in the extra work that would allow me to break new ground in this emerging discipline that I believed would revolutionize the world.

Twice a week, I drove to the submarine base in New London, Connecticut, where I taught classes in the new and emerging fields of advanced digital signal processing for sonar and radar.

When people say, "America is the land of opportunity," this is what they mean. Only three years after arriving in America, I was standing in front of a class of 40 leading Naval scientists and engineers.

They had more practical experience than me, so they weren't

interested in just sitting back and absorbing a lecture. They constantly challenged me with questions, and in some ways, I was learning more from them because of their persistent inquiries.

Their enjoyment of my courses and excellent student evaluations fueled my confidence, and ignited my desire to share even more of what I was learning.

* * *

With all of these things happening so quickly, I gained new ground through what again could be called "coincidence" or "serendipity."

One afternoon in the spring of 1982, a senior faculty member in the department was looking for help to review a technical publication. He walks into my office and hands me a paper. He says, "You're the expert on modern spectral analysis methods. This paper's in that area. Can you please review it for me?"

There are moments in your life after which you are never the same. For my career, you can easily mark the stage before and after I read this paper. It was about an approach to spectral analysis using the *bispectrum*. Despite years of study in my area of expertise, I had never heard of the *bispectrum* before. Everyone in the field of spectral analysis was hard at work on parametric techniques, which employ models to analyze the patterns in a signal (sort of like using a simple formula to determine the shape of a mountain.) However, at the time, everyone was studying parametric techniques for the *power spectrum*, but not the *bispectrum*.

The power spectrum methods most people in the field studied looked at how much energy a signal has at different frequencies, like different pitches in music. But signals have interactions between frequencies that the power spectrum misses. These interactions between frequencies can provide valuable new information about the system that generates them. The *bispectrum* method spots interactions that can tell, for example, whether a signal is from a submarine or ocean noise. In the case of brain waves, it can detect unusual patterns, especially after injury.

Reading the paper on the bispectrum method was a revelation. I immediately rushed to the library and searched for any material I could find about it. At the time, there was very little information in signal analysis and applications about higher-order spectra, of which the bispectrum is a special case.

But I was able to learn about the concept of higher-order spectra (one of which is the bispectrum) in statistics, which was introduced in a published paper in the mid-1930s by Andrey Kolmogorov, perhaps the most brilliant Russian mathematician of the 20th century.[3] Since that time, there have been papers published by statisticians on the *bispectrum*, but very few addressed the applications using conventional methods.

As I read, I imagined a new area of research using higher-order spectra for digital signal processing applications based on parametric methods. My heart was racing with excitement because, to the best of my knowledge, no one in the modern spectral analysis community was working in this area of signal processing.

But to take advantage of this new opportunity, I had to move quickly. Over the next two decades, working with a growing team of talented graduate students and postdoctoral fellows, we were able to advance the field of signal processing, bringing many other researchers around the world into this orbit.

* * *

In any profession, a sign that you are on the right track is when the luminaries in your field begin to recognize and validate your work. This happened after my first graduate student and I published the very first IEEE tutorial paper on the *bispectrum*.

In 1985, Professor Alan Oppenheim, the "father of digital

signal processing," reached out to me and invited me to give a talk about the *bispectrum* at MIT. It was a nerve-wracking experience, but it went so well that Dr. Oppenheim encouraged me to write a textbook to be published under his digital signal processing series with Prentice-Hall, which, of course, I enthusiastically agreed to do.

Along with one of my Ph.D. students, I published the very first textbook on Higher-Order Spectral Analysis for signal processing. And in the summer of 1989, with the support of the Office of Naval Research, I was the co-organizer of the very first workshop on the same topic in Vail, Colorado.

After years of waiting and skepticism, the newfound validation of our work was a breath of fresh air. This new area of research would define me as one of the pioneers of digital signal analysis.

It would be an incredible ride and I was eager to see where the future would lead.

* * *

During the summers from 1982 to 1989, I was still collaborating with Dr. John Siegel, who was now working as the deputy director at the Maryland Institute for Emergency Medical Services Systems.

It was then that another opportunity appeared to me by chance. At UConn, there was a recruiter who came to campus to scout our senior engineering students and convince them to work at the naval weapons center at China Lake, California. Although it's located near the Mojave Desert in Death Valley, China Lake is the largest base for the U.S. Navy.

Karen Altieri was traveling to universities in rural and cold-winter areas because China Lake was very isolated, and she felt it would be difficult to convince students from urban areas to work there.

Although her ultimate goal was to recruit engineers, it was part of the process to build relationships with certain faculty in the department. In the process, she either heard about my work or noticed that I had introduced the curriculum in digital signal processing.

So, one day, she came to my office and introduced herself. She was very smart and I was very impressed. I told her about my curriculum, describing the areas I covered, and she said she was surprised that my students knew how to design digital filters, which at that time was a big deal.

As we continued talking, I mentioned the other classes I was teaching, including those at the naval base in New London.

She said, "Oh, you're teaching there too? We have the best radar group of the United States Navy in China Lake. I have the best engineers and scientists."

Then I started telling her about the research I was doing in modern spectral analysis.

She said, "I want you to come to China Lake to give a talk. We'll invite you and cover all your expenses."

And that's exactly what happened. In October of 1983, I left the cold of Connecticut and it was suddenly summer in California.

They set me up in a special residence that's normally reserved for admirals or naval officers, the sort of suites that were located on the naval base. Remember, this was 1983. And I still had H-1B status. Suddenly, I felt like I was being given the red-carpet treatment.

When I went to give my talk, I understood why they treated me so nicely. This was just the beginning of all military hardware going digital.

It was a large auditorium and there were about 100 people there. But these weren't students. These were managers, technical leaders, vice presidents, and people whose titles I would never know. These were the bosses, the head of the radar division, and people like that.

Although I knew my area of expertise, I was nervous because

after only four years in America I still had a strong accent. I wondered if what I had to teach them might get lost in translation.

Feeling the pressure to perform, I believe I gave a great talk and they were really engaged.

After it was over, the head of the radar division approached me and said, "You're really an inspirational speaker. We loved what you presented. Can you teach these techniques for us?"

"Sure," I said immediately, without any idea about how I would actually teach these experts anything.

He said he'd have Karen talk to the person in charge of continuing education and training. It turned out to be a woman named Vicki Monroe, who had grown up right next to the Los Angeles Airport in Westchester.

I had a meeting with Vicki and told her they wanted me to create a course for them.

She said, "You can do a five-day course, where you teach every day and is a combination of teaching and consulting. That's usually what we do. What's your overhead?"

Working with major institutions, there's usually a large overhead charge. But in this case, it was just me.

Because I'd never done consulting before, I had no idea what to say. Finally, she suggested a price of $10,000 for the week.

My mind started racing. At the time, my university salary was only $23,000 per year. Here she was offering me $10,000 for five days!

She advised me to set up an account as Nikias Associates, and then walked me through the process of creating my first consultancy.

I thought back to my flight from London to Buffalo, watching *Rocky*, and hearing that question, "Do you believe America is the land of opportunity?"

Now I knew the answer. Yes, I do. But I believe the opportunity is rewarded based on merit.

Looking back, I am very grateful to all of the people in China Lake who recognized my work and understood that I could help them.

In March 1984, I taught my first course, delivering 35 hours of instruction and consultation in a single week. It was intense—much more advanced than the graduate courses I was teaching in New London– but I had a lot of energy and enjoyed giving inspiring lectures filled with practical examples.

Vicki Monroe called me to her office. Not only did they want me to teach another course; they wanted me to do it for a number of years.

The timing couldn't have been better. Our first daughter, Georgiana, was born, which made me feel the insecurity of fatherhood. One of the first things that I did was to get life insurance through the IEEE Society!

Looking into the eyes of a little baby made me feel the full weight of responsibility for providing for a family for the first time. To be honest, it was frightening, and I wasn't sure how I would do it. But it also kindled my entrepreneurial spirit, inspiring me to create new ideas for consulting opportunities.

Later I reached out to the New London, Connecticut, naval base and the Newport, Rhode Island, submarine base, and they wanted my classes and consulting too.

Just like that, I doubled my consulting fees, charging the same amount on both coasts.

In a short time, I was flying around the country to Warminster, Pennsylvania; Bethesda, Maryland; and Panama City, Florida. For the next decade, I would provide consulting services in advanced digital signal processing methods for sonar and radar to all these naval laboratories.

Better yet, as I was teaching these new technologies, I was the only one doing it. Over a decade, more than 2,000 naval engineers and scientists would take my courses.

I wasn't even a U.S. citizen yet, but I had a Green Card, and everyone was treating me with the highest respect. Never once did I feel overlooked or discriminated against.

That's why I have always said that the U.S. Navy has always

been very, very good to me!

⁂ ⁂ ⁂

Over the years, my experience at China Lake also produced some other interesting stories. After I had been consulting there for a few years, Steve Smith from the Office of Naval Research contacted me and asked for a favor. Apparently, in his spare time, one of their engineers had built a radar device that he claimed could detect stealth planes. I wasn't sure why they needed my help, but they flew me to China Lake for a weekend and I met with this person at his house. We talked about his work and he came across as a very eccentric and talkative scientist. Then I examined his advanced technology.

After the weekend, I reported back to the Office of Naval Research. I said, "I have to be honest with you, Steve. This guy is nuts. There's no way it can work."

⁂ ⁂ ⁂

Innovation always takes a willingness to go beyond established boundaries. While I appreciated all of the new prospects that had opened up for me, I was beginning to get restless.

I didn't know what the next step in my career would be, but I could feel that it was time for a change.

For both Niki and me, the city lights were calling us once again. And we would not be able to resist the opportunity.

PART THREE

EARLY ACADEMIC CAREER

CHAPTER 9

Second Homecoming

"Those who can contribute most to this country,
to its growth, to its strength, to its spirit
will be the first that are admitted to this land."[1]

PRESIDENT LYNDON B. JOHNSON
REMARKS AT THE SIGNING OF THE IMMIGRATION BILL
OCTOBER 3, 1965

Although UConn had been nothing but good to me, I was beginning to feel that my opportunities for growth were limited.

After three years, I was becoming increasingly frustrated that all but one of my grant proposals had been rejected. Without new sources of funding, I couldn't recruit doctoral students to work with me. The UConn campus was also isolated, lacking nearby technology companies to collaborate with or provide financial backing. I knew digital signal processing with higher-order spectra was a promising field, and I felt I was missing opportunities.

At the same time, Niki and I were missing the excitement of living in a major city. After our daughter, Georgiana, was born, Storrs felt too isolated for us. I had several job interviews—including one at USC—but my résumé wasn't strong enough yet.

Finally, in 1985, the Department of Electrical Engineering at Northeastern University made me an offer. To be honest, I had reservations about Northeastern, especially its overall academic reputation, but I believed the status of the College of Engineering was on the rise.

Boston was also a great city, with its beltway of Route 128 serving as a major technology corridor for companies doing defense and other engineering work. I saw that as an ideal opportunity for expanding my research and my network of connections.

When I turned in my resignation at UConn, I received an unexpected response. The chairman of the Department of Electrical Engineering didn't want me to leave, so he set up a meeting with the engineering dean to convince me to stay.

I met with Dean McFadden in his large office with modest New England-style furniture and large windows. He invited me to sit on the couch and he sat across from me. He was very respectful and polite. At first, he tried to see if he could get me to stay by increasing my salary and offering me internal support for my research.

But I reiterated the reasons I wanted to move. I explained that UConn had been really good to me and that I didn't have any complaints about how the university had treated me. On the contrary, everyone had gone out of their way to treat me well.

Then I told him the truth. The reason I was considering the offer from Northeastern was more personal. I explained that now that we had a baby Niki was not really happy. She felt isolated and we were both missing city life.

He looked at me and said, "I don't want you to make the same mistake I did. Therefore, my advice is for you to take the offer and move to Boston."

I was shocked. The entire purpose of the meeting was to convince me to stay and here was the dean telling me to take the job.

Then he said, "Years ago, I was at the University of Illinois and it was very isolating there. My wife didn't like it. And she kept telling me that. But I didn't listen to her, and then she divorced me. I don't want this to happen to you."

He continued, "Once you're married and you start having a family, it is no longer just about you and what is best for your career. You also have to pay attention to what is best for all of your family members overall, even if you have to compromise part of your career."

To this day, I think that was not only wise, but also compassionate advice. Although his university would have to replace a faculty member, he saw the larger picture and I appreciated his candor.

With Dean McFadden's endorsement, on July 1, 1985, I started as an assistant professor at Northeastern University.

Shortly after we moved to Boston, Niki returned to Cyprus for the month of August to visit family and let them see our beautiful baby, Georgiana.

Still frustrated with the lingering doubt of not getting funding at UConn, I drew a personal line in the sand. I felt that this was a crossroads in my career. I needed to prove to myself that my research could get strong support. Otherwise, I wouldn't have been able to establish myself as a researcher, and not just a teacher.

So, for the entire month, I locked myself in our apartment in Boston. I transformed our living room into a "war room," papering the walls with charts and graphs, working feverishly around the clock from morning until night. Amazingly, I completed drafts of seven grant proposals.

At the end of the summer, I submitted proposals to the National Science Foundation, the Office of Naval Research (ONR), the Air Force Office of Scientific Research (AFOSR), the Whitaker Foundation, ALCOA, Battelle-Pacific Northwest Laboratory, and the National Institute of Health with Dr. Siegel.

Incredibly, with the exception of the grant proposal to the AFOSR, all six were funded.

Six months after I locked myself in that apartment, I was big news at Northeastern University. No other faculty member in the history of the engineering school had ever had so many grant proposals funded at once.

However, one senior faculty member—an expert on radar—invited me and Niki to his house for dinner. At one point in the evening, he said, "I want you to know that, early in my career, I had five grant proposals funded at the same time!"

I was amused that the news of my success had revealed the friendly rivalry among my colleagues, but I also appreciated their congratulations and support. Sometimes I wonder what would have happened to my career had I traveled with Niki to Cyprus, or simply decided to take some time off before beginning the fall semester.

There are times where we don't know where the road will lead until we've gotten lost in the wilderness and discovered our true capabilities. For me, August of 1985 was a watershed moment, which led to a flood of new opportunities.

The funding from those six grant proposals helped me attract a talented team of Ph.D. students and postdoctoral fellows. In my six years at Northeastern, I graduated nine Ph.D. students. It was a record. Four of those students went on to have long and successful academic careers at very prestigious universities.

* * *

The success of my career as an engineering professor depended on establishing a well-funded research program. Though I had begun to doubt myself after many rejections, I did not give up easily. Instead, I made a sacrifice: I skipped the summer trip home to my beloved Cyprus. In the end, a number of developments proved the decision had been a wise one.

The funding jumpstarted a whole new area of original research, especially our work with the Office of Naval Research. By the 1980s, a new generation of submarines was developed to have quieter engines that were extremely difficult to detect in shallow waters. Although the technology required for these engines had been developed in the U.S., it was apparently stolen by the Soviets and used in their submarines. In the midst of the Cold War, the ONR anti-submarine warfare program funded the development of sonar signal processing methods that could detect submarines from transient acoustic noises generated inside of a submarine, such as a door opening to fire a torpedo.

I had also received a biomedical engineering grant from the Whitaker Foundation, which was very prestigious research funding for young investigators in bioengineering. Several previous faculty members at Northeastern University had attempted to acquire this grant, but had failed.

One day I received a congratulatory letter from Karl Weiss, the vice president for research at Northeastern, who asked to meet with me because he was very impressed that I was the first professor from the university to win six major grants, including one from an organization as distinguished as the Whitaker Foundation.

Over the years, his mentorship transformed into a friendship. He shared with me his personal story of how he and his wife, Madeline, were Jewish children who had been smuggled out of Nazi Germany to escape Hitler. For three years, Madeline and her family hid in the basement of a house in Belgium, which was located right next to a Gestapo office.

In 1936, Karl was brought from Germany to a farm in England. During World War II, his half-brother, Hans, was a German pilot who was taken prisoner by the British. And yet, after the war, they remained close all of their lives.

Karl generously passed on a wealth of professional knowledge to me, and taught me everything he knew about corporate fundraising. In his role as vice president of research, he had connections to a large number of engineering and defense companies located in and around Boston.

He took me to meet many of the CEOs of those companies, and I learned so much just by observing how he interacted with them. He charmed them with small talk, never getting into details, letting the technical people review all of the proposals. He was a master at what he did and everyone loved him.

Karl also helped me understand the "soft skills" that were necessary to be successful, beyond the technical skills that I had already developed. He always told me how important it was to "get into the mind of the other person."

He often laughed and said, "Max, you are not Jewish enough. You need to get into the mind of the other person and understand how *they* think."

Over the years, in every position where I was a candidate, I asked him for his astute advice during the interview process.

When I had an offer to become a faculty member at USC, I went to Karl for guidance. He set up a meeting for me to talk to Northeastern's president, but he also told me that I should take the offer!

When I later became the founding director of USC's Integrated Media Systems Center (IMSC), Karl was named the chair of IMSC's Board of Councilors. As he had always been, he was enormously helpful, especially giving me advice when I was a candidate for dean and later provost at USC.

❋ ❋ ❋

Meanwhile, though Niki and I felt very blessed that we had spent several years in America, we knew we would only qualify to apply for citizenship in 1989.

In 1988 I was presenting a paper on higher-order spectral analysis for the blind equalization problem at the IEEE communications conference. I was offering a completely new approach, with new mathematics based on cumulants for information extraction from communication channels.

After my talk, a person from the Department of War approached me and asked if we could have dinner. That was the beginning of a new research collaboration that lasted 12 years. It helped me get funding for my research, a grant to finish my book, and it also helped me get a security clearance with the U.S. government. Although the work was unclassified, it gave us the opportunity to have some technical discussions in a classified environment.

However, the problem with getting a security clearance was that I wasn't a citizen yet. It was a time-consuming process because they have to do an extensive background check, interviewing the vast network of people you've met throughout your life.

He didn't hesitate. He asked that we start the paperwork and the background check right away, so that it would be ready when it was time to apply for citizenship and meet with the Immigration and Naturalization Service (INS).

Not long after paperwork was finished, he called to tell me that the clearance had been approved and that I should be hearing from the INS soon.

When Niki and I prepared for the citizenship exam, we took it very seriously. At the time, there was a book they gave you to help study and we quizzed each other every night at the dinner table.

We arrived at the federal building in Boston and Niki was called in first for the exam. I waited outside for 15 or 20 minutes, and then she reappeared.

"How did it go?" I asked.

She said, "I think I did well. She was asking me questions about the Civil War."

I thought, "Wow! The Civil War."

So, I go in and the INS officer is an older lady with a Southern accent. She didn't even look up at me. She was still filling out the form, finishing up Niki's paperwork.

Finally, she says, "Please sit down."

She's still writing and says, "When is Maria's birthday?"

"November 22, 1988," I said.

Without looking up, she says, "Does the date remind you of anything?"

"Yes," I said. "November 22, 1963, was when President Kennedy was assassinated."

"And what are the responsibilities of a good citizen?" she said. That was one of the questions at the time.

I started listing the items, "Serving in the armed forces if they ask you, voting, volunteering, always paying taxes."

When I got to the fifth item, she cut me off.

"That's enough," she said.

Then she changed her tone.

"So you studied in Greece?" she asked.

"Yes," I said.

"You have a communist government in Greece, don't you?"

"No, that's not true," I said. "I believe you're referring to Andreas Papandreou, who was the elected Prime Minister of the Socialist Party. It's a parliamentary democracy in Greece."

"But in Cyprus, you do have a communist government," she continued.

At that moment, although I wanted to be respectful, I got a little upset. My family's home was in ruins and this person had no understanding of what was really happening to Cyprus.

"No ma'am," I said. "I'm afraid you're not very well informed. The Constitution of the Republic of Cyprus has a lot of similarities to the United States. It's a republic, not a parliamentary democracy. The executive branch—the President—gets elected every five years, there is the judiciary, and there is the parliament."

I was going on and on, explaining similarities and differences between the American Constitution and the one in Cyprus.

Finally, she looked at me and said, "That's enough. You passed."

So that was the citizenship exam. Niki had the Civil War, and I was defending the democracies in Greece and Cyprus!

In September 1989, we took our oath to become American citizens. It was one of the happiest moments of our lives. The ceremony took place in Faneuil Hall of Boston, an important gathering place during the American Revolution. Known as the "Cradle of Liberty," it symbolizes the birth of American independence.

We finally belonged somewhere outside of Cyprus. And we were going to have equal rights with all of the people around us. It was like a "second homecoming."

* * *

Additionally, in 1990, when I was 38, I became an IEEE Fellow because of my research on higher order spectra. After many years of insecurity and hard work, my efforts finally paid off.

At the time, of the approximately 350,000 members of the IEEE, only 2 percent are fellows based on their technical contributions. But of that 2 percent, only 5 percent of those electrical engineers are under the age of 40 when they are elected.

The climb up the mountain of academia had been a long and arduous one. In addition to becoming an IEEE Fellow, I had also been promoted from assistant to associate and then full professor.

After all we had been through together, it finally felt fulfilling, especially because Niki was so proud of my achievements. Little did we know that some of the most exciting adventures were just ahead.

CHAPTER 10

The Fall and the Rise

"It is not the mountain we conquer, but ourselves."[1]

OFTEN ATTRIBUTED TO
SIR EDMUND PERCIVAL HILLARY,
NEW ZEALAND EXPLORER

Throughout its long and vibrant history, California has always been the place to be. It's a place where people from across the nation and around the world have come to pursue their passions and discover their dreams.

If America is the "land of opportunity," California was "the promised land."

And for us, on our great journey, it was also a return to a climate very similar to the town where we had grown up in Cyprus.

Moving to the promised land all began with an exciting new opportunity.

In the summer of 1990, I learned the Signal and Imaging Processing Institute (SIPI) at the University of Southern California was losing a senior faculty member, who had relocated to the East Coast.

While I was attending an international conference to present a paper, the chairman of USC's Electrical Engineering Department approached me and encouraged me to apply to the position.

Despite the many things we loved about Boston, I felt like it was important to explore opportunities, if nothing else to meet and interview with a new group of potential colleagues.

The interview in November 1990 was intimidating. I met with

acclaimed figures in the field of electrical engineering and felt that the two-day interview went well.

I returned to Boston with a good feeling. On Thanksgiving Day, the chairman of the department called to tell me that the faculty had voted unanimously to support my appointment.

* * *

While we found a community we loved at USC, we still had to find a house. In the spring of 1991, every two weeks I flew back on weekends, searching for just the right place to live. By April, we had made an offer on a house on a hill. It had a gorgeous view of Catalina Island and the vast Pacific Ocean. That did it for us.

In a poetic coincidence, in the same month that Niki and I made an offer on our first house in Southern California, Dr. Steven B. Sample made the transition from president of SUNY Buffalo to the University of Southern California.

Although I had never met Steve Sample in person, his signature was on the diploma that I would soon be hanging in my office. And he would play a key role in many aspects of my career over the next few years.

On July 1, 1991, I started my first day at USC, making the long commute on the 110 freeway, with the feeling that the future was filled with possibilities.

* * *

For those who know me now, 1991 was a very different time. During my first year at USC, I was much more laid back, enjoying the casual life of being a faculty member and living in a beach city.

I wore running shoes and casual clothes to teach my classes. And for our first time in America, it never got cold in the winter!

We began to enjoy outdoor life as a family, taking advantage of weekends and holidays to explore the many pleasures of Southern California. I was also feeling an immediate change in my work environment. I found USC's engineering school to be much more entrepreneurial, and the research environment was much more collaborative.

I transferred all my grants, brought all of my graduate students with me, and started recruiting new graduate students who would help us pioneer new paths of innovation and discovery.

In a short time, I was fully devoted to research with my graduate students, teaching new courses, and building relationships with my colleagues across the school.

Little did I know that my time as a laid-back engineering professor would soon be coming to an end.

⁂ ⁂ ⁂

One year after I joined USC, the dean of the engineering school invited me to lunch. In addition to a wonderful meal, he presented me with a surprise. He wanted me to consider becoming his associate dean for administration and research, a promotion that would essentially make me the second-in-command for the entire school.

While flattered by the offer, I also felt that I was too young. At 39, I wasn't sure that I was ready to enter the academic leadership arena. To get advice, I consulted an aerospace executive, who laughed and said, "Oh, well. It happens to the best of us."

Then he told me he believed I was at the right age to test the waters of academic leadership. If it didn't feel like the right fit, I could always return to my research and teaching just like before.

I came up with a compromise. I agreed to accept the position of associate dean for research, but only for 50 percent of my time. The rest of the time I wanted to continue my research and teaching duties.

I had no idea that I had just signed up for two jobs, each of which would require 100 percent of my time and attention! I also couldn't have predicted the challenges that USC, the School of Engineering, and the entire L.A. basin would soon be facing.

* * *

Southern California had grown very dependent on the aerospace and defense industry. For several decades, this was great news for the region and our engineering school.

After the cutbacks in defense spending following the end of the Cold War, the transformation of the region's economy was swift and shocking, like suddenly pulling the plug from an electrical socket. Within only three years, half of the entire aerospace workforce in the L.A. basin was laid off.

Given the longstanding dependency on the aerospace industry, the engineering school began facing its own serious financial challenges.

The fate of the aerospace industry would only be the beginning of the seismic shifts reshaping the L.A. basin. In April 1992, there was the acquittal of several police officers who had been involved in the terrible beating of Rodney King.

It had only been a year since Niki and I had made an offer on our house. To be honest, being new to the area, I didn't realize the implications of the verdict. At the engineering school, colleagues and staff started talking about leaving campus to go home early.

One person even told me, "Whatever you do, don't get off the freeway on your drive home. Stay on the freeway, even if it takes longer."

I really didn't understand why people were concerned, but I think I left campus a little early. Later that night, watching the results of the riots, I began to see the implications. And I wondered what it meant for the university.

* * *

As my responsibilities were increasing at USC, I also found that my new leadership role was expanding my interaction with the larger Trojan Family. A couple of years into my tenure, I was invited to give my first speech to the USC Alumni Club of San Diego. I was very nervous and still learning about the Trojan Family spirit.

Before I spoke at that breakfast event, the person introducing me pulled me aside. He said, "I just want to make sure I pronounce your name correctly. Is it Nick-ias or Ny-ky-us." (It's Nick-ias.)

I gave him the correct pronunciation. "Good," he said. "I just don't want it to be like the time when I introduced Spiro Agnew and I pronounced it Spy-ro."

My mind instantly flashed to a moment when President Nixon's communications director famously mispronounced Agnew's name. Spiro Agnew was Greek, and all of Greece was amused when he was introduced as Spy-ro.

Years later, here I was in San Diego with the same man, USC Trustee Herb Klein, who was now introducing me.

It was the beginning of a long and valued friendship with Herb, who was not only a wonderful man, but also someone who would play a key role with his political connections a few years later.

* * *

As I was getting settled into my new role as associate dean for research, I was about to learn the sometimes-painful lessons of dealing with a fall, followed by a rise. For an individual or an institution, the time right after a fall can create a period of deep soul searching.

In the fall of 1992, interdisciplinary efforts at USC led to a new opportunity. The deans from several schools—engineering, cinematic arts, music, communications and journalism, and libraries—began having conversations. At the same time, the internet made the transition from a tool of government and academe to a commercial endeavor.

In engineering, given the decline of support for the aerospace and defense industries at the end of the Cold War, there was a need to diversify our funding sources. In Los Angeles, our biggest potential partner was the entertainment industry.

The dean of engineering gave me the assignment of fleshing out the concept of an Entertainment Technology Center—a groundbreaking new center to help USC capitalize on its strengths in technology and entertainment and take advantage of its location in Hollywood.

I was tasked with figuring out what we could do and how we could do it.

This was an important moment because it was the first opportunity to meet with deans and faculty in other schools at USC. It was a great learning experience, offering a glimpse of the culture and priorities for each school, as well as the different policies that existed across campus.

It would also be both a challenge and an opportunity to bring together people from disparate disciplines, virtually all of whom had never collaborated with each other before.

While there were many interesting conversations involving truly brilliant ideas, it became clear that for an interdisciplinary center to work, it would need serious and steady funding that only the federal government could provide.

In December of 1992, I visited the National Science Foundation's Engineering Research Center (ERC) program. Although the program directors viewed them as "out of the box," I clearly sensed that they were interested in our ideas. An additional benefit of the ERC was that approved proposals received federal support for up to 10 years.

I was immediately excited about putting together a proposal. Competing for an NSF ERC grant was very competitive and prestigious.

In my enthusiasm and naiveté, I may have underestimated how challenging this new task would be. I learned that our engineering school had tried to win this type of grant three times before—twice in photonics and one in brain sciences—but the process had ended without success.

At a Christmas party, a fellow engineering faculty member asked me, "What makes you think you can win an ERC?"

It was a reminder that there were many challenges in front of me and this was only the beginning.

* * *

The question from my engineering colleague made me reflective. I remembered a story about a researcher at the RAND Corporation named Keith Uncapher, who in 1972 was issued a challenge by the United States' Defense Advanced Research Projects Agency (DARPA)—to create an institute to continue the development of the internet, which was very experimental at that time.[2]

Keith took the proposal suggested by DARPA to UCLA, but they told him it would take 15 months to decide. So, he brought it to USC's Zohrab Kaprielian who was the Provost and Dean of Engineering.

Years later, when our flight was delayed from Washington, D.C., to LAX, Keith shared the full story of how it happened during dinner at the airport.

He gave a presentation during lunch at USC. Zohrab was there, but he just listened, said nothing, and then left. Keith was crushed, thinking Zohrab wasn't interested in the center.

The next evening Zohrab called him at home and asked to get

together for a drink at a nearby bar. They met that night, but just socialized together. There was no mention of the center.

As they were saying goodnight, Zohrab said, "We'll get back to you about the center, I hope soon."

The next morning, Zohrab called Keith at home.

"I can commit the $500,000 you need to start the center," said Zohrab.

"Wait a minute, don't you need the Board of Trustees' approval?" asked Keith.

"Make sure you do your job. I know how to do mine," said Zohrab, and then hung up.

Keith had tears in his eyes telling me the story in the airport.

"This is what leadership is all about, Max. Getting together for drinks, he was calibrating me, wanting to get to know who I was as a person."

Within five days, USC's Board of Trustees authorized the center and the Information Sciences Institute was born, becoming one of the pioneers in the development of the internet.

* * *

In 1993, we were finally ready to fully pursue a grant for an ERC for a new Multimedia Technology Center. I coordinated the collaboration of faculty from key schools, the libraries, and researchers from the Information Sciences Institute.

At times the process was very challenging because each school had different priorities. There's always sort of a "clash of cultures." Throughout the process, it was never easy.

While we were preparing the proposal, I also felt that it was very important to get advice and perspectives from people who worked at the intersections of the public and private sectors. I traveled around the country, talking to a Viacom executive in Times Square, a top research director at AT&T's Bell Labs, a deputy director at the MIT Media Lab, an executive at National

Semiconductor in Silicon Valley, and many of the best minds in a variety of industries.

These interactions helped me organize the very first "multimedia workshop" at USC, which brought to campus leading speakers from Microsoft, Apple, and several other large and small technology companies.

⁂ ⁂ ⁂

When we finally submitted the proposal, all of us not only felt that we had a great chance of winning, we believed that we were going to win. We didn't have to wait long. Not only did we fail to get the proposal funded, we didn't even make the final round for a site visit.

For me personally, the aftermath of the failure was devastating. I wondered how I could have been so overconfident, and I was sure there were many people on and off campus who behind my back were saying, "Max screwed up."

Because I put so much extra time, energy, and effort into getting this proposal ready, the failure was crushing. I was haunted by that comment from a colleague who'd said, "What makes you think you can get an ERC?"

Maybe he was right. Maybe the problem was me.

I went to my office in the dean's suite and asked my assistant to take all of the binders and material related to the proposal and throw them in the trash.

One morning, when I was getting ready for work, I looked at myself in the mirror and said, "How can you be so stupid? You forgot. Never take anything for granted!"

For the rest of my career, I would never make that mistake again.

⁂ ⁂ ⁂

While I was still recovering from the ERC news, I turned my attention to helping other faculty and stumbled into a project that opened my eyes to what had been missing. During the process of working on a very different proposal in computer networks to get federal funding, I worked with a group from TRW, a local aerospace company.

TRW was collaborating with several universities and corporations all around the nation. When I walked in, I was amazed. They had created a "war room" for proposal writing, with concepts and ideas taped up all over the walls. They approached the process like a political campaign, which was eye-opening for me.

During the process, a top executive from a company in Minnesota pointed out something else that I hadn't understood up until that point.

"Excellent research will get you at the door," he said. "But it's the way you put the partnership together that will really stand apart."

Instantly, I realized what we had done wrong on the first ERC proposal. We had focused on making the technical aspects as compelling as possible, but we hadn't been thinking about a partnership beyond the university. We had limited the scope of our vision.

* * *

In the fall of 1994, I also started collaborating with a group of faculty to try to define the future of the internet and the World Wide Web. Our goal was to try again to get funding from the NSF to create an ERC known as the Integrated Media Systems Center (IMSC).

The memories of our earlier failure still lingered in my mind. We borrowed the idea of TRW's proposal "war room," setting up our team in a similar manner. We worked relentlessly to build relationships with corporate partners recruiting 40 companies from across the country, expanding our idea into a truly *national* partnership. Significantly, more than half of those companies were located in Silicon Valley, expanding USC's presence in the Bay Area.

The key to those new relationships would be a USC alumnus I had never met before.

In 1995, a development officer in the engineering school was traveling with me to build partnerships in Silicon Valley. At the very end of a long week, right before we needed to get back on a plane to Los Angeles, she had scheduled a meeting with Mark Stevens of Sequoia Capital.

She said, "It's a venture capital firm, so he doesn't represent a company. But he does have a large network of contacts and maybe he can help us."

By the end of the week, I was exhausted. The meeting was late on a Friday afternoon, and I just wanted to get on a plane back home. I told her to cancel the meeting.

To her credit, she begged me to change my mind.

"No, no, Max. Let's just talk to him," the development officer said.

Reluctantly, I went to the meeting with no expectations.

It's Friday afternoon at 4:00 p.m. Mark walks in with his casual clothes and his Nike sneakers, looking like he's dressed for a round of golf. It was normal end of the week attire for Silicon Valley venture capitalists, although I didn't know that at the time.

After some small talk, we began to hit it off and he clearly laid out what he could do.

He listed off about 16 major companies that had just gone public and were doing work in multimedia and the internet. He generously offered to write letters to the CEOs of these companies on our behalf.

When I asked Mark why he was being so helpful he said, "Listen, I'm up here in Silicon Valley. I'm a Trojan and I'm surrounded by Stanford and Cal alumni. If USC has a chance to win and beat even Berkeley in this area, I want to be part of it."

Mark Stevens later became one of USC's youngest trustees, and he has been one of the most important people in increasing the university's presence in Silicon Valley. During my years as president of USC, Mark and his wife Mary donated more than $120 million to the university.

And it all began with a meeting that, thankfully, I didn't cancel in 1995.

* * *

After months of tireless work, we submitted the ERC proposal. We felt good about our preparation and our chances, but we refused to make any predictions. The final decision was now out of our hands.

One morning in September 1995, I walked into my office in the dean's suite to find several messages. In those days, it was common for assistants to screen phone calls and leave important messages on Post-it Notes on your door. As I flipped through the notes, and entered my office, I noticed one was from the NSF ERC program director.

I thought to myself, "They don't usually call with bad news. Bad news usually arrives in a letter in the mail."

As I dialed the number, I tried to contain my hope and anxiety. The program director had good news. Out of 117 proposals that had been submitted, 10 had been chosen for a site visit. USC had made the top 10.

All of the proposals were in different areas of engineering and the NSF planned to fund four or five projects. However, of the remaining proposals, only two were in multimedia—USC and Columbia University. The multimedia proposal from UC Berkeley didn't even qualify for a site visit.

While it was exciting to be among the top 10 ranked proposals, there was no time to celebrate or relax. We were about to enter a new level of intensity.

But before we could get started, tragedy would strike once again.

⁂ ⁂ ⁂

Later in the same week I got the good news from the NSF, we received a call from Cyprus. My father had passed away. His funeral would be held on my birthday.

On the way back to Cyprus, I thought of how Niki's father had passed away just as I got the bad news about our previous ERC proposal. Coming face to face with my own mortality made me determined that nothing would be left to chance.

After the initial visit, the center directors were asked to give a presentation to the NSF final review panel, which we did.

And then we waited until May 1996 when the announcement was made. Out of 117 proposals, USC's was ranked number one. It was a major boost to the morale of the engineering school and the entire university.

When he heard the news, President Sample called me directly to congratulate me. It was a sign that things were beginning to turn around for USC and Los Angeles.

⁂ ⁂ ⁂

Before the announcement was made public, President Sample set up a meeting with me and Elizabeth Daley, the dean of the cinema school, with the editorial board of the *Los Angeles Times*.

We were all sitting together around a large conference table, and they offered each of us a glass of water. Steve led off with a few words about the importance of the ERC, and then he said, "Of course, I have my dean here of the cinema school and I also have our new leader, the founding director of this center. They're going to be partners."

He looked at me and said, “So Max, why don’t you tell them all about it?”

When I speak, I’m very animated. I move my hands and gesture a lot. As I began talking, I started to get nervous. So I tried to show my enthusiasm, emphasizing a point with a dramatic gesture—when my hand hit my glass of water.

It was like everything went into slow motion. I watched the glass fall. I watched it spill all over Steve Sample’s suit. And I watched the expressions on the faces around the table.

I was mortified. An uncomfortable silence fell over the room. I looked at President Sample. He looked at me, my face burning red with embarrassment.

Without missing a beat, Steve said, “No, no, please continue.”

Then he looked around the table, smiled, and said, “Don’t worry. I’m used to cleaning up all of the messes my faculty make.”

After that, I relaxed, and everything went smoothly.

As we were walking back to the parking structure, I said, “President Sample, I’m really sorry.”

He said, “Don’t worry about it. You did a great job.”

And then Elizabeth Daley said, “Well, Steve, from now on you’re going to have more than just the cinema school to talk about.”

USC’s academic reputation was now truly on the rise. An important part of that would be the university’s new Integrated Media Systems Center, a National Science Foundation Center of Excellence.

CHAPTER 11

The Human Element in Tech Progress

"E debbasi considerare, come non é cosa più difficile a trattare, né più dubia a riuscire, né più pericolosa a maneggiare, che farsi capo ad introdurre nuovi ordini."

NICCOLO MACHIAVELLI, *IL PRINCIPE*, VI

"And it ought to be remembered that there is nothing more difficult to take in hand, more perilous to conduct, or more uncertain in its success, than to take the lead in the introduction of a new order of thing."[1]

NICCOLO MACHIAVELLI, *THE PRINCE*, CHAPTER VI

From the very beginning, there was great excitement about The Integrated Media Systems Center. And we were very grateful that we would have the opportunity to conduct research and experiments that would define the future of the internet and digital media.

Looking back, it was a heady moment that I must admit I wasn't fully prepared for. Although our team of faculty investigators was doing pioneering work in a new technological frontier and we had articulated a compelling vision for the future, we didn't really know how things were going to work out.

While we were celebrating the National Science Foundation's announcement of our new center, I was humbled when Mal Currie, then the chairman of USC's Board of Trustees, walked across the room, introduced his wife, Barbara, and said, "You're going to be one of our university leaders now."

It was a shocking moment, as this path had never occurred to me before then. I knew Mal Currie, of course. In addition to leading USC' Board of Trustees, he had previously served as CEO of the renowned Hughes Aircraft, and, before that, as U.S. Under Secretary of Defense for Research and Engineering.

More than a decade later, I'd be named the holder of the Malcolm R. Currie Chair in Technology and the Humanities, the first endowed chair at USC, or any university, to honor technology and humanities.

On that night, I was elated just hearing the chairman of the board suggest that I would play a bigger role at USC. I could also sense an immediate change in the way I was perceived by people throughout the university. Reflecting on that night, I can now see this moment was also the beginning of a subtle shift in my personal identity.

Until that celebration, I hadn't spent a lot of time outside of my technical specialty. I was good at giving inspiring presentations as long as I had my PowerPoint slides. But that night, the audience was filled with USC's trustees, alumni, and members of the university community. These were extremely successful people, many of whom owned or operated some of the most powerful and prosperous organizations in California.

Without any visuals or even a script, I was admittedly a lousy speaker. Fortunately, the people at that reception didn't focus on what I lacked as a speaker, but instead saw who I could become as a leader: a futurist, technologist, risk-taker, and humanist, who would help chart a new and inspiring path for university research.

* * *

Little did I know that getting the IMSC funded would only be the beginning of a series of new struggles that would teach me many hard-earned lessons about leadership and human nature.

First of all, despite the excitement, there were painful personnel issues from the very beginning. For instance, one faculty member from the School of Music was unhappy with his initial budget. He had asked for a lot of money and we simply couldn't afford to give it to him. I patiently explained that the funding had to be allocated to many different areas, which we were trying to launch at the same time. But he got upset and immediately quit.

Getting people to understand the technology was also difficult. But the biggest obstacle was the realization that we weren't so much creating a new research center as we were launching a startup from scratch.

When we started IMSC, we didn't have the equipment we needed or the laboratory infrastructure. We had to build the backbone that connected all of our labs and computers.

These growing pains led to a lot of disagreements, and for some of our faculty it became very contentious. Following the enthusiasm of getting the center established, it was disheartening to see our early momentum dissolve into disagreements.

That's what the first few years were like. Constant challenges and quarrels and changes in technical leadership positions, day after day.

But like all startups, you either perish or persist through the growing pains. And that's what we did.

* * *

The question was, "How do you create a startup from scratch?" We had no guidebook, no blueprints, for how to begin. For two or three years, it was a very steep hill to climb.

And while we were still scaling this hill, we also felt the pressure of having to please all our external corporate partners.

One example was our partnership with IBM. To help us get up to speed, they had donated a large computer for visualization experiments. From the outside, it looked like a charitable gesture. In reality, they wanted to use their donation as a showcase to their customers to demonstrate that they were a pivotal partner in our futuristic center.

But there was a problem. From our perspective, there was no sense hooking up the large computer until we built the IT infrastructure that would allow them to communicate with each other. And that takes time. You can't just throw it together overnight.

That wasn't good enough for IBM. When one of their vice presidents came to campus six months into the beginning of our new center, he found the equipment still stacked in the original boxes.

He was furious and he took out his frustrations on me because I was the director. He was very angry and very rude. To be honest, I had never experienced behavior like that before.

My deputy director at the time, Sandy Sawchuk, and I listened to him yell and scream and threaten what would happen if we didn't do exactly what he wanted on his timeline.

Sandy and I sat silent until the storm of his anger blew over. It was one of those abuses you take as part of the job. It's one of those moments where you figuratively get on your knees and beg for forgiveness. And as the director, I ultimately had to take responsibility for every aspect of this new startup, even if I wasn't making certain decisions.

After the meeting, Sandy Sawchuk said, "Max, I really admire you. If I was the director, I don't think I could take that. I would have said something back."

"Sandy, we take it, we apologize, and we move on." I said. "And if he doesn't like it, he can take his equipment back and that's the end of the relationship."

Following his abusive outburst, the IBM representative never apologized. But he did once make a reference that he'd probably overreacted.

That was one of the many examples of how painful it was at the beginning of the IMSC.

* * *

In 1996, we started with essentially nothing. Within five years, we had established a center with nearly 200 people—29 faculty, 102 graduate students, 23 research staff, and 15 administrators—as well as a new technology transfer program. In just five years, our little startup had grown to a thriving center with a $10 million annual budget, $3.5 million of which came from the NSF. The rest of the money came from our other partners, primarily our corporate sponsors.

But you have to remember that some of our corporate partners, even those who contributed amounts as small as $50,000 per year, still needed the same level of attention as the NSF. Some of them would just show up on campus with their people, requesting tours.

It was a constant challenge. Luckily for our graduate students, it was also an important experience in interacting with industry representatives. They were often the ones who guided the tours, frequently leading to further conversations and job opportunities for many of those students.

* * *

Despite the many difficulties in the beginning, there were also several advantages to the groundbreaking work we were doing. One of those advantages was that we gained an entirely new team of innovators and collaborators.

One of the key faculty researchers for the IMSC was Tom Holman, who was a professor at the cinema school. Holman is probably best known as the inventor of the THX sound system, which is used in almost every movie theater in the nation.

When we received the award for the ERC, he took us to Skywalker Ranch—George Lucas' large ranch and workplace for making movies in Northern California— to give us a private tour. It was very impressive to see all of the advanced technologies and the beautiful theaters that George Lucas had built for the people who worked there.

Many people forget that George Lucas created Skywalker Ranch, and his company Industrial Light and Magic, because the technology didn't exist for him to realize his vision for the first *Star Wars* movies.

* * *

IMSC was also experimenting with digital avatars and the communications infrastructure required to connect people from different places together in one virtual environment. We understood the incredible applications these technologies held for education in the classroom, productivity on the manufacturing floor, the newsroom, the museum, or the home theater of the future. And we did demonstrations with haptics, giving people gloves that allowed them to touch an object in a virtual environment and feel the sensation as if it were real.

However, with new technologies, there is always the possibility that some people will misunderstand how they might be used. Once the NSF sent me to Capitol Hill in Washington, D.C., to give a talk at a luncheon.

It was widely attended, with an audience of mostly Congressional staffers. I gave a presentation, which included a demonstration of haptics. After my talk, a Congressional staffer accosted me and offered me his strong opinions about what we were doing.

"I have a problem with your presentation," he said. "Because when you present haptics—and you talk about touch, and feel, and sensation—using the internet, and you come from Hollywood, then what comes to my mind is virtual sex. And I don't want the federal government funding something like that."

I kind of laughed, wondering if he was kidding. Then I

patiently explained, "Haptics can be used to improve the experience of blind people so they can experience the exhibits in a museum. Imagine what they can learn from those interactions. We can't be responsible if others want to use the internet for bad things. That's not our intent."

"Yeah, but I just want you to know that haptics and Hollywood means sex," said the staffer.

Then he elbowed his way through the crowd and was gone.

* * *

We also discussed ideas like "the book of the future," the "newsroom of the future," "the classroom of the future," etc. We would talk about how television, computers, and home theaters would eventually converge. And we debated how these advances might one day help people pay bills without writing or signing checks. At the time, that was a big deal.

Even in small talk, people would say, "Wow, you mean we're going to pay bills without signing a check?"

Today it seems obvious, but back then it seemed like science fiction. But if you were presenting to a layperson, there was a "wow" factor. And I loved those moments because you could see people's eyes light up with possibilities they'd never considered before.

* * *

As I was learning more about launching a startup from inside a university, a personal transformation took place inside of me. I was now promoting research that everyone could understand, and for the first time, I discovered I liked "selling" the work we were doing.

By this time, everyone had some level of understanding about the internet and web browsers. But when you told them about immersive environments and digital avatars, everybody would get very excited.

Suddenly, just by talking about our research, I had become much more interesting at dinner parties!

I was also learning USC's various schools, their internal cultures, and the loosely federated structure of the university administration.

I was discovering the frictions and disagreements among the various deans, understanding what was important to them and which territories they claimed for their schools. It would be information that would be useful in the growth of my academic career.

However, while those things were happening in the background, my attention was mostly absorbed by the many things happening at IMSC.

In 2002, IMSC pursued a Grand Challenge Experiment with a project that we hoped would amaze audiences from coast to coast. To do this, our immersive audio group decided to put on a concert.

They recruited Trojan alumnus Michael Tilson Thomas, then the conductor of the San Francisco Symphony Orchestra, who provided a brief address along with the New World Symphony.[2]

There was a live concert from Miami, which was broadcast through a very fast network to create an immersive environment with a three-dimensional audience in the Bing Theatre on the campus of USC.[3]

This was the first time a live event was streamed into a theatre on a university campus.

And it was a huge success. We got a lot of positive attention for demonstrating these new technologies in a way that the general public could understand.

Projects like our futuristic concert started putting IMSC on the map.

And it would be IMSC that would lead to many other

partnerships for me and the university.

* * *

The NSF required all ERCs to establish a program for local underprivileged students to get excited about new technologies.

So, as soon as the IMSC had been approved, the NSF program director suggested I make a connection halfway across the country. He proposed that I travel to Detroit to meet with a Catholic priest named Father William T. Cunningham. In the heart of the most economically-disadvantaged area of the city, Father Cunningham had established an innovative manufacturing academy that gave new skills and new hope to children who were often overlooked.

Many of the kids were minorities or high school dropouts, who would have had little chance of getting ahead without the special training they received to help them find jobs in the automobile industry. More importantly, the academy offered new opportunities for those whose career prospects might otherwise be grim. The program made Father Cunningham very popular, earning him visits from President George H. W. Bush and later President Clinton.

So I went to Detroit and spent an entire day with him, along with two faculty members from USC. He was a wonderful man and it was clear that he had created a model that could be replicated in other urban areas.

As we toured the facilities, it sparked the idea that IMSC could create our own outreach program, which became the Multimedia University Academy.

We decided that we could recruit high school dropouts, or high school graduates, from inner city schools who weren't planning to attend college. We could then design a 22-week training academy, where students attended 20 hours per week.

We recruited a full-time career placement person to help

them prepare their resumes and help them get jobs in the film and television industries. We set up that program with additional funding from the NSF, and it became a very popular and successful program.

One of the best stories that came out of the academy was a dropout who was working as a janitor at his high school. However, the college counselor at the school had noticed that he had artistic inclinations. Thanks to the academy, he went from being a janitor to one of the best animators we ever trained.

* * *

With the lessons we learned with IMSC, we became extremely good at developing interdisciplinary research proposals and forming the partnerships necessary to give us the extra edge to win.

We ended up winning three more national centers in the next few years.

But in 2000, our second research center originated from an unusual source.

One Friday afternoon, I got a call from the office of Mike Andrews, who was the assistant secretary of the Army. He wanted to learn more about our capabilities and how that could impact the modernization of our military for simulation and training. They wanted to establish an institute to bring together engineering, digital media, and Hollywood industry talent.

The Army was going to visit three universities: UC Berkeley, UCLA, and USC. I was given the assignment to handle the site visit on our campus.

USC won the competition, and the Institute for Creative Technologies (ICT) became a reality. (Immediately afterwards, there were some political tensions between the cinema and engineering schools about who should be the director.)

In many ways, if not for the creation of IMSC, those

groundbreaking research collaborations may never have happened. Today the ICT has a more than 20-year track record of pushing the boundaries of military training through advanced virtual environments that provide soldiers with highly-realistic scenarios. At one point, the institute had annual funding of around $35 million per year.

* * *

After all of our efforts over many years, yet another opportunity arose as a new millennium arrived. In 2000, after 17 years of leadership, Dean Silverman announced that he was stepping down.

A number of the school's faculty came to me and said they planned to nominate me to be the next dean. To be honest, I felt like I had gained a lot of experience and I was ready for a new challenge.

When I accepted the nomination to become a candidate, I did my homework. I asked myself, "What is the bold vision for the future of the school? What would be the best strategic plan? If I were to become the dean, what were the metrics to monitor moving forward?"

I prepared, like a good engineer, what I thought was a very compelling PowerPoint presentation for the search committee. Surprisingly, I was the only candidate who used PowerPoint.

My presentation to the search committee was about 40 minutes long. I talked about the broad vision, emphasizing biological engineering and how the 21st century was poised to be the Age of Medicine and Biology.

Then I talked about the first elements of a strategic plan, how to move the school forward, and how we could take advantage of new breakthroughs in biotechnology that would open up entire new sectors of the global economy.

The presentation generated a lot of discussion because it wasn't just about engineering, but also a vision that involved other schools in interdisciplinary efforts.

I was one of four finalists, and I think two of them were outside candidates. In addition to the presentation to the search committee, I was interviewed by the provost, by the other senior officers of the university, and finally by President Sample. I tried to show Dr. Sample my PowerPoint presentation, but he didn't even want to see it.

He said, "No, no, no, we don't have to."

But I insisted. When I was meeting with him, I had a printed copy and I started to walk him through all of the slides. And then we talked about the school and a few other things.

At one point, as we were going through the slides, he said, "Okay, I get it, I get it."

I could tell he'd had enough.

Then, he looked at me, and in his contrarian way, he said, "Max, what is your opinion of the two Greek philosophers, Plato and Heraclitus?"

It came out of nowhere, but I quickly responded.

"Well, according to Plato, virtue is knowledge," I said. "However, for Heraclitus, virtue is character."

I said, "I'm oversimplifying the difference between the two philosophers. Clearly, Plato is the greatest, but in terms of virtue, this is how they differ in very simple terms."

"Okay, Max," he said. "Very nice spending time with you."

And that's how the interview ended. As I was leaving the suite, I heard his voice again, "It was really nice spending time with you, Max."

"Thank you, Mr. President," I said and walked out.

For the first time, I felt that Sample was trying to get to know me personally, which I saw as a good sign.

Everybody must have liked the case I made for the future of engineering. In 2001, I was appointed as dean of USC's School of Engineering.

CHAPTER 12

Back to the Roots

«οὐκ ἂν γένοιτο τοῦθ', ὅπως ἐγὼ λαβὼν
σημεῖα τοιαῦτ' οὐ φανῶ τοὐμὸν γένος.»
ΣΟΦΟΚΛΈΟΥΣ ΟἸΔΊΠΟΥΣ ΤΎΡΑΝΝΟΣ, 1058–59

"It cannot be that when I have obtained such indications,
I shall not bring light to my ancestry."[1]
SOPHOCLES, *OEDIPUS TYRANNUS*, LINES 1058–59

My experience at USC opened up new avenues of possibility for me personally and professionally. But I didn't expect that it would once again take me back home to Cyprus.

In 1996, we visited during the summer, with Niki often staying longer with our daughters to reconnect with family and friends, but my growing responsibilities at USC kept me so busy that I could often only stay for a short time.

Even though our visits were limited, I felt somehow that returning to the island was an important way of reconnecting with my roots.

A few years earlier, in 1988, my parents had transferred the titles of all of our family's properties located in the occupied areas of Northern Cyprus to me and my sister. At the time, my mother was very emotional, describing our homes as "lost properties." But my father made sure that I would never forget that they were "frozen assets."

He believed strongly that the properties that had belonged to our family for several generations would one day return to us in future generations. Even if this meant that our daughters or their children had to do it, he needed to believe that a day would come when we would legally reclaim them from Turkey.

At that time, the University of Cyprus was summoning me to return home to reconnect with my past and close a chapter of my life. They selected me as an honorary degree recipient at the commencement ceremony in June 2000. I was simultaneously honored, humbled, and surprised.

⁂ ⁂ ⁂

As we prepared for commencement, I was asked to provide a list of names of friends and relatives to invite to the ceremony. My busy schedule had kept me from thinking about my early days in Cyprus. But now, as we listed names, the memories came back to me at first slowly, but vividly.

The ceremony would become a sort of reunion, bringing together old friends and families, some of whom I hadn't seen since I was a kid running through the streets of that small village. It would also be a valuable experience for our two daughters who were born in the United States by helping them maintain a connection to Cyprus and Athens.

Although many of the guests we invited were able to attend, there was one who could not make it that day.

For some reason, when I first learned about the honorary degree, I felt compelled to invite the American Ambassador to Cyprus, Donald Bandler. I figured it was a long shot, but I sent the invitation anyway.

He received my message and promptly faxed a letter from Cyprus to my office at USC, apologizing that he wouldn't be on the island that particular day. However, he replied that he would be returning shortly. If we were still on the island, he said that he would love to meet me and Niki, and offered us an invitation to visit him at the American Embassy in Cyprus.

His faxed letter turned out to be the beginning of a long and enjoyable friendship that would last until his untimely passing from early-onset Alzheimer's in 2017.

Niki and I went to the embassy to meet with Ambassador Bandler and his communications director. The American embassy in Nicosia is a modern building that combines the ambassador's residence and administrative buildings. Its bombproof construction makes it look like a fortress with imposing command posts.

The ambassador wanted to know more about who we were, asking about our family history. He also displayed great admiration for the technologies we were developing at USC, expressing optimism about the future of the internet. At one point in the conversation, I told him about the work I had done for the U.S. Navy and the security clearance I had with the U.S. government.

He was elated. He started talking excitedly, saying, "One of the big things we're trying to do here is find ways to bring the Greek and Turkish Cypriot communities together."

Then he suggested an idea. He said, "It would be really nice—under the auspices of the American Embassy—if we could bring the two communities together. We could organize an event in the buffer zone."

He was speaking, of course, of the "green line," a neutral zone that resembled the demilitarized zone (DMZ) in Korea, a "no-man's" land which separates the two territories.

"If you're available in the next few days, I would like to give you the same tour I gave to Michael Dukakis when he visited the island," he said. "I will take you to the occupied part of Cyprus."

"My god, Mr. Ambassador," I said.

I was stunned not just because of the special offer, but also because of what I knew about the region's history. Very few Greek Cypriots had crossed the line into occupied territory since the Turks had invaded the island in 1974, and only under extreme circumstances as part of the negotiations for the settlement of the Cyprus issue.

Niki didn't hesitate for a moment. She said I should do it.

Ambassador Bandler smiled and nodded, pleased with the decision.

"I know a Turkish-Cypriot businessman," he said. "I'm going to call him and ask him to host us for lunch."

* * *

From the back seat, I watched as a small American flag fluttered on the front the embassy's dark car. I felt my heart beat a little faster as we slowed to 10-15 miles per hour and prepared to drive through the buffer zone.

To make the journey, we would have to pass through three separate checkpoints. I knew that making such a crossing as a Greek Cypriot was rare, and I feared what might happen if anything went wrong.

The first checkpoint was the Greek Cypriot National Guard. Ambassador Bandler lowered his window just enough so the guards could see his face, but not anyone else in the car. He waved and smiled and the guards gestured for the car to continue.

At the British and United Nations checkpoint, he followed the same routine, waving and smiling as we went through.

But as we reached the Turkish checkpoint, I could feel the car slowing even more. Through the dark windows, I could see the stern faces of the soldiers, tilting their heads trying to get a better look inside the car.

But then at the last moment, the guards relented and waved us through, Ambassador Bandler still looking as calm and cool as ever.

As far as I knew, I was one of the very few Cypriots that had just crossed into the buffer zone for the first time in more than 25 years.

* * *

Once we crossed into the Turkish zone, Ambassador Bandler said, "Open your window so you can see clearly outside."

I hesitated for a moment, but my curiosity compelled me to get an unblemished view of Northern Nicosia. Although time had taken its toll on the city I remembered from my childhood, in many ways the past had been preserved.

At the time, there was little real estate development in the northern part of the island, so the landscape was still dotted with houses that had been built in the 1940s and 1950s. Although the houses were still standing, the area had a ghostly presence, as if all of the region's people had vanished overnight.

After touring most of Northern Nicosia, we drove to a restaurant where we met the Turkish Cypriot businessman that Ambassador Bandler had mentioned at the embassy. It was during that lunch that Bandler proposed a bicommunal professional summit, a way to bring the two sides together. It would not focus on the past, but rather help people imagine a future in which technology and economic development might bring us together.

The businessman agreed to help us set up the summit, offering to pull strings to attract Turkish Cypriot entrepreneurs from the occupied area.

Soon I found myself collaborating with the American Embassy, working out the details of a summit that might finally bring the two communities together for a common cause.

However, first Ambassador Bandler had to use his diplomatic skills to convince Rauf Denktas, the Turkish Cypriot leader of the self-declared republic of Northern Cyprus, to allow the summit to take place.

Denktas had always been adamantly opposed to any meeting between the two sides, but Bandler told him that if he didn't agree he would be "cutting off his nose to spite his face."

Finally, Denktas agreed, but they had to set up their own rules. There would be 100 IT professionals attending, 50 of them Greek Cypriots and 50 Turkish Cypriots.

Although the government in Cyprus didn't appear to be

opposed to this summit, Ambassador Bandler wanted to cover all of his bases.

He said, "Max, I'll set you up with a meeting at the Ministry of Foreign Affairs in Cyprus, so you can inform them what we're planning. It's better that they hear it from you."

I'm not a trained diplomat, so I didn't know what to expect.

But when I arrived, they had already done their research on me. They knew who I was and they were very cordial. I asked if they had any problems with our efforts to bring these professionals together.

The man said, "As far as we're concerned, the Turkish Cypriots are citizens of the Republic of Cyprus. It's just the northern part that's under occupation by the Turkish Army. That's the position of the Cyprus government."

Everyone was finally on board.

From my work with the government, I knew that complex political problems are approached in a multitude of ways—through diplomatic discussions, technological innovations, and even popular culture, which can change perceptions on both sides.

However, in Cyprus the challenge is even more complex. Most people think of it as an island divided by two distinct communities from different ethnic backgrounds—Greek Cypriots and Turkish Cypriots. But there is one more division: religion. The two faiths—Christian Orthodox and Muslim—create almost a double division, making it even more difficult to find common ground.

I had many discussions with Ambassador Bandler and the Greek Cypriots who would be attending the conference. Because of this double division, we believed that the only way to bring the two communities together and reunify the island was through economic success. In many ways, we viewed this event not as a technology conference, but also an economic development conference.

It was a long shot, but one worth taking. We just had to get everyone involved to make it as successful as possible, so we could get the media coverage that would help the idea gain ground.

⁂ ⁂ ⁂

We organized two conferences, giving us a chance to share ideas that would be beneficial to both sides. Ambassador Bandler pointed out to me at the end that our bicommunal conferences were the most successful ever organized since 1974.

I still have the pictures from the event, showing 100 Greek and Turkish Cypriots sitting at the same tables, eating dinner, and having conversations together. It was very emotional for everyone because it was such an unusual event.

We felt like it was a great success and we got a lot of attention in the Greek Cypriot press. But on the other side, Denktas was reluctant to promote anything that suggested any type of reunification. Unfortunately, even after all of our efforts, it didn't really gain ground with Turkish Cypriots.

⁂ ⁂ ⁂

As a follow-up to the event, Ambassador Bandler wanted to introduce me to Glafcos Clerides, the president of Cyprus. I must confess I was excited to visit the presidential palace.

Surrounded by pine trees, the palace is designed in the British colonial style, highlighted with traditional elements from Cyprus—a central tower dome, limestone walls, and gutters carved with human and animal figures.

By the time I met with him, President Clerides was an 82-year-old man, whose early challenges were now tempered with the wisdom of someone who had seen and lived so much history.

Ambassador Bandler and I arrived in the embassy car, the media camping out at the presidential palace, the cameras clicking and the questions flying as we approached the entrance.

At one point, Ambassador Bandler stopped and told everyone that he would give a brief press conference after the meeting.

Inside, we sat down for a discussion with President Clerides.

He turned to Ambassador Bandler and said, “Donald, when you called me over the weekend, I was on my yacht in Limassol. And you wanted to meet urgently today and I said, why not? You know, I always make myself available if you have something important to talk about.”

Ambassador Bandler took a moment to introduce me, but he probably took too long, giving him my detailed resume.

When he finished, President Clerides looked at me and said, “So, you’re teaching in our technology college here?”

“No, Mr. President, I’m a professor at the University of Southern California,” I said.

“And where are you from? You were born here in Cyprus.”

“In the village of Komi Kebir,” I replied.

“Oh, that’s a very small village,” he said.

After a few minutes, we turned the subject to the conference we had organized, and then he understood the point of the meeting.

“That was a great thing you did,” said President Clerides. “I even want Turkish Cypriots to be able to come to work in the south. We need labor for construction. Instead of bringing workers from other countries, or from the Middle East, why not give those job opportunities to Cypriots?”

We met for about 30-40 minutes, talking about the success of the conference and the possibilities moving forward.

After the meeting, Ambassador Bandler pulled me aside and said, “Max, don’t rush to go out. I know what the media want. I want to give you a tour of the presidential palace. And you have to see the gardens, they’re beautiful.”

So the two of us took a long walk around, taking in the scenery and the serenity of the gorgeous gardens, building up anticipation for the reporters waiting at the entrance.

When we finally headed back to the car, it was a media circus.

Everyone wanted to know what we discussed with President Clerides about the Cyprus issue, and what we told him.

Ambassador Bandler took the opportunity to introduce me, talked about the importance of the conference, and what it had done to unify the two groups. It was great publicity and he understood how to make the most of the moment.

Although the Cyprus problem remains unsolved, I have very fond memories of that time.

I just wish we could say our efforts brought the two communities together. But all of these years later, I am still hopeful that they will once again sit together at the same tables and share the same interests as we did at the Ledra Palace Hotel.

* * *

Even after the IT summit and our meeting with President Clerides, Ambassador Bandler wanted to set up a meeting between me and the Turkish Cypriot leader Rauf Raif Denktas.

It was one thing to have a Greek Cypriot travel into Turkish Cypriot territory. It was a completely different thing to actually sit down with Denktas, who was hated by all Greek Cypriots.

In his younger years, Denktas was very extreme. During the island's bicommunal violence that took place in the 1950s and the early 1960s, he was involved in acts that Greek Cypriots considered terrorism.

From the very beginning, he was pro-Turkey, pushing for partition of the island, insisting that the two communities remain separate.

For me personally, meeting with him would be a tremendous risk at that time. There was the danger that my fellow Greek Cypriots would see me as a traitor, someone who had left the island for America, and then returned to meet with a terrorist. To some of the people I grew up around, meeting Denktas would be like sitting down to talk to Osama bin Laden. That's how much people hated him.

But I have to admit that my feelings were much different than the general consensus. I was grateful that Ambassador Bandler would offer to arrange such a meeting, and I have to say that I was actually excited.

Yes, he was the leader of the Turkish-Cypriot self-declared republic in Northern Cyprus. But no one else recognized it as an independent state.

What did I have to lose? I was just going to talk to him.

When I did meet with him, I was surprised by a few things. First, his so-called palace was in an old British colonial building, made of red brick with red tiles on the roof. Compared to President Clerides palace, it lacked the extravagance you would normally associate with a major leader.

The other thing that surprised me was Denktas himself. For many years, Greek Cypriots had lionized him. When we met, he was a short, small man who was much less intimidating than his public reputation. I thought he would project power rather than pity.

I was also very careful never to address him as "President." I couldn't do that.

Instead, I said, "Very nice to meet you, sir."

His chief of staff handed him my business card and he studied it for a moment.

Then he said, "Dr. Nikias, so you're Greek American, aren't you?"

"No, I am Greek Cypriot. I was born in a village in the Karpas Peninsula."

"Oh," he said, a look of mild confusion forming on his face.

"When I was 10 years old, my family moved to Famagusta and I'm a graduate of the gymnasium of Famagusta."

I paused for a moment to let it sink in that both places where I had lived were now occupied by the Turks.

"Oh, but your wife is American, isn't she?," said Denktas.

He couldn't accept the fact that a Greek Cypriot was involved in an effort to bring the two communities together. He was searching for a connection between me or Niki and America.

"No, my wife is not American," I said. "We're both naturalized citizens, but my wife was born and raised in Famagusta and she's also a graduate of the gymnasium of Famagusta."

"Oh," he said again, trying to figure what to say to someone whose families' and friends' villages and homes had been locked away in Turkish-occupied territory for more than a quarter of a century.

"Our daughters, however, are American," I said. "They were born in the United States."

Suddenly, he perked up and spoke to me in fluent Greek, which he would never do in public.

"*Na sas zisoun kai oti epithimite*," he said, which means, "I wish them a long life, and anything you and your wife wish for them."

After the somewhat uncomfortable beginning, we began to talk about the IT summit. Now he started to warm up and eventually became very cordial.

* * *

After two trips to Cyprus, I returned to my busy schedule at USC and had less contact with Ambassador Bandler and others.

Then the attacks of September 11, 2001, shocked the world. On that morning, I felt compelled to send a message to Ambassador Bandler, so I wrote him an email, including a short excerpt from Thucydides' Peloponnesian War, the funeral oration of Pericles.

Thucydides writes:

> We throw open our city to the world, and never by alien acts exclude foreigners from any opportunity of learning or observing although the eyes of an enemy may occasionally profit by our liberality . . . We live exactly as we please and yet are just as ready to encounter every legitimate danger.[2]

On September 17, President Clerides and the entire government cabinet came to the American Embassy to express their condolences and declare their support for U.S. efforts against terrorism.

It was a major media event and Ambassador Bandler made brief remarks, reading the excerpt that I had sent him which was included in the Embassy's press release.[3]

Donald emailed me, writing: "It was nice to have the Pericles reading from you. So nice that I incorporated it on the spot into my televised statement today when President Clerides came to the residence to sign our condolence book." Apparently, most of the media outlets publishing the story made a reference to Pericles' quote from the funeral oration.

Later, I joked with him, saying, "Donald, I made you look good in front of the Greek Cypriots and they loved you!"

* * *

In 2003, for the first time since 1974, the Turkish army allowed Greek Cypriots to return to the northern part of Cyprus to see the homes they had been forced to abandon.

Niki and I took our two daughters, as well as my sister and mother-in-law. It was very emotional, and they were in tears most of the time. It's not easy seeing Turks from Anatolia, who had been brought in by the army to change the demographics, now living in your homes.

I will always remember the sadness and anger we felt when we saw the crumbled cross that marked my grandfather's grave, a historical remnant of the looting and the vandalism from nearly three decades earlier. It's unfair and unjust, but there's also very little you can do about it.

I will never give up on returning the rightful properties back to our families, but in many ways that was the closing of a chapter in my life. We are an American family now. Our home is the

United States. It was time for me to start a new chapter in my life, one in which I would be taking on even more responsibility by becoming dean of the USC School of Engineering.

PART FOUR

THE RISE OF USC

CHAPTER 13

Act With Intention

« Έγώ δέ οῗμαι, έφη, τόν άρχοντα ού τώ ραδιουργεῗν χρήναι διαφέρειν τών άρχομένων, άλλά τώ προνοεῗν καί φιλοπονεῗν.»

ΞΕΝΟΦΏΝΤΟΣ ΚΎΡΟΥ ΠΑΙΔΕΊΑΣ, Α 1.6.8

"I hold that the ruler should be marked out from other men, not by taking life easily, but by his forethought and his wisdom and his eagerness for work."[1]

XENOPHON, *CYROPAEDIA*, BOOK I, 6.8

In May 2001, a call from Provost Lloyd Armstrong came on commencement afternoon.

"Max, I'm calling to tell you that you are my choice, and you are President Sample's choice, to be the next dean of USC's School of Engineering," he said.

I thanked him, and he suggested we get together that next Monday, so we could talk about the position and he could present me with the offer.

On Monday, when I received the official offer, I was shocked. It was supposed to be a promotion. But he was offering me $40,000 less than what I was already making. Essentially, he was asking me to take a major pay cut.

"Lloyd," I said. "I'm already making more than this."

"Yeah," he said. "But we look at the comparative data with other deans of engineering, and usually we begin at the 50th or 55th percentile."

"Yes, but how many of those other deans have won National Centers of Excellence, and then became founding directors of major institutes? How many of them have the experience I already have?" I asked.

Surprisingly, he wasn't budging, so I had to get creative.

"In this offer, you're including an at-risk bonus, right?" I asked.

"Yes," he said.

"Do you believe that I'm not going to perform and, therefore, I'm not going to get the bonus? Is there any dean you haven't given a bonus to every year?" I asked.

"What do you mean?" he said.

"Why don't you add the bonus to the salary, and then at least you make me whole," I said.

"Oh, I see. So, your issue is that you don't want to face a reduction in your monthly paycheck. Is that it?" he asked.

"Yes!" I said, as if that shouldn't have been obvious.

"Okay, let me think about it and I'll let you know," he said.

I was really disappointed with his response. I seriously considered turning down the offer. But then I realized that throughout my career, I've never tried to maximize a single transaction. Instead, I always tried to see it as a series of transactions that get bigger and better over time.

The next day Lloyd called and told me he would accept the deal we had discussed. That's how I began my tenure as dean of USC's School of Engineering.

* * *

Looking back, although I was disappointed about being offered a lower salary for promotion, it was probably for the best. It fueled a fire within me to prove myself and to be a successful dean.

Having learned the school inside and out serving as associate dean of engineering, and then director of the Integrated Media Systems Center for 10 years, I'd begun to develop my own ideas for what USC needed for the future.

At the time, the school had a strong foundation, but it also had several underlying challenges. There were budget issues that needed to be addressed right away and I needed to position the school for the changing landscape of the future.

I met with the university's comptroller and budget director, quickly identifying 10 percent of the money we needed. I immediately announced a six-month budget freeze, which gave us time to reorganize the school and redirect its priorities. These were difficult decisions to make, but I wanted to take care of everything at one time, rather than draw out the inevitable changes over several months.

To the surprise of some, I reduced administrative costs and gave mid-year salary increases to ensure equity among our faculty. I also invested heavily in a new team of communications and development staff.

For advice, I also met with the dean of the Stanford engineering school. Beyond elevating the engineering programs, he told me about the importance of building teams for development, corporate relations, communications, and alumni relations.

Stanford had 30 development staff, just for engineering. At the time, USC only had three. I also knew that our donor pool had relied on the same names for many years, and I believed we needed to find new people to support the exciting things we were planning to do.

I left the meeting at Stanford feeling like we had a lot of catching up to do. We needed to make major investments and take advantage of interdisciplinary partnerships, which my experience at the Integrated Media Systems Center told me would be the future for faculty and students.

* * *

As I was making structural changes in engineering, I met someone who would become an important working partner for the next 17 years.

In July 2001, I was walking across campus when I heard someone say, "You're my kind of dean."

It was Katharine Harrington. She was talking about my decisive actions to enact a budget freeze and get the school's budget in order from the very beginning.

In her no-nonsense way, Katharine was truly a pioneer in higher education. At the time, she was in the Office of the Provost, where she was responsible for increasing graduation and retention rates. But it was her impressive use of data analytics that set her apart from her peers.

When we talked about our challenges with retention rates at the engineering school, her data analysis was truly extraordinary. Her innovative ideas would make her the very best student enrollment expert in American higher education.

She would also become an important partner in helping engineering, and the entire university, attract more and more of the best and brightest students from around the world.

❊ ❊ ❊

In those early days, I was also forming my leadership team. To become the second-in-command at the engineering school, I wanted Yannis Yortsos. When I was associate dean, Yannis was the chair of the chemical engineering department and I've always been impressed by his leadership abilities and his impeccable character. So I asked him to come up with a list of all of the changes that would need to be made in order for the school to reach the next level.

I met him for lunch. As always, he came prepared. He'd already written a detailed paper, describing all of ways we could elevate the school. As he gave me an overview, I told him that I wanted him to become my Senior Associate Dean.

For a moment, he hesitated. Then he began to tell me why he wasn't the right person for the job. I looked at him and smiled.

"You already have the plan," I said. "Now you just have to implement it."

With Yannis in place, I added Randy Hall to head our research efforts. Randy had been in charge of the advanced transportation program at Caltrans, the California Department of Transportation, which manages the entire state's highway systems and infrastructure. I was always impressed by how Randy led a very complex program and was delighted when he joined the school as a faculty member and chair of industrial engineering.

The combined track record of these two leaders speaks for itself. Randy Hall later served as USC's Vice President of Research for 15 years. And Yannis Yortsos became by far the very best and longest-serving dean of engineering.

Together, they also helped us build an excellent team of associate and assistant deans, who would help the school navigate the future.

* * *

There were some donors with different temperaments and idiosyncrasies. I found that out quickly with USC trustee Ron Tutor.

Tutor served on the engineering school's Board of Councilors. He was also infamous for getting what he wanted.

In June 2001, I held my very first BOC meeting, with high hopes that everything would go well. A few minutes after the meeting started, Ron Tutor stormed in, screaming at the top of his lungs.

"I donated more than $10 million for a building! I want to know, when are you going to build my building? I have been waiting for five years and nothing has happened!"

He wasn't really screaming at me, but rather for the benefit of everyone else in the room. And he wouldn't stop.

A few days later, I went to Ron Tutor's office. He was still upset. In fact, he wouldn't even look at me.

"All I want to know is when is USC going to build the building that I've already paid the naming rights for," he said.

"Ron," I said respectfully. "I want this building as much as you do. And to be honest, I'm the only hope you've got."

"Oh," he said dramatically, rearranging his feet on the desk so he was now facing me.

"But the building you originally supported needs to be updated," I said. "To really help our engineering students, we need to change the designs and its location. I think we need to add labs for biochemical engineering and nanotechnology."

I slid the plans across his desk and waited for the backlash.

"I know it's not the same, but it will be a much better and bigger building," I said.

The outburst never came. He just wanted someone to finally finish *his* building.

Along the way, there were challenges. Initially, the look of our modern engineering building was rejected by Steve Sample because he believed in the importance of maintaining consistency with USC's Italian Romanesque architecture.

In the end, Steve was right. We went back to the blueprints and made the necessary changes. When we finally held the groundbreaking ceremony for Tutor Hall of Engineering in 2003, Ron was no longer upset. He was elated.

Although we got off to a rocky start, the construction process was a great experience and I worked closely with Ron on several structures over more than 15 years.

* * *

When you are in a leadership position never assume that those who are constantly praising you are really your friends.

I have a personal story that taught me this important lesson as soon as I became dean of engineering.

In 1991, one year after I arrived at USC, I was promoted to be associate dean for research in the engineering school.

Along with the school's CFO, this promotion gave me significant say on the allocation of research funds from certain foundations.

Right away, I got a visit from an electrical engineering professor.

He was the nicest guy, praising my academic work, my publications, my record of accomplishments. You name it, he loved it!

"I'm thrilled that we recruited you," he said. "And I want you to know that I was on the dean's faculty committee that reviewed your tenure appointment to join USC."

I have to admit. It was very flattering.

For the next decade, I worked with him and provided substantial support for his research.

Fast forward to 2001. I'm named dean of the engineering school.

Out of curiosity, I asked my assistant for my file that was kept in the dean's office.

Looking through the paperwork, I found the recommendations from the dean's faculty committee in 1991.

The vote for me to join the faculty was unanimous . . . except for <u>one</u> person.

Guess who? The guy whose research I'd supported for the past decade!

Instantly, I realized his first visit was not out of friendship. It was to cover his tracks!

Like all followers, he was acting out of his own self-interest.

And he probably thought I'd never find out.

❊ ❊ ❊

No matter how much you prepare as a leader, there are simply some things beyond your control. For all of us, one of those moments was the morning of September 11, 2001. There were many traumatic days for our nation that followed. But for engineering, there were also serious concerns about how the attacks would affect the enrollment of our international students.

An engineering professor, Dr. Raghavendra, told me, "Don't you worry, Max. There will always be students from India no matter what."

He reasoned that there was no language barrier for Indian students, and that they always had excellent training in engineering and the sciences, as well as a strong desire to get a graduate degree from an American university.

We immediately planned to send a USC representative to India, with a new strategy to recruit graduate students.

The plan worked. In fact, it worked so well that two years after 9/11 USC had the only engineering school with an increase in international students. Our success caught the attention of politicians, who had seen a dramatic decrease in the enrollment of international students around the nation.

During an audit requested by a Congressman from Pasadena for the U.S. Government Accountability Office, I provided an interview. They were curious how we accomplished something that no other university in the entire nation had done.

I told them that after 9/11 many universities put their international recruitment plans on hold. But USC redoubled its effort to recruit the very best students from India, which made all of the difference.

* * *

Only a few weeks after 9/11, I also got a deeper appreciation for the close connections among the members of the Trojan Family.

I traveled by train with USC's fans to the annual game against Notre Dame. I hosted a group of engineering alumni, and although the mood was subdued, we were excited to see the Trojans play.

It was Pete Carroll's first season as coach and USC lost a game in the rain, 27–16. Although it's difficult to believe now, the Trojans finished that season 6–6 overall, ending with a loss to Utah in the Las Vegas Bowl!

During that train ride, I was doing much more than just traveling to a college football game. It was the first moment that I really experienced how much Trojan alumni love their traditions.

⁂ ⁂ ⁂

At almost every social event for the school and the university, from alumni receptions to President Sample's pre-game football parties, Niki was always there by my side.

To be honest, she read the briefings for most events more carefully than I did. She talked about this material in the car, both before and after events. It was like having a trusted colleague focused specifically on social events. And she's always been my most important partner, both personally and professionally.

We both became deeply immersed in the traditions of the Trojan Family. During the Pete Carroll era, the pre-game presidential football parties were one of the hottest tickets in town. For home and away games, all of these parties were oversubscribed because of the popularity of the football program.

In the beginning, I had to really study what was happening with the football team because it was so important for "small talk" at these parties. If you didn't know about the quarterback situation—or whatever else was happening with the team at the moment—you could appear ignorant in conversations with alumni.

⁂ ⁂ ⁂

As things were changing at USC, I had an epiphany.

I looked in the mirror while I was getting ready one morning.

"What's happening to me?" I thought. "I love this job. Every minute of it."

I couldn't say that before, but suddenly I felt I really had an opportunity to elevate the school of engineering academically.

But to reach the next level, we needed a vision for what the school could become. And that began by establishing new priorities and creating a new strategic plan.

❊ ❊ ❊

First, we needed to identify the most exciting areas of engineering that we believed would shape the future. Then we had to retain and recruit the very best faculty in each of those disciplines. We even overhauled the budget to focus on three main areas: recruiting new faculty, academic programs for students, and interdisciplinary research.

We also built an external relations office from scratch in order to bring together fundraising, alumni relations, corporate relations, and communications under one umbrella. Once we'd staffed that office, we were ready to hit the ground running.

As everything began to fall into place, I wanted to find a way to quickly and clearly communicate where we were headed. Some leaders prefer mission statements, but I felt they were too difficult to memorize and often ignored.

Instead, I created a motto: "10 in 5 and 5 in 10." I believed we should become a top 10 engineering school in five years, and then a top five school in 10 years.

It would be a challenge, but the motto made it clear where we were headed. And everyone from the most experienced faculty to the newest students could understand it.

The motto wasn't the only reason for our success, but four years later when I became provost the school had risen to number six in the nation.

❊ ❊ ❊

Just as we were gaining momentum, there was another unexpected surprise.

I discovered that USC's central administration was seriously considering spending $50 million on an outdated technology for distance education—the National Technological University (NTU) satellite system.

There was one major problem. Satellite delivery was soon going to be replaced by streaming via the internet, giving users interactive features—all for free!

I rushed straight to the provost and begged him not to waste $50 million. Fortunately, cooler heads prevailed and we passed on the old satellite technology.

However, this decision led to an unexpected predicament. We had to let our remote faculty and students around the world know we were "pulling the plug" on our satellite transmission with the school's Distance Education Network (DEN).

Before we went completely online, there was serious concern from some of our faculty who were worried we could be flooded with complaints from remote learning students.

But I knew we eventually had to make the decision to begin webcasting. One morning I said, "Just do it."

Amazingly, we received zero complaints. None whatsoever.

I call that DEN's "Spotify moment." We embraced the new technology and it quickly paid off.

In only four years, enrollment grew from 200 remote students to 1,200, making it the largest program of its kind in the nation.

❊ ❊ ❊

From the very beginning, our goal was to retain and recruit the world's best faculty. But you can't recruit the best with the same strategy as everyone else.

So, we decided we weren't going to list job openings. We didn't want people coming to us. We were going after them.

We hired recruiting firms to do national searches for the best potential candidates in computer science, nanotechnology, and biomedical technology. If we didn't find the right candidates, the job simply went away because we wanted to make sure that all of our new hires were the best and the brightest.

During this process, I also received some very valuable advice from Keith Uncapher, the former director of the Information Sciences Institute. He told me that in emerging fields such as biological engineering and quantum computing, we may not find many senior faculty. Instead, he suggested hiring young assistant professors—the young Ph.D.'s.

"Besides," he said. "They're not going to be that expensive. So hire many of them, but give them the resources. Because they're the ones who are going to develop these fields."

As we recruited more and more top faculty, I had another realization. Of the 160 engineering faculty, only 15 of them brought in about 50 percent of the entire school's research funding! These faculty were the very best research performers and other universities would try to recruit them from time to time.

For these 15 faculty, I had an open-door policy. Anytime they had a problem or needed to see me, I would drop whatever I was doing and make myself available to them.

* * *

In enhancing our faculty, there was also one major area that we clearly had to rectify: we needed to recruit more women.

For decades, engineering has been a notoriously male-dominated field. In 2001, USC had only three women—out of 160—on the engineering faculty. I was shocked to learn that the chemical engineering building didn't even have women's restrooms!

When we announced that we were making it a priority to recruit more women, I was surprised at the resistance I received from some of the faculty, especially the department chairs who were all men. Some believed there simply weren't enough qualified female candidates. That was not the case, of course.

I also have to give all the credit to Yannis Yortsos, who really took our recruitment of women to the next level of national prominence, helping the school stand out in terms of gender diversity.

The result was that the composition of the school's faculty changed forever.

Yannis also was instrumental increasing the percentage of female students in engineering to more than 50 percent during his tenure as my successor dean,[2] when the national average was around 16-17 percent.[3]

It took a major effort, but the work led to positive change. I was very proud that in only four years we recruited 30 new faculty members. And, yes, we added a women's restroom in the chemical engineering building.

To everyone, it was a sign that times were changing for the better.

* * *

The biggest challenge we had in the engineering school was student retention. After a year, nearly one-third of our students would transfer to business or other majors. We believed the nation was losing future talented engineers and resolved to fix it.

Through student surveys we learned that the problem was that the faculty who taught physics, chemistry, and mathematics were from the College of Letters, Arts and Sciences, so they weren't giving our students any relevant examples for engineering. Our solution was to create a center with our own faculty teaching those courses.

Yortsos then had the innovative idea of creating freshman academies, which talked about the wonders of engineering and got students really excited about these professions.

After we made those changes, our retention "leakage" eventually went down to zero.

* * *

In those early days, I also had several other interactions with people who have now become notable names in the school. One of the most memorable meetings was with alumnus Dan Epstein.

When I gave my inaugural speech, he immediately understood the vision and got very excited. Noting Dan's enthusiasm, I traveled to San Diego to have a meeting in his office. This was going to be a major ask to endow the naming of the Industrial and Systems Engineering (ISE) department, and I was anxious about taking such a big step with a major donor.

Everything went according to plan until I mentioned the amount of support we were asking for: $15 million. Dan hesitated for a moment, his head turning slightly from side to side, as if he was thinking it over. I thought I may have lost him.

Then he said, "I'm ready to close the deal today for $10 million, but if you still want $15 million, then I need to think about it."

Of course, he was a businessman. And he was negotiating.

I tried to hide my excitement, calmly agreeing to the deal. I was thrilled.

Even with his negotiation, Dan Epstein had just agreed to make the largest gift by an individual to name an academic department in USC history.[4]

Forty years after he had attended USC, the department where he once took classes was renamed the Daniel J. Epstein Department of Industrial and Systems Engineering.

It was a major boost to the department and the school. It helped fund two endowed chairs, which supported two leading senior faculty members. But more importantly, it was a sign to other potential donors that major things were happening in engineering.

⁂ ⁂ ⁂

Some donors needed more convincing than others. It's difficult to believe now, but one of those people was John Mork, a graduate of the school's petroleum engineering program. John went on to create the Energy Corporation of America (ECA), one of the nation's most successful energy exploration companies, which discovered vest reserves of natural gas in the Marcellus Shale of Pennsylvania and West Virginia.

The Mork Family's generous support has since become esteemed among members of the Trojan Family.

But when I first met him, John was disengaged with USC. On Friday, September 13, 2002, I traveled to meet him in Denver. It was the day before the USC football game against Colorado.

Our department of petroleum engineering had been closed down by the previous dean. Naturally, the graduates of that department weren't pleased with the decision. All of the alumni were angry and disconnected from the school, including John.

I learned later that he had agreed to meet with me as a courtesy, thinking that I was only in town to attend the USC game the next day.

I also didn't know that John had asked his executive assistant to come in after 30 minutes to pull him out of the meeting. Once we started talking, I could see him getting interested in the vision.

We talked for 90 minutes, with his poor assistant coming in every 15 minutes to remind him of another important appointment.

It was one of the most important meetings that I've ever had. John and Julie Mork became some of the most generous supporters in the history of USC. First, they created the Mork Family Department of Chemical Engineering and Materials Science.

Then, nearly nine years after our initial meeting, the Mork Family made the largest gift for student scholarships in USC's history. They donated $110 million to create the Mork Family Scholars Program, which helps provide scholarships to students with the dream of a world-class education.[5]

It's a tribute to the entire Mork family that they have forever changed the future for so many members of the Trojan Family. And I'm forever grateful that John didn't decide to end that first meeting after 30 minutes!

* * *

In June 2003, I was at an event on campus to celebrate the conclusion of USC's Building on Excellence Campaign, which raised $2.85 billion and at the time was "the most successful fundraising campaign in the history of higher education."[6]

As I was listening to President Sample's speech, something dawned on me. Because the campaign was ending, all of the fundraising initiatives at USC's other schools were closing down. They were celebrating their accomplishments, not planning for the future.

I immediately saw the advantage. The School of Engineering was the only one preparing to launch a new fundraising campaign in November 2003. It was called "Destination: The Future," and it was going to be a major fundraising initiative.

Everything is timing. And it was time for us to seize the moment.

CHAPTER 14

Seize the Moment

"Dum loquimur, fugerit invida aetas:
carpe diem, quam minimum credula postero."
QUINTUS HORATIUS FLACCUS, LIBER 1: XI, TU NE QUAESIERIS

"In the moment of our talking, envious time has ebb'd away:
Seize the present; trust tomorrow e'en as little as you may."[1]
HORACE, *ODES*, BOOK 1, POEM 11

In the fall of 2003, I scheduled a lunch at the California Club. We were about to announce our fundraising campaign and we needed a donation that caught people's attention.

So, I met with alumnus and venture capitalist Mark Stevens, who had been very important in helping USC expand its relationships in Silicon Valley. Now I was asking him to play an even greater role by helping our students and faculty create startups and spinoffs.

I asked him for $30 million. We settled on $22 million to establish the Mark and Mary Stevens Institute for Technology Commercialization (SITeC).[2]

The institute centralized tech transfer at the school of engineering, which entailed assessing faculty research innovation, conducting market research, preparing drafts for business models, performing feasibility studies, and helping spin innovations out into startups, licensing them to other entities, and promoting them to venture capitalists.

When I became provost, I expanded the institute to the entire university.

I'm very proud that it's still helping our students and faculty today as the USC Stevens Center for Innovation. And I'm very grateful to the Stevens family for their tremendous generosity.

* * *

While major gifts serve as a catalyst, planning a fundraising campaign for the engineering school was a challenge.

Fortunately, I worked closely with Ken Leventhal, who freely offered his wise counsel to USC's Board of Trustees for more than 35 years.[3] He was a celebrated certified public accountant, the chairman emeritus of the Ernst & Young Kenneth Leventhal Real Estate Group, and the namesake of the USC Leventhal School of Accounting.

He'd been part of the financial planning committee for USC's Toward Century II fundraising campaign, as well as the architect and national chairman of USC's Building on Excellence campaign.[4] Both were highly successful.

Although I knew Ken, I didn't know him well. But I was advised to talk to him because he was the "master" of planning campaigns. Those meetings were the beginning of a close working relationship that lasted until his death in 2012.

I met with Ken and Alan Kreditor, Senior Vice President for Advancement, both of whom I admired greatly. While Ken was a master planner, Alan was a brilliant tactician. No one understood human psychology better than Alan.

There were only a couple of areas where I disagreed with him. Alan told me, "Max, don't waste your time with too many alumni events. This is not where your money will come from."

When I started talking about launching a fundraising campaign, everybody advised me to hire a consultant, who would talk to our pool of potential donors and then help us decide the goal for the overall campaign.

So I went to Alan to get permission to hire a consultant. But he wouldn't give it to me.

"It's a waste of time," he said. "Don't do it. Only high schools and churches hire consultants because their goal is usually to raise $200,000 or $300,000, with everyone contributing $10,000 or $15,000."

I tried to plead my case, but he continued.

"Are you going to have a consultant meet with Mark Stevens? And do you think Mark Stevens is going to tell a consultant exactly how much money he's going to give? If I had a consultant ask me that, I'm going to lowball. I'm not going to commit to a consultant. Max, it's a relationship. You build it first."

I didn't listen. We hired a consultant. She went around, met will all of our prospects, came back and said, "If you add up all of the numbers, it's $6 million."

Then I said to myself, "Oh, my god, Kreditor is right!"

Lesson learned. I should have listened to him and saved the money.

I called him to let him know.

"Yeah, don't listen to them," he said. "You said you want to announce a campaign for $250 million. Be ambitious. If you say $250 million, people are going to think you calculated. Round the number to $300 million."

"But if we don't make it . . ." I started to say.

"Nobody remembers the duration of a campaign. But they all remember the number," said Kreditor. "If you extend the campaign for a few more years to meet the goal, so be it. In the end, the only thing anyone remembers is the amount you raised."

Once again, he was right. At first, I didn't listen to him. But I did learn an important lesson: that I should have been a better listener.

* * *

After months of planning, we were finally ready to officially launch our fundraising campaign.

It was going to be a big gala at the Ritz Carlton in Marina Del Rey. But then a major issue arose.

As we were preparing for the announcement, our number two and three senior development officers came to meet with me. They told me they were quitting. They'd found jobs somewhere else.

I was devastated. I felt betrayed in some ways. And I worried that their departures might cause our donors to hesitate in their support of the school.

Again, I went to Kreditor with the bad news. But he was unfazed.

"Why are you worried about it?" he said. "You're going to hire new development officers. Max, you have to understand that you're the continuity for this campaign, not your development officers."

Once again, he turned out to be right.

That Saturday night at the Ritz Carlton was a critical evening. Andrew and Erna Viterbi were sitting at the head table. Viterbi was the communications pioneer who invented an algorithm used in billions of cellular phones around the world.[5] He later served as co-founder of the digital and wireless communications giant Qualcomm Inc.[6]

That night Niki was sitting next to Andrew. She later told me that as I was walking up to deliver my speech, he turned his chair, so he could get a better view of the podium. Then he said to Niki, "I have to listen very carefully to what Max is going to say."

I gave a passionate speech about the future, with an expansive vision of all of the major initiatives we planned to pursue.

It would turn out to be a turning point for the school of engineering.

⁂

We were also competing against Harvard and the University of Pennsylvania for a new research center from the Department of Homeland Security.

During the site visit, I made sure the lead person of the review team never left my sight, so I could always be there to answer his questions.

He kept asking me, "If USC wins this center, is there going to be a protest on campus?"

"I don't know," I said. "But I don't think there will be."

"What about the English department?" he asked.

A month later, he called me with the good news. USC would establish the Center for Risk and Economic Analysis of Terrorism Events (CREATE), the nation's very first Homeland Security Center of Excellence.[7]

I rushed to the Davidson Conference Center, where President Sample and Provost Armstrong were hosting a leadership retreat.

When I told them, President Sample perked up immediately. "What?" said Sample. "Another center of excellence? The very first from DHS?"

He was impressed, informally announcing the news to the audience.

Although the English department did write a letter opposing the center, we never had any protests on campus.

❋ ❋ ❋

In December 2003, only a few weeks after the gala at the Ritz Carlton, Andrew Viterbi called the engineering school's development office. He didn't call my office or my executive assistant.

He let them know that he was going to be in Los Angeles, staying at the Beverly Wilshire Hotel. If I was available, he would like to have breakfast with me that Saturday morning.

I wondered why he didn't call my office, but I agreed to meet him at 8:00 a.m. on Saturday morning.

Earlier, President Sample and Ken Leventhal had tried to get a large gift from him without success. Up until that point, the only thing the Viterbis had endowed was a chair for Professor Sol Golomb for $2 million.

What I didn't know was that Provost Armstrong and the College of Letters, Arts, and Sciences had prepared a proposal to ask for a $10 million gift.

That morning at the Beverly Wilshire, Andrew and I had breakfast. I brought him up to date on things happening at the school. We talked about geopolitics, Israel, the future of engineering, and a number of other topics.

At the end, he said, "Max, I didn't bring you all the way out here for breakfast just to have our usual talk. Erna and I have decided that we would like to name the school."

I couldn't believe it. It wasn't just any name. It's Viterbi, which is legendary in engineering.

I thanked him and then I said, "Andy, you do realize that university protocol requires that as soon as I leave this meeting, I have to call my president and my provost because you're a trustee."

"No, no, no, Max," he said. "You're not going to do that. As far as I'm concerned, this meeting did not take place. Erna and I wanted you to know first. On Monday morning, I have a meeting with your provost, who I know is going to solicit me for $10 million and I'm going to tell him 'no.' Then I'm going to have a meeting with President Sample and let him know about the naming gift. Once I'm done, then I'm going to give you the heads-up."

I left breakfast and I was on the moon!

* * *

Although I had been sworn to silence, I needed to share the good news with someone. I called Sol Golomb from the car and gave him the confidential news.

"Oh, my god, Max. This is wonderful news," he said. "Congratulations! We brought Andy Viterbi home."

* * *

On Monday morning, I went to the office and didn't tell anyone. I was sitting there wondering, "When is my phone going to start ringing?"

Finally, I got a call from Andrew Viterbi, telling me the deal had been done.

As soon as I hung up, Steve Sample called me directly.

"Congratulations, Max," he said. "I'm giving the assignment to Ken Leventhal to negotiate the gift. This is wonderful news. Congratulations!"

The minute I finished that call, Alan Kreditor and Ken Leventhal called me together. I heard Kenny on the phone, "Kreditor, can you tell me how many donors you had . . . that they came to you . . . you didn't solicit them . . . that they came to you . . . how many?"

I could hear Alan laughing.

"I know the answer," Leventhal continued. "None. But the dean of engineering, Viterbi went to him!"

"Yeah, I told the provost," said Kreditor. "You never solicit Andrew Viterbi. Only he decides what he wants to do. But he didn't listen to me."

* * *

The Viterbi's $52 million gift was the largest naming gift ever received by an engineering school.[8]

After 99 years of history, the school had a new name: the USC Andrew and Erna Viterbi School of Engineering.

For the school and my deanship, it was the crowning achievement.

❊ ❊ ❊

By May 2004, I felt very good about how things were going with the newly-named Viterbi School of Engineering.

Around that time, I got a call from a senior faculty member at Northeastern University, where I had also been on the faculty.

He said, "We want to award Steve Sample an honorary degree. Would he accept it? And we would like you to come with him."

I called President Sample and explained to him how excited Northeastern was to recognize him for all he had done for USC and our local communities. He agreed to be honored, but what I didn't know was that there was something else on his mind.

❊ ❊ ❊

I arrived early and met Steve Sample at a hotel in downtown Boston. There was a dinner the night before, the honorary degree ceremony the next day, and then we were going to fly back to Los Angeles together.

As dean of engineering, that was my only time to spend with the president.

That night at dinner we were seated at the same table as Robert Kraft, the owner of the New England Patriots and his wife, who was also receiving an honorary degree.

When we got back to the hotel, Steve said, "Are you tired? We're used to Pacific Time. It's still early for us. Do you want to sit by the bar, Max? Do you like apple martinis? I love apple martinis. Let's have apple martinis. Come on, let's go."

He was the president. What else was I going to do?

We sat at a table by the bar and he ordered apple martinis.

Then the surprises began. He began praising my leadership qualities, which was totally unexpected.

At one point, he said, "Max, from now on, watch carefully how I do things. The way I go to the podium. The way I say things. You learn by watching."

It was so odd that when I got back to the room I called Niki. I told her that he spent the entire evening praising my leadership skills, the Viterbi gift, everything.

But Steve Sample was hinting at something I didn't know. Three weeks later, he announced that Lloyd Armstrong was stepping down in a year and he was going to do a national search for a new provost.

He knew the announcement was in the works, but he couldn't tell me.

* * *

In September 2004, USC's CFO Dennis Dougherty approached me at a pre-game football party.

"We need to have lunch together," said Dennis.

I agreed and met him downtown at the Pacific Dining Car, where Dennis had his own table next to the bar.

"You have to be our next provost," he said.

I was surprised and shared my reservations with him. I was happy with how well things were going at the engineering school. I also feared that if I applied and didn't get the job it would undercut my leadership as dean.

Dennis listened to my concerns, but remained adamant that I should be a candidate. In November, we met again for lunch and he kept encouraging me to throw my hat in the ring.

Over the holidays, Niki and I discussed the situation seriously and I had lunch with Dennis for a third time. I was still hesitant, but I was listening.

Then, in January 2005, I organized an evening event on

campus, where President Sample addressed engineering students. Afterward, he asked me to walk with him to his car. As we stood in front of Tommy Trojan, he encouraged me to become a candidate for provost. Later, I would come to believe that he had sent Dennis Dougherty to find out how I felt about the position.

But that evening on campus, Steve made his pitch to me. Without mentioning Dougherty's name, he tried to address my concerns.

"Max, listen, I've been watching you now for some time," he said. "I have no doubt you're going to be a successful university president someday. But if you look at university presidents today in the Association of American Universities, only about 10 percent really understand the complexities of medicine and medical schools. There are universities that don't have medical schools and that's a blessing. But we do, and I have a crisis on my hands."

He mentioned a crisis, but at that time it didn't register for me. I was too busy trying to accept the idea that he was selling me on becoming a candidate.

"If you were to become the provost—and, by the way, I'm not promising you the job—I'm just giving you advice. If you were later to become the president of an AAU university, becoming provost here would teach you how to manage a medical school. And then you're going to be ready."

That made a strong impression on me, and it began to change my mind about participating in the process.

"By the way," Steve Sample continued. "Medical schools and medical doctors can bring a president down."

At the time, it seemed like casual advice. Looking back, those words seem prophetic.

"So, Max, I don't want you to become a candidate," President Sample said. "We're going to call you an 'advisor' to the search committee. You're going to go through the entire process. We're talking to you, but you're an advisor, not a candidate."

* * *

The week before my meeting with the search committee, I wrestled with what I was going to say during my opening statement.

Seeking advice, I had a phone conversation with my mentor Karl Weiss, who said, "Didn't you get an award in history during high school? Steve is right. They're not going to talk to you about research. Max, focus on the importance of the humanities."

It was then that I came up with the idea for Visions and Voices,[9] a university-wide arts and humanities initiative, which has become incredibly popular among students from all disciplines at USC.

The search committee was comprised of several luminaries, including President Sample, Warren Bennis, and Kevin Starr.

It was an intimidating atmosphere, but my strategy was set. For the first 10 minutes, I delivered a passionate speech about the importance of the arts and humanities, outlining the Visions and Voices initiative.

The excitement in the room was palpable and it generated a 20-minute discussion, with lots of questions about how I planned to do it and who would pay for it.

After about 30 minutes, a booming baritone voice brought the conversation to a halt. It was Kevin Starr, who shouted, "I think we've had enough of your Hellenistic background. Can we discuss research now?"

Of course, I was happy to talk about research. The discussion shifted to areas where I was very comfortable, but I didn't know that Warren Bennis was saving the most difficult question for the end.

"Over the past 11 years, Lloyd Armstrong has been a great provost," Bennis said. "But you are a very different personality from Lloyd. So, why do you believe you can be a great provost?"

That was a tough question. Fortunately, I had done my research, reading several of Bennis's papers and a few of his books.

"I understand. And this is a question I have wrestled with in becoming a candidate for this position and preparing for this interview," I said. "Warren, I think the answer is in your book. You describe good leaders as those who shine under the spotlight."

"Yes, that's true," Bennis said.

"So, the president always has to shine under the spotlight," I said. "The deans—in the way they run their schools—also have to shine under the spotlight. But Warren, in your book, you also say that there's another type of leadership. Truly great leaders are the ones who help others shine under the spotlight. Therefore, I believe that's the role of the provost. It's a different leadership role. The provost should help his deans shine under the spotlight, and always make sure that the president shines under the spotlight."

Then I heard President Sample's voice at the end of the table.

"Okay, Max. Thank you. That's the end of the interview," he said.

For almost six weeks, I didn't hear another word. I wasn't sure what was going on. Finally, at 4:00 p.m. on a Monday during the last week of March, I received a call from Steve Sample.

He told me that I was his choice to become the next provost.

"I want to share some numbers with you, so we can wrap it up because I want to make the announcement by Wednesday," he said.

I thanked him and then said, "Steve, I'm fine with it. I just don't want to face a pay cut."

"What do you mean?" he asked. "Why would you face a pay cut?"

I explained what happened four years earlier when I became dean. He burst into laughter. He didn't know I'd been asked to take a pay cut, and he assured me that he wasn't asking me to work for less.

We agreed on the salary and by Wednesday the announcement went out.

⁂ ⁂ ⁂

As soon as I learned that I was going to be named provost, I asked my daughter Georgiana, who was an undergraduate student at USC, to come to my office.

I shared the news with her confidentially, and I was a little bit apologetic that she was going to lose her privacy. From her last name, everyone would recognize that she was a student in the College of Letters, Arts, and Sciences.

"Dad, they already know you as dean of engineering," she said.

"That's different," I said. "I'm going to be the provost now. So all schools will report to me."

As the conversation ended, Georgiana started to walk out the door, and then she came back into my office.

"Okay, I think I know why you wanted to see me," she said. "Don't worry, I will never embarrass you."

I was scheduled to take over as provost on June 1, 2005.

CHAPTER 15

Sea of Change

«Εὖ δὲ χρὴ καὶ τοῦτο εἰδέναι ὅτι ὁπόσους ἂν ἀξιοῖς σοι πείθεσθαι,
καὶ ἐκεῖνοι πάντες ἀξιώσουσι σὲ πρὸ ἑαυτῶν βουλεύεσθαι.
μηδέποτ᾽οὖν ἀφροντίστως ἔχε, ἀλλὰ τῆς μὲν νυκτὸς προσκόπει
τί σοι ποιήσουσιν οἱ ἀρχόμενοι, ἐπειδὰν ἡμέρα γένηται, τῆς δ᾽
ἡμέρας ὅπως τὰ εἰς νύκτα κάλλιστα ἕξει.»

ΞΕΝΟΦΩΝΤΟΣ ΚΥΡΟΥ ΠΑΙΔΕΙΑΣ, Α 6.42

"This too you must know well, that all those whom you expect to obey you will expect in turn that you make plans on their own behalf. So never be unthinking, but at night consider in advance what your subjects will do for you when day comes, and in the day how things will be finest for the night."[1]

XENOPHON, *CYROPAEDIA*, BOOK 1, 6.42

To start my tenure, Steve Sample said, "Max, the best way to learn the job of the provost is to be acting president."

Then he announced he was taking a three-month sabbatical. He sent out an executive order that no one—not even the trustees—should disturb him while he was away. The only one who could contact him in an emergency was me.

So, on my first day as provost, I found myself as acting president. Everyone had to come through me for anything they wanted.

⁂ ⁂ ⁂

After the president, the provost is the second ranking senior officer at the university, equivalent to the COO of a major corporation. (Unlike at many other universities, the provost position at USC was also even *more* complex: At the time, all of our schools and the medical enterprise reported to the provost.)

When I was in the position, I used to joke that the only large operation that the provost didn't get much involved with was the athletic department. Longtime USC trustee Ken Leventhal referred to the provost as the "shock absorber" of the university.

So, with many presidential responsibilities delegated to the provost, my first 100 days were intense.

Immediately, I began having two types of cabinet meetings every week—the meetings with all of my new direct reports—my vice provosts and vice presidents, and then a separate meeting with all of the senior vice presidents of the university.

The responsibility was immense. With more than 30 different lines reporting into the provost's office, I would soon learn other challenges were already awaiting me.

On my very first day as provost, my first major challenge was already waiting for me outside my office. The faculty of the English department had arrived bright and early with a petition, demanding that the dean of the College of Letters, Arts and Sciences be fired.

We were able to come to an agreement that kept the dean, who later became the president of Northeastern University.

It would be a daunting task, but it was only one of the many challenges I would face moving into my new office. I was about to get a major surprise.

❊ ❊ ❊

One day when I was provost designate, I was headed to the USC Bookstore and bumped into the university's budget director and associate comptroller. He was a great resource for financial planning and budget information.

I was just making conversation when I said, "We need to get together to talk about the budget for the Office of the Provost."

"What budget?" he said.

At first, I thought he was joking, but I could see that he was serious.

"What do you mean?" I asked.

"The problem is that the provost doesn't have a budget," he said.

It seemed incredible, but it was true. All of USC's deans had budgets for their schools, but the university's chief academic officer had only about $5 million to promote academic initiatives.

I was shocked. How can you do anything without a budget?

From my point of view, this would hold the university back from creating incentives to encourage interdisciplinary partnerships and collaborations.

Fortunately, I had a great working relationship with the CFO of the university, Dennis Dougherty, who had complete control of the university's budget. He understood the importance of interdisciplinary efforts and, gradually, we began to make changes.

Five years later, when I became president, I'm very proud to say that I provided the provost's office with an unrestricted budget of $75 million.

I truly believe that transformed the university for the better, allowing us to design programs and recruit prominent faculty the university needed to elevate its academic reputation.

* * *

One area where I wanted to make a change was the leadership in USC's admissions office.

I explained to Steve Sample that, although USC had done an extraordinary job of improving the academic quality of its undergraduate programs over the previous decade, we were now competing with elite institutions for a smaller and smaller pool of top students.

I believed that we could be much more entrepreneurial, expanding our recruiting nationally and internationally. We could become a global university by recruiting young men and women who truly represented the diversity of the 21st century.

After listening to my ideas, President Sample nodded and said, "You call me only if you decide not to make the change."

I didn't have to interrupt his sabbatical.

Thanks primarily to the talented new leader in admissions, Katharine Harrington, the Trojan Family was about to expand beyond Southern California to regions around the world.

* * *

While many of the challenges I faced early on as provost were very serious and difficult, there were some that seem almost comical now.

In May 2005, I learned some surprising news. Elizabeth Daley, who had been appointed as dean of the cinema school in 1991, was going to step down to become the Executive Director of the USC Annenberg Center for Communication.

After I met with Elizabeth and her leadership team, I asked her to walk with me as I left the school.

"I heard that you are stepping down as dean," I said.

She confirmed what I had heard.

"I don't understand," I said. "I know in the past when I was director of the media center, we didn't always see eye to eye. But I admire you and I would love to work with you. Why would you leave the forest to direct a tree?"

"They didn't give me a choice," she responded.

"Really?" I said.

I couldn't believe the dean of a school that was consistently listed as the best in the nation was being forced out.

"If you don't mind, let me have a conversation with Steve Sample," I said.

She was elated and said, "Okay, let me know how it goes."

A few days later, Steve and I had dinner at the Langham Hotel in Pasadena. While we were waiting for our cars at the valet, I brought up the subject of Elizabeth Daley.

He told me that toward the end of his tenure my predecessor found her difficult to work with and wanted to make a change. Steve had always been big on delegation, so he simply went along with the decision.

But there was another issue. Ten years earlier, USC had approached George Lucas with a gift proposal to name the school. But it didn't succeed. Some members of the administration were frustrated that nothing had happened for a decade.

"Steve," I said. "Can we try one more time with George Lucas? I mean, that was 10 years ago. He may not have been ready back then, but maybe he is now. He's had a lot of success recently."

I had piqued Sample's interest and, to his credit, he was willing to listen.

"I know you've never given any dean, including me, a bonus for getting their school named. But what if we succeed in getting the cinema school named, we reward her with a bonus?" I said.

"I love it. Why don't you talk to her," Sample said.

So I scheduled a meeting with Elizabeth in the middle of our chaotic office, which was still under renovation.

I told her about my conversation with the president and the suggestion that we approach George Lucas again.

"No," she said. "I've already talked to George about this. It's up to him if and when he wants to do it."

"I know. I understand how difficult this is, but if we are able to secure a naming gift for the school, you will receive a bonus," I said.

"A bonus?" she asked. "How much?"

"Mid-six figures," I said.

Immediately, her eyes got wide, and she literally popped up

out of her chair.

"That's very nice," she said.

"Let's just start talking about it. Preparing the proposal and how we approach him this time."

A few months later, several of us were in northern California for the football game against Cal Berkeley. Elizabeth visited Skywalker Ranch to talk with George about the possibility of a naming gift.

It turned out to be the right time. A short time later, George Lucas made a record donation of nearly $200 million, providing $100 million for the buildings and another $100 million for the school's endowment.

It turned out to be a great partnership. To his credit, even with his extraordinarily generous gift, George Lucas didn't want his name on the school. He requested that we name it the USC School of Cinematic Arts, reflecting his belief that the future would be about digital arts beyond just film and television.

George once told me that, "The School of Cinematic Arts is the Harvard of cinema."

And that's how he really sees it, a place of educational exploration that is renowned as the very best at what it does.

* * *

When we held the groundbreaking ceremony for the new cinematic arts complex, several Hollywood luminaries attended the event, including George Lucas and Steven Spielberg.

During the event, Niki was sitting next to Kathryn Sample. At one point, Kathryn leaned over and said, "Remember this wouldn't have happened if Max hadn't convinced Steve to keep Elizabeth Daley."

There is one other story I remember from that day. After the ceremony, on the walk back to his office, Steve Sample was very upset.

At the event, several people were lining up for photos, which had drawn the Hollywood paparazzi because of all of the celebrities in attendance.

Steve was the only one dressed in a suit and tie, wearing his signature dark-rimmed glasses. As Lucas, Spielberg, and others were lining up for a photo, one of the paparazzi started shouting.

"Excuse me sir, can you please step aside?"

Sample froze, not believing he was being asked to step out of a photo on his own campus.

"Step aside," the photographer said impatiently, waving him away from others.

They didn't know who he was—and they didn't care!—they just wanted a photo of the celebrities.

Finally, Sample got out of the picture, but he wasn't happy about it.

On the way back to his office, he said to me, "I'm the f***ing president of the university and he asks me to step aside."

* * *

In the summer of 2005, just as I was getting a handle on all of my new responsibilities, a retired engineering alumnus reached out to me and asked me to have lunch at the California Club.

It seemed like a normal request, but his advice turned out to be a "cold shower" that woke me up to the realities of the current situation.

In 2001, Steve Sample announced to USC's community that he had been diagnosed with Parkinson's Disease. That was one of the reasons the Board of Trustees had approved a three-month mini-sabbatical for him. It gave him time to rest and recuperate from the strains of the academic year.

"Max, do you realize what you are getting into?" the engineering alumnus said, with real concern on his face.

"What are you talking about?" I said. "I'm so excited."

"No, no, no," he said. "Listen to me. You need to be very careful."

I'll admit I was taken aback by his serious tone.

"Steve Sample has Parkinson's," he said. "You really need to read up on Parkinson's as an illness."

I didn't know what to say, but he was right.

"I hope he stays well for many years. I really do," the alumnus said. "But Parkinson's is progressive. For some it goes slower, for others it goes faster. But there is no turning back this disease."

He slid an article about Parkinson's across the table.

"You need to do your homework," he said. "And you need to be very careful. Because if it's progressing, you're going to get overloaded with more and more assignments. You need to protect yourself, or you're going to burn yourself out."

It was definitely not the meeting I was expecting, but it turned out to be the best thing for me. It made me really study Parkinson's Disease and understand its symptoms and side effects. And I'm grateful that it made me wake up to the realities around me.

* * *

In September 2005, I was honored to have my installation as provost at Town and Gown at USC.

To everyone's surprise, more than 750 people from both campuses showed up. There were so many people that the events team had to set up video screens so people could watch the ceremony on the patio.

To the astonishment of many, I gave a speech about the arts and humanities, where I announced Visions and Voices.

Over the years, we brought in incredible writers and artists from the novelist Isabel Allende to playwright David Henry Hwang to directors like Spike Lee.

At another Visions and Voices Signature Event, the National Theatre of Cyprus staged scenes from Sophocles' *Antigone* in

USC's Bing Theatre.

I had no idea how it would turn out and was actually concerned about how the students and faculty would receive it.

Again, to our amazement, 800 students showed up, so we had to arrange for video screen projections outside the theatre to accommodate everybody watching it. The performance was in Greek, with English subtitles—just like at the opera.

To my pleasant surprise, students were quoted the next day in a *Daily Trojan* article saying that what they liked the most was that the performance was in Greek!

Over 15 years, USC held more than 1,700 Visions and Voices events, on and off campus. They were all free to students, with total attendance reaching over 400,000.

I'm very proud of that legacy. Thousands of students from every discipline were introduced to the arts and humanities through Visions and Voices.

⁂ ⁂ ⁂

There were many other ways our office tried to advance academic excellence.

Together we were also able to quickly move forward on several other initiatives. My team had a motto: "Our visions have deadlines."

We introduced micro-seminars, which taught specialized topics in 90 minutes. It was a way for leading faculty to interact with our first-year undergraduates, and I even volunteered to teach one to incoming freshman on Athenian democracy.

⁂ ⁂ ⁂

As I gained my footing as provost, I also found myself with increasing responsibilities.

With the help of the CFO, we set up a strategy to reduce administrative costs across the university, providing us with budget surpluses. After a few years, we'd saved up enormous reserves, which increased the working capital for the entire university.

When Steve Sample saw the amounts adding up, he wanted to keep the working capital low and put the reserves in the university's endowment. At the time, that was a strategy being employed at other private universities and it would improve our endowment rankings.

It went all the way to the finance committee of the Board of Trustees, but I took a stand making the case for why we needed access to large working capital.

To this day, I'm surprised I didn't get fired. I was going against the wishes of the president. But ultimately the finance committee decided to put a small amount in the endowment and keep the rest in the reserves.

A year later, that turned out to be a major decision. When the financial markets crashed in 2008, all of the major private universities had to borrow taxable bonds to meet payroll. Fortunately, we'd built a war chest of working capital.

We did borrow $400 million during the Great Recession, but unlike other universities we borrowed non-taxable bonds. This allowed us to purchase two hospitals at the Health Sciences Campus (HSC).

We weren't borrowing to meet payroll. We were borrowing to invest in the future.

❋ ❋ ❋

New technology infrastructure also provided us with new opportunities. At the time, USC had only a few distance learning programs in engineering, gerontology, and a handful of classes in medicine.

I was worried USC was falling behind in this important area.

In 2005, hurricane Katrina had nearly destroyed on-site operations at Tulane University and its hospitals.[2]

I was concerned what would happen if there was a major earthquake. We needed to make sure the university could remain operational no matter what happened.

For online education, we created incentives for our deans to be entrepreneurial, developing their own online degree programs.

Within five years, USC went from just three schools offering a few online classes to every school having robust distance learning programs for master's degrees and executive education.

In only a few years, those distance learning programs enrolled some 13,400 students from 40 different countries.

People forget that when the Covid-19 pandemic lockdown arrived in March 2020, the university was able to go fully online quickly because the hard work had already been done a decade earlier.

* * *

There was one area where I refused to expand our remote learning options. Some deans gave me proposals, and even pressure, to create USC campuses abroad.

I started to get calls from trustees asking, "Why is USC not doing this? Are we falling behind?"

From the very beginning, I made it very clear that establishing campuses abroad could do two things. First, it could dilute the quality of a USC degree. Second, when you begin establishing satellite campuses in other countries, you are beholden to their laws and values.

The significance of an undergraduate degree from USC is not just the learning of a discipline, but also a grounding in our core values such as gender equality, freedom of expression, and a relentless search for truth. I still believe that. And that's why we refused to establish campuses abroad.

❋ ❋ ❋

While we were succeeding in many areas, my next challenge as provost happened in student affairs.

Our vice president for student affairs made the decision to suspend a popular fraternity, which created a firestorm.[3] President Sample's office received thousands of complaint letters and assigned me to handle the issue.

I asked my vice provost to help me reexamine the entire case. Like a good lawyer, she looked into what rules were violated, how the case was tried, and how decisions were made.

After a week of going through all of the evidence in a massive binder, she came to me and said, "Look, Max. The freshmen and the sophomores in the fraternity were going to the student affairs office, complaining that the more senior guys were breaking the rules. They were asking for help, they didn't want to be part of it."

Student affairs didn't help them and probably could have handled it better, according to the vice provost.

We decided on a "Solomon" solution. We reopened the fraternity, but only for the freshman and sophomores who were trying to do the right thing. The juniors and seniors received the punishment because they were the ones breaking the rules. But this allowed the fraternity itself to continue.

That was my final ruling. The complaints to the university stopped and there was an unexpected response. My decision became popular with the fraternity. When they reopened in the fall, they held a dinner for parents and invited me to speak.

It became a tradition that I spoke to the parents of fraternity and sorority members each year because they didn't perceive the administration as against the Greek system.

❋ ❋ ❋

Another major challenge came when I was given oversight of the design and construction of the Tutor Campus Center, as well as securing the naming gift from Ron Tutor.

We had several meetings with Ron. I told him that everyone was very grateful for the engineering building, but this would solidify his legacy with a facility at the center of USC's campus. It would be there for 100 years and students of all disciplines—not just engineering—would benefit from it every day.

Initially, he resisted the idea, but I wasn't going to give up. We set up a breakfast meeting with me, Ron, and Ken Leventhal at a very unassuming diner in the valley, which was frequented by construction workers.

We worked out the terms of the deal right there. I'm sure no one else knew we were finalizing a multi-million dollar deal at that little diner!

Later, I worked with student affairs on the programming and with the architects for the design of the building.

I felt very strongly that the Trojan Family Room should have high ceilings and a stairway that led to the second floor up to the admissions offices. I wanted the parents who were visiting campus with their kids to walk through the plaza, and then enter what is now Sample Hall. Then they could go through the Trojan Family Room and take the stairs to the admissions office.

I thought it would be a great first impression of the campus, something that very few other universities could match. And those images and experiences would remain in their minds when they were choosing which university to attend.

* * *

With all of the innovations and improvements we were making in the provost's office, there were many challenges lurking under the surface.

I was about to be tested like never before.

CHAPTER 16

Being Tested

«Τίπτε καταπτώσσοντες ἀφέστατε, μίμνετε δ' ἄλλους;
σφῶϊν μέν τ' ἐπέοικε μετὰ πρώτοισιν ἐόντας
ἑστάμεν ἠδὲ μάχης καυστειρῆς ἀντιβολῆσαι·»

ΌΜΉΡΟΥ ἸΛΙΆΔΑ, Δ 340–42

"Why are you cowering here, skulking out of range?
Waiting for others to do your fighting for you?
You—it's your duty to stand in the front ranks
and take your share of the scorching blaze of battle."[1]

HOMER, *ILIAD*, BOOK 4, LINES 340–42

During my five-year tenure as provost, I found myself being tested with one difficult assignment after another. Some of these were Herculean tasks.

In many ways, that was how I proved myself to the Board of Trustees. Besides, it's an excellent training ground assuming you don't fail!

And yet, each new challenge brought the possibility of failure to the forefront of my mind.

The first major challenge appeared unexpectedly. For many years, one of the most important archives in the world has been the Shoah Foundation, a collection of more than 50,000 testimonies of survivors of the Holocaust.[2] But it almost didn't happen at USC.

Steven Spielberg, who was a member of USC's Board of Trustees, spent nearly a decade of his life filming these very emotional testimonies. But at the time, this precious footage was simply housed in a series of trailers on the lot of Universal Studios.

Being brilliant as he is, Spielberg realized the testimonials needed to find a permanent home. He felt very strongly that this should an academic environment, which could teach lessons to future generations and ensure there would never be another Holocaust.

Several colleges and universities wanted the archives, but he was looking for a secular institution so they wouldn't be perceived as only for the Jewish community.

As a trustee at USC, he saw the university as a natural home for the archives. Through his attorney, Bruce Ramer, he was trying to negotiate a permanent home for the Shoah Foundation.

By April 2005, Ramer and his team believed they had a deal with USC. To their surprise, my predecessor called them up one day and essentially pulled the plug on the whole deal.

Naturally, everyone got very upset. Spielberg was filming in Poland. As soon as he got back to the U.S., he called Steve Sample at 10:00 p.m. and expressed his concerns.

I don't know all of the details of that call, but Sample apparently told Spielberg, "I've just announced a new provost, who takes over June 1. And I'm going to ask him to look into it."

The chairman of the board, Stanley Gold, called me and said, "Why don't you get a copy of what everyone thought they had agreed upon. And let's review it carefully, you and me, Max."

During a five-hour plane flight, that's exactly what we did. Some parts of the agreement seemed repetitive, but I ended that flight with a much better understanding of what we were negotiating.

We set up a meeting in my office. Stanley Gold invited Bruce Ramer and Doug Greenberg, who at the time was the executive director of the Shoah Foundation.

I knew Bruce Ramer, but not well. Stanley said, "Listen Max, I've known Bruce for many, many years. He's going to come to this meeting and he's going to want to give us the whole thing—how it happened and why they thought they had a deal. Okay, so *do not* interrupt him. Let him get it off his chest!"

And that's exactly what happened. Bruce spoke for the first 15 minutes. He was clearly, visibly, quite unhappy.

I told Bruce I needed some time to do my homework. I also said I needed to have follow-up meetings with the two of them, and probably their entire team. I wanted to make sure I understood the importance of the archives, and what they were hoping for in an agreement.

Then we set up a timetable to begin negotiations.

We had a long meeting in Bruce Ramer's office in Beverly Hills. At one point, Bruce looked at me and said, "Max, you need to understand essentially what we're negotiating here. Giving the Shoah Foundation's archives to USC is the equivalent of cutting out our beating heart and handing it to you. That's how important it is."

"Okay," I said.

"Will you keep it alive and take good care of it? It is sacred," he said.

I realized a key component would be the digital preservation of the archives. Every four years, everything has to be backed up. And then the process begins all over again. It's never-ending, really.

So I was thinking of all of the technology upgrades we would have to make. In fact, we had to work with Information Technology Services to find space next to the university's supercomputers on Grand Avenue just to house the Shoah Foundation's preservation center.

There was a lot of work to be done, but finally we thought we were getting close.

We agreed to meet in my office in Bovard for an entire day, beginning at 8:00 a.m. On my team, there were only two people: our general counsel and one of her associates.

When the Shoah Foundation's team arrived, there were nine of them, including some of the most respected attorneys in L.A.

From the university's perspective, I clearly recognized that the Shoah Foundation was a unique asset that no other college or university in the world would have. It could be the epicenter of incredible amounts of interdisciplinary research and scholarship.

From a personal perspective, I took very seriously our responsibility to preserve the archives if we reached an agreement.

At 4:00 p.m., I looked at Bruce Ramer and the eight others sitting across the table.

"Is there anything else?" I said. "I think that's it."

They looked at each other and nodded in agreement. Then Bruce said, "However, we need some time to caucus amongst ourselves."

We offered to leave and let them have the office, but Bruce said they wanted to get some fresh air. They went outside and formed a little circle outside Bovard. Through my office window, I could see them talking.

We saw one of them on the phone and the general counsel said, "I bet they're calling Spielberg."

An hour later, 5:00 p.m. passed, "What's taking so long? I don't think we have a deal," said the general counsel.

"I don't know," I said. "But you're probably right."

A little bit after 5:15 p.m., I saw them walking into the building. They were lined up one-by-one, almost in a kind of receiving line. It seemed they were coming in to offer us their condolences, and that unfortunately we didn't have a deal.

Jerry Breslauer, Spielberg's accountant, came in first. As he walked in, he took my hand, and then he gave me a big hug. Then he said, "Thank you, Max. We have a deal."

Then he wiped tears from his eyes. After that, each person came up to me and shook my hand. It was a very emotional moment.

To this day, I'm very proud that the university is deeply committed to the USC Shoah Foundation.

⁂ ⁂ ⁂

Another person who had a major impact was Eli Broad. Eli had donated $25 million for the naming rights to a building on USC's Health Sciences Campus. However, the construction costs on the building had ballooned to $250 million.

When the gift agreement was first reviewed by the Board of Trustees' finance committee, it was rejected because the naming gift was now only one-tenth of the cost of constructing the building.

In all of the years Steve Sample had been president, this was the first time a naming gift had been rejected, making it politically sensitive, especially with a prominent donor like Eli Broad.

I got the assignment to renegotiate the gift and met with Dan Hollander, the director of Scientific and Medical Research Initiatives for The Broad Foundation.

We ended up proposing an $80 million stem cell research building, with a $35 million gift from the Broad Foundation.

Eli offered to help us get another $35 million in funding from the California Stem Cell Initiative, which would help cover the construction of the building. USC put up $10 million and that was the deal.

Eli wanted to control the look of the building, and USC would control the programming inside of it.

In all my dealings with Eli Broad, I found him to be a gentleman. He was a tough negotiator, but he was fair.

* * *

As the challenges got bigger and more complex, I found myself serving as "acting president" more often.

It was a double-edged sword and I had to be very careful. On one hand, I had more visibility, taking on more public and speaking events. Trustees from various committees began to reach out to me for ideas and advice.

On the other hand, I had to perform no matter how difficult

the challenge. At one executive committee meeting, President Sample was concerned that a particular issue was too controversial.

"The provost should perhaps handle that," he said.

"No, we need to protect the provost too!" said Ken Leventhal. "The university's general counsel should handle this one."

At that moment, I realized the trustees wouldn't hesitate to speak up to protect me. And I greatly appreciated their support.

* * *

At one point in 2007, I wondered if I was being asked to take on too much responsibility. I was being recruited to be president of another elite, private university on the East Coast.

I was interviewed secretly in Los Angeles, and then had a follow-up interview with the hiring committee at the Red Carpet Club of a Midwestern airport.

Later the chairman of the university called me and said, "I cannot make you an offer unless you come with your wife to meet more of my trustees."

At that point, I felt like I had the obligation to tell President Sample. However, I couldn't get ahold of him to set a meeting.

I had a long discussion with Niki, and then another long phone call with an elderly alumnus, who I greatly respected.

"Don't do it, Max," he said. "You have a moral obligation to Steve Sample to stay and help him, given his illness. This is how you get to be tested in terms of 'loyalty' and to 'whom.'"

Again, it wasn't a legal obligation, but this alumnus believed it was a moral one.

In the spring of 2008, Chairman Gold reached out to me and asked me to come to his office. He wanted me to know that the board had come to an agreement with Steve to stay on for only two more years. After that, he was going to retire.

The information wasn't to be made public. It was important

that it remain secret, otherwise Steve Sample would become a "lame duck" president.

The chairman handled it masterfully, doing it in a way that President Sample's reputation was fully protected.

Without giving me any assurances about the future, he said, "I hear other universities are coming after you for president."

He mentioned two private universities in particular, which was true. But I was very surprised that he knew about both of them.

"I hope you stay at USC and help us with this transition," he said.

"If there is any other university coming after you, let me know," he said.

"Okay," I said. And, of course, I never went back to him.

I had a moral obligation to stay.

* * *

I was just getting my rhythm when the Great Recession hit.

I was very concerned about USC's students and families. I didn't know if admitted students—or even the ones who were already enrolled—could afford tuition.

We froze hiring across the university for at least a year, and quickly restructured administrative operations. We redirected our financial aid, doubling it in only two years from $90 million to $180 million.

Schools and units across the university were asked to come up with very conservative revenue projections, with contingency plans for cutting 5 percent of their budgets.

We also increased international student enrollment in undergraduate programs from 7.5 percent to 15 percent without compromising academic quality. International students, to this day, pay full tuition.

With all of those changes, we could have afforded to give

salary raises to faculty and staff, but we felt it would have sent the wrong signal given how many families were suffering financially. So we froze salary raises too. However, we did give raises to faculty who were promoted.

In the end, USC weathered the storm and survived not only "unscathed," but also far ahead of the competition because we invested in the recruiting of students and faculty.

* * *

During my final two years as provost, with the "blessing" of Steve Sample, I was having weekly 7:00 a.m. breakfast meetings at the Cal Club with Ed Roski, who became the chairman of the Board of Trustees in 2008.

I went into every meeting very well prepared, with a list of important activities to brief him on for both of USC's campuses. Many times I would get important advice on certain issues from him.

However, as soon as it was announced that there would be a national search for a new president, I suggested to Ed that it wouldn't be appropriate for us to continue meeting.

"Are you kidding me?" he said. "There's a university to run and as chair I need those briefings from you as provost."

I wanted to continue to be helpful, but I explained that the optics wouldn't look good if I became a candidate for president.

Reluctantly, he agreed to discontinue the meetings. By the time the presidential search was completed, we hadn't met for seven months.

* * *

In the first week of January 2010, I got a call from Pete Carroll.

"Can we meet at my house in Hermosa Beach?" he said.

When I got there, we went inside so no one walking along the Strand could see us.

After a few minutes, he told me that he was planning to leave USC. He didn't tell me who was pursuing him, but he said that an NFL team had agreed to give him much more authority and control than he'd had during his first experience in the league.

I was surprised that he called me first, and not President Sample or Mike Garrett. At the time, I suppose he saw me as a candidate to become the next president.

We had a very interesting conversation and I said, "You do realize that we have a moral obligation on behalf of the university to do our best to keep you. You have to give us the opportunity to present you with a counteroffer."

"Max, I don't think it's right for me to ask for more money from the university," he said. "I'm already getting paid well. I'm already the highest paid coach in college football. And am I going to ask that you pay the mortgage of my second home here in Hermosa Beach? I just don't think it's right."

"Please do not sign on the dotted line," I said. "Let me speak with the president and Mike Garrett."

Then I asked him, "How was your relationship with Mike Garrett?"

"When I took the job, people warned me about Mike," he said. "Told me that he wasn't easy to get along with. But I have to say, it was better than what I thought at the beginning, based on what others had said."

We agreed to meet again at his house in Hermosa Beach after I spoke to the president.

I tried over and over to get ahold of Steve Sample, but he was away in Arizona. Although I left him a voicemail, he hadn't called back.

So I contacted Mike Garrett, who was still upset that the Trojans had to play Boston College in the Emerald Bowl, although we won 24-13.

"No counteroffer," said Garrett. "Let him go."

I tried to explain that one year playing in a less prestigious bowl shouldn't override the overwhelming success of his teams since 2003. But he refused to make a counteroffer, or even work with me.

So, finally, I called Ed Roski.

"Are you kidding me? We cannot afford to lose Pete Carroll," he said. "There has to be a counteroffer. You've got to get ahold of Steve."

We finally located Steve and he said, "Call Mike Garrett back and tell him we have to make a counteroffer."

We put together the terms of an offer and set up a meeting with Pete Carroll.

In the meantime, Mike Garrett was saying, "I'm going to bring in Lane Kiffin. He'll get the right assistants to keep the recruiting class intact."

"Pete Carroll is recommending Sarkisian as his successor," I said.

"Over my dead body," said Garrett. "I'm going to get Lane Kiffin."

So I go to meet with Pete Carroll, with an offer that included several incentives, including more money.

"Max, I thought about it," he said. "The team that is recruiting me has a great quarterback that I'm going to work with. You need to understand that for me at this point it's not about the money. I'm getting paid well whether I stay here or whether I go to the NFL."

Then he added, "I just want to take one more bite out of the apple."

Considering our earlier meeting, it was disappointing, but not unexpected.

"Besides, what's the worst that can happen to me?" he said. "I get fired? So what? I was fired before."

Then he said, "General Patton said that great generals never die . . . they just fade away."

"Pete," I said. "That wasn't Patton. It was General MacArthur who said that!"

Then we both started laughing.

As I was getting ready to leave, I said "Pete, you need to realize what people are going to say. The NCAA Infractions Committee is going to come out with their findings from the Reggie Bush case in the next six months. People are going to say you're leaving because you're afraid of the findings. And you're going to get the blame for that."

"I realize that, Max," he said. "But honestly, I don't care at this point. I want to take one more bite out of the apple. This is a great opportunity for me."

Then he said, "And let's face it, people are going to say whatever they want to say anyway."

I thanked him for what he'd done for the university, the football program, and for the great memories that he'd created for all of us.

And I felt sad that I was the first one to officially know that the Pete Carroll era at USC had come to an end.

Then I said, "I don't know about my future, but if I'm here at USC I will make sure that what you have done is recognized and that you're honored by the university."

Six months later, the NCAA handed down severe sanctions that placed USC's football program on probation for five years. They were "near death" penalties.

We waited until those sanctions had passed, and then invited Pete Carroll to receive an honorary degree in 2015. The faculty committee unanimously voted on his nomination. That was the promise I had delivered to him five years earlier, and it was the right thing to do.

* * *

With all of the challenges I faced during my time as provost, none of them proved so daunting and demanding as the issues on USC's Health Sciences Campus.

The results were sometimes tragic and at other times almost comic. I compare it to trying to get 25 horses into the gate simultaneously just so they could begin the race. But before our medical enterprise went anywhere, there were several problems that had to be fixed—and quickly.

And I finally realized what Steve Sample meant that night in front of Tommy Trojan when he said he had a crisis at the medical school.

CHAPTER 17

In the Eye of the Storm

«ὣς εἰπὼν σύναγεν νεφέλας, ἐτάραξε δὲ πόντον
χερσὶ τρίαιναν ἑλών· πάσας δ› ὀρόθυνεν ἀέλλας
παντοίων ἀνέμων, σὺν δὲ νεφέεσσι κάλυψε
γαῖαν ὁμοῦ καὶ πόντον· ὀρώρει δ᾽ οὐρανόθεν νύξ.
σὺν δ᾽ εὖρός τε νότος τ᾽ ἔπεσον ζέφυρός τε δυσαὴς
καὶ βορέης αἰθρηγενέτης, μέγα κῦμα κυλίνδων.»

ὉΜΉΡΟΥ ὈΔΎΣΣΕΙΑ, Ε 291–96

"With that he rammed the clouds together
—both hands clutching his trident—
churned the waves into chaos,
whipping all the gales from every quarter,
shrouding over in thunderheads the earth and sea at once
and night swept down from the sky—
East and South Winds clashed and the raging West and North,
sprung from the heavens, roiled heaving breakers up."[1]

HOMER, *ODYSSEY*, BOOK 5, LINES 291–96

Before I became provost, I really didn't know that much about USC's medical enterprise.

However, as soon as I took the job, I started to get an avalanche of emails and messages pleading with me to visit the HSC.

One day, Brian Henderson, the interim dean of the medical school, called with an urgent message. He needed $10 million right away. I was shocked.

"Brian, you have to understand that I'm not used to those

kinds of numbers," I said. "They usually have three fewer zeroes."

I told him I needed to do my homework before committing that kind of money.

I was stunned to learn that the medical school was running a $35 million deficit, with no hope of ever balancing their budget.

I didn't know it at the time, but major budget cuts by Tenet Healthcare were causing all kinds of headaches. Because of their legal problems, Tenet was drastically reducing the salaries of our medical doctors, who were threatening to leave if we didn't find a solution—and fast.

One evening I got a call from a prominent cancer doctor. She was very emotional and very angry. Tenet hadn't properly maintained her equipment, and now she felt it was putting her patients at risk.

At one point, she said, "Provost Nikias, can you please hold on a second? I'll be right back."

Then I heard a strange noise in the background.

A moment later, she returned to the phone.

"I'm really sorry," she said. "I had to go to the bathroom and throw up. Every time I talk about Tenet, it makes me sick."

* * *

It wasn't just the doctors and the staff who were upset. The Keck Foundation was also furious.

They believed USC wasn't living up to the terms of the foundation's original gift agreement. They were threatening to stop payment, or even remove the Keck name from the medical school. That would have had a disastrous effect on the school's reputation, and it would have been very embarrassing for the entire university.

I needed to solve multiple problems, but I couldn't do that until I knew exactly what they were.

The Keck School was responsible for three main areas—the

teaching of students, research in the medical sciences, and patient care.

Because years earlier USC had entered into an agreement with Tenet Healthcare, the university had no control over patient care! None whatsoever. And that had become a major problem.

At the same time, some units—such as the USC Norris Cancer Center and the USC Hospital—had patient care that fell under Tenet Healthcare. The rest of patient care fell under L.A. County at LAC + USC Medical Center, which is also where students had their teaching programs and residents had their fellowships.

This created all kinds of complications, especially for billing. Patients were visiting our faculty physicians, many of whom had their own faculty practice plans as separate corporations.

If you had surgery at the hospital, you might get a bill from one of the faculty practice plans. But you might also get a bill from another plan, or for follow-up visits, from the hospital. It was truly the Wild West!

I even experienced the frustration personally. I was scheduled for a minor procedure at USC Hospital. I got a call from someone asking for a credit card number in advance.

After asking who was calling, the person said, "Oh, we're from USC's Health Sciences Campus."

"Yes, but who are you?" I asked.

In the end, the caller admitted they were actually from Tenet Healthcare, but they were saying they were from USC.

When all was said and done, I ended up getting *three* different bills for the procedure from *three* different entities!

It would be comical, if it weren't so infuriating. If this was happening to me, I knew it must be happening to hundreds of other patients.

It had to stop. The only question was how to fix all of the leaks before the entire ship went down.

* * *

In 1999, the gift from the Keck Foundation was supposed to be the catalyst that would signal the academic ascent of USC's medical school.

After receiving the $100 million donation, USC had agreed to raise another $350 million for that purpose.

But the Keck Foundation was correctly concerned that the school couldn't fix its most pressing problems, let alone raise that much money.

The biggest challenge was the doctors. The best physicians always have options. When they became unhappy, they threatened to leave. And if you lose your top talent, it's only a matter of time before the reputation of the school goes with them.

To his credit, I always found Robert Day, the chairman and CEO of the Keck Foundation to be a gentleman and a very smart businessman who wanted to find a mutual solution. But those early days and early meetings were really rough because everyone was unhappy.

When Robert and I realized we could work together, I said, "I'll try my best, but I don't know exactly if things will work out or not."

"You've got to help me," he said. "My cousin Bill is putting a lot of pressure on the Keck Foundation board to remove the name right away."

It was that bad.

Chairman Gold had lunch with Bill and Nicole Keck. "We have this new provost," he said, channeling Steve Sample's advice about the Shoah Foundation. "Why don't you meet with him and see if you can build a relationship with him."

* * *

Beyond the visible challenges for the medical school, there was one major crisis that very few knew about.

And I was about to learn just how bad things had gotten.

A year before I accepted the provost position, there was a fiscal scandal on the HSC.

The provost took the issue to the USC Board of Trustees' audit committee, without giving the heads up to the president first. The audit committee, of course, took immediate action, opening up an independent investigation.

But the president was upset that he was left out of the picture. Later he told me the situation was so bad that one night he drafted a letter of resignation.

In the end, the decision was made to create two senior vice president positions, one for administration and one for finance. But it could have become a major scandal.

To add to the difficulty, I soon realized that many trustees didn't really want the university to be in the healthcare business. Five years earlier, USC Norris Cancer Hospital, which had only 45 beds, started losing money. Rather than figure out why it wasn't profitable, the board simply sold it to Tenet Healthcare.

Many of the board members were in other industries like real estate, and they didn't want to deal with the challenges of running a complex medical enterprise.

There were also other surprises that we discovered. For instance, USC hadn't received an increase in funding from L.A. County for 15 years.

I realized that I needed a comprehensive understanding of everything that was happening at HSC.

Otherwise, we would keep applying band-aids when it really needed major surgery.

❊ ❊ ❊

I asked the general counsel to do a deep dive on all of the legal entities at HSC. Ken Leventhal used to refer to them as "wild horses running in all directions, uncontrollably." He told me jokingly, "Good luck, Max, getting them all back in the corral."

I wish I could tell you that I anticipated what we would find, but I could have never imagined how bad things had gotten.

The general counsel's briefing took about two hours, but when it ended I was more confused and concerned than before it began.

The complexity alone was mentally exhausting.

One of the first things I learned was that the L.A. County contract needed to be modified. In the 15 years since it had last been renegotiated, costs for everything had skyrocketed.

We were providing clinical services to a hospital with 1,000 beds. Salaries had to be adjusted for the cost of living, but the contract had remained steady at $73 million per year.

At the same time, it was difficult for the medical school to generate any revenue because all of the clinical care payments were going directly to the 19 faculty practice plans.

So the medical school only made about 9 percent of its budget from tuition revenues. They were totally dependent on L.A. County, which was reluctant to raise the amount of the contract.

Everything was in the red and without a sustainable business model. It's possible to raise some money through research grants and philanthropy, but there wasn't even an endowment to sustain the school for the future.

Surprisingly, the school had apparently always operated that way, or at least for the past several decades.

In addition to all of those issues, we hadn't even started with the facilities. When you walk onto virtually any college campus, it's fairly easy to determine which school owns and operates a building.

But at HSC, this was a mystery even to the people who worked there. There were parcels of land and parking structures, which were partially owned by L.A. County or USC. Some buildings were owned entirely by one of the 19 faculty practice plans. Others were owned by Tenet Healthcare.

The medical school's faculty and staff were wearing several hats. Their salaries came from a composite of many different legal entities. Centrally, the university had very little control or oversight.

It wasn't surprising that many of them had no connection and no loyalties to the overall medical school or the rest of the university, with one exception: Trojan football!

* * *

Over the years, USC had hired a number of different consulting organizations to offer reports about how to address the crisis at the medical school. Like they were going to give us the secret recipe.

One report mentioned a study about a financial crisis that took place at the University of Pennsylvania from 2000 to 2005. It was so serious that when it was all said and done, the crisis placed the entire university—not just the hospitals or the medical school—into a deficit of $800 million. All of that happened because of issues with the medical enterprise. And it happened at a prestigious Ivy League university!

Suddenly, I realized what Steve Sample understood when he was selling me on becoming provost. His office had provided me of a copy of that exact report.

* * *

Late one night, while reading through one of the binders, I was also struck by a report by one previous consultant. They had concluded that the leadership team of the medical school was "understaffed, and in some cases, not qualified to lead the school's initiatives and deal with the challenges."

It was clear that no matter what changes we made, we were also going to need to recruit new leadership for the school.

We also understood that USC needed new expertise on the

Board of Trustees. Since many of the trustees didn't understand, or didn't want to be involved in healthcare, we needed to find people with very specific expertise in that area.

The board elected as a new trustee Bill Schoen, an L.A. native, a Trojan and proud marine, whose company operated hospitals around the country to help us understand how to restore order at our hospitals and the HSC.

* * *

It was Bill Schoen who suggested I visit other medical centers around the nation to learn from their leadership.

So, in the middle of everything else, toward the end of the summer in 2005, I took a tour of America's very best medical centers, meeting with their key administrators.

I visited the University of Pittsburgh Medical Center and Boston University, where I met with a cardiologist named Aram Chobanian, who was the interim president and had served for many years as the dean of their medical school.

During my conversation with him, I got advice about how to integrate all of USC's faculty practice plans because he had done the same thing many years before at Boston University.

He generously agreed to meet with me for two hours for breakfast and I went to his office with a list of 20 questions. He patiently listened to my questions, and then offered a lot of very good advice.

As he walked me out of the boardroom, we stopped to shake hands.

He smiled at me and said, "By the way, I don't see Tenet being at USC four years from now."

Honestly, I didn't believe him. At that moment, I just wanted to fix the bleeding, but I didn't see any way for us to get out of our agreement with Tenet.

I had no idea that just a few years later his words would

become prophetic. It would take another year for me to see a clear path toward the future, but maybe his observation planted the idea in my mind.

* * *

In the end, we chose a model in which the medical enterprise reports to the central administration. Ken Leventhal strongly believed that the university should have direct oversight. If a crisis occurred, the university would have to step in and bail out the medical school no matter what.

As he saw it, we weren't going to shut down the medical school or walk away from the HSC. If that was the worst-case scenario, then he believed the university had a responsibility to be in charge of the medical school.

Otherwise, it would operate as a separate campus that could have a potentially negative impact on the overall university, just like at the University of Pennsylvania.

* * *

It was a very tough time. There is a risk with every decision you make, of course. In the end, I think we made the right decisions considering the situation.

We were dangerously dependent on Tenet Healthcare. When they began to have financial difficulties, they passed their problems onto USC through major budget cuts.

It deeply damaged our relationships with doctors and patients, although most people who came for treatment didn't understand that we had little to no control of the patient care in our own hospitals.

The larger question for the future of our medical school was this: How do we end our agreement with Tenet Healthcare?

Without letting it be widely known, Chairman Gold reached out to a renowned litigator, who had a reputation as a "pit bull." The answer to our problems with Tenet was named Marshall Grossman.

* * *

By the time USC reached out to him, Grossman already had established himself as one of the most respected and sometimes feared lawyers in Los Angeles. We needed him to do one thing: find a breach of contract by Tenet Healthcare that would get us out of our limiting, long-term agreement.

We also hired a consulting firm called Alvarez Marsal (A&M), which could help with the assessment and restructuring of the HSC. From A&M, we hired a woman who was very experienced in the healthcare business, giving her the title of CEO reporting directly to me.

During her audit, we learned several shocking things. First of all, there were no files in the office of the dean with annual evaluations of the chairs of academic departments, or any annual merit evaluations of the faculty of the medical school.

There were doctors practicing elsewhere in the L.A. basin who hadn't visited their HSC offices for years. Some faculty controlled large laboratory spaces and yet they hadn't had research grants in recent memory.

But the most egregious discovery was a faculty member who had been living permanently in Colorado while drawing a salary from the medical school. And he hadn't been to the office in years!

I immediately told our legal office to terminate payment of his salary and there was never a complaint or a lawsuit. He knew what he was doing and he'd been allowed to get away with it for too long.

* * *

However, the most alarming discovery wasn't about any individual. It was about the school itself.

USC's medical school hadn't received a full accreditation since 1981. From 1991 to 2006, the school had only received provisional accreditations from the Liaison Committee on Medical Education (LCME). One of the primary responsibilities for any dean of the medical school was its teaching program, which now wasn't even fully accredited.

Incredibly, outside of a small circle of people, the medical school's leadership just didn't tell anyone!

* * *

After all of those initial findings, it became very clear that we were going to have to recruit a new dean for the school.

I asked the provost to lead the effort and worked with Korn Ferry, who specialized in searches for medical schools.

With all of the changes that needed to happen, there were some people who weren't just counting on a new administration, but also holding out for a miracle to turn around the situation.

To demonstrate the sense of desperation at the time, you'd have to know the story of the Saudi princess.

The princess was the daughter of Fahd bin Abdulaziz Al Saud, who died in 2005. She was in her early 30s and she was involved with an American who drove her around on a motorcycle, something of which her family definitely didn't approve.

Somehow a renowned cancer surgeon at USC was introduced to the Saudi princess. He saw her as the savior of the medical school because she had mentioned the idea of donating $500 million to expedite a cure for cancer.

The cancer surgeon even brought the princess as a guest to a USC-UCLA football game, where she and her boyfriend wore jeans and leather jackets, riding in on his motorcycle. Throughout the game, the cancer surgeon treated her like a trophy, most likely because he was hoping to control her money and how it was spent.

To me, the whole thing looked comical, but there were some who took it seriously. However, after a number of discussions between her and the people who managed her trust, it became clear that we were not going to see any money.

After that game, she and her boyfriend rode off into the sunset on his motorcycle and we never heard from them again.

* * *

More bad news arrived during spring break week in March 2006. I was serving as acting president again because Steve Sample was in Hawaii.

I was working late in my office when the phone rang around 8:00 p.m. It was a trustee who had shocking news.

"I just heard that Vaughn Starnes is going to UCLA," he said. "He received an offer and he'll take a big group with him."

Immediately, I felt a freefall inside of me, like gravity was pulling me down emotionally. After all of the work we'd done, this was the worst-case scenario for USC's medical school.

Dr. Vaughn Starnes wasn't just a great cardiac surgeon, he was a legend in his profession.

This wasn't just a phone call, it was an emergency. And I had to find a solution fast.

* * *

The rumor was that UCLA had not only offered him a new position, but also an entire wing of the Ronald Reagan Medical Center.

A few years later, I verified the story with the provost of UCLA, who told me, "Max, I've never seen a package like that and I don't believe UCLA will ever prepare another one like it."

At the time, I thought about the morale at the HSC. It was already very low, but if we couldn't keep one of the most renowned surgeons in the world, there would be no hope.

Keeping Vaughn Starnes was equivalent to saving the medical school.

* * *

I began calling Starnes' home but I kept getting an answering machine. I didn't want to leave a voicemail for such an important matter.

From my office, I kept calling every thirty minutes. Finally, at about 10:00 p.m. a voice answered softly. I suppose he was already asleep and my calls woke him up.

I introduced myself and then he said, "I know who you are. We met briefly at an event a few months ago."

I asked if it was true that he'd received an offer from UCLA. There was a pause on the other end. He was probably wondering how I'd learned about the offer so quickly. Then he told me that the rumors were true.

"Have you signed on the dotted line?" I asked.

Then he said the magic words.

"Not yet," said Starnes.

I breathed a sigh of relief, feeling that I still had a small chance to find a way to keep him.

"But I have to sign soon," Starnes continued.

"Please don't until the two of us have had a chance to get together." I said. "I owe it to you, to the Keck School, and to the university to discuss the situation with you first. And you should allow me to present you with a counter-offer. USC cannot afford to lose you."

There was another pause on the other end. I thought maybe I'd lost him.

"Can we get together for dinner tomorrow evening?" I asked. "Just pick the restaurant and I'll be there."

"Okay," he said. "I'll have my assistant reach out to your office tomorrow."

I thanked him and left the office to go home to Rancho Palos Verdes. It was a long drive home, to say the least.

But that was all I needed to hear from him that evening. I felt like I still had a chance.

* * *

The next night we met at the Parkway Grill in Pasadena, sitting against the wall so we could talk privately.

I let him pick an expensive bottle of red wine, which we shared.

I wanted to take the evening to really get to know the man beyond the renowned surgeon. We shared a lot of personal information about our humble beginnings, our career paths, and so on. I loved learning the fact that he had grown up on a farm, and I mentioned that Greek farmers during the Homeric Age came up with the principles of democracy.

Toward the end of the evening, the conversation changed from personal to business. I told him that there was something that didn't add up for me.

"I did my homework on you," I said. "You were trained at Stanford to become the successor of the legendary heart transplant pioneer Norman Shumway. But what did you do, my friend? In the summer of 1992, you surprised everyone and left Stanford to come to the middle of nowhere in East Los Angeles."

"When the occupancy rate of the USC Hospital was only 10 percent," he said.

"Yes, that's true," I replied.

"I guess I was young and immature," he joked.

"But it doesn't add up," I said. "Why would you do that?"

At that moment, he became very emotional. I saw his face start to get red. He was holding a paper napkin and he ripped at it with his hands.

"I didn't want to become the boss of the people who trained me," he said. "I wanted to build something on my own."

That was the moment Vaughn Starnes earned my infinite respect. It was then that I realized I wasn't just dealing with a very talented surgeon, but also a very special man.

Our dinner signaled the beginning of a long and productive working relationship between the two of us. More importantly, that night was the beginning of the ascent of USC's medical enterprise.

"Okay, how do we get to that?" I asked. "How do we help you continue building something of your very own?"

Our conversation moved forward on two fronts. First, we needed to figure out how we could keep him at USC and reject the offer from UCLA. Second, we needed to figure out what we needed to do in the long run for the future of the university's medical enterprise.

I told him that I was there to do everything possible to keep him at USC. But I also said that if he accepted our offer, I couldn't promise him that we were going to buy the hospitals.

That night it was Vaughn Starnes who finally explained in a way that I understood why USC had to buy the two hospitals. He made the case so clear and compelling that, in my mind, it was the pivotal moment that made me decide we had to find a way to make the purchase.

Although I left dinner that evening feeling like we were on the right track, the next morning I would be dealing with a whole new set of challenges.

❋ ❋ ❋

I came to the office that morning with a new feeling of optimism. We didn't have a deal to keep Vaughn Starnes yet, but I believed he had been willing to listen and consider options.

But before I could dig into the negotiations, I was hit first thing in the morning with several emails and phone calls from faculty chairs at the HSC. The rumor had spread like wildfire. The spirits at USC's medical school were already dampened, but now the faculty chairs were distraught. They believed Vaughn Starnes and his entire team were already gone.

As I was flooded with these emails and phone calls, I said nothing. I couldn't tell anyone that I'd just had dinner with Starnes and that we were doing everything we could to keep him.

I asked the vice provost to work with me and our legal office, drawing up a retention contract. I had several meetings with Vaughn, and his wife, Julie, who was the business manager of his faculty practice plan. By April, we finally had a deal.

This is how the USC Cardiovascular and Thoracic Institute (CVTI) was born. Considering the offer he had been given by UCLA, $25 million to support the institute seemed like a modest investment. We made the commitment to help recruit more transformative faculty members and to raise even more money to support the CVTI.

When we made the announcement that we had retained Starnes, it was a sign that we had stopped the bleeding. There was immediately a change in the morale at the medical school, with a glimmer of hope that we might be able to turn things around.

Now we needed to find a solution to the second challenge Starnes had identified.

We needed to figure out a way for USC to buy the hospitals.

CHAPTER 18

Catalysts of Change

"At the mention of anything he was counted to do, Hamilton nodded dismissively, as if he had it under control. Jefferson and Madison had noticed at that dinner table what a smile of triumph the man had . . . The glowing future he had foreseen was, it seemed, like a living picture before his eyes."[1]

CHARLES E. CERAMI,
DINNER AT MR. JEFFERSON'S,
CHAPTER 12

It's true that getting deeper into the healthcare business would mean taking on greater risk. But it would give us the power to make decisions and changes, rather than being controlled by Tenet Healthcare.

At that time, Steve Sample and USC's Board of Trustees were still wary of this approach. But Stanley Gold clearly saw the importance for USC to control all of the university's clinical operations. Without controlling clinical operations and patient care, medical schools can't create a sustainable business model and can never balance their budgets.

He began having conversations with Ken Leventhal and other key members of the board.

Over time, the sentiment among our trustees began to shift. This was the beginning of the end for Tenet Healthcare at USC.

❋ ❋ ❋

By the summer of 2006, the challenges on the HSC were still ongoing. It's true that we'd kept Vaughn Starnes, but that was the only real success worth mentioning.

Steve Sample was on another three-month sabbatical for the summer when I received a call from USC's vice president for external relations, who told me about yet another crisis. This time with L.A. County.

After years of approving the same $73 million agreement, L.A. County had decided they were no longer going to sign it.

This would have been a disaster. Although the funding from L.A. County hadn't raised in 15 years, we needed *more* money from them, not a complete elimination of funding.

This time our challenge was political. For years, L.A. County Supervisor Gloria Molina had taken an adversarial stance against USC and its plans for a biotech park adjacent to the HSC. She was a formidable presence with a lot of political power.

To be fair, Gloria Molina may have had reason for taking an antagonistic position. In the 1990s, she wanted the County to commit to building a new 1,000-bed hospital. However, County Supervisor Zev Yaroslavsky only supported a hospital with 500-600 beds.

At the time, USC's senior vice president for Government Relations was a close friend of Yaroslavsky's. She convinced Steve Sample that the university should remain neutral and let the politicians work it out themselves.

In Los Angeles, County Supervisors have no legislative body. Instead, they are like kings and queens, with about 2.5 million people under each of them. By sitting on the sidelines, USC had essentially chosen not to support their own supervisor.

Gloria Molina never forgave USC for staying neutral. Politically, this was a major mistake.

In the end, Molina was right. The hospital eventually got built, but it was too small. It should have been 1,000 beds as she suggested.

But the political damage had already been done. By June 2006, it had become a crisis.

That summer the Keck School was negotiating a small increase from $73 million to $80 million. However, Molina was insistent that they include in the contract a clause about the minimum wage. This essentially would give L.A. County the right to audit all salaries at USC, not just the salaries in the County contract.

As a private institution, we believed L.A. County had no right to audit all of USC's salaries. It would be like giving up our 501(c)(3) independent status.

Now the entire contract was being held hostage. And Molina had decided this was the hill she was willing to die on.

USC's vice president for external relations and I went to Molina's office. It was a tense meeting. She was always tough and demanding, and she had no intention of budging on this issue.

Knowing the history I had inherited, I was very respectful to her.

"You're asking me to essentially change the DNA code of the university," I said. "I cannot do that. We are a private institution, and we must retain our independence."

"All the companies who do business with the County accepted those clauses," Molina said. "Why not USC? It's unacceptable."

"Well, we were founded in 1880 and have retained our independence all of that time," I said. "No other corporations that work with the County have survived that long."

Then I added, "I'm here to tell you that we are going to fully comply with the County's minimum wage standards. I told you that before coming here. In fact, I asked our CFO to do an audit. He found that there were four cafeteria workers whose salaries were slightly less than the County's minimum wage. I asked him to give them a raise. So, I'm here to tell you that we are fully complying with the County minimum wage."

Then I proposed that the USC Board of Trustees would have the independent auditors Ernst & Young do an annual audit and to certify the university was fully complying.

I even offered to call a press conference and publicly share all of the things we would do, just to satisfy the unions that were likely pressuring her to hold out for these changes to the contract.

She paused for a moment, and then said tersely, "No. This is not acceptable. We don't have a contract."

And with that, the crisis on the HSC suddenly got much worse. Without that contract, the fallout would be immense because of our dependence on them for funding.

But there was little else I could do. I felt she was being stubborn, but I couldn't allow a public entity to audit the salaries of a private university.

I got up and stood at the door. There was really nothing left to say, but I felt that I needed to be honest while still being respectful.

"Supervisor Molina," I said. "You give me no choice. As soon as I go back to my office, I'm going to have to issue layoff letters to all of the doctors and staff who work with L.A. County Hospital. I'm sorry, but we're not changing the independent DNA code of the university. Both of us may as well commit political suicide. Is that what you want? Have a good afternoon."

And I walked out the door.

By the time I got back to my office, one of Molina's senior staff members called me with a message. Supervisor Molina had accepted my proposal. USC could hire independent auditors to certify that the university was complying with the County's minimum wage requirements.

In August 2006, the L.A. County Board of Supervisors approved a new contract for $80 million.

A few years later, we continued to work with Molina's office and were able to get the annual contract raised to $120 million.

She was a very tough negotiator. I really thought I may have to lay off hundreds of people because we simply couldn't come to an agreement. I wasn't bluffing and she knew it. And she didn't want to be responsible for hundreds of layoffs.

* * *

In August 2006, we also held the most critical meeting for the future of USC's medical enterprise.

It was a Board of Trustees' executive committee meeting. Attorney Marshall Goldman was there to present his findings about our agreement with Tenet Healthcare.

President Sample was there, but he didn't say anything during the entire meeting. The board chairman had asked me to prepare a presentation. I made the case that the only way to achieve a sustainable financial model was to control the hospitals and all of the clinical operations. It was also the first time that I tied USC's future as an elite research university to having a first-class medical school with an academic medical center.

After my presentation, one of USC's trustees said, "I wouldn't have taken this risk in my business."

I politely replied, "I agree with you. If the decision is strictly a business one, then my recommendation is not to own the hospitals. However, our decision must be academic first and foremost and not a business one. Otherwise, in the long run, USC will be marginalized as a research university."

In the end, it was this argument that carried the day.

While we provided the vision for the future, Marshall Grossman provided the ammunition we needed to achieve our most important goal. He had found exactly what we had been hoping for—a breach in our longstanding agreement with Tenet Healthcare. Now we had the basis for a lawsuit, one that would come as a surprise to everyone but the people in that meeting.

* * *

The next day—on August 22, 2006—we crossed the Rubicon. *Alea iacta est*, as they say: the die is cast.

We filed a lawsuit to terminate our agreement with Tenet Healthcare, and to take ownership and control of USC University Hospital and Norris Cancer Hospital.

That same day one of our senior officers called Tenet's General Counsel, who was quite angry and said he was prepared to take the case to trial.

At one point, his anger got the best of him when he said: "Now I know why they call USC the University of Spoiled Children."

It was a telling phone call. While they may have really believed we had a weak case, fear is always behind an outburst of anger. If USC could find a breach in its contract, that could lead other hospitals and medical centers to review the terms of their agreements.

It was only the first shot across the bow, but it was the beginning of a battle that would continue for another year.

On the same day that we announced the lawsuit, the department chairs of our medical school held an emergency meeting. When the news was shared with them, they broke out in spontaneous applause. It was an inspiring moment of truth. And it was one that would begin to transform the morale across our entire medical enterprise.

On August 30, 2007, just over one year after we filed the lawsuit, we defeated an appeal from Tenet. Unless Tenet filed another appeal with the California Supreme Court, which we fully expected, we were prepared to proceed to trial.

To our surprise, the CEO of Tenet Healthcare came to Los Angeles to begin discussions to settle the case and sell the hospitals to USC.

* * *

With the possibility of acquiring the hospitals now a real possibility, it was important for us to take the first steps in recruiting a new leadership team for the medical school.

After several interviews, Korn Ferry helped narrow the search to four candidates. Our first choice was the chair of the Department of Surgery at one of the very top universities in the country. He was a wonderful man, who impressed everyone. He also happened to be the parent of two USC students, so he and his wife knew the university well.

He considered the offer very seriously, but in the end decided he couldn't leave his university.

* * *

With our first offer now off the table, we turned to another finalist: Carmen Puliafito. He was in Australia on a trip, so I made him the offer on the phone. When he returned to the U.S., he called me back and accepted the job.

Throughout the process, as we do with every major search, we relied on the experience and expertise of Korn Ferry, who assured us they had done their due diligence and there were no issues.

Our medical school leadership and some senior faculty in Ophthalmology were very positive after receiving excellent recommendations for Puliafito. Again and again, we heard he was an excellent recruiter, which was an important skill we were going to need as we built up our medical enterprise.

In 2007, USC's hiring policies were also very different than they are today. For tenured or tenure-track faculty positions which included deans of the schools, the Academic Senate resisted endorsing a policy for doing background checks on faculty candidates. We conducted background checks for part-time faculty and all staff positions, but the Academic Senate requested that we not do background checks for full-time tenure or tenure-track faculty hires.

It seems incredible, but that was the Academic Senate's position then. In April 2010, as president-elect, I asked the Academic Senate to reconsider the issue. Their executive board voted to implement background checks for all faculty hires moving forward.

That was one of *my first accomplishments* as president of USC.

But for those who had been hired prior to the policy change, they were already on the university's payroll.

* * *

In my offer letter to Carmen Puliafito, I was very clear that the hospitals would not report to the dean of the Keck School. I remember that he argued with me about it a little, but I explained that we were planning to implement a different reporting structure.

He seemed to understand and accepted the offer that was presented to him. However, within a year, I realized that he hadn't given up on the idea of persuading me that the hospitals should report to him.

One morning when I was provost, Puliafito invited me to a breakfast at the California Club, along with two USC trustees, one of them being the chair of the Keck School's Board of Overseers.

We chatted for a little bit about general things happening at the medical school, and then at the end of the breakfast Puliafito announced that he had to leave. Very quickly I realized that the breakfast had been a setup.

The chair of the Board of Overseers began by raising the issue that I was too busy as provost to have the hospitals reporting to me. He said the hospitals should report to the dean because he knows the healthcare business, and on and on.

I got very upset. This was the first time I really pushed back and argued.

"I will talk to the president," I said. "But I think it's a big mistake to have everything reporting to one person."

I was still fuming on the drive back to campus. As soon as I got back to the office, I called Puliafito to let him know how I really felt.

"Listen," I said. "If you ever do that to me again, I will ask the president to fire you immediately."

The idea of the hospitals reporting directly to the dean never came up again.

* * *

On April 14, 2008, after months of negotiating and planning, Tenet agreed to sign a non-binding letter of intent for the university to acquire USC University Hospital and USC Norris Cancer Hospital.

It had taken nearly two years from the time we filed the lawsuit, but we were finally one step closer to our original goal. We'd won one battle, but the war was not yet over.

We still had to come to terms on a price for the hospitals, and the negotiations were not easy.

In October 2008, Chairman Gold flew to Dallas to meet with Trevor Fetter, the CEO of Tenet, to negotiate a price for the two hospitals. Gold told him firmly that USC needed a discounted purchase price, explaining in detail how Tenet's long-term neglect of infrastructure had increased the amount of renovation that would be needed to restore facilities on the HSC.

They went back and forth, arguing over the purchase price.

Finally, as a tactic to make Tenet fear that USC was "walking away" from the negotiations, Gold suggested that they work together to draft a press release stating that the purchase wasn't going to happen. He also noted that USC would have to notify the judge that the settlement had broken down and the university would need to resume litigation.

The chairman asked Fetter to think about it over the weekend and contact him early the next week with his decision. Fetter said he would consider a reduction in price, but that the new offer might disappoint him.

"Work on the offer," the chairman said. "Then let me decide if I'm disappointed."

Fetter mentioned an earnings call that would be taking place in a couple of weeks, noting that he'd certainly get questions about the USC deal.

"If we're still negotiating, or if the discussions have been terminated, you should tell shareholders that," said Gold.

He could see that Fetter didn't like the idea of telling his shareholders that the deal had fallen apart. But Gold left the meeting thinking USC would likely have to re-start litigation in order to get the best deal.

* * *

After all of our hard work, in October 2008, it seemed like it all might fall apart, along with the entire global economy. As the stock market took a dive, layoffs swept away jobs around the world.

And yet, USC was sitting in a great position with substantial working capital. In January 2009, USC's bond request of $400 million was oversubscribed by a factor of three—meaning that financial institutions on Wall Street believed strongly in the future of USC!

* * *

With things beginning to move in the right direction for acquiring the hospitals, we needed to untangle another thorny problem to ensure the future of USC's medical enterprise.

We needed to integrate all of the faculty practice plans under the USC Board's fiduciary control, since they were composed as separate, independent non-profit corporations. In addition to the services the medical school faculty provided to the department in which they worked, each chair also had their own 501 (c) (3) non-profit corporation on the side. The faculty underneath each chair were also members of that particular faculty practice plan.

When each plan billed for clinical services—patient procedures, consultations, and surgery follow-ups—the revenue was shared with all of the faculty members who provided care for patients.

The entire system was mind-numbingly complex. And we had 19 faculty practice plans!

Getting faculty to agree on anything is difficult. Persuading 512 medical faculty and doctors—from 19 different practice plans—to give up fiduciary control to USC's Board of Trustees and transfer all their assets (and liabilities) to USC could be nearly impossible.

There was initial resistance and the outcome was uncertain. So I invited two key people to breakfast at the California Club because I believed they would be the most important in helping us get an agreement.

Vaughn Starnes and Ed Crandall, the chair of the Department of Medicine pledged their support and offered to work with the rest of the chairs to try to make it happen. Together, they really provided the leadership to explain and sell the idea to everyone else.

Later, I invited all of the chairs to a private dinner at the Cal Club to talk about the integration plan. I ordered a good wine to serve with dinner, and then before we got down to business, I told them a story about a famous dinner that took place in Thomas Jefferson's house, with James Madison and Alexander Hamilton attending.

In a single evening, Hamilton succeeded in persuading bitter rivals to federate the states, and then create a federal bank that turned all of the states' debt into a federal obligation.

I described the wines, the food, and the ice cream they served at that dinner as they celebrated and finalized a deal. The faculty were laughing, especially when they realized that our entire dinner that evening was a metaphor.

Then I told them that Virginia was the only state that had a surplus in their budget and Massachusetts had the largest debt. So, naturally, they did not want to federate the states and subsidize the states who were broke.

However, by agreeing to move the capital to Northern Virginia—Washington, D.C.—the real estate value of properties in Virginia would all go up, Hamilton reminded them.

Then I told all of the chairs that we had a similar task before us. I surprised them by saying: "You draft the agreement of integration for us, but on one condition: the integrated faculty practice plans will be under the fiduciary oversight of USC's Board of Trustees. That's non-negotiable. Everything else is negotiable."

It was a long evening, but overall the atmosphere was positive. Within six months, we had a deal!

Now we just had to get everyone to vote on it for final approval.

* * *

In October 2008, all of the medical school's faculty and doctors gathered in a large auditorium on the HSC. We honestly didn't know how it would turn out.

As the vote approached, my vice provost gave me the best advice. She said, "Max, you shouldn't address the faculty in the auditorium. Let me do it. You should not show up at all. If they vote 'no,' at least you don't feel directly rejected, and you have one more chance to directly work with them."

I thought this was very sound advice.

Later, she called me.

"We did it, Max," she said. "The vote was unanimous!"

* * *

After all of our efforts, we were finally able to take a moment to celebrate. I remember the event on the hospital quad, seeing the enthusiasm and smiling faces on the HSC for the first time in many years. I couldn't help thinking back to the dinner I'd had with Vaughn Starnes in Pasadena three years earlier where he said, "We must buy the hospitals."

If he had left for UCLA, I'm not sure if any of our other efforts would have happened. Convincing him to stay was the moment that turned everything around. After all of the trials and tribulations, it finally felt worth it.

For all of us, it felt like a new beginning.

CHAPTER 19

Pinnacle of Leadership

«Οἱ πολλοὶ ἄνθρωποι, ὅταν μὲν θαρρῶσιν, ἀνυπόστατον τὸ φρόνημα παρέχονται.»

ΞΕΝΟΦΩΝΤΟΣ ΚΥΡΟΥ ΠΑΙΔΕΙΑΣ, Ε 2.33

"Large masses of human beings, when they are inspired with confidence, display a spirit that is irresistible."[1]

XENOPHON, *CYROPAEDIA*, BOOK 5, 2.33

To be honest, my final year as provost was the most difficult. Given all of the challenges I had to navigate, and my previous life experiences, I had learned to take nothing for granted.

Although the board had nominated me to become the next president of USC, there were no guarantees that I would be chosen for the position. The point, of course, was not to come across as someone who expected the job, or was lobbying for the presidency, but as someone whose everyday actions proved that I was the best candidate to lead USC into the future.

However, the process was very challenging at times because everyone assumed correctly that I was eventually going to be a candidate. There were many faculty and staff, as well as alumni and even trustees, who would approach me on campus or at events and tell me confidentially that they believed I should be the next president. I would always smile, say very little, and then politely change the subject.

While I appreciated their confidence, I also knew that some of them were simply telling me what I wanted to hear or hoping to gain my favor if I did become president.

In addition to being careful about talking about the presidency, I was cautioned to avoid controversial issues, steering clear of areas where I might find myself entangled in disputes or disagreements.

I was also counseled to be very careful of all of my interactions with USC's trustees. It was important to limit my interactions with them, avoiding socializing with them and keeping all of my discussions with them focused strictly on the business of the university. The most important thing was to make sure that I didn't appear to be "campaigning" to be the next president.

But the most important advice might have been about my interactions with Steve and Kathryn Sample. They would have their own anxieties as Steve stepped down from a prominent position he had held for so long, and it would likely be an emotional time in their lives. If you include his time as the leader of both SUNY Buffalo and USC, he had been a university president for nearly 30 years. When you hold a position for that long, it becomes an important part of your identity.

Because Steve and Kathryn would be making a major life transition, I was advised to continue to show them the utmost respect and keep a low profile during all of the celebrations that would fill their final year.

* * *

With both possibility and uncertainty in front of me, I viewed being a candidate for the presidency as an assignment, which I took very seriously. Five months before my first interview, I began the arduous task of preparing for my interview with the search committee.

Besides not knowing what questions I might be asked, I felt that I needed to clarify for myself what would be the best strategy for the future of USC. Although the university had made major strides over nearly two decades, it still had far to go in order to truly reach the top tier of American research universities.

I needed to think deeply about USC's long and rich history, as well as develop a strategy for how to elevate and advance the university in the years ahead. USC had made great progress in undergraduate education, which provided the foundation for the next steps that would take the university to new heights.

But I also realized that any approach needed to not only appeal to the Board of Trustees, but also the larger university community. I needed to ensure that all of USC's stakeholders felt like they could claim ownership and that they were part of the university's vision for the future.

However, the first step in the plan was finding the right strategies.

As I quietly considered and developed my plan, I gave it a name: the Manhattan Project—a moment after which the university would never be the same.

* * *

In the process of preparing my personal Manhattan Project, I understood that while I was interviewing to become the president of USC, my focus couldn't just be on the university itself. I had to look across the landscape of higher education to find peers and competitors that had already made a similar journey to what I envisioned for USC.

I settled on two private universities that had both dramatically enhanced their academic reputations over a period of 30–40 years: Duke and Stanford.

It was also very important for a university not to copy the plans or strategies of another institution, but rather to establish a unique identity. In the past, I had been frustrated when I'd heard USC's previous provosts talk about making the university the "Stanford of the south" or the "Harvard of the west." In a competitive business like higher education, it didn't make any sense to me to describe ourselves as another university. We had our own ambitions, our own strengths, and our own brand.

We understood that we had to rely on original thinking and unconventional approaches.

The guiding question became: What is it that sets USC apart from all of its competitors?

When establishing a vision it is always important to have one close competitor in mind. For Steve Sample it was UCLA and how to surpass it in quality of undergraduate students and education.

Doing my homework on USC's future, I concluded very quickly that in my mind it was going to be Stanford.

* * *

As I prepared for my interview and planned my opening statement to the search committee, I received helpful advice from several people. But there was one person whose coaching and guidance was particularly valuable: Bob Iger.

In 2000, Iger had been named president and COO of The Walt Disney Company. When Michael Eisner announced that he would step down as Disney's CEO in 2005, Iger was just another candidate with no assurances that he would rise to the role which would earn him the reputation as one of the greatest dealmakers in the Fortune 500.

He generously offered to speak with me by phone on a Sunday afternoon, one week before my meeting with the search committee. He listened to my thoughts and concerns, and then offered me a wealth of wisdom from his own experience.

He stressed the importance of focusing on only three priorities—and no more than three!

"If you use five or six, they won't remember them all at the end. Bring it home with three priorities," said Iger.

I had been planning to use five priorities, but I greatly respected his advice. Over the course of an hour, he talked about how internal candidates cannot win by playing defense. He encouraged me to think about who would win if I won.

"You have to define yourself and the future of the institution," he said.

Then he explained how the candidate who does the best job of defining that future will gain control of it.

Finally, he returned to the idea of three key points, urging me to develop a clear, concise message that revolved around those three areas.

"A strategy that is too complex, will be difficult to articulate. A strategy that has too many facets, will be too hard to remember," he said.

He ended by saying something very wise. "Remember, this is a political campaign!" he said. "Good luck, Max."

After our call, I kept thinking about how I could transform my five priorities into only three main points.

It was difficult to do, but I was grateful for his insights because they helped crystallize how I should revise my remarks and also gave me a new strategy.

This wasn't just a job interview, it was a political campaign!

* * *

You can prepare as much as possible, but the true test of leadership is to adapt during unexpected circumstances. After months of study and planning, the night before my interview, that's exactly what I found myself doing. Around 10:00 p.m. on that Friday evening, I started experiencing severe pain: diverticulitis.

I called our family physician and he told me that if the pain didn't improve by morning I would have to go to the emergency room. I told him that wasn't possible because I had an interview the next afternoon with the presidential search committee.

"Oh, my God," he said. "We've got to get you some strong antibiotics right away."

He wrote me a prescription and Niki and I drove from Palos Verdes to a pharmacy in Torrance, which was fortunately still open at 1:00 a.m.

By morning the pain was better, but I was exhausted. I slept until 11:00 a.m., and then ate lots of bread and drank tea instead of coffee. I felt weak, but I was also strangely calm.

Fortunately, the meeting wasn't until 3:00 p.m. I had done everything I could to get ready, and I had overcome an unexpected challenge right before the interview.

Now it was up to me to deliver.

* * *

As I walked into the interview, I decided not to wear the USC pin that I normally had on my jacket. In order for me to put it back on, I felt that I had to convince the search committee to select me as the next president.

There were 12 members of the committee, seated around a large table. Chairman Ed Roski asked me to take the first 5-7 minutes to present my opening statement.

"Just tell us whatever you want," he said.

My mind was focused and ready, and I opened by tying my personal history to the history of the university. I shared with them how Niki and I dreamed of coming to America to pursue a better life through education. I shared my passion for USC and its future, focusing on the importance of accelerating the university's ascent.

I concluded by assuring the committee that I not only believed in this vision, but also that it should inspire the entire Trojan Family.

After finishing my opening statement and answering a few

questions, Stanley Gold nearly threw me off track.

"Tell me a mistake you made and how you corrected it," he said.

I paused for a moment to gather my thoughts, and then responded.

"Stanley, I did make a mistake, but unfortunately I haven't been able to correct it yet. When our daughters were growing up, I didn't spend as much time as I should with them because I have always been busy with USC over the past 19 years. But Niki comforts me by telling me that I can correct it by spending time with our grandchildren in the future!"

* * *

On the drive back home to Palos Verdes after the interview, I called Niki to tell her that I thought it went well.

"Drive carefully," she said. "The rain's going to be very heavy."

Before I got home, my cell phone rang, and I answered. I heard Ed Roski's voice, telling me that of the seven finalists, I was the search committee's unanimous choice to be USC's next president.

He told me he planned to call an emergency meeting of the Board of Trustees for the next Tuesday. In that meeting, they would finalize my selection.

"I'm concerned that if we don't move fast, it's going to leak," Roski said.

* * *

That night Niki and I celebrated quietly. The good news brought back all of the memories of our long journey together.

We were both slightly exhausted from the previous sleepless night and now, more than excitement, we both felt gratitude and relief.

But very quickly, we also felt the weight of the responsibility that would come with our new reality. We were going to be the next President and First Lady of USC.

The next Tuesday, the Board of Trustees held a telephonic meeting to vote on my election. Ed Roski had asked me to be on standby. If the board voted in my favor, then I would be called to join the meeting.

I waited patiently and finally the phone rang. To my surprise, trustees from around the world were on the call.

I'd prepared a brief opening statement in which I thanked them and told them how humbled I was by this extraordinary opportunity.

At some point, I think it was trustee Lorna Reed who said, "We want to hear from Niki. Put her on the phone!"

Niki spoke spontaneously and it was just a great celebration. It was wonderful that they were not only welcoming me as the new President, but embracing Niki as First Lady.

After the call, Niki and I shared a glass of champagne with our daughters.

"Never forget why America is great," I said. "The American dream that built this nation is still alive."

* * *

Although we were excited about our new opportunities, there wasn't a lot of time to celebrate. The announcement of my promotion came in March, but Niki and I wouldn't officially assume our new roles until August 3.

The chairman formed a committee of faculty, students, and staff to plan for the inauguration ceremony, which was scheduled for October 15.

While it seems like we had some time to prepare all of these events, it's difficult to understand how much time and effort goes into a presidential transition.

In addition to assuming a new role as First Lady and getting involved with numerous details for the upcoming inauguration, Niki soon found herself managing the massive operation of planning the move to the USC President's house.

❋ ❋ ❋

At the same time, I was also receiving a steady flood of personal letters, congratulating me on my new role, from the President of Cyprus to Pete Carroll to members of Congress. Many came from those I knew well, but the majority of them came from people I didn't know at all.

One letter that really stood out was from a 90-year-old USC alumnus, who was a retired judge living in Arizona. As a person of Greek-American descent, he told me the story of how, when he was a child, his Greek-American, immigrant father had taken him to an event in USC's Bovard Auditorium.

After USC's president at the time delivered a speech, his father turned to him and said, "When you grow up, I want you to become USC's very first president of Greek descent."

The retired judge wrote, "I'm thrilled that you are, Dr. Nikias. My father is smiling from up there. You did it for me and my father."

❋ ❋ ❋

It was nice to receive congratulations from throughout the Trojan Family, but I still had to keep on top of everything at the university and assemble my cabinet.

As I had done when I became dean and later provost, I had already been assessing the abilities of those around me, and I'd thought about who would make a great team.

I was also keeping in mind many leadership lessons from

the classics. One lesson that stood out in my mind was that a new leader should be careful not to dismantle the traditions and symbols of the past, especially when following a popular predecessor.

The Trojan Family has a number of traditions that had been established over more than a century. It was important for me to preserve them and respect them.

I made a decision not to say anything negative about the past, but rather to always focus on an even better future.

With that in mind, I kept many of the cabinet members from Steve Sample's administration because I'd worked closely with them as provost and thought that the continuity would be important in helping us quickly move forward.

* * *

One area where it is important for all leaders to take care of themselves is their employment contract.

Historically, the corporate world has done a great job of establishing contractual agreements with their executives, hiring attorneys to represent both the executive and the organization in the negotiation process.

However, in American higher education, this process was nearly non-existent. The contracts for my appointment as a faculty member, founding director of a national center of excellence, dean and provost, were no more than two to three pages. And there were practically no protections for the individual.

I was very fortunate with my personal employment contract, and I like to say it was a sign that God was looking after me.

When I became president-elect, I reached out to Bruce Ramer, who was a longtime member of USC's Board of Trustees, to seek his advice about my upcoming contract negotiation. After a brief discussion he said, "I will be honored to represent you in your contract negotiations."

I was flattered, but I didn't know what to say. Bruce was already a celebrated lawyer, whose list of celebrity clients included Steven Spielberg, Clint Eastwood, and Robert Zemeckis among many others.

We checked with USC's General Counsel and learned that there was no conflict of interest because he served as a Life Trustee, with no voting rights or fiduciary duties to the university. He also recused himself from any discussion about me and my employment contract at the board level all the years I was president.

I'll never forget the meeting Bruce had with the compensation consultant hired by the executive committee of the board to discuss my contract renewal.

"Because Max serves at the pleasure of the board, in the case of stepping down without cause, the package you're offering is not enough," said Ramer. "Having achieved all of these goals in USC's academic ascent, what does Max get if he's asked to step down?"

The consultant seemed surprised because academic contracts are usually accepted with little or no negotiation.

"This guy has said that he is gonna raise $6 billion, and they will. That's never happened before in American higher education," said Bruce. "And he's gonna elevate USC academically, as well as the quality of the students and faculty. And the medical enterprise will reach new heights and achieve enormous growth. He's going to do all of that."

I could see the consultant's eyes widening, feeling like he was clearly out of Bruce's league.

"And when he does it, the board is gonna wake up one morning and say, 'Okay, you did it. Get the fuck out of here. We don't need you anymore. So, what you are offering here is not enough. It's not fair.'"

The consultant looked at Bruce and said, "Okay, I see your point. We need to do better if all these goals are met. So yeah, sure. If they are met, he has to be rewarded."

After we left the meeting, I looked at Bruce and I said, "Bruce, come on. You were too rough on the guy. The board will never do that to me."

Bruce stopped and looked at me, "From my experience in these business deals, we trust nobody. Trust, but verify."

❊ ❊ ❊

As soon as I officially became president, I noticed that things began to change. Many people asked me, "What surprised you the most?"

To be honest, I didn't think much would be different. As provost, I had served as acting president many times and worked with many of the same cabinet members for several years.

Other than moving my office down the hallway, I thought everything would be basically the same. Wow, was I wrong. Becoming president was a rude awakening that made me rethink everything about how I normally operated.

As provost, when a problem needed to be solved, I could quickly get answers or take action. In that position, the deans reported to me, so they were very responsive to my requests.

But as president, I had to be careful. Although it was tempting to pick up the phone and demand changes, I couldn't do that. At such a large, decentralized university, there were simply too many things happening to get involved with every detail.

Being president is more than a full-time job on its own, so I had to learn to rely on my direct reports to develop and execute plans, rather than doing it myself.

I had to learn to delegate, trusting that my team would make solid plans and good decisions.

❊ ❊ ❊

There was another surprising thing that I noticed after becoming president. People who had known me for years suddenly changed. Everyone was incredibly nice, with people on campus going out of their way to make eye contact and say "hi" to me.

Before I was president, I could walk across campus often without people recognizing me or feeling obligated to talk to me. It was an unexpected change, and there were times when I missed the anonymity of being just another academic leader.

Although people were suddenly friendlier, I learned something very quickly. I always recognized that people were "saluting the flag"—meaning the president of USC—and not me personally.

When you first become president, everyone is your friend. But when I stepped down eight years later, it was then that I truly found out how many were truly my friends. It turns out, very few.

* * *

Like I had done in preparing my opening statement to the presidential search committee, I knew I had to spend a tremendous amount of time planning for my inaugural address. However, this would be a much larger audience and the stakes were much higher.

I wanted everyone connected to the university and the local community to feel like they were part of the transformation that was happening at USC.

To make sure that I had a clear and compelling message, I worked on the speech off and on throughout the entire summer.

I wanted everyone to walk away from the inauguration, inspired and energized to lift USC to new heights of achievement and recognition, by articulating the vision for an "undisputed, academically elite" university.

After many hours of thinking and searching, I ran across the metaphor that would serve as the guiding symbol for the entire speech: The Destined Reign of Troy—"*Fas Regna Trojae.*"

⁂ ⁂ ⁂

After months of anticipation, the big day finally arrived.

I was humbled and grateful that so many people were able to attend, including Dr. Peter Scott, my thesis advisor from SUNY Buffalo; Dr. John Siegel and his wife; and our good friend Andreas Polydoros.

For the first time ever, students from more than 120 different nations carried the flags of their countries as part of the procession, creating a new tradition that would be adopted for future new student convocations and commencement ceremonies.

We also started another new tradition with the Presidential Medallion, which historically was only worn by the current USC president at appropriate events. I created a second Presidential Medallion to be displayed in the Office of the President, listing the names of all of the university's past presidents.

It was a way of honoring USC's history, showing respect for those who had built the university into what it had become.

⁂ ⁂ ⁂

When it came time for me to deliver my inaugural address, I looked out at a jubilant crowd of 10,000 people, including so many colleagues from across higher education, city and state leaders, and members of the local Southern California community.

After many months of contemplating and preparing, I was focused and ready. As I began my speech, the words, phrases, and images seemed to flow naturally out into Alumni Park.

I could sense that the vision I presented resonated with the crowd, and I felt grateful that everyone was so proud of USC's history and optimistic about its future.

Over the next year, I was surprised by how many alumni reached out to tell me that my speech was the most inspirational they'd ever heard.

❊ ❊ ❊

Even after the inaugural ceremony, the festivities and the surprises continued.

During the evening at a black-tie dinner at the California Club, the dean of the College of Letters, Arts and Sciences came to my head table and whispered in my ear: "The Dornsifes would like to chat with you briefly. They were so inspired by the events of the day that I think they may decide to name the College."

The next Saturday USC played football against Cal Berkeley in the Coliseum. At one point, I looked down on the field and noticed the Trojan Marching Band maneuvering into a new configuration, spelling out "Max" on the football field.

In the moment, it made all of us laugh. But later, when I went to the locker room after the Trojans' 48–14 victory, Matt Barkley, who tied a school record that day by throwing five touchdowns, said: "We had to beat Cal today for you President Nikias."

But even with all of the wonderful celebrations, I was always careful to never take anything for granted.

❊ ❊ ❊

After the inauguration, former USC president Jack Hubbard requested that we have dinner together. I always admired his wit and appreciated his wisdom, so of course I agreed.

Before becoming USC's eighth president, Jack was a naval aviator who earned four air medals as well as the Distinguished

Flying Cross.[2]

During his first year as president, USC became a member of the Association of American Universities the elite group of top research universities in the United States. So, when he wanted to talk, I was willing to listen.[3]

One evening, the two of us had dinner alone at the Cal Club. He gave me some unexpected advice that would foreshadow the future.

"I've been watching you since you became dean," he said. "And let me tell you, you work too hard. It's not worth it."

"Jack, are you kidding me?" I asked. "I love what I'm doing. I get up every morning and feel blessed to be president of this great university."

I went on, telling him how grateful someone with my background was to even have such an opportunity.

He listened quietly, and then finally raised his voice.

"You don't understand," he said loudly. "There is no tenure in administration, only in the professoriate. So listen to me when I tell you that it's not worth it."

He was very insistent, and I didn't expect this reaction from him.

Then he leaned in and said something I will never forget.

"USC is like a mistress," he said. "You passionately love her, but she'll never love you back!"

Looking back, his words seem incredibly prophetic. Many years later, I would continue to reflect on his advice from that night. In some ways, maybe he was right.

USC is a mistress that will never love you back.

igure 1. First, second, and third grades of the elementary school in the village of Komi Kebir on the Karpass Peninsula, Cyprus. I was in the first grade in the fall of 1958. Third from the right in the first row of boys.

CLM Nikias

gure 2. I'm the flag bearer of the First Gymnasium of Famagusta celebrating National Holiday in October 1969. Niki is wearing glasses (second row in the middle).

CLM Nikias

Figure 3. When I was training to become second lieutenant in the army, I underwent military exercises on Mount Psiloritis on the Island of Crete in February 1971.

CLM Niki

Figure 4. USC Trustee Ratan Tata, the chairman of the Tata Group, introduced me to the Prime Minister of India, Manmohan Singh, at Parliament House in New Delhi in February 20

© 2011 Photograph provided by the Prime Minister's Office, Press Information Bureau, Government of Ind
Reproduced in accordance with government polic

nder the auspices of the USC President's Distinguished Lecture Series, I had the honor of wel-oming and introducing to the university community President George W. Bush and First Lady aura Bush in 2013 (Figure 5), President Bill Clinton in 2014 (Figure 6), and the Prime Minister of he U.K. David Cameron in 2017 (Figure 7).

igure 5. President George W. Bush and First Lady Laura Bush

© 2013 University of Southern California (Photo by Steve Cohn)

gure 6. President Bill Clinton

© 2014 University of Southern California (Photo by Karen Ballard)

gure 7. Prime Minister of the U.K. David Cameron

© 2017 University of Southern California (Photo by Steve Cohn)

Figure 8. We unveiled the new female symbol of Troy—Hecuba—on USC Village opening day in August 2017. The sculptor Christopher Slatoff stands next to Niki.

Figure 9. In May 2015, Niki and I hosted Japan's Prime Minister Shinzo Abe and First Lady Akie Abe on the USC campus. PM Abe studied at the University of Southern California in the 1970s.

CHAPTER 20

Successes and Embarrassment

«Θεσσαλός Ἱπποκράτης, Κῷος γένος, ἐνθάδε κεῖται,
Φοίβου ἀπὸ ῥίζης ἀθανάτου γεγαώς.
πλεῖστα τρόπαια νόσων στήσας ὅπλοις Ὑγιείης,
δόξαν ἑλὼν πολλῶν οὐ τύχᾳ, ἀλλὰ τέχνᾳ.»

ANTHOLOGIA GRAECA, II, 7.135

"Here lieth Thessalian Hippocrates, by descent a Koan,
sprung from the immortal stock of Phoebus.
Armed by Health he gained many victories over Disease,
and won great glory not by chance, but by science."[1]

ON HIPPOCRATES OF KOS, *THE PHYSICIAN*,
GREEK ANTHOLOGY, BOOK II, 7.135

After we purchased the hospitals and integrated the faculty practice plans, USC Health emerged from the "dark ages" into a new medical renaissance. For the first time in nearly 30 years, we ensured that the Keck School received its proper approvals.

In 2010, the school was granted the maximum eight-year accreditation from the Liaison Committee on Medical Education. We also made sure the Keck School was again fully accredited in 2018.

As our medical enterprise continued to gain momentum, it was very important to secure the financial support that could help us take advantage of the opportunities available to us.

As soon as I became president, I met with Robert Day, chairman of the Keck Foundation asking for a $200 million gift. Eventually, we settled on $150 million. But he also wanted to make sure that his cousin, Bill Keck, who was a USC trustee, would support the donation.

I had a good relationship with Bill, so I agreed to talk to him about it. I met Bill and his wife, Nicole, in his office. He talked for most of the first two hours, and then surprisingly said he would agree to a gift of $100 million, but not $150 million.

The Keck Foundation had the money, so it wasn't that. There seemed to be no rationale, other than the fact that Bill wanted a different number than Robert was offering. After several attempts to convince Bill failed, he never supported the gift and ultimately resigned from the USC board. It was too bad really, but there was nothing we could do to change his mind.

Nevertheless, the Keck Foundation Board almost unanimously approved the gift of $150 million. The provost negotiated the details of the contract, stipulating that USC would commit to raising three times the gift amount. We reached that goal in less than two years, raising nine times that amount—$1.3 billion—in only seven years.

In all of my interactions with Robert Day, I always admired how much respect he had for the Keck name.

"I want to honor my grandfather," he said. "He was the one that built the wealth, and I want his name to be associated with the healing of patients and diseases in perpetuity."

It was also Robert's idea that everything should be branded with the Keck name. That's why we have The Keck Medical Center of USC, the Keck Hospital of USC, the Keck Doctors of USC, and the Keck School of Medicine of USC.

In the end, it was a brilliant branding strategy. Before our patient care was always confused with the L.A. County Hospital, which was called "The LAC+USC Medical Center." But the Keck name gave everything a clear identity.

* * *

As we made structural changes to improve the Keck School and our entire medical enterprise, we also needed to find new leaders who could keep up our momentum and lead us into the future.

Within a year of acquiring the hospitals, we announced a national search for a senior vice president and chief executive officer for USC Health. Tom Jackiewicz was the one candidate who really understood what we were trying to do. When he interviewed, Jackiewicz was the CEO of the UC San Diego (UCSD) Health System.

In his opening statement, Jackiewicz said, "From all of the material you sent me, I did not see a plan for how you are going to grow. How are you going to expand your presence in Southern California?"

We spent time together just the two of us talking about the future of medicine at USC. I was very honest with him about the current state of our medical enterprise, but also shared our compelling vision for the future and what a special opportunity this would be for him.

"Yes, there are high risks," I said. "But we have a chance to truly make a difference."

Keck Medical Center at that time was much smaller than UCSD, and without the infrastructure one would have expected.

From the very beginning, he was in sync with our ambitions to become a top tier medical enterprise.

For the first time in years, we amended the bylaws of the university to create a new senior vice president, who was an officer of the corporation, reporting directly to the president.

At the beginning of his tenure, Tom called me one day to say that the job may be an impossible task, given how badly behaved some of the medical leaders and chairs were.

"Tom, nothing great ever comes easy," I said. "This will get better."

"That's exactly the right amount of empathy and optimism I

needed," he said.

* * *

While many people think of advances in medicine coming from new technologies and new discoveries, we understood that it was all about people.

In a five-year period, we were able to attract 120 new professors, 12 new chairs and 6 new directors of centers and institutes to our medical school, including some of the world's most transformative faculty.

We needed a strategy for retaining and recruiting what I called "better-than-excellent" faculty, focusing on key areas where we could gain a strategic advantage.

One of our most impressive hires was Dr. Indy Gill, who was recruited away from the Cleveland Clinic. He had such a renowned reputation that several celebrities such as Annette Bening, Shirley MacLaine, and Warren Beatty helped us during his recruiting process.

Four years later, however, we had to do our best to retain Dr. Gill. The Cleveland Clinic came back to him and made him a very generous offer.

It was summer and Niki and I were in Sun Valley, Idaho. I arranged for him to fly in for a day and picked him up at the airport. We had lunch at the Round House restaurant at the top of Bald Mountain, where we discussed a new retention package for him. As soon as we sat down for lunch, I took the piece of paper with his list of requests and went over it one by one saying "check, check, check, some modification here, another here, check," and so on. After a few minutes I looked at him and said "We have a deal, let's eat."

He smiled. "Don't worry, Max," he said. "We're just warming up!"

I had Tom Jackiewicz on the phone, who was very concerned

that we not lose him. In the end, we made a deal.

Tom felt that it was very important to give Dr. Gill the acknowledgement he deserved for his work at the Keck School. I also felt a connection to him because we were both immigrants who had moved to the United States and felt we needed to achieve great things in order to prove ourselves.

* * *

Another major personnel breakthrough came in 2013 when the Keck School recruited world-renowned brain sciences researchers Arthur Toga and Paul Thompson. They moved their Laboratory of Neuroimaging from UCLA to USC along with their entire team of 110 faculty, researchers, and talented graduate students.

Toga and Thompson were already looking for other possibilities, and the dean of the Keck School learned they were entertaining an offer from the University of Pennsylvania, which it appeared they were going to accept.

Figuring he had nothing to lose, our dean reached out to them and suggested that if they came to USC they wouldn't have to move their entire team across the country. With that many people involved, surely some had kids that they didn't want to remove from schools and, again, there was the contrast in the weather between Philadelphia and Southern California.

In the end, the story of their recruitment played well, especially at USC alumni events!

The headline in the L.A. Times read: "USC steals two star brain researchers from UCLA."[2]

Then Mark Stevens and his wife, Mary, decided to donate $50 million to support Toga and Thompson by creating the USC Mark and Mary Stevens Neuroimaging and Informatics Institute.

Suddenly, everyone knew that USC was becoming a place where the very best researchers wanted to be because we were willing to invest in the future.

* * *

In addition to "above excellent" researchers, we also needed people willing to make a major statement about the Keck School's value by supporting groundbreaking research.

One of our doctors, David Agus, recommended that I meet with Larry Ellison, the visionary co-founder and chairman of Oracle Corp. Dr. Agus had a special professional relationship with Ellison and there was a mutual respect between them.

Since this was my first time meeting Larry Ellison, I went with Brad Grey, the chairman and CEO of Paramount Pictures, who was a patient of Dr. Agus and was battling an aggressive form of cancer. Grey knew Larry because his son, David, and daughter, Megan, were both film directors and alumni of USC's School of Cinematic Arts. David and Megan were also alumni of USC's School of Cinematic Arts. I also happened to know Grey because he was an alumnus of SUNY Buffalo, where I'd received my Ph.D.

On a rainy Saturday afternoon, Brad Grey and I drove to Ellison's massive compound in Malibu. We were greeted at the door by Ellison's girlfriend. She asked us to remove our shoes, a custom Ellison had likely acquired from his fascination with Japanese culture.

We were only scheduled to meet with him for 30 minutes. But two hours later, the conversation was still going, shifting from movies to Israel to technology trends, finally winding its way back around to our proposal.

Ellison talked about how much he appreciated that his children had been able to attend USC. We were hoping for a significant gift and had decided on $200 million, which would have been one of the largest gifts ever for cancer research and treatment.

It was a big ask, even for Larry Ellison. When we came to the amount, I expected a moment of hesitation, which was normal for many donors. But Ellison immediately said he'd do it, suggesting we'd just need to negotiate the details.

After the attorneys prepared the first draft of the proposal, I had one call with Larry and the deal was done. It was one of the easiest agreements I'd ever been involved in.

⁂

A lot of press was devoted to Dr. Paul Aisen, a world-renowned Alzheimer's researcher from the University of California, San Diego, and USC didn't fare very well in those stories. There were allegations that Dr. Aisen's move to the Keck School did not follow the policies that UCSD had established.

The truth is that nobody from USC was really recruiting him in the beginning. Aisen had reached out to some members of USC's faculty, expressing his dissatisfaction with his current situation at UCSD.

At some point, the administration at the Keck School learned that he might want to leave and began to pursue him. One night, I got a call from the university's general counsel, who wanted me to know that the University of California was planning to file a lawsuit against us the next day.

They were upset because Dr. Aisen's group had more than $200 million in research grants that would move to USC if he left. I didn't really know much about Dr. Aisen until that phone call on the eve of the lawsuit.

It wasn't unusual for schools to pursue a leading faculty member. But this was a big deal that would certainly make headlines.

I wasn't president when the final deal was reached, but all of higher education was surprised when USC eventually settled the lawsuit for $50 million.

If there is a happy ending to the story, in 2022 USC trustee Dan Epstein brought the two universities back together when he and his wife, Phyllis, and the Epstein Family Foundation donated $50 million to establish the USC-UCSD Epstein Family

Alzheimer's Disease Research Collaboration.

Dan's identical twin brother had passed away from Alzheimer's, bringing a personal connection to their investment in this important area of research.

❊ ❊ ❊

While there were many positive things happening during this time, there were also challenges.

Unfortunately, the relationship between USC and the Doheny Eye Institute ended through litigation. But, fortunately, Gayle and Ed Roski quickly stepped up to donate $25 million to name the Roski Eye Institute at USC, which is ranked #1 nationally for its research.[3] The Roski family has been very philanthropic to the university. Ten years earlier, Ed Roski donated an endowed gift to name the Gayle Garner Roski School of Art and Design after his wife.

As the school's reputation rose and we expanded our medical enterprise, donors were now willing to invest in the excellence of our faculty and physicians. It felt like a completely different world from only a few short years before.

A few years after the purchase of the hospitals, I returned to USC's Health Sciences Campus to talk about the larger vision of our medical enterprise and its place in the history of Southern California.

It was a satisfying feeling to look back over the previous four years since I'd delivered the first address on our Health Sciences Campus and see how far we had come.

Although we had made great strides, there were projects that unfortunately didn't work out.

❊ ❊ ❊

During my final year as president, I worked closely with Charlie Munger on a project that could have merged Good Samaritan Hospital with our Keck Medical Center.

Several times I went to his house so the two of us could have dinner and discuss the possibilities. Good Samaritan made international news when Robert Kennedy was taken to its emergency room after being shot at the Ambassador Hotel in 1968.[4] Charlie had been chair of the hospital's board for 40 years, as well as its most generous benefactor.

In addition to major surgeries, Good Samaritan Hospital had an emergency room and delivered babies, two things that Keck Hospital did not do. L.A. County Hospital had those two services, but a partnership would create new offerings for USC. Also, it would have allowed the Keck School to establish residency and teaching programs, helping it to be less dependent on the L.A. County Hospital. In the long run, we projected that the gains for USC would have been enormous.

There were historic and business reasons for us to create a collaboration. I also saw Good Samaritan Hospital as an important part of our extended presence in downtown L.A. If you drew a line from USC to downtown, and then north to East L.A., we believed there shouldn't be any patients in that area who were driving all the way to the west side for healthcare. Everyone should be able to get the services they needed near USC.

Over a period of several months, Charlie and I discussed all of the details, including a partnership in which USC would make a commitment of $450 million over 10 years. After all, it would be much cheaper than raising $2 billion to build another hospital.

In the summer of 2018, we were still working on the details, but we had a deal. When a new administration started the following year, they rejected the idea.

Unfortunately, that was a major partnership that I think would have transformed medical care throughout the region.

❖ ❖ ❖

Beyond expansion, an important part of the renaissance for our academic medical enterprise was the beautification of the Health Sciences Campus (HSC).

But before that happened, I had to deal with the lingering negative perceptions from many people, including members of the Trojan Family. One day early in my presidency, a wealthy Trojan alumnus made a comment that stuck with me.

"No one from the west side will go there because it looks like a slum, with all those wires everywhere," he said.

He was apparently irritated by the cables that crisscrossed the HSC, supplying power to our hospitals and research labs.

To be honest, I was angry about the comment, although I didn't say anything. Instead, it made me more determined than ever to transform the HSC. It ended up being a massive effort that took nearly seven years and required an investment of $35 million.

At one point, a very prominent real estate developer from Orange County had knee surgery conducted by one of our top orthopedic surgeons. I was having a phone conversation with him, but he kept changing the subject.

"Max, every time I visit HSC to see my doctor, I notice new trees! You know I have an eye to notice these things in my business," he said. "You are changing the face of the medical campus . . . and it's beautiful."

Finally, people were beginning to notice the transformation that took so much time and effort. It also took seven years of working with the L.A. Department of Water and Power, but we eventually even found a way to put all of those "wires" underground.

And the wealthy Trojan alumnus, who had called the HSC a "slum" a few years earlier phoned me one day. He told me he had a prostate issue and his urologist had recommended that he see Dr. Gill.

"Can you please introduce me to him?" he asked.

I agreed to connect him with the best prostate doctor in the nation.

Then I hung up the phone and said to myself, "Yes . . . it's no longer a 'slum.'"

* * *

In the end, the dramatic ascent of Keck Medicine of USC would not be without its controversy. In the *Cyropaedia*, Xenophon reminds us that what separates leaders from followers is self-restraint. A major controversy that unfolded in those days reminded me of the durability of his insight.

Dean Carmen Puliafito arrived at USC in 2007. Puliafito had graduated *magna cum laude* from Harvard Medical School,[5] where he met his wife, the psychiatrist Dr. Janet Pine. He later earned an MBA from The Wharton School of the University of Pennsylvania.[6] Over time he became a gifted surgeon and even helped invent an imaging technique known as optical coherence tomography (OCT), a process that earned him awards and acclaim.[7]

But due to his lack of self-restraint, his alleged powerful addiction to methamphetamines and other drugs damaged the reputation of our medical enterprise and the entire university.

After decades of steadily rising through the ranks of leading academic medical enterprises, he would lose so much—including his job and his medical license.

However, as I mentioned earlier, when he first arrived at USC in 2007, USC's Academic Senate didn't allow background checks for tenured or tenure-track faculty. As such, USC did not perform a background check and did not know about any addiction problems when he was hired (even assuming he had any such problems at the time).

For those who suggested that I knew about his addiction, and chose to tolerate it and cover it up, the idea is outrageous—and a cheap shot to me personally.

I once fired a senior member in the office of the provost for being intoxicated at an event. I would never risk the reputation of a school for any single person, let alone someone with a dangerous addiction.

⁂ ⁂ ⁂

I first learned about the allegations of Puliafito's drug problem from an article published in the *Los Angeles Times* in July 2017.

Puliafito had chosen to resign as dean of the Keck School in March 2016 and was on sabbatical leave. In the fall of 2016—more than six months after he had resigned as dean—a member of USC's communications staff received an unsubstantiated tip about an incident at a Pasadena hotel.

When university officials contacted Puliafito about the incident, he claimed that a friend's daughter had overdosed at a local hotel and he had accompanied her to the hospital.

In March 2017, a year after Puliafito's resignation as dean, USC's administration received several detailed questions from the *Los Angeles Times*. They also sent a copy of a 911 recording from the incident at the Pasadena hotel. In that transcript, Puliafito referred to the woman in medical duress at the hotel as his girlfriend. This was the first time that any of USC's administrators had any idea the twenty-one-year-old was his girlfriend and not the daughter of a friend.

Since Puliafito was a doctor at the hospital, the 911 recording was immediately referred to the Medical Staff Services Office, an independent body with the sole authority to remove a medical doctor from patient care. The Medical Staff Services Office determined there were no existing patient care complaints and no known clinical issues.

⁂ ⁂ ⁂

On July 17, 2017, the *Los Angeles Times* published an article asserting that Puliafito not only routinely hung out with a circle of alleged criminals and addicts, but also that he used methamphetamines and other drugs with them.[8]

After this article was published, USC's Medical Staff Services Office reopened its investigation and the California State Medical Board initiated a review.

However, it's important to note that no one knew about any of Puliafito's illicit activities until after that article was published.

* * *

When USC administrators were presented with evidence of Dr. Puliafito's egregious behavior, the university immediately suspended him from all activities related to his faculty position, including patient care. We also initiated dismissal proceedings, which would strip him of his tenure.

Some may wonder why the university didn't hire private investigators to track down information on Puliafito. It was university policy never to hire private investigators to look into faculty or staff outside of our two campuses based on unsubstantiated tips. If a tip could be substantiated, then we reported the incident or person to the authorities such as the LAPD or the FBI.

Virtually all members of the Association of American Universities have the same policy.

In the fall of 2017, I raised this issue with USC's Academic Senate, asking them to examine the policy and work with the administration to institute changes if they were needed.

We even used Puliafito as an example. If USC had hired an outside investigator to track his whereabouts, there was a good chance we would have discovered what was published by the *Times* nine months later.

However, the Academic Senate never seriously conducted a serious discussion about changing this policy. And I understand it.

If the administration had the power to hire private investigators, who is to stop someone from calling in an anonymous tip on any faculty member for any reason?

And they did not want the university "spying" on the private lives of faculty off campus based on tips to the senior administration.

* * *

USC's Board of Trustees ultimately hired Debra Yang of Gibson, Dunn & Crutcher to conduct an independent investigation to see whether there were signs in Puliafito's behavior that were perhaps ignored and not reported properly to central administration, which she did. As a result of her findings, my leadership team created an action plan that revisited the university's core values, improved the campus culture, restructured a number of university operations, and revised employment policies across both of USC's campuses.

We established the Office of Professionalism and Ethics (OPE) that now serves as the centralized place for all of the university's complaint monitoring and investigation. And we created the USC Office of Ombuds Services, which provides a safe space for the entire university community to address difficult workplace situations, and for our employees on both campuses to seek impartial guidance on a range of work-related issues.

In the end, I played no role in the Board of Trustees' decision not to release the findings of Debra Yang's independent investigation of the Puliafito matter. It's a decision that lies solely within the province of the Board.

However, if they ever decide to release those findings, I would have no objection to their doing so. And I'm confident that those findings would provide further confirmation of all of the details I've listed above.

Looking back, I feel that Puliafito betrayed the university, but also his own reputation and that of his family. With his bad behavior, he embarrassed all of us.

Despite all of the work we'd done to elevate the medical enterprise, his actions fueled years of negative press from the *Los Angeles Times*, which wrote more than 100 articles just about him.

* * *

When I look back on the precarious journey of USC's medical enterprise, I'm still amazed at how much was accomplished in such a short period of time.

From 2009 to 2018, the revenue of our clinical operations grew from around $390 million to nearly $1.8 billion. When we integrated the practice plans, there were 512 medical school faculty involved. Eight years later, there were more than 1,200. We reached the point in which the Keck Hospital was doing more than 100 transplants per year, surpassing the number of the UCLA Medical Center.

By 2018, we crossed one million patient visits per year on USC's Health Sciences Campus. Medicine and health sciences were suddenly 52 percent of the entire university's budget.

There will always be critics, but I still think we achieved an incredible amount. In time, when people look back on those years, I believe they will say they were the renaissance years. During that time, we built the foundation of the academic medical enterprise, elevated USC among the best research universities in the world, and improved healthcare for millions of people throughout Southern California and the Pacific Rim.

Years later, after talking to Tom Jackiewicz, I received an email from him that summed everything up. He wrote: "We did some amazing things. We wrote a script for organizational change and growth. Those years will be the highlight of my career."

CHAPTER 21

Learner Centric

"Per varios casus, per tot discrimina rerum
tendimus in Latium; sedes ubi fata quietas
ostendunt; illic fas regna resurgere Troiae.
Durate, et vosmet rebus servate secundis."

P. VERGILIVS MARO, AENEID I.198–207

"Through so many hard straits, so many twists and turns our course
holds firm for Latium.
There Fate holds out a homeland, calm, at peace.
There the gods decree the kingdom of Troy will rise again.
Bear up. Save your strength for better times to come."[1]

VERGIL, *AENEID*, BOOK 1.198–207

While the transformation of USC's medical enterprise was monumental for the future of the university, it was also essential to enhance the academic environment for our students.

Before I became president, USC had gained attention for its extraordinary improvement in undergraduate education. This was reflected in the university's steady rise in the rankings over many years.

However, I never allowed myself or any members of my leadership team to be driven by those rankings. We understood that students and parents paid attention to the rankings when making decisions about which college to attend. But our first priority was always improving the academic quality and educational experience for our students.

Part of the problem with the rankings was that their metrics were constantly changing, especially for publications like *U.S. News and World Report*.

Then, in 2016, we got a major surprise. The *Wall Street Journal* featured USC in an article titled, "The Biggest Surprises in College Rankings."[2] There was even a picture of the USC campus below the headline.

We didn't know exactly how the *Journal* made its decisions, but we did learn that their criteria were much more comprehensive than other publications. There was no way for anyone to game the metrics because we simply didn't know what they were!

Before the story appeared, the *Journal* requested that I sit down with them for an interview. I traveled to New York and met with reporter Melissa Korn.

At the end of the interview, I asked if she could confidentially share with me where USC was going to land in the new rankings.

"No," she said curtly.

"Can you at least tell me if we will be in the top 20?" I asked.

She paused for a moment.

"Yes," she said.

I couldn't help but ask the next question.

"Is there any public university in the top 20?" I continued.

She smiled.

"No," she said.

I didn't express any emotion, but inside I was celebrating. USC had officially surpassed UCLA and UC Berkeley.

In the end, USC landed at #15, which was much higher than any of our previous national rankings.

Finally, we were about to take our rightful place among the nation's academically elite universities.

The *Journal* looked at more than 1,000 universities across North America. USC was listed ahead of prestigious institutions like Emory, Carnegie Mellon, Rice, Dartmouth, and Brown.[3]

Shortly after the rankings were published, I met on campus with Jose Antonio Mead, the Secretary of Finance and Public

Credit of Mexico.

I shared the *Journal* article with him, noting that west of Chicago, there were only three universities in the top 20: USC, Caltech and Stanford.

He smiled and said "Max, I can see how cleverly you define the geography for your bragging rights!"

* * *

Beyond the recognition in the rankings, one of the most important accomplishments during my tenure was becoming a student-centric university.

In 2010, USC was receiving about 35,000 applications for the 2,700 places in its freshman class.[4] By 2018, that number had passed 64,000—more than any other private research university in the nation.[5,6]

And it wasn't just American students that were making USC their top choice. At one point, we had students from more than 128 different countries around the world.

Niki and I also took a personal interest in our students. One of our favorite moments of each academic year was Move-In Day.

As parents ourselves, we understood the mix of excitement and emotion that comes with such a major transition for an entire family.

We loved meeting parents and students who were often surprised we were there to greet them and even take selfies with them.

We didn't have to be there. But we felt that it was important for us to get to campus early each year to welcome all of the students and families who had chosen to become part of the Trojan Family.

* * *

Personally, I also felt that it was vital for me to keep in touch with USC's students.

With all of the responsibilities of running a major university, it's very easy for a president to become detached from the heart of the institution, which is the students.

That's why I scheduled regular afternoon teas with about 25 students. We served British tea with milk, along with lemonade and cookies.

I always loved hearing what was on our students' minds. I would go around the room, asking them to tell me one good thing about the university and one thing that we needed to do better. In those sessions, I even took notes!

After the teas, I always shared the students' suggestions with the members of my cabinet and we always took them seriously.

During one of the teas, a student mentioned that there were no "yellow jacket" security guards on Sunday evenings, although the person was there every other night.

I was shocked. We promised parents that we would provide security every night of the week.

I called a senior member of my administration and shared what the student had told me.

"That's impossible," he said. "We have them seven nights a week."

A week later, I realized he hadn't called me back, so I contacted him again.

"I promise you the yellow jacket guard will be there Sunday evenings," he said. "Because of budget concerns, apparently, they decided to reduce the commitment. We'll get it fixed. Immediately."

That's what you learn from talking with students. And that's how you transform a university by listening to what they're experiencing every day.

* * *

Besides the teas, there was another way I kept in tune with students.

Soon after I became president, I met with Derek Bok, the former president of Harvard University, who offered me advice.

"Max, you'll constantly be under a lot of pressure, especially from the deans, beating up on you and on the provost. Each one of them is going to want a new building," he said. "My advice is twofold: be laser-focused on academic excellence by improving the quality of students and faculty you recruit. And second, teach an undergraduate class to keep in touch with the students."

It was good advice, which I took to heart.

I reached out to the late Professor Tom Habinek, the longtime chair of USC's Department of Classics. Together, we developed and taught a freshman class on "The Culture of Athenian Democracy."

* * *

I was always impressed with the quality of our students. And yet, we were always focused on bringing more of the best and brightest to USC.

One day Katharine Harrington was driving on the freeway when I called to talk to her about the strategy for undergraduate recruiting.

I told her that we wanted to increase the number of high school visits from around 400 to more than 2,200 every year—in all 50 states and 15 other countries.

It was a dramatic increase, with the vision of admitting at least one student from every school we visited.

"I'm going to need more people," she said on the other end of the phone.

"We can add up to 50 new positions to help you recruit nationally and internationally," I said.

There was a pause on the other end of the phone.

"Katharine? Are you there?" I asked.

Then she told me that she nearly had an accident on the freeway!

She couldn't believe we were making such a major commitment. But she also knew it was going to take a tremendous amount of work to reach our lofty goals.

I have to give Katharine credit for putting together an excellent team, led by Tim Brunold who was an exceptional dean of admissions.

There's no doubt in my mind that they were the very best in the business.

As USC was getting more and more popular, we were being forced to turn away more than 3,000 students with straight A's—and with SAT scores in the 99th percentile—every year!

One day I realized that Caltech has an annual freshman class of around 200 students. Each fall USC was enrolling 600 students with almost perfect grades and test scores. In other words, our campus had three times as many Caltech-caliber students as Caltech itself!

We also had about 1,700 freshmen with the same academic credentials as those who enrolled at Stanford.

* * *

Of course, as USC became more selective, there were some who worried that students were getting left behind. To make sure that didn't happen, we increased USC's pool of financial aid from $180 million in 2010 to $336 million per year. It was the largest amount at any university in America—and we did it with our own money![7]

We also did our best to ensure that students who took out loans graduated with manageable debt. Many people were surprised that, on average, USC students left with only $24,000 in debt and had a default rate of less than 1.6 percent.[8]

After working very hard to improve access to USC, one in seven members of our freshman class were the first members of their families to attend college. One in five were "SCions," students who had family members who had attended USC. And more than one in five were underrepresented minorities.[9]

Twenty-four percent of USC's enrolled undergraduate students received Pell Grants.[10] If you looked at the nation's private colleges and universities at the time, USC ranked second or third in Pell Grant recipients![11]

❊ ❊ ❊

Beyond Pell Grants, USC also expanded access by recruiting the very best students from community colleges. Often these students had the academic ability, but sometimes they came from challenging socioeconomic backgrounds.

Historically, these students become very loyal alumni because they always remember that USC gave them a chance. However, there were times when I faced pressure from some who thought we were admitting too many transfer students.

In fact, one year some trustees were upset that we weren't planning to increase the size of the freshman class to let in more students. Essentially, they were implying that students from community colleges may not be of the same quality as students who had attended top private schools.

"I'll tell you why," I said. "Ed Roski was a transfer student. Ron Tutor was a transfer student. Wayne Hughes was a transfer student. Ron Sugar was a transfer student."

I paused for a moment, waiting for the names of those members of the Board of Trustees to sink in.

"They become very loyal alumni and you'll see their names on faculty chairs and on buildings all across our campus," I said. "So, I rest my case."

Unlike virtually all of our private competitors, USC enrolled more than 800 students from community colleges every year.[12] And it turned out that they had exactly the same graduation rates as the rest of the university—92 percent![13]

❊ ❊ ❊

Eventually, with all of the improvements we were making, the composition of USC's freshman class began to change.

In the past, 60 percent of the university's students came from California. We wanted to become more of an international university, with about 14 percent of our students coming from other countries.

There was something else that set USC apart from other research universities. At the time, USC had 6,000 students majoring or minoring in our arts schools. In all likelihood, it was the largest number of art students at any research university in America.[14]

With students from so many different backgrounds flocking to USC, one of my most important responsibilities as president was building on the traditions established by those who preceded me.

While we wanted to honor the university's enduring traditions, we also wanted to create new traditions for the entire university community. One of those new traditions helped us reach a group that had rarely been recognized in the past.

When I first became president in 2010, Chairman Ed Roski and University Professor Kevin Starr came to me with an idea of a veterans appreciation dinner. As veterans themselves, they knew that USC and Notre Dame were the only two private universities in the nation to maintain their relationship with ROTC during the 1960s and 1970s.[15]

The university was home to more than 1,100 ROTC members and veteran students, who were studying under benefits of the Yellow Ribbon program.

In preparing and hosting our veterans appreciation dinners, one of the very first people I engaged with was General David H. Petraeus.

I first met him in Washington D.C. at a dinner when he was the Director of the CIA.

Peter Bergen, a national security analyst for CNN, noted that, "Historians will likely judge David Petraeus to be the most effective American military commander since Eisenhower. He was, after all, the person who, more than any other, brought Iraq back from the brink of total disaster after he assumed command of U.S. forces there in 2007."[16]

Military historian Victor Davis Hanson also had high praise for General Petraeus in his book, *The Savior Generals*.

* * *

In addition to the veterans appreciation dinner, we also created a new tradition for incoming students.

Before I became president, USC had hosted "welcome week," which held several indoor events to welcome new students and families.

We decided to design a new event in Alumni Park, a beginning "bookend" for students' academic careers, which would come full circle when they earned their diplomas and participated in their final commencement.

In August 2010, we held the first ever New Student Convocation ceremony. Like commencement, this new convocation was steeped in tradition, with participants dressed in academic regalia and members of the administration, faculty, and the student body officially welcoming our incoming students.

Over the next few years, we also held a convocation to welcome transfer students at the beginning of the spring semester.

And we found new traditions that elevated our already impressive commencement ceremonies.

Because commencement represented the closing of one chapter and the beginning of another, we decided to add a "charge" to our graduating students. The charge was chosen from the *Aeneid*, Virgil's great epic describing the journeys and destinies of the mighty Trojans, and which was read at the ceremony in English, Latin, and ancient Greek.

In 2011, USC presented Girish Karnad, the famous Indian playwright, with an honorary degree. After seeing all of the pageantry and tradition of our commencement ceremony, Karnad said, "Max, you do it as well as Oxford!"

Another year my provost sent me an email that read: "I had several law students come up and say they really liked the readings from Virgil in Latin and Greek—one said she cried."

⁂ ⁂ ⁂

For me and Niki, we always felt that the university's students were like our own children. Whether they came from Southern California or distant regions around the world, we believed it was our responsibility to provide them with the very best educational experience possible.

We would soon learn, however, that for every day of joy there are also days of tragedy. And those days would test the resolve and resilience of the entire Trojan Family.

CHAPTER 22

Confronting Tragedy

«Κἀνακωκύει πικρᾶς
ὄρνιθος ὀξὺν φθόγγον, ὡς ὅταν κενῆς
εὐνῆς νεοσσῶν ὀρφανὸν βλέψῃ λέχος·»

ΣΟΦΟΚΛΈΟΥΣ ἈΝΤΙΓΌΝΗ, 423–25

"She cried out bitterly,
the shrill cry of a bird when it sees its home empty,
its nest stripped of young."[1]

SOPHOCLES, *ANTIGONE*, LINES 423–25

There are many wonderful things about leading an organization. But there are also many unexpected events that happen and you must simply respond as well as possible. I've often described these crises as a "torpedo into the mothership of the university."

I'd only been president of USC for 18 months when the first of three tragic incidents struck the university.

According to police reports, at around 1:00 a.m. on April 11, 2012, a tragedy occurred that would horrify the entire campus community.[2] In a few hours, the Trojan Family would wake up to a changed world and begin the mourning process together.

Police and others later informed me that two Chinese electrical engineering students—Ming Qu and Ying Wu—had been shot nearly a mile northwest of USC's University Park Campus.

They were both rushed downtown to California Hospital Medical Center, but it was too late. They were pronounced dead on arrival.[3]

It was a terrible and tragic event, felt deeply throughout our campus community, resonating throughout the City of Los Angeles, across the nation, and around the world.[4,5]

Like everyone, I was shocked and saddened by the horrible events of April 11. But my respect and appreciation for the city's leadership grew enormously. The mayor of Los Angeles and chief of LAPD stood side-by-side with USC during a moment of great crisis.

They assigned 35 detectives to the case, who quickly were on the trail of the killers. During the robbery, one of the suspects had stolen a cell phone that belonged to one of our graduate students. Police traced the phone signal,[6] leading to the arrest of Bryan Barnes, 20, and Javier Bolden, 19, just over a month later.

Both were later charged with two counts of murder, as well as attempted murder for another incident in December 2011 that allegedly injured a man and a woman at a party in South Los Angeles.[7]

Barnes eventually received life in prison, while Bolden is serving three consecutive life terms without parole, along with an additional 22 years.[8]

However, on the morning of April 11, 2012, the tragedy captured the headlines of newspapers from Boston to London to Shanghai.[9,10,11] At USC, we immediately reached out to the family and brought them to Los Angeles.

A few days later, it just happened that there was an Asian American Society event at the Langham Hotel in Pasadena, honoring me and the UCLA Chancellor. I agonized over my speech for that evening, finally deciding that it had to be a eulogy for our two slain students.

Later, two prominent people came up to me and said that they were wondering what I could possibly say, but that giving a eulogy in honor of our students was exactly the right thing to do.

On campus, the dean of religious life brought together the entire university community and quickly planned a memorial. Thousands of people attended the moving service in the Shrine

Auditorium.[12]

As I approached the podium at the memorial service, I bowed for five seconds at a 45-degree angle before the pictures of Ming and Ying. It was an image that would travel the world on the front pages of newspapers across China.[13]

As parents, Niki and I could only imagine the incredible sorrow the families of such young people felt. It was a heart-wrenching loss and I was determined to help bring something positive out of it.

* * *

As our community was experiencing grief and sadness, we were also dealing with another potential crisis. On April 1—only 10 days before the tragedy—acceptance letters had gone out to USC's next freshman class. The deadline for students to respond was May 15.

Immediately, we started receiving phone calls and emails from families who had USC as their first choice, telling us that they had changed their minds because of security concerns.

Throughout the process, I was in close contact with Katharine Harrington, vice-president of admissions and planning.

"You're my admiral on this one," I said. "Deploy all of your reserve strategies. Hopefully, we can still make the class without lowering academic quality."

That year we had more than 1,000 students, who filed appeals on their admissions decisions. In previous years, we would have admitted around 25 of those cases. In 2012, we admitted hundreds of students who were equally qualified.

We also learned something very interesting. We discovered that "SCions"—the children and grandchildren of USC alumni who had applied for admission—had no concerns about the safety and security of our campus.

It was a reminder that even in moments of crisis, the Trojan

Family always stands by the university. And I never forgot that.

⁂ ⁂ ⁂

After the tragic events of April 11, we unveiled a host of new security measures to enhance safety and held a series of meetings with the mayor's office. I even offered for USC to cover the cost of security improvements.

In those discussions, USC agreed to add more DPS security officers, extend the hours of yellow-jacketed "security ambassadors," increase the number of security cameras and the people monitoring them, and expand the service area of USC's Campus Cruisers, which were free for our students.

We also made safety education mandatory for all incoming international graduate students, just like it was for undergraduate students.

The LAPD came to the table with several ideas, including a detective specifically dedicated to the area, adding 30 police officers to the Southwest Division, and adopting a computerized system for preventative policing.

By working together, the LAPD and Clery crime statistics showed that crimes were reduced significantly on campus and in the neighborhood.[14]

⁂ ⁂ ⁂

For more than a year, USC thankfully returned to normal, a kind of quiet tranquility falling over the campus. But on Halloween night—October 31, 2012—I received a call that gunshots had been fired outside the Tutor Campus Center.[15]

From midnight until 6:00 a.m., I received updates every 30 minutes from an officer at the scene. But it would take days to unravel the details of what exactly had happened that night.

It turns out that it all started with an off-campus promoter.

A USC student group was holding a Halloween party on campus.

The campus was mostly empty as it normally was on a Wednesday evening. The party was supposed to be limited to USC students but someone had hired a third-party promoter, who sent out an invitation through social media to the entire city of Los Angeles.[16]

Soon hundreds of people descended on campus, looking for something to do on Halloween.

The trouble began before they even got to the ballroom of the Tutor Campus Center, where a line had formed outside. In that line, members of two rival gangs noticed each other. Someone pulled a gun and shots were fired.[17]

The terrified USC students joined everyone else, running for their lives, creating chaos on campus.

As soon as I learned about the incident, I called USC's DPS Chief Carey Drayton. But he didn't answer! I kept getting a voicemail.

Finally, I learned that one of Drayton's deputies, John Thomas, was on the scene with LAPD. I was able to reach Thomas, who gave me valuable updates every 30 minutes for the next six hours.

In between his updates, I was also in close contact with the LAPD.

At 3:00 a.m., when the chaos began to clear, I called Thomas again.

"JT, I need to know if we have any USC students injured," I said. "It's really important because we will have to notify their parents."

"I have the LAPD South Division Chief right next to me," said Thomas. "Let me put him on the line."

The South Division Chief offered to send two officers to the emergency room to find out.

I thanked him and prayed that the Trojan Family wouldn't have to mourn together again.

Half an hour later, JT called me back.

"They're not USC students," he said.

Although I was troubled that anyone was injured on our campus, I was relieved our students weren't involved.

It had already been a long night for John Thomas, but I told him that I had one more favor to ask.

"What is it?" he asked.

"Can you work with DPS and LAPD to make sure that the crime scene has been cleared by 5:00 a.m.?" I asked. "I don't want students coming to class and seeing crime scene tape, or blood on the sidewalks, and taking pictures of it and putting it on social media."

"Got it," JT said.

"We've never had a crime scene near Tommy Trojan in the middle of the campus," I said.

"Consider it done, President Nikias," said JT.

Over the course of that evening, I realized Thomas was a humble servant, who did his job and never asked for acknowledgment.

A few months later, he was appointed the new chief of USC's Department of Public Safety. And I will say that I believe he was the very best chief USC has ever had. And I was happy for him when he was appointed as UCLA's chief of police in 2024.[18]

* * *

The Halloween incident couldn't have happened at a worse time.

For several months, we had planned to host the very first Widney Society Gala, a gathering of the most loyal and generous philanthropists supporting the university. We were expecting a "who's who" of the most prominent people from around Southern California and other areas.

The gala was scheduled for the next day, and only a few hundred yards from the previous night's crime scene.

By the time I spoke at 8:30 p.m. that evening, I'd barely slept in 24 hours. Despite all of the uncertainty of the previous day, several people reassured me of their commitment to the ongoing mission of the university—to serve the next generation of students, who we were entrusted to educate and protect.

The killings in 2011 had happened off campus. But this incident had happened at the heart of our university. We would need to make even more changes to protect our students, faculty, and staff, even if some of those decisions would be unpopular.

* * *

To begin with, we added extra security measures, requiring all visitors to campus events to show identification.

We decided to close the campus in the evenings to events, which I believed drew unfair criticism. But it would have been incredibly expensive to provide security every day of the week throughout the year.

Instead, we hired a security consulting firm run by former LAPD Chief Bill Bratton, which did a thorough assessment of security measures at USC, as well as in the "bubble" area that immediately surrounded the campus.

We also paid for partnerships with ridesharing services Uber and Lyft, providing transportation for our students in an extended area that stretched from Normandy to Hill, and Exposition to the 10 Freeway.

From sunrise to sunset, our students could take Uber or Lyft free of charge, as long as they were located within this area.

Then one day, Chief Thomas came to me with a concern.

"President Nikias, I found out that when they're off duty several of our DPS officers are driving for Uber and Lyft inside the bubble," he said.

"Chief, it's okay," I said. "Encourage *all* of your DPS officers to do that. They know the area, they've been background checked, and we trust them. Why not?"

We were just trying to solve a challenge to keep our students safe. But we ended up being the very first university in the nation to establish a transportation service for our students in that way.

A few years later, other universities noticed what we were doing and copied us. But we had to be innovative because we needed to find a solution quickly.

In the end, all of the extra security we provided was not free, of course. Our security budget increased to $50 million per year, and I suggested that USC pay for the increased partnerships with the LAPD to provide greater security on and around campus.[19]

But as parents, it was also personal for me and Niki.

Every August, before students returned for classes, we toured all of USC's security procedures.

We always started in the command center, and then Chief Thomas would give us a driving tour of the community surrounding the campus, pointing out the issues we faced and the steps we'd taken to address those challenges.

Niki and I were intimately involved in these decisions because our own daughters attended USC and we felt that protecting all students was like looking after our own children.

During one tour, Chief Thomas mentioned that DPS officers were assigned to watch for suspicious activity on surveillance cameras. But at the time, we only had two people doing that.

"You know, JT, I really think you need more general operators. You don't have nearly enough," I said. "You need four to six people on duty all of the time."

He agreed. But, of course, everything costs money. So the first thing we needed to do was understand what we really needed.

* * *

Through some of the university's contacts, we scheduled a tour of Las Vegas. Casinos had years of experience in using technology to enhance safety.

From what we learned there, we began to build our own model of what 24/7 security would look like on our campus. We learned about how to use cameras and analytics, and we also realized that we needed people with entirely different skillsets.

In my conversations with Chief Thomas, we realized that DPS officers on patrol had a different type of background and training than people who were watching activity on a camera all day. This realization led us to think about what abilities were needed for these new positions. And we found those skills in young people who were interested in gaming and computers.

We ended up building specifications for new positions based on the idea that you're on patrol, but in a virtual video environment rather than an officer making rounds in the neighborhood.

I think it was a pioneering approach to the challenges we faced, and several other universities later placed similar technologies on their campuses.

* * *

Sadly, we learned that no matter how many officers are deployed or how many technologies are implemented, tragedy can still strike at the heart of a community.

In the summer of 2014, at around 12:45 a.m. on a Thursday morning, a Chinese graduate student named Xinran Ji was robbed and violently assaulted.[20]

He managed to make it to his apartment building, which was only a block away on 30th Street. Later that morning, he was found deceased in his apartment.[21]

Police were able to quickly reconstruct what had happened because it was reported that there was a trail of a "significant amount of blood," leading from his apartment back to 29th Street and Orchard Avenue.[22]

Although the assault happened off camera, police used

technology to reconstruct the awful events of that night.

At one point, I was told that it looks like he's having trouble walking, weaving his way down the sidewalk. The command center didn't know he'd been assaulted because they didn't see it happen on camera.

When all of the clues were pieced together, it eventually led to the arrest and conviction of four suspects.[23]

Chief Thomas remembers meeting with an LAPD detective and the parents of Xinran Ji.

When detectives showed the parents the suspects' pictures, Xinran Ji's mother pulled out a pen and crossed off each of their faces with a large "X."

Without a word, she communicated both her loss and her emotions.

It was another shocking tragedy for Xinran Ji's family and the entire Trojan Family.

It also caused us to change our protocols again. From that moment on, any time our camera operators saw a student walking alone at night, they followed them on video until they returned home safely.

Although the headlines often made it seem otherwise, by 2016 our massive investments in security led USC to be ranked "safer" than UCLA, Cal Berkeley, UCSB, and many other urban universities in terms of annual crime incidents.[24]

CHAPTER 23

The Gothic Revival

«Μετὰ μεγάλων δὲ σημείων καὶ οὐ δή τοι
ἀμάρτυρόν γε τὴν δύναμιν παρασχόμενοι
τοῖς τε νῦν καὶ τοῖς ἔπειτα θαυμασθησόμεθα.»

ΘΟΥΚΥΔΊΔΟΥ ἹΣΤΟΡΊΑΙ, 2.41.4
ΠΕΡΙΚΛΈΟΥΣ ΕΠΙΤΆΦΙΟΣ

"Mighty indeed are the marks and monuments of our empire that we have left. Future ages will wonder at us, as the present age wonders at us now."[1]

THUCYDIDES, *HISTORY OF THE PELOPONNESIAN WAR*, BOOK 2, 2.41.4, FUNERAL ORATION OF PERICLES

There is something about stepping onto a university campus that transports you to another world. Maybe it's the elegant architecture that connects centuries of human history, or the optimism of people who are pursuing their passions, but I've always felt that the sanctuary of the university brings order to the chaos that often exists in the outside world.

I believe a university should evoke a strong, positive emotion in everyone who sets foot on campus. It needs to be an ideal environment for living and learning, a place to create new knowledge and offer excellent patient care, and that the beauty of our campuses should be exciting and uplifting.

I was determined to give the entire university the branding it deserved in both physical and digital spaces. We needed to make sure all of our logos and designs worked online and on smart phones. And we needed to create a new identity system that would provide our schools and units with flexibility, but also could be used across all types of media. That design had to be consistent across digital spaces, as well as on physical signage on our two campuses.

We also had an expedited timeline. We completed the branding redesign and launched it in less than six months. I suggested that the new logo should feature the shield, which appears on the university seal.

I loved the idea of the shield because I felt it was a great symbol for USC. On the university seal, the shield featured a representation of the sun shining over waves from the Pacific Ocean.

I believed the image set us apart from other universities—as a symbol of strength, but also a traditional academic symbol. And it also depicted one of our greatest assets—our location in "sunny" Southern California.

* * *

With the branding efforts underway, we needed to find someone who could lead the university's physical transformation.

We recruited Lloyd Silberstein. I really liked his personality, but I also appreciated his past experiences and entrepreneurial mindset.

At one point, he had started his own construction company, so I knew he understood how to watch costs and meet deadlines. It was a skillset that we would need with so many construction projects in the planning stages.

During my early conversations with Lloyd, we talked about dramatically changing the hardscape and landscape on both campuses, adding plants, trees, shrubs, and flowers, as well as several new fountains.

In the same spirit of the Academy described by Aristophanes in *The Clouds*,[2] we planted 2,000 trees on the UPC, including an olive tree grove at the Trousdale entrance from Jefferson Boulevard!

On the HSC, we added 400 new trees, as well as several shrubs and flowers. On both campuses, we built new fountains, with the most prominent ones in the UPC's central plaza and at the USC Village.

We also rebuilt all of the campus entrances, pathways, and open spaces, adding red brick designs to give everything a consistent look that matched the Italian Romanesque style of the buildings.

During our large-scale beautification efforts, I received many letters from faculty, staff, and alumni about the changing looks of the campuses.

One older alumnus from Bakersfield wrote to me: "I visited and toured the campus before a football game, and I got tears in my eyes to see how it has changed."

And yet, with all of the positive responses, I also got a very nasty letter from a senior professor at USC's School of Architecture, accusing me of planting too many trees on the periphery of the campus. He insisted that my intent was to "block the neighborhood out."

I responded that I did want to block the view of the many cars passing by on the city streets, but it wasn't to hide the view of the neighborhood. I wanted the campus to be place of refuge, a physical and intellectual sanctuary in the same tradition as the original Academy. But it was proof that no matter what you do, you can't please everyone!

* * *

For such a major physical transformation, we knew we needed a consistent "look" and style that connected the university of the present to the great history and traditions of USC.

We asked the Board of Trustees' campus planning committee to approve our use of Collegiate Gothic architecture in all of our new buildings.

I explained how the modern university is a brainchild of the intellectual movement of the Italian Renaissance. The classic architecture makes everything look older. In higher education, the perception is that "the older a university is, the higher its academic quality."

I once hosted a lunch at USC in which a former Congressman was a guest.

"My God, Max," he said. "Your campus looks like Yale." I shared the story later with Governor Arnold Schwarzenegger, who smiled and said, "You made USC a Renaissance child!"

* * *

Over an eight-year period, from 2010 to 2018, the physical transformation of both of USC's campuses was unprecedented. We expanded the square footage by 30 percent, adding a total of 20 new buildings.

We also changed the living and learning environment for our students by adding new residential and honors colleges.

Only a few years earlier, USC was viewed mainly as a commuter campus. But we helped usher in the transformation to a truly residential university.

With our residential colleges we also revived an educational model that has existed since medieval times, a moment when the essence of the university revolved around the relationship between students and faculty.

* * *

For many years, we also wanted undergraduate students at the USC Marshall School of Business to have a place of their own. Thanks to a Marshall School alumnus Frank Fertitta and his wife, Jill, we were able to make that happen. Their generosity helped create Fertitta Hall, which has an iconic, cathedral-like design.[3]

One afternoon, during the construction, Father Michael Engh, an American Jesuit priest and former president of Santa Clara University, happened to be visiting campus.

When he got to my office, he smiled and said, "Max, are you building a church at the southeast corner of the campus? It looks beautiful."

"Father Michael, our business school can make it available for mass on Sundays," I said. "But for a fee!"

He laughed.

* * *

Another example is the Annenberg School for Communication and Journalism.[4]

To keep up with demand for the school's popular curriculum, we envisioned a new Wallis Annenberg building at the very heart of campus, in the middle of the four oldest structures at USC.

I went to Wallis' house for lunch to show her renderings of the building and get her "blessing" on the architectural style. I didn't know that behind my back some of Annenberg's senior faculty had been lobbying her, saying that the building should reflect 21st century architecture to make it consistent with the teaching of modern journalism.

When I displayed the renderings, they were in USC's traditional Collegiate Gothic style. I could sense her hesitation and she brought up the idea of having a more modern look. I explained to her the significance of the building's location at the center of campus and the importance of the matching architectural style.

Before I could finish my pitch, Wallis' partner, Kris, walked in and saw the large renderings on display.

"Oh, my God," she said. "This is a beautiful building, Wallis. Gorgeous!"

And that was that.

Wallis turned to me and said, "I'm okay with whatever you want, Max! Just make sure there's state-of-the-art, hands-on media technology inside the building to help students learn."

* * *

While we worked very hard over many years to transform USC's physical and digital identity, our biggest project was just getting started. It would be an architectural masterpiece, and we would call it the USC Village.

We envisioned it as a medieval Tuscan village redefined for the 21st century. It would be a place offering residential colleges for undergraduate students, as well as retail and dining establishments that would give it a sense of community that could only be found in a historic town square.

At the time, it was the largest development project in the history of USC and in the history of South Los Angeles. It will likely remain the largest single project undertaken by USC for the next 50 years.

* * *

When I became president in 2010, I inherited the Village project where several private developers, including two trustees, who were interested in building a shopping center that would include student apartments. However, when I looked at the future, I really believed it would be a mistake for USC to lease the space to private developers.

Although having private developers build student apartments would alleviate some of the university's student housing issues, apartments alone don't give the feeling of a learning community. So I started having brainstorming conversations with my senior leadership team. I wanted us to be prepared to make the case that the area should be developed as an extension of the campus.

To make that happen, I first had to convince the finance committee and later the entire board that this vision for the project was the right one for the university.

But I had to be more persuasive than normal. Remember, I was making my pitch for the largest project in the university's history during the uncertain aftermath of the Great Recession.

I told the board there were two "motherships" for investments at USC: the medical enterprise and student quality, which provided tuition revenues.

We'd already made a major investment by buying the hospitals. However, by far our biggest and most important mothership was tuition revenue.

Although USC had greatly improved its selectivity in recent decades, the university had done very little in 23 years to expand residential housing for students.

Then I pointed out the challenges that USC faced if we failed to take action. As the university climbed in the academic rankings, our competition for students was changing. We were now competing with the likes of Stanford, UC Berkeley, UCLA, NYU, Cornell, Northwestern, Penn, Harvard, and other top tier universities.

To attract the very best students, we had to do much more than just offer full scholarships. We needed to offer a very special residential experience.

Then I noted the investments some of our competitors were making. Harvard was investing $1 billion in renovating residential halls, even with a much smaller student body. Stanford had announced that upgrading and building new residential halls was a top priority. UCLA had recently added four new residence halls with 1,800 beds.[5,6]

I hammered home the point that elite research universities compete on the quality of the experience, not on cost. And USC was badly in need of a unique, residential undergraduate experience.

The only place for the university to expand—over at least the next 50 years—would be the USC Village.

I told the trustees this was their moment to make a change that would impact not only the next freshman class, but also generations of the future.

Then I presented a plan that allowed us to borrow from ourselves by using the working capital that I had put in place and through our fundraising campaign.

Fortunately, both the finance committee and the entire board could see the vision and gave us the green light to pursue the next steps in the process.

* * *

Lloyd Silberstein and I had several brainstorming sessions, ultimately deciding to focus on the USC Village and put all other construction projects momentarily on hold. We also had several conversations about the basic principles that would help us plan and design this massive project.

"The safety and security of our students has to be of paramount importance," I said.

"Yes," Lloyd agreed. "Then the USC Village shouldn't become a destination for people throughout the L.A. basin. We don't want to make it like L.A. Live, which is just a few miles away."

"Okay," I said. "Then it shouldn't have a movie theater or a hotel either. Because those things would make it a destination, which would require extra security."

"And USC already has a hotel," said Lloyd. "Right next to the Galen Center on Figueroa."

"I agree," I said. "The Village should be a natural extension of the campus. And that means it should have the same security measures as the rest of the campus. Our priority should be students first."

"True," said Lloyd. "But we want to make sure the retail, the restaurants, and the shopping are open to students and the neighborhood."

"Rather than apartments, I think the design should be focused on residential colleges," I said. "It makes it more of an extension of the academic environment. A great place for living and learning."

"So how do we create that sense of connection in the design?" Lloyd asked.

"Well, we can have the residential colleges from the second to the fifth floors, and then the restaurants and retail could be on the ground floor," I said.

"Then you connect it all with courtyards, gathering spaces, and study areas, giving it a sense of community," said Lloyd.

"Exactly," I said. "But we also can't forget the security."

"So, the residential colleges require fingerprint ID's to enter," Lloyd said.

"Right, in the lobby of each of the residential colleges," I agreed.

I paused for a moment to consider the architecture.

"We want the Village to last for more than 100 years," I said. "We need to give it a timeless look, so we can't build it with wood frames. If we did that, we'd have to tear it all down and rebuild in a few decades."

"If we build it to last, it also saves the university money in the long run," said Lloyd.

"We also need to pay attention to the sustainability," I said. "It's important to our students and we want to make sure we get that right."

"Maybe we put the parking underground?" Lloyd suggested.

"How much will that cost?" I asked.

"It won't be cheap," Lloyd said. "But that means we could use all of the surface space for either buildings or green space."

After several brainstorming sessions, we took the designs to the Board of Trustees. They finally agreed that the USC Village was the right project at the right time.

* * *

With the board's approval, we now had to get the master plan approved by the L.A. City Council.

It was an ambitious plan that laid out a vision for the next 20 years, including not only the development of the USC Village, but also commitments the university would make to the surrounding community, like investing in affordable housing.

As with all major undertakings, challenges arose along the way.

USC had agreed to do 100 percent union work. But when it came to providing funding for affordable housing for the local community, the City kept moving the bar.

In the beginning, both sides agreed USC would pay $2 million. When we went to the next meeting, the amount had raised to $4 million. At another meeting, they asked for $6 million. One day we learned the amount had ballooned to $20 million.

Trustee Ron Tutor, who did a great job as our chief negotiator, exploded.

"No more than $10 million," he yelled. "If you don't like that, we'll see you in court."

Then Ron stormed out of the room.

Apparently, the City's negotiators had read that Columbia University had paid the City of New York $20 million for affordable housing for one of their building projects.

First of all, our project was going to have a much larger impact on the area and the local economy than the one in New York. Second, Columbia's endowment was nearly three times larger than USC's.

While we wanted to do the right thing, we were being asked to increase our contributions by 10 times in just a few months.

It didn't seem right.

⁂ ⁂ ⁂

Niki and I were on layover at the tiny Twin Falls, Idaho, airport when my cell phone rang. It was the mayor of Los Angeles at the time, Antonio Villaraigosa.

The airport terminal was so small that I stepped outside to keep the conversation private. It was snowing and the wind was freezing.

"I can't get the final approval through the City Council unless USC commits $20 million for affordable housing," said Villaraigosa.

I argued that it was too much, and I expressed my frustration that the amount kept rising.

"And now, Antonio, you are asking for $20 million?" I asked.

"Well, Columbia University had a similar project and committed $20 million to New York City," said Villaraigosa.

"I'm very familiar with that project," I said. "But Columbia committed a $20 million, zero percent interest loan to New York City. Is this what you want?"

"No, no, no, it can't be a loan," said Villaraigosa. "Look, Max, I can't get it through unless USC makes this commitment."

I was freezing and I had to think quickly on my feet.

"Antonio, I'll agree to $20 million in affordable housing under three conditions," I said.

"Okay, I'm listening," he said.

"First, I would like the Village to be fenced and have the same security measures as the rest of the campus. That means nobody enters from 10:00 p.m. to 6:00 a.m., unless they show an ID and tell the guards the purpose of their visit."

"I'm okay with that," said Villaraigosa.

"Second, I have to appeal to you as a father," I said. "As part of our local hiring, we don't want to include convicted felons going through remediation. It makes the parents nervous."

"Consider it done," he said.

"Finally, I would agree to increase the affordable housing

from $10 million to $20 million, but the final $10 million should be paid in two installments. One on the 10th anniversary, and the second on the 20th anniversary, of the signing of the development agreement."

"I'm okay with that," he said. "However, I want the first $10 million in cash right away, with the signing of the agreement."

"Antonio, it will be $10 million in cash, but only *after* we receive the building permits for the Village."

It was so cold that I didn't know if I could stand it any longer. But his next words warmed my heart.

"We have a deal, my Greek brother!" he said.

In the end, although it was a hefty amount to pay, I think the deal was worth it. I had enormous respect for Mayor Villaraigosa and he clearly understood the importance of USC to Los Angeles.

It was a great moment for all of us. But we also knew there were still several hurdles that we would need to overcome before the Village became a reality.

* * *

When it came time for final approval by the Los Angeles City Council, I trusted that Mayor Villaraigosa would keep his word and deliver on what he'd promised.

For that reason, I chose not to attend the day of the final vote. Although we were confident we had done everything right, I was cautious not to be overconfident.

City Councilman Bernard Parks, who is a USC alumnus, had voiced his opposition throughout the entire process. But on the day of the vote, his fellow City Councilmember Jan Perry persuaded him to reconsider, noting that his would be the only vote against the project.

He only needed to look at the chambers and the rotunda of City Hall, which were packed with more than 1,100 members of the local community.[7] They were elated that the Village would bring new businesses and 12,000 new jobs to the area.[8]

In the end, the project was approved with a unanimous vote of 15-0, which brought a massive cheer from the gathered crowd.[9]

❊ ❊ ❊

A very important part of creating a better environment for our students was the Village Dining Hall, which is located inside McCarthy Honors College.

Inside the dining hall, the most distinctive feature is the large, colorful stained-glass windows.

It's true that some would later call it "Harry Potter Hall,"[10] but I've had so many compliments from students and parents who understand that the look brings the great tradition of the academic hall of the past to current students.

❊ ❊ ❊

The early morning of August 17, 2017, seemed like the beginning of any other academic year at USC. Thousands of people gathered in Alumni Park for the New Student Convocation.

That morning my mind was on the many students and parents who filled the park with hope and optimism for a new year. But I was also reflecting on how the ceremony served as a bridge between the university's past and its future.

Just a few hundred yards away, that future awaited the incoming class of 2,700 freshman, who would be the first to call the beautiful USC Village their home.

I also remembered how, in 1885, eight USC graduates had gathered together in the office of Widney Alumni House—the university's very first building—which still stood only a minute away in the other direction.

When those former students gathered to form an alumni

association, they wouldn't have believed USC would grow from a single building into a research university with global reach and influence. And they couldn't have imagined that we were about to unveil the finishing touches on the largest construction project in the history of South Los Angeles.

As I finished my speech welcoming everyone, the Trojan Marching Band led the thousands of attendees out of Alumni Park and across Trousdale Parkway.

The heat rose from the streets as more than 10,000 people crossed Jefferson Boulevard into a new world that represented decades of dreams and years of construction.

As the platform party took their seats, I thought about how the USC Village had been a labor of love that began seven years earlier, from the very first day I became president.

The project benefited from the hard work and the dedication of so many people, including those involved in construction, university relations, neighborhood relations, student affairs, and hospitality services. In many ways, it took a village to construct the USC Village.

That morning I ended my remarks with a line I had written in the margins of my speech:

"This village gives us 1,000 years of history we don't have!"

* * *

In the end, after all of our efforts, the USC Village added 1.25 million square feet of space, six large buildings for housing, a beautiful dining hall, and a new fitness center.[11, 12] We had estimated the USC Village would cost $700 million. Thanks to the cost-saving strategies of Lloyd Silberstein and his deputy Willy Marsh, it came in at $640 million. It was the best kind of construction project—on time and under budget.

It also had something else for students and the larger university community. It was a figure that had been covered by a large cloth during the opening ceremony.

To the audience, it had been a mystery for most of the morning. But I was about to reveal a new addition to the Trojan Family.

CHAPTER 24

The Rise of Hecuba

« Ἐν τοῖς κακοῖς γὰρ ἀγαθοὶ σαφέστατοι
φίλοι· τὰ χρηστὰ δ' αὔθ' ἕκαστ' ἔχει φίλους.
εἰ δ' ἐσπάνιζες χρημάτων, ὁ δ' εὐτύχει.»

ΕΫΡΙΠΊΔΟΥ ἙΚΆΒΗ, 1226–28

"Hard times prove the honest friendship of good men,
while prosperity always has friends."[1]

EURIPIDES, *HECUBA*, LINES 1226–28

A large crane carefully removed the drape from the figure near the stage. White doves fluttered into the air. Fireworks popped and sparkled. And cardinal and gold confetti rained down on the excited crowd.[2]

As the crowd celebrated, I thought about how the sculpture symbolized more than just a new work of art on our campus, but also a new moment in the history of the university.

For more than 85 years, an iconic figure had been part of USC's campus. Thousands of students, parents, alumni, and visitors have taken their pictures with perhaps the most recognizable member of the Trojan Family—Tommy Trojan.

But on this day, Tommy Trojan finally had a companion—a beautiful bronze sculpture of Hecuba, the mythical Queen of Troy.

As we were planning the USC Village, we realized that there was a transformation happening throughout the academic community. We wanted to find a new symbol of female leadership. After much research and debate, we decided that the best symbol would be Hecuba.

We were very fortunate to have been introduced to a brilliant sculptor named Christoper Slatoff. Trained in abstract and conceptual art, Slatoff had made a name for himself with fine art and public sculptures.[3]

After taking a tour of his studio, it was clear that he had the skill and the background to bring this beautiful new sculpture to life. Over a period of months, we had a series of meetings, thinking about what the sculpture needed to convey, and I had the good fortune of being part of the creative process.

In the summer of 2015, Niki even contributed to the project. We were taking a tour of the Acropolis Museum in Athens when we reached the exhibit of the Caryatids of the Erechtheion, considered one of the most complex buildings on the Acropolis.

We noticed the beautiful hair on a figure etched in the stone. I took a picture and texted it back to Slatoff, writing, "Christopher, this should be the hair of Hecuba!"

And he was able to do exactly that. He even used a live model, an African American actress who was in the movie *Straight Outta Compton*.

However, the most important part of the process was talking about the philosophy behind the sculpture. I suggested that USC needed not only a symbol of female leadership, but also a symbol of "diversity." And not just the incredible diversity represented by our student body, but also the intellectual diversity embodied by our many academic disciplines. Slatoff had the great idea to morph the faces from six different ethnicities into the countenance of Hecuba.

Our philosophical conversation was deep and wide-ranging, exploring the ideas that would soon be captured in bronze.

"When I shared the ideas of a female monument of Troy, a lot of people asked me, 'Why not Helen?'" I said to Slatoff. "Homer refers to 1,000 ships for Helen, but the fact of the matter is that Helen wasn't truly a Trojan. Hecuba is a mythical figure, the legendary Queen of Troy, who was married to King Priam and had

19 children. So, I feel that it's a poetic coincidence that today USC has 19 independent schools, just like the children of Hecuba."

My ideas immediately resonated with Slatoff, who shared his own inspirations.

"My major influence—in how I saw and designed Hecuba—is this marvelous Greek vase," said Slatoff. "Both Hecuba and her husband, King Priam, are dressing their son Hector in his armor. For me, the idea of USC as an entity that gives you the protection, the knowledge, everything you need to go out into life and succeed. That's a marvelous metaphor for me."

I thought that was wonderful, but I also expressed my concerns about how to communicate so many complex ideas in a single work of art.

"In my mind, there's a very amorphous shape of what this monument is going to look like. It has to be very majestic. It has to represent not only gender equality, but also the diversity of our university. And yet it has to look imperial," I said.

"So, some of that comes through the right gestures," said Slatoff. "Finding the right pose is extremely difficult. And you'll say, 'Oh, I know I'll do this.' And it doesn't always work. But with an open hand, inviting the people in, plus the hand over the heart, it conveys sincerity."

"Like a very welcoming gesture to anyone who is approaching the statue," I said.

"Exactly," said Slatoff.

"It's very maternal in some ways," I said. "Because let's face it, Hecuba wasn't just the queen of Troy. She was also the matriarch of the city of Troy."

"We also know that we need a base to raise the figure of Hecuba. So, we could use a Greek Chorus, a group of women that echoes what the primary character says," said Slatoff.

"That's a great idea," I said. "When we look at our university in the 21st century, it's all about gender equality. That's one of our core values, along with diversity. So, we could have these six women, each one representing the humanities, the sciences, technology, medicine, the arts, and the social sciences."

"Right," said Slatoff.

"But then you could also represent the diversity of our campus, where each one of the faces is different, with an African American face, an Asian face, a Hispanic face, a Native American face, an Eastern Mediterranean face, and a Caucasian face."

"Yes," said Slatoff.

"We should also include Troy and the Greeks, meaning a Middle Eastern face," I said. "And the ribbon the six women will be holding will be very symbolic. Not only representing the different disciplines or diversity, but also representing humanity all coming together."

"And we'll need to see it on site," said Slatoff. "In general, scale is a very misunderstood aspect of art. Because it doesn't matter how good the sculpture looks in my studio. It doesn't even matter how well it's sculpted; what matters is the impression it makes at the site."

"It's the emotional experience you create inside the person looking at a piece of art," I suggested.

"Right," he said. "It's experiential."

"We always wanted to have a grand, imperial presence. But I have to admit that I wanted a monument that students can take pictures with, and, therefore, if that's going to be too high, then probably it would be difficult. But if it has to be at least two stories high to get that effect, then that's what it ends up being," I said.

"This is a very large piece, which will have to be cast in many smaller pieces, and then welded together," Slatoff said. "What I love is basically casting in the dark. There is incredible fire, with this whole magnificent liquid metal on the top, you know. All the impurities that come to the surface, and we scrape that off and throw it away."

"It's amazing, the entire process," I said.

"Then each of these pieces is welded together like a three-dimensional jigsaw. Then we're all going to get together. And we're going to do the patina, which is a coloration on the surface," said Slatoff.

I nodded like a student enjoying a lecture from a wise professor.

"And I'm hoping that when it's all put together, nobody would ever think that it was anything other than one piece. You know, the really hardcore art lovers, if my work was in a museum, would see it in person three to four times a year. Whereas this is something that's going to be part of people's lives," he said.

❊ ❊ ❊

Even after all of Slatoff's thought and preparation, when we got the final mockup finished, it didn't look quite right.

It was beautiful and exquisitely crafted, but when Lloyd Silberstein saw it in Slatoff's studio, he immediately said, "It needs to be taller."

We all kind of looked at him, wondering if he was right.

"It looks tall in the studio," said Silberstein. "But you don't realize when you get it out there in the piazza, it's going to look short. It needs to be at least two stories high."

To us, that seemed like a giant statue. But when we got it set up at the site, he was right.

Then Lloyd had one more suggestion, which I have to give him credit for.

"Okay, to make it look bigger," said Silberstein. "Behind Hecuba, we're going to plant the tallest tree in the Village. Then when you look at the sculpture from a distance, it's going to make Hecuba look bigger."

Once again, he knew what he was doing.

So, at the very heart of the USC Village, we planted a single, grand oak tree. For centuries, that type of tree symbolized strength and endurance across many different cultures.[4] The tree was planted several months before any students set foot in the Village, giving it time for it to take root to welcome the first of many generations at USC.

❊ ❊ ❊

One interesting piece of positive publicity came surprisingly from UCLA.

In previous years, it had become tradition for the student body presidents at both of our universities to make a bet. The student government president of whichever team lost the annual football rivalry between UCLA and USC was required to publish an op-ed in the opposing school's student newspaper.

In November 2017, UCLA lost and the female president of their student body posted a wonderful tribute to Hecuba. In part, she wrote:

> It is not easy being a woman in leadership. Whether we are running to serve as president of the United States or president of our undergraduate students' associations, women today face a slew of challenges and obstacles not faced by our male counterparts.[5]

She continued:

> It matters that one of the top 20 private universities in the country has a female mascot to stand alongside her male counterpart. It matters that her face is the combination of faces of women who have seen, heard, smelled, tasted and lived different experiences. It matters that one of her hands is placed over her heart, while the other is outstretched to every passerby.
>
> Hecuba matters. And it matters that she is now leading the charge...
>
> There are very few Trojans I can get behind. But Hecuba is definitely one of them.[6]

It was a wonderful tribute by a student about a monument on the campus of her crosstown rival. And her op-ed was widely applauded by members of the Trojan Family.

❋ ❋ ❋

With the addition of Hecuba, we also created new traditions. For many years, the university had a live camera feed that let people see what was happening near Tommy Trojan at all times of day and night. We did the same for Hecuba at the USC Village.

In 1921, the Trojan Knights started the tradition of guarding Tommy Trojan during the week we played football against UCLA to protect the statue from being disfigured by our crosstown rivals.[7]

The USC Helenes—the women of Troy—were also founded in 1921. They began a new tradition of covering and guarding Hecuba during the same week.

As the First Lady of USC, Niki also started a new tradition of bringing cookies and baklava to the Trojan Knights and the USC Helenes, who slept overnight in sleeping bags, ensuring that the statues remained safe and pristine.

❋ ❋ ❋

For some reason, the *New York Times* wrote glowingly about the USC Village, while the *Los Angeles Times* only seemed to write negatively about it. The *New York Times* focused on what the Village would do for our academic and local communities. Their story pointed out that the project created a welcoming home to 2,700 students and provided 8,000 permanent jobs for people in the local communities.[8]

In addition to bringing in Trader Joe's and Target, they also noted that we planted more than 390 trees and added "nearly 500 underground parking spaces and about 1,500 bike racks."[9]

But what did the *Los Angeles Times* choose to focus on? They wrote a scathing review of the entire project, topped off with the ridiculous title, "Disneyland meets Hogwarts at $700 million USC Village."[10]

❊ ❊ ❊

In October 2017, a few weeks after the grand opening of the USC Village, we held a black-tie gala to thank all of the donors who supported the project, especially the key benefactors who provided naming gifts for residential colleges.

It was a spectacular evening for more than 1,000 guests, who enjoyed dinner on the central piazza as well as performances that displayed USC's strengths at the intersection of arts and technology.[11]

In the center of the piazza, students from the USC School of Thornton Music performed around the reflecting pool, their beautiful voices filling the gorgeous new space.

Niki and I chose music from our favorite composer, the renown Yannis Markopoulos. The USC Thornton Symphony, under the direction of Brent McMunn, along with classical guitarists, choral artists, and a soloist from USC's vocal arts department performed a selection from his *Mother, Magnanimous*.[12]

I also offered a special tribute to the donors who made USC's residential colleges possible. It was an honor for me to recognize the generosity of the visionary philanthropists, who truly transformed the undergraduate experience for generations of USC's students.

On that night, everyone understood that the USC Village was much more than a major construction project. It was a gift to the university's academic community and the local community. A gift from one generation to the next, and one that will keep on giving for generations to come.

CHAPTER 25

Invaluable Asset

«Μοῖραν δ' οὔ τινά φημι πεφυγμένον ἔμμεναι ἀνδρῶν,
οὐ κακὸν οὐδὲ μὲν ἐσθλόν,
ἐπὴν τὰ πρῶτα γένηται»
ΌΜΉΡΟΥ ἸΛΙΆΔΑ, Ζ, 488–89

"And fate? No one alive has ever escaped it,
neither brave man nor coward, I tell you—
it's born with us the day that we are born."[1]
HOMER, *ILIAD*, BOOK VI, LINES 488–89

It seems fitting that the first official event held at USC's president's house was a Thanksgiving meal for students. Looking back, it seems incredible that this special gathering took place only one day after we moved into the residence in San Marino.

The dinner was Niki's idea, of course. She remembered the cold and lonely time in Buffalo when everything was closed on Thanksgiving. She planned and organized a day that would be the opposite of what we had experienced many years before. A celebration that would be warm and welcoming, providing a sense of camaraderie and family for everyone, especially our international students who may not have had friends or family to share the Thanksgiving break.

That first dinner in 2010 would also be a sign that the president's house would not be closed off to the rest of the university community, but would open its doors to the larger Trojan Family.

In an article in *Outlook San Marino* magazine, Niki explained her philosophy of hosting other people. She said, "In Greek culture, you never sit down to have dinner alone. There's always the neighbor, the cousin, the mother-in-law, the father-in-law who will drop by and say, 'Well, what's up for dinner?' And you don't even plan on it. Not only that, but you also plan a lot of parties—birthdays, celebrating by hosting dinners at the house. It's something that I've done a lot."[2]

In another interview she said, "If my daughters wanted to bring a few friends who had nowhere else to go, I would tell them, 'Have them come over; there's always plenty of food.' So that's how the idea came about because I knew we were going to be in the president's house, and I wanted to follow this tradition that we had."[3]

Initially, we imagined a small gathering, a chance for us to get together with a few students who had no other place to go for the holiday. But when the day came, Niki and I—along with our daughters Georgiana and Maria—greeted nearly 400 students at the door, shaking hands with each one as we welcomed them into our home.

In an interview with *The Daily Trojan*, one student said, "I was really glad to have this, because I didn't have anywhere to go for Thanksgiving dinner. It's a great way for people to meet each other and to spend time with people from school you don't know."[4]

Following the meal, I spoke to the students again. As an immigrant myself, I had carefully studied the holiday, so I used the opportunity to share the history of Thanksgiving.

⁂ ⁂ ⁂

We have many wonderful memories of events with students. But as they often do, they sometimes surprised us.

One year at Thanksgiving, a student came running up to the door, out of breath. We asked him if there were any other students or buses outside.

He said, "Oh, I don't know. I live in Pasadena, but told my family I'm going to the president's house for Thanksgiving."

Niki asked another student if he was from Korea. He said, "No, I'm from Arcadia. My mother works today, so I signed up for your Thanksgiving."

A freshman from India, who was studying electrical engineering, called his parents from the party and said, "Mom, dad, this house is beautiful. I want to be a president of a university one day."

And yet another year, the property manager found several students wandering in the basement of the house. Apparently, they'd gotten lost and couldn't find their way back to the party!

To this day, when I run into younger alumni, they will bring up the Thanksgiving dinners as the event they remember the most.

⁂

Over the eight years we spent in USC's president's house, it was much more than just our home.

For the thousands of people who entered and enjoyed their time there, it was a place to connect with other Trojans and the larger history of the university.

I met many USC alumni who shared fond memories of visiting the president's home over nearly 50 years. Some recalled great times with James and Marilyn Zumberge who lived there in the 1980s, or Steve and Kathryn Sample who resided there from 1991 to 2010.[5]

For them, the Seeley G. Mudd Estate was an important bridge between the university's present and its past.

⁂

As we were moving in, Niki later discovered from the USC

Libraries archives that the home's paneling was delivered from a manor house in England, and that the rooms in the house were designed to match those panels.

But what was most exciting about moving into the house was the "poetic coincidence" that we learned connected our home in Cyprus with the estate in San Marino.

As we were about to move into the Seeley G. Mudd Estate, I wanted to do all of the research I could, studying the history of the home and its connection to the university.

In the process, while looking through material in the university archives, I discovered several yellowing photographs of murals that had been painted on the walls of the house.

Seeley Mudd had commissioned the noted muralist Alson Clark to paint scenes of Cyprus on the walls along the staircase.[6]

Although the murals had long been painted over, I had a file of old photos and could see where the murals had once been. The amazing thing was not just that these were photos of our beloved Cyprus, but also that one of them portrayed the Greek theatre of Salamis[7]—only two miles from where Niki had grown up!

Another wall featured a beautiful mural of the Byzantine Monastery of Antifonitis, which was constructed in the twelfth century and was famous for its detailed frescoes on its walls and pillars,[8] and was now at the base of the stairs in San Marino.

After being named president, I had my first interview with the *Los Angeles Times* in a meeting in my office at USC. At the end of the interview, the reporter said, "Anything else, Max? I think we covered it all."

"There are two things I would like to say," I said. "I assume this new responsibility, this commitment, but I don't take anything for granted. Our life experiences and our journey thus far have taught us not to take anything for granted."

After a pause for him to take notes, I told him about the poetic coincidence of the murals.

"Even the playwrights of antiquity would have been intrigued by this connection among USC, the president's house in San

Marino, and Cyprus. Is it a poetic coincidence, or is it destiny?" I asked.

Then I told the reporter that one of the reasons we bought a house in the Palos Verdes Peninsula was because it was like a Greek island in the Pacific.

I felt that the interview went well and the story was soon published.

Steve Sample called me soon after. He laughed and said, "I didn't know you were living on a Greek island in the Pacific!"

* * *

From 1979 to 2018, the Seeley G. Mudd Estate became the official residence of the president of the University of Southern California.[9] It had been left to the university in Dr. Mudd's will, on the condition that it remain the official residence of the president's family.[10]

Considering its extraordinary history, Niki and I felt very strongly that the house shouldn't just be a place where the president and the first lady live, but it should be opened to even more members of the Trojan Family.

We believed it should become USC's Heritage Campus, essentially a *third campus* strategically located between USC's University Park Campus and Health Sciences Campus. It was only a short drive from both campuses, less than 30 minutes from the UPC and about 15 minutes from the HSC.

Over the eight years we lived in the residence, we hosted around 26,000 people as guests, which we felt was our duty as leaders of the university.

In an article in *Outlook San Marino*, a description read, "There seems to be no evidence whatsoever that the hospitality of Max and Niki Nikias is forced. Or rushed. This really does come naturally to them. 'The interesting thing,' said Lorna Reed, 'is that though it is the Nikiases' home, they truly believe it is all of the university's house . . . 'Come to your house.' It's a wonderful feeling you get as having a little bit of ownership.'"[11]

❊ ❊ ❊

For every event over eight years, Niki was the consummate hostess as well as the most diligent student. She read all of the briefing binders and took careful notes.

Sometimes she would give me a quick summary of key people right before the dinner, just to make sure I knew what was important to them! It was a team effort, but few people knew how hard Niki worked or how important she was to making sure everyone had a great time.

Each year, we hosted 10 holiday dinners for faculty and staff, alumni groups, donors, parents, and government officials, as well as an afternoon reception for students.

These weren't small events. Around 300 people attended each of them, meaning that we had about 3,000 people coming to the house over the course of just a few weeks.

Each year, Niki also hosted several events for the leadership teams of several USC women's organizations such as Town and Gown of USC, the Association of Trojan Leagues, the Alumnae Coordinating Council, and the Norris Cancer Center.

During some of these luncheons, it was tradition for many of the women to wear large, colorful hats, adding to the pageantry of the event.

❊ ❊ ❊

One of our favorite dinners each year was an evening to thank the donors and supporters of USC's Good Neighbors Campaign.

Many years earlier, USC had created its own fundraising campaign, which directly benefited the schools and neighborhoods surrounding the university's two campuses.

By 2018, the Good Neighbors Campaign had raised more than $23 million from USC faculty and staff, with 100 percent of proceeds directly funding nearly 550 community partnerships.[12]

Each year we enjoyed hosting the top donors to the Good Neighbors Campaign. Many of the most charitable donors were staff members, who gladly gave 1 percent of their incomes every year.

I especially remember the year Tristan Baizar spoke. A graduate of the Neighborhood Academic Initiative, he had turned down offers from 13 different colleges because his dream was to attend USC.[13]

That night, dressed in a formal white shirt and a black bow tie, he stood at the podium in front of 400 guests and said, "I don't believe I would be standing before you tonight as a proud new Trojan if it wasn't for NAI and wonderful folks like you who donate to programs you believe in. As you can see, I am a true-life example that it works."[14]

It was always a warm and joyous gathering for the most dedicated members of the Trojan Family, and we were always very grateful that so many people were eager to give back to the communities surrounding USC.

* * *

In late 2014, we welcomed another guest who would become a fixture of the house over the next few years.

Around that time, a small, mixed-breed tolling retriever Australian shepherd dog began showing up at the house. From time to time, I would see him wandering around and wonder where he'd come from.

We were involved in so many off-campus events and traveling so often that the additional responsibility of taking care of a pet was out of the question.

Then, in February 2015, I was returning from speaking to a group of LAPD Cadets. Normally, my driver, Koji, would drop me off at the front door, and then park the car in the garage. As I was walking to the house, I realized that I'd left my cell phone in the car, so I went to the garage to retrieve it.

As soon as I got my phone and closed the door, I saw this little dog staring at me. When I walked toward the house, he began to follow me.

I was confused. I didn't understand why this random dog was following me around.

So I called Niki and said, "There's this dog and he keeps following me. Is it the same dog that's been hanging around, or is it the neighbor's dog?"

Niki said, "Why don't you come inside. We need to talk."

When I got in the house, she explained that she and the property manager, Jim, had been feeding the dog and she wanted to adopt him.

Niki had sworn everyone to silence—the property manager, the gardener, even my driver—telling them that they couldn't tell me anything about the dog, who by this time she had named "Buddy."

It turns out that the dog hadn't been returning to the property—he'd never left!

"How long has this been going on?" I asked.

"Six months," Niki said.

Later, I asked Koji, "You've known that they've been feeding this dog for six months and you didn't tell me anything?"

"I'm sorry, sir but you don't live in this house. You only come here to sleep," he said.

I laughed. He was right.

My initial reluctance to Buddy's presence quickly changed. He transformed our lives, becoming a full-fledged member of the family. Sometimes I felt like we were living in Buddy's house, and he was training us on how to take care of a dog.

Not only did Buddy move into the house, he slept in the master bedroom on the floor on Niki's side of the bed. Sadly, after ten years with Buddy, he was diagnosed with lung cancer. In October 2024, he passed away peacefully. We still miss him.

* * *

While I am very proud of the hundreds of events we held, and of the thousands of guests we hosted over eight years, I am very aware that it was a team effort. I have to give credit my wife, Niki, who always worked tirelessly to make sure everyone felt comfortable and welcome.

We always believed the president's house was an asset for USC. Like any other asset, there was a return-on-investment. But that ROI was not in dollars and cents, but rather in memories, goodwill, and shared experiences of the Trojan Family.

Rick Caruso and his team of architects visited the Seeley Mudd estate on two occasions, expressing interest in the "looks" of the house and the special features designed by Reginald Johnson. They spent a lot of time taking pictures all around the structure, I suppose looking for ideas for their own commercial properties.

Unfortunately, after I stepped down as president, he supported selling the property. USC did sell the estate in 2021.[15]

When you don't take advantage of an asset's value, it's simply another house for a couple to live.

The residence in San Marino gave the president easy access to both campuses, sending a signal that the leader of the university was there for everyone from downtown L.A. to East Los Angeles.

Unfortunately, I believe that legacy and tradition have been lost now that the *third campus* is no longer part of USC.

But I have confidence that the shared experiences that took place there will be carried on in the minds and the memories of thousands of Trojans who found it a warm and welcoming place.

And Niki and I will always be grateful for that special time in our lives.

CHAPTER 26

Relentless Planning

«Ἀρχὴ γὰρ λέγεται μὲν ἥμισυ παντὸς ἐν ταῖς παροιμίαις ἔργου, καὶ τό γε καλῶς ἄρξασθαι πάντες ἐγκωμιάζομεν ἑκάστοτε.»

ΠΛΆΤΩΝΟΣ ΝΌΜΟΙ, Ζ, 753Ε

"For, as the saying goes, 'well begun is half done,' and every man always commends a good beginning."[1]

PLATO, *LAWS*, BOOK VI, 753E

Philanthropy is not a new concept. In a 2011 *Trojan Family Magazine* column, I noted that the word first appeared in the tragedy *Prometheus Bound* by Aeschylus, which is where many people turn when trying to understand the beginnings of philanthropy.[2]

The word comes from the Ancient Greek phrase *philanthropia*. When broken down into its component parts—*phil*, which means love, and *anthropoi*, which means people—it essentially translates to "love of humanity."[3]

In my experience, everyone who chose to donate their money to the people and programs at USC had a great love of humanity. They understood that they were giving the gift of a life-changing education to our students, and the support for life-saving research to some of our faculty.

Philanthropy has long been a great tradition at USC. During the summer of 1880, the university's very first trustees voted to sell land to help create an endowment and construct USC's first building, Widney Alumni House.[4]

Judge Robert Maclay Widney also set aside around 30 lots to

sell at a higher price. At the time, the market value of each of those lots was only $50.[5] But according to legend, friends of the university purchased them for $200 each—four times the market value—to raise additional money for the university's first endowment.[6]

That type of deep devotion to USC and its people carried on to the time when we were planning a major fundraising campaign. But it wasn't just any campaign, it was an effort that would transform the future of the entire university.

⁂ ⁂ ⁂

After months of planning behind the scenes, on the evening of September 15, 2011, we gathered hundreds of trustees, alumni, and friends outside of Widney Alumni House to make a very special announcement.

Remember that this was in the aftermath of the Great Recession, when the unemployment rate was nearly 9 percent.[7] But, together, we displayed our faith in USC's future by declaring our intention to raise $6 billion over the next eight years.

At the time of the announcement, it was the largest campaign in the history of American higher education.

⁂ ⁂ ⁂

When people read the headlines of fundraising campaigns, especially for major private universities, they sometimes have strong feelings about the need for raising money.

In truth, private universities like USC depend deeply on philanthropy. Public universities receive hundreds of millions of dollars from their state budgets and federal research funds, and then also raise support through fundraising campaigns.

Private universities are on their own, raising the money they need to educate every student, compete for the best faculty, and purchase increasingly expensive technologies required for research.

Without philanthropy, the cost of education would quickly skyrocket. Even full-tuition-paying parents at USC were getting a 10-percent subsidy because the costs of infrastructure, the quality of the faculty, and other essential services were partially paid for by philanthropy.

If we didn't have fundraising campaigns, the medical school and the research enterprise wouldn't break even. And that doesn't include all of the amenities that students and parents demand in the escalating arms race among colleges and universities around the nation.

* * *

For USC, one of the most important decisions was not just how much money we planned to raise during our fundraising campaign, but also the timing of when to make that news public.

It was common practice for most universities, including Stanford and Harvard, to wait until they had raised 50 percent of the campaign goal before announcing it publicly. The reason for this is so there is no embarrassment if, for some reason, the goal is never reached.

However, when we talked to our alumni and stakeholders, we found such enthusiasm for our efforts that we decided to make the announcement when we had raised only 16 percent of the total goal.

To some, it seemed like we were overconfident. But during my first year as president, the optimism of the Trojan Family helped us raise an unprecedented $1 billion in cash and pledges.[8]

* * *

For any major fundraising campaign to succeed, you must have a strong commitment from the members of the Board of Trustees. Their generous giving not only sets a great example for their colleagues and peers, but it also sends a signal about the importance of philanthropy in advancing a university's overall academic excellence.

Our campaign gained ground early on because several members of USC's board stepped up to show their confidence in the university and what we were doing.

On the day of my inauguration, I had the privilege of announcing two $50 million gifts from Wallis Annenberg and Eva and Ming Hsieh. Julie and John Mork and their family established and endowed the Mork Family Scholars for $110 million. The Keck Foundation named the USC Medical Center and Hospital with a $150 million donation. And David and Dana Dornsife decided to name USC's College of Letters, Arts and Sciences for $200 million.

During my first year as president, those five major gifts invested $560 million in the university's people and programs, giving us extraordinary momentum for the long road ahead.

* * *

In the quiet phase of the campaign, I had several conversations with John Mork, who was going to succeed Ed Roski as chairman of the Board of Trustees.

As soon as I became president, John told me that he and his wife, Julie, were very interested in making a major gift to USC.

"Julie and I really want to help," Mork said. "We want to make a difference, especially for students."

They were very passionate about making it possible for students from all walks of life to receive a USC education.

Then he added, "Remember, Max, if you want to be among the elite, it takes continual investment."

We had a series of discussions about how much they were willing to invest in student merit scholarships. I was under the impression that their gift would likely be around $25 million, which would have been very generous of them and life-changing for countless students.

The last football game of the season that year was held at the Rose Bowl in Pasadena. USC was playing UCLA on December 4, 2010.

Niki and I hosted Julie and John, along with several other guests, in our private box at the stadium. Julie is a proud supporter of the UCLA Bruins, but also very enthusiastic about being part of the Trojan Family. USC and UCLA competed on the football field only one day per year, but she was a major Trojan supporter for the other 364 days of the year!

At halftime, John and I stepped out of the box, and he pulled me aside.

"Max, Julie and I discussed the student scholarships gift, and we'd like to move forward with it," John said.

"This is great news, John. Thank you. Should we prepare the gift proposal with the number of scholarships we discussed in our last meeting?"

"Well, we want a larger number of students to benefit from this program," he said.

"How many more?" I asked. "Should we double the number?"

"No, quadruple it," he said.

"John, do I hear you correctly?" I asked. "That's more than $100 million for student scholarships."

He looked at me straight in the eyes.

"Yes, that's what we're talking about. We want to have an impact not just on this generation of students, but also on the next. That's what we want to do."

Four months later, we held a very emotional ceremony to announce and celebrate the Mork Family's historic gift.

When we say that the origin of philanthropy means "love of humanity," John and Julie—and the entire Mork Family—are a perfect example of this. They could have kept their money for themselves, or invested it in another business venture, but instead they chose to change the course of hundreds of students' lives.

❋ ❋ ❋

In addition to the incredible support from trustees, there was one other reason I felt strongly about making the campaign public after only one year.

I'd carefully studied the fundraising campaigns of our private university peers and I noticed something very interesting. The majority of them had recently closed campaigns or were going through a transition in leadership.

I shared my findings with Alan Kreditor, former senior vice president for development at USC.

"Alan, if we go public now there won't be another university announcing a campaign any time soon, at least for a few years," I said.

"Really?" he replied. "Then go public now. You'll be noticed and all the new gifts you secure will stand out."

Then he laughed.

"Max, be bold," he said. "And please do me a favor . . . break all my fundraising records!"

In that moment, I recalled Aeschylus' expression, "When the person is willing and eager and determined, even the gods join in."

And I was hoping that the gods were all Trojans!

❋ ❋ ❋

Even with all of our preparation and support, the campaign soon faced competition.

In the fall of 2011, Stanford was scheduled to conclude their campaign. But as soon as we announced that we were planning to raise $6 billion, they extended their campaign until February 2012 so they could declare that they'd raised $6.2 billion![9]

In 2013, two years after we launched our campaign, Harvard announced that they planned to raise $6.5 billion.[10]

It was clear that they were reacting to our ambitious goal and that we were setting a new bar for fundraising in American higher education.

The competition was expected. But the skeptics who questioned our goal also came quickly after we made our initial announcement.

The *Los Angeles Times* quoted Rae Goldsmith, vice president of the Council for the Advancement and Support of Education, who said that it was rare for universities to go public with such ambitious goals without first sounding out donors privately.

"They don't want to set themselves up to fail. The institutions would have to have some confidence in their ability to raise that kind of money," said Goldsmith to the *L.A. Times*.[11, 12]

Another person said, "Even during normal economic times, it would be ambitious. Coming now, it's doubly so."[13]

Even the *Chronicle of Philanthropy* seemed to question our ability to raise so much support.

One article titled "Can USC Really Raise $6 Billion?" began ominously: "Some fundraising experts are questioning whether the University of Southern California can really reach its audacious goal of raising $6 billion by 2018. No private organization has ever tried to collect that much from a single drive."[14]

And *Philanthropy News Digest* stated, "Typically, universities wait until they have received commitments of at least 40 percent of their goal before publicly announcing a campaign. But at a time when many colleges and universities are struggling with budget cuts and shrinking endowments, the campaign has generated a good deal of controversy."[15]

I told *Philanthropy News Digest* we were not afraid to take the risk in order to boost the university's endowment as long as it helped USC achieve "academically elite status."

* * *

Looking back, I think we have to address the question that some people have since posed. Was our goal reckless?

Some said it was overreach. Some said it was too bold. Many people saw the number attached to our final goal. But we didn't just make it up out of thin air.

What *nobody* saw or knew was the thoughtful planning and hard work that took place over two years in preparing for this campaign. It wasn't something we just decided upon in a meeting. It all began when I was provost, even though I didn't know for sure that I was going to be the next president.

Two years before I became president, during one of my breakfast meetings with Chairman Ed Roski, he said to me, "Max, now that we're in the process of buying the hospitals from Tenet, USC will need to expand its fundraising efforts."

"Yes, Ed, I can see the need for that," I said. "But my concern is that since the ending of President Sample's campaign six years ago, central development operations have been downsized significantly."

"Really?" he said. "You need to look into that and give it a priority."

I agreed to do my homework and follow up with him at our next breakfast. At that meeting, I suggested we hire a consulting firm, with an expertise in fundraising to do a thorough assessment of our overall development operations, not just central development. I also recommended that we include both campuses, all of USC's schools, and athletics.

Then Ed added, "Do it, Max. You need resources and money to build academic excellence. Those are the keys to the kingdom. Otherwise, it's just talk and pipe dreams."

* * *

As I began looking into consulting firms, a trustee called with a recommendation. "I've been told that John Glier of Grenzebach Glier Associates (GG+A) is the best," he said. Shortly thereafter, we scheduled a meeting with Glier in my office a month later.

We had a long talk, but at some point in the conversation he said, "Max, I'll be honest with you. We do ongoing fundraising work for UCLA, so it might be a conflict for us to be working on a future fundraising campaign for USC."

"John, it's only going to be a one-time assignment for you and your firm," I said. "We just want you to do a comprehensive study to assess our fundraising performance, our current level and deployment of resources, and how we compare philanthropically to other private institutions of our size and complexity."

I could see he was still unsure, so I continued.

"I want you to look at central development carefully, their interactions with the schools and other units, our planned giving programs, annual giving, data analytics, alumni relations, and so on," I said.

He agreed to create a list of comparative metrics for 10 leading private universities, and told me that his team may have to interview as many as 200 USC leaders, ranging from development staff and supporters to deans, alumni, and trustees.

"No worries, I'll make sure you have everything you need," I said. "And I'll encourage everyone to give you and your team their full and candid participation in this review process."

"Max, this is a big undertaking that may take us six months or more to complete," he said.

"I'm okay with that," I said. "Send us a draft of an engagement contract for our legal office to review."

We shook hands and very quickly the agreement was signed. He started the study in the second half of 2008. It was in the midst of the market crash and the beginning of the Great Recession.

Amid all of that uncertainty, I felt good that we were planning ahead for the future.

However, the downturn in the market was only one of the shocking things that would happen during that time. The other would be GG+A's findings.

⁂

I knew the findings were going to be bad. But I had no idea how unsettling they would really be.

In almost every area, USC had fallen behind in its ability to raise fundraising support. In terms of personnel and infrastructure in development, we were woefully behind.

Our overall development team, which included central operations and those of all our schools and units had a combined 180 people. Stanford and some of our other competitors had more than 400 people in these positions.

For all of the talk of the loyalty among the members of the Trojan Family, our annual alumni giving rate was very low.

And one area where Harvard set the standard for excellence was raising money from $1 million donors, with a schedule of payments over five years at the most. For us to get better at this, we would have to greatly increase the number of development officers, and then train them to pay attention to smaller gift donors. It's important because those smaller donors might become larger donors in the future.

For example, trustee David Dornsife began as a $200 donor in the 1980s. By 2011, he and his wife, Dana, increased their giving to $200 million!

That type of relationship and cultivation is very important. Because you just never know how someone's career or giving will change over time.

GG+A also had another shocking finding. Our medical school was a major underperformer in fundraising. Over five years, our private competitors raised about 35 percent of their support for medicine. At USC, it was less than 20 percent.

Despite all of the surprising news, I found the study and its findings very important. We now had a road map and a comprehensive plan to build the infrastructure and move forward.

We presented GG+A's finding to the Board of Trustees, but the actual implementation of the plan would have to wait.

The university was getting ready to announce a national search for a new president.

* * *

As soon as I became President-elect in March 2010, I reached out to John Glier again. I asked for his help in recruiting a new senior vice president for development at USC. Because he specialized in this area, he knew everyone.

He helped us find five candidates. Some of them were veterans, who had run, or were still running, major development operations and fundraising campaigns at top universities.

However, given the completed GG+A study, I felt we needed a chief development officer to build the new infrastructure, working closely with the deans by implementing the study's recommendations.

I felt Al Checcio was the right person to lead this effort. His previous work experience was at second-tier universities, with significantly smaller operations. The largest gift his previous campaigns had ever raised was $10 million. Some of USC's trustees also expressed serious concern that throughout his career Checcio had changed jobs every five years.

Personally, I liked him and felt he was someone we could work with to build and implement the recommendations in GG+A's report.

I got the approval of the Board of Trustees right away, and we recruited him to begin his appointment when I was starting as president.

I immediately enlarged the central development budget from $8 million to $40 million annually. Within a few years, the university increased the number of development officers from 180 to 460 people across both campuses.

The new plan was executed quickly and the campaign started gaining momentum.

* * *

Exactly five years later, I was told very confidentially that Checcio was considering leaving USC for a university on the East Coast.

He even had a secret meeting with his direct reports, asking them all to join him. I was told that they refused. We were in the midst of a very successful fundraising campaign and some of them had just moved to Los Angeles. As a result, he backed off.

From a leadership perspective, I didn't think there was any need for me to bring up what I'd heard. And I didn't. We never discussed it!

By then the campaign had reached a critical mass and had great momentum. I always felt I have been the continuity of the campaign, as I was in my years as dean of engineering.

If he'd chosen to leave, I'm certain we still would have surpassed our original campaign goal.

* * *

In addition to building up our advancement infrastructure, we realized that we also needed to do a better job of investing the money we already had.

As soon as I became president, I was talking with former chairman Stanley Gold, sharing my fundraising plans.

"Max, the time has come for USC to do the investments of its endowment very professionally," he said.

"What do you mean *professionally*, Stanley?"

"Let me give you some history," he said. "When I became chairman, our Board of Trustees didn't have an investment committee to provide oversight of the endowment investments. They were handled by the CFO, with the help of the Treasurer."

"Okay," I said.

"So the board created an investment committee and I recruited Suzanne Nora Johnson. A few years later, with your recommendation, you remember, Mark Stevens became a co-chair of that committee."

"Sure," I said. "I remember."

"Now you're planning for a big campaign, new money will start coming into the endowment, and we need a team of full-time professionals to manage the investments," he said.

"I see your point," I said. "So we'll need to recruit a Chief Investment Officer, who will then recruit the team, right?"

"Exactly. You need to make this a priority. It's as important as announcing a new campaign," he said.

At that time, USC's endowment was only $2.5 billion. We put together a search committee to recruit the first CIO for the university's endowment.

We ended up with three finalists. Towards the end of the search, Trustee Joan Payden of Payden & Rygel Investment Management called my office and said she'd like to give me her feedback on the finalists. On Christmas Eve, we met for lunch.

"Max, you recently bought two hospitals, so should I give you my feedback with medical metaphors?" Payden asked.

"Please, go ahead," I said.

"This is the very first CIO you are going to hire for USC, correct?"

"Yes, we never had one before," I said.

"When you have a patient in the surgery room, what do you need?"

I must admit, I was puzzled for moment.

"Do you need someone who is a leader in medical research? Do you need a hospital administrator type? Or do you need a brilliant surgeon to take care the patient?" Payden asked.

"A brilliant surgeon," I said.

"That's exactly what I think. And Lisa Mazzocco is the person for you," she said.

We ended up hiring Lisa and she built an excellent investment team around her. When she stepped down eight years later, the USC endowment was more than $7 billion, a combination of her investment strategies and new money coming in from the campaign.

Joan Payden was right. Lisa was a great surgeon, and just what the patient needed at the right time. Thanks to Lisa, USC was in much better financial health than before.

* * *

In addition to all of the planning, it was also important to clearly communicate my expectations for the upcoming campaign. On August 23, 2010, I gathered all the deans and senior development officers in the spacious Town and Gown ballroom for a breakfast.

From the mood in the room, everyone seemed to be looking forward to a nice, relaxing morning with the new president. In fact, one of my staff members later told me about a dean who joked that he was sitting at a table near the door because he wanted to slip out early without being noticed.

However, I'd spent weeks preparing my message. One person would later call it my "marching orders" speech. That morning I revealed GG+A's shocking findings, and I talked about the serious work that needed to be done to build up our development infrastructure in order to succeed in our upcoming campaign. I also announced the opening of USC development offices in New York City and San Francisco.

It was a blueprint for the future, and I needed everyone to

understand that it wasn't going to be easy.

A few minutes into my remarks, the dean who planned to leave early, quietly called his office and told them that he'd decided to stay for the entire event!

I concluded the morning by saying that "our goals are very ambitious, and our journey will be difficult, our courage will be questioned, and our endurance will be tested."

With everyone on the same page, it was now up to all of us to execute the strategy we had put in place.

* * *

When preparing for any endeavor, it's important to get ideas and advice from people who have experience in similar efforts. I remembered that Ken Leventhal had served as campaign chair for a decade under President Sample. He'd also been on USC's Board of Trustees since the 1970s.

I knew he would have important insights for our upcoming campaign, so I had several conversations with him.

During the summers in Sun Valley, Idaho, we used to ride our bikes together for about 30 miles every day. I loved studying the history of USC and I ran across accounts of the university's very first fundraising campaign, which was announced by President Norman Topping.

"Kenny, did you know about Topping's campaign in the 60s?" I asked.

"Yes, I remember that," he said. "That's why the Board of Trustees and President Hubbard decided to double the goal of the campaign in the 70s."

"I read that the focus back then was athletics, especially football," I said. "President Hubbard was quoted saying that the success of the campaign depended on the success of the football team."

"That's no longer true," said Leventhal. "With Sample's

campaign we proved that it's about investing in academic excellence."

"What about the 80s with President Zumberge?" I asked.

"We needed to be ambitious. That's why the goal was doubled from that of the 70s, and we ended up raising $640 million."[16]

"And then with Sample you broke all records, raising close to $3 billion over ten years," I added.[17]

"Without complete commitment from the president you can't raise that kind of money," he said.

"Kenny, if I were to follow the ambition of past decades, what should be my campaign's goal?" I asked. "The Trojan Family has been very ambitious for sure. And their enthusiasm about USC is infectious."

"Do your homework," he said. "We've been raising about $280 million per year, even without a campaign. How much more can you raise in the future? Double that? Triple that? Every year?"

"We've done a comprehensive study, planned a strategy, and I honestly feel very comfortable with a new campaign aiming to raise $600 million per year," I said.

"But if you really want to be bold, set a goal of $700 million per year," he said.

Then he laughed.

"I'm not suggesting that. Just think about it," he said.

Over eight years, that would be $6 billion. That conversation was in my mind throughout the summer of 2010.

If we were really going to be ambitious like all of USC's previous campaigns, it seemed like we needed to do something that had never been done before.

After talking to Ken Leventhal, I also went back to Alan Kreditor for advice.

"Max, people remember the goal of the campaign and not the duration," he said. "If the economy goes to hell, everybody will understand why the campaign took longer. I told you before, be bold. This is what the Trojan Family expects us to be."

⁂ ⁂ ⁂

After one year of a "silent phase," we were getting closer to announcing our new campaign publicly. Al Checcio came to me with a proposal for a $4 billion campaign. When I pushed back, he relented.

"Okay, $4.5 billion and that's it," he said.

But over the previous 12 months, I'd done my homework and consulted with the right trustees. I clearly realized that the extra $1 billion—assuming we were aiming for $6 billion instead of $5 billion—was going to be a "stretch."

However, I'd experienced the enthusiasm of the Trojan Family. And I really believed we'd built tremendous momentum during my first year as president.

In the end, I made the final decision to set the goal at $6 billion.

It was ambitious. It was bold. But it wasn't *reckless*.

We had relentlessly prepared for it!

CHAPTER 27

The Campaign

"There is a Tide in the affayres of men,
Which taken at the Flood, leades on to Fortune."[1]

SHAKESPEARE, *JULIUS CAESAR*,
ACT IV, SCENE III, 2217–18

In the early stages of the campaign, I felt it was very important to establish a few guiding principles, so that everyone would understand what we were trying to accomplish.

During a meeting with the development committee of the Board of Trustees, I laid out those principles in detail.

I told them that we needed to establish a *sense of urgency* in order to excite the members of the Trojan Family and make them want to become part of the journey.

In order to keep the gift agreements precise and simple, we established *strict rules for how to count money* for the campaign by adopting the Council for Advancement and Support of Education's (CASE) guidelines.

We also made the decision to *never file a lawsuit against a donor,* even if the donor broke their promise on a pledge or gift agreement. We had seen other universities take legal action against a donor and it was a mistake.[2]

We also needed to make sure that we offered *flexibility in structuring gifts,* giving donors options of cash gifts, a schedule of payments, transfer of stock, estate planning, life insurance, real estate, and other assets.

I told the committee that we needed to *pay attention to North America.* While I often said that the sun never sets on the Trojan

Family and the university is truly international, the wealth and culture of giving is primarily located in North America. It is important to have fundraising programs internationally, but I asked them not to expect big gifts beyond the continent in which we lived.

I also wanted to *establish transparency and accountability with our quarterly reports*, monitoring the progress for each school and unit, with expectations and performance goals established by our central development office.

And we needed to *pay attention to donors of every giving level*, keeping in mind that smaller donors to this campaign could become major donors in future fundraising efforts. For this reason, we also established several donor recognition programs to acknowledge those who had made important contributions.

It was imperative to *show the proper respect to donors*, inviting them to be stakeholders in the university. It was important to cultivate them by asking their advice and keeping them engaged while also making it clear that they couldn't be involved in management decisions.

And finally, I told the development committee that all of our *relationships are based on trust*. People do not donate money unless they trust the leadership and believe in what the organization is doing. They need to see returns on their investments in academic excellence.

* * *

Despite the doubts and the criticism in the early stages of the campaign, we pressed forward with our plans. We understood that the timing and the numbers were on our side, and we were determined to take advantage of the moment.

We not only had to elevate our expectations, we also had to change our approach. In the past, USC held most of its fundraising events in Southern California, bringing the Trojan Family closer to campus.

We decided this time to take the university to our alumni, meeting them in places we had never visited before. Over three months, in nine cities, Niki and I met and talked with more than 4,000 members of the Trojan Family.

But this outreach wasn't just an alumni tour or a fundraising effort. It was all about academics.

On all of our tours, we brought trustees, senior administrators, academic deans, and star faculty. And we introduced them to alumni, parents, and friends who were delighted that we were traveling across the country to display what made USC so special.

❋ ❋ ❋

Four years later, in 2015, we did the same tour of nine cities in three months to re-energize the Trojan Family during the heart of our campaign.

We also hosted events in Houston, Dallas, and Austin, where we were greeted by an incredibly enthusiastic group of USC alumni and parents.

During many of those alumni events, people would ask me, "What exactly do you do as president?"

"It's very simple," I said. "Whatever I do, I try very hard to add value to your degrees! That's why it's very important for you to give back to your *alma mater*. Your degree is worth far more now than when you graduated!"

No matter where we were when we hosted events, those lines always got lots of laughter.

❋ ❋ ❋

In addition to trustees and senior administrators, I also felt that

I needed to get perspectives from the faculty. During the campaign, I had lunch with USC Distinguished Professor Warren Bennis.

"Max, I've been at USC for almost thirty years, and you are the first president who made us all feel proud we're at USC," he said. "This is what Gandhi did for India as a nation for the first time."

I laughed out loud.

"Warren, I ain't Gandhi!" I said.

"All these years, many of our faculty looked down on USC, and many of them wished they were somewhere else," he said.

"Not only that, the quality of students, of research programs, and now the goal of the campaign, all of that makes us feel proud," he said. "The word is out in the academic community, Max. USC is now the place to be."

Then Warren added a concern.

"The only threat that I see in the future is from the faculty in the humanities and social sciences," he said. "They usually develop an undercurrent of resentment when fundraising campaigns raise large gifts for medicine, the sciences, and engineering."

"But Warren," I said. "Look at the Dornsifes' gift of $200 million to the College of Letters, Arts & Sciences, as well as all of the gifts we've secured for the arts," I said. "It's for them and we secured those donations early in the campaign."

Warren shook his head.

"It doesn't matter," he said. "They have a short memory, Max."

As time would reveal, he was right.

* * *

Soon the campaign reached a critical mass thanks to many generous philanthropists, including the university's largest anonymous donor. Along with his daughter, this person donated around $340 million.

But he didn't want anyone to know. I asked him if he was sure that he didn't want any recognition and he told me, "Max, I want to be a whale that doesn't rise to the surface. A submerged whale never gets harpooned!"

* * *

Sometimes you don't know the true impact of a gift for many years. And often the story behind the scenes is more complex than the narrative that fits in a press release.

Because universities can outlive large corporations and the governments of nations, the gifts they pursue have the potential to not only benefit the students of the present, but also generations of the future.

When Zohrab Kaprielian was USC's provost in the late 1970s, he convinced Thomas Lord to establish the Lord Foundation of California. Through the foundation's grants, our business and engineering programs enjoyed generous support for nearly four decades.

In 2016, when I was president, the executives of the LORD Corporation requested a secret meeting where they informed us that the company could be acquired. Surprisingly, we learned that this might result in a lump sum payment to USC of around $200 million.

After that meeting, I told one of my senior officers, "If this happens, we should all pay a visit to Kaprielian's grave, light a candle, and thank him for closing the gift 40 years earlier."

The deal didn't go through while I was president. However, a couple of years after I stepped down, another company acquired the LORD Corporation. When that happened, USC received $260 million. In May 2023, part of that money was used to rename USC's Computer Science Department after Thomas Lord.

While it appeared that the $260 million was a new gift, it was actually one that was set in motion four decades earlier. And I still think we should light a candle at Kaprielian's grave.

* * *

There are some fundraising stories that are interesting and some that are legendary. Al Mann's story is the latter.

In his long life, Mann was a celebrated entrepreneur who created 17 aerospace and biomedical technology companies.[3]

Al and his wife, Claude, loved USC. Niki and I also loved hosting them at many football games in the Coliseum.

"Every time I hear UCLA in his conversations, I make sure Al remains *only* a Trojan," Claude used to joke. Of course, when Al heard her say that, he would break out in loud laughter.

But back in 1998, Al wasn't connected to the Trojan Family. He was just trying to find someone to help him create a biomedical engineering institute. He'd earned his bachelor's and master's degrees from UCLA,[4] so it made sense to try to set it up there. But he was told that it would take several months for UCLA's Board of Regents to formally approve it.

President Steve Sample found out about his desire for an institute and our board said they could do it much more quickly. It was Steve's brilliance reaching out to Al Mann and very quickly negotiating a deal. Soon they announced the establishment of the USC Alfred Mann Institute for Biomedical Engineering.

Right away it made headlines—and for many years it was a funny story at internal events—when a two-time UCLA alumnus donated $100 million to USC, and then joined our Board of Trustees.

It symbolized the essential difference between public and private universities, showing that we were more nimble simply because we were burdened by less bureaucracy.

When I was president, Al extended his generosity by endowing a chair in music. Before he passed away in 2016, he also donated an additional $60 million into the endowment for his institute, bringing his overall giving to more than $170 million.[5] Over time, thanks to market investments, the institute's endowment had grown dramatically to more than $250 million.

In 2023, with the permission of the trustees of Alfred E. Mann Charities, Inc., USC redirected $35 million from the institute's endowment to name the biomedical engineering department,[6] $50 million to name the School of Pharmacy,[7] and $40 million to expand research collaborations with Children's Hospital Los Angeles.[8]

Again, it looked like those were three new and separate gifts. But in reality, all of the money was simply reallocated from market gains in the USC endowment.

Either way, the university is still fortunate that 25 years earlier, Al Mann got frustrated with his *alma mater* and Steve Sample convinced him to establish his institute at USC, leading to him and his wife, Claude, becoming Trojans for life.

* * *

For another donation, we learned that Robert Price and his brother wanted to find a way to honor their father, Sol Price.

In 1936, just seven years after the School of Public Policy was founded, Sol Price earned a bachelor's degree in philosophy from USC.[9]

Over the years, Sol's businesses, charities, and philanthropy dramatically improved the quality of life for so many people in Southern California and throughout the world.

Robert and his brother chose to generously donate $50 million from the Price Family Charitable Fund to name the USC Price School of Public Policy.[10]

They were a wonderful and generous family, and Robert said he didn't want to become a trustee.

He simply wanted to ensure that the school's students, faculty, and alumni could carry on Sol Price's passion for social justice, which helped lift people out of poverty and help them rise up the social ladder.

* * *

We also received a generous gift from former California Governor Arnold Schwarzenegger, who came to me right after his final term in office.

Shortly before that, I'd run into him at a restaurant in Sun Valley, Idaho. He told me that he really wanted to talk to me, and I suggested we have our assistants set up a meeting.

When he came to my office, he told me that he wanted to secure his legacy in some way at USC. After a few conversations, he chose to donate $20 million to create the USC Schwarzenegger Institute for State and Global Policy.[11]

In 2012, I hosted the institute's inaugural symposium, which drew a crowd of nearly 1,000 thought leaders and representatives from more than a dozen national and international news and media outlets.

He later became the inaugural Governor Downey Professor of State and Global Policy,[12] and he was our keynote speaker during an international trip in South Korea, where he was a huge hit. Clearly, he was a celebrity wherever he went in the world!

I was also very grateful for the generosity of Suzanne Dworak-Peck, a renown graduate of USC's School of Social Work.

She's someone who cares about the major challenges of our society, including homelessness, addiction, mental illness, as well as helping veterans. She's a wonderful person and we couldn't have found a better name for the school.

At the same time, an anonymous couple wanted to donate $25 million, so the USC Suzanne Dworak-Peck School of Social Work not only has the perfect name, but also a healthy endowment.[13]

* * *

With all of our fundraising success, there's sometimes the perception that we would have taken money for any cause. But that's simply not the case.

One gift we declined was from Charlie Munger, who I deeply respected. He was a brilliant businessman, and I found him to be a very nice person. Over the years, he gave me a lot of great advice about building the USC Village and creating residential colleges.

Charlie had offered a major gift to support housing for graduate students at the USC Village. Years earlier, he'd supported a similar project at the University of Michigan. Unfortunately, our priority at the time was to build more housing for undergraduate students. So we turned down his proposed donation.

After we turned down the gift, I was asked to do a radio interview along with Charlie. He refused to join us, but he knew when the interview was happening. During the discussion, the reporter was baiting me, trying to get me to say something bad about Charlie.

But I simply praised him, talking about how much I valued his support and advice. I said that I was grateful for his offer, but that I couldn't change the priorities of the university just to take his money.

As soon as the interview ended, I got a call from my assistant in the president's office, saying that she had Charlie on the phone.

He didn't mention the interview, but clearly he'd been listening.

"Max, how are you doing?" he asked.

"Oh, Charlie. Thanks for calling, we should get together for dinner again soon," I said.

Charlie was a character. And we did get together for dinner several more times over the years.

* * *

Despite turning down certain gifts that didn't directly advance our academic excellence, we surprised everyone by reaching our goal of $6 billion 18 months ahead of schedule, in February 2017.[14]

With our achievement, we'd raised as much support in 6.5 years as we had in the previous 6.5 decades. And we constantly ranked in the top three for annual fundraising in higher education, along with Harvard and Stanford.[15]

It was an incredible achievement that took the hard work and dedication of hundreds of people throughout the university. And I'm still very grateful that over a short period of time we helped ensure that thousands of students will receive a world-class education for several decades into the future.

Although we had reached our goal early, we decided there was no need to have a major celebration. During the course of the campaign, we'd had many events where donors were properly recognized and thanked. So I didn't feel like we needed yet another celebration.

Much has been written about the extension of our campaign, but no one really knows the reasons. We decided to keep it going because we had a discussion with the development committee of the Board of Trustees.

We chose not to set a new campaign goal because we didn't feel the need to prove ourselves for a second time. We'd already accomplished our overall goal and that was enough.

We simply did what our private peers had done in the past. Harvard and Stanford had continued raising money after their campaigns had officially ended. So we figured, "Why shouldn't USC do the same?"

Also, if we suddenly stopped fundraising, the entire infrastructure of development officers that we'd spent years building would have had to be downsized significantly.

We received criticism because we continued to raise money. But if we'd laid off hundreds of people who'd just helped us break all of the university's fundraising records, I'm sure there still would have been numerous complaints.

It was a no-win situation, I suppose. After eight years of

fundraising, in August 2018, the same month I stepped down as president, we closed *Fas Regna Trojae*, with a final total of $7.16 billion.[16]

In the end, about half of the money came from 33 transformative gifts of $25 million or more. And we also had five astonishing gifts of $100 million or more.[17]

While there are still detractors who will say it was all about the money, I will remind you of all of the students who attended USC with scholarships, or the faculty members who can now do life-saving research, or the beautiful buildings, or the first-class laboratories and classrooms, which would not exist without those donations.

Much has also been said about the campaign and USC's admissions.

But the truth is that our policy regarding prospective students was very strict: no *quid pro quo*.

Many times I had people say "so and so are very philanthropic," suggesting that their donations should somehow be taken into consideration.

I would always say, "Stop, let's not go there. If their kid gets into USC and they have a good experience, and the parents would like to make gift, we will consider it down the road. But we're not going to discuss that now."

If anything like that came to my attention, I wouldn't tolerate it.

And when the Varsity Blues scandal hit the headlines, I wasn't even president anymore. More than six months after I stepped down as president, I first read the story like everyone else. I never met Rick Singer and I'd never even heard his name until I saw the news in March 2019.

To this day, if I do an online search about the scandal many stories are accompanied by a picture of Tommy Trojan. And yet, there were other universities involved.

In the media, it seemed like Varsity Blues was only about money. But the truth is that the total contributions from the parents involved in the scandal did not exceed $1 million. That's less than .0001 percent of the entire amount raised during USC's fundraising campaign.

The big question is why so many prominent parents would take such a risk, using athletics to cheat to get their kids into top colleges. In 2019, a USC alumna published an op-ed in the *Wall Street Journal* titled "Scandal Brings USC into the Elite Ranks."[18]

The op-ed was somewhat tongue-in-cheek, but it had a point. USC was no longer the "University of Spoiled Children." It had become an elite institution "mentioned in the same breath as Yale, Stanford, and UCLA."[19]

* * *

Shortly after I stepped down as president, I had another dinner with Charlie Munger. We were negotiating the possible merger of Good Samaritan Hospital with USC's medical enterprise. He wanted to know more about the results of our fundraising campaign.

"On average, we've been raising $2.3 million per day or $895 million per year," I said. "Our total budget for all of our development officers is about $84 million. So, basically the actual cost to the university is about 10 cents for every dollar. For other non-profits, it's sometimes 30 or 40 cents per dollar."

"That's impressive," he said. "How many people have donated?"

"We've had more than 400,000 donors and half of them have given for the first time," I said.

"And what are you using all of that money for?" he asked.

"It's all about academic excellence," I said. "One hundred and ten faculty chairs, seven schools and divisions named, 25 new centers and institutes. And we've expanded the facilities on campus by 30 percent."

"That's an incredible achievement. No different from Stanford and other Ivy League schools in terms of raising funds," he said.

"Yes, Charlie, but the success of the campaign is now being trashed, as if it was the only thing we cared about," I said. "The truth is that I had my staff go through my calendar and I never spent more than 15 to 20 percent of my time on fundraising. My schedule was packed from early morning until late evening, but most of my time was spent on initiatives to improve the quality and diversity of students and faculty, especially in recruiting."

"It's envy, jealousy, and madness. That's what it is, Max," he said.

* * *

As soon as I stepped down, one of the very first people who called me to get together for lunch was Eli Broad. We had lunch in a private room at the California Club.

He wanted to thank me for the collaboration we had together, but also for what I'd done for USC and the City of Los Angeles.

At one point, we also chatted about the campaign.

"Did everything work out the way you planned it?" he asked.

"Of course not, Eli," I said. "Besides the obvious, although we reached the goal ahead of schedule, there were a lot of things that surprised me."

"Such as?" he asked.

"Originally, I thought half the money we raised would go toward the endowment. But it ended up only being about one-third," I said. "Big donors didn't like giving money for someday in the future. They wanted to have an immediate impact."

"That's not a bad thing," he said.

"No, of course not. But I was also surprised that about 65 percent of the money came from non-alumni. I expected it to be the other way around."

"Again, it shows they're investing in excellence like our foundation, not just because they love the university," he said.

"And it turned out that around 63 percent of the gift proposals that were given to donors were funded. I thought it would be higher for some reason," I said.

"How much went to medicine?" he asked.

"About 35 percent," I responded.

"When you became provost, USC didn't have much in the medical sciences and patient care," he said. "It took a serious investment and look where it is now. Be proud of that, Max."

* * *

Whenever you meet so many people during the process of a campaign, you also get to know some eccentric characters who provide you with strange and often funny stories.

There was the Greek-American gentleman from Chicago who showed up outside my office, without an appointment, demanding to see me. He was waving around a movie script, telling the receptionist that since I'd raised so much money, I should fund his movie and introduce him to Steven Spielberg.

Instead, my office called the Department of Public Safety. Then he became a very persistent stalker on social media, trashing me at every opportunity.

And all because I wouldn't introduce him to Steven Spielberg!

* * *

And then there was a USC alumnus and, at the time, a big fundraiser for the Democratic Party. He reached out to my office, wanting to introduce me to members of the Royal Family of Saudi Arabia, who he said wanted to donate money to USC.

But I refused to take a meeting with him. I didn't like the tone of his emails or the conversations he had with my Chief of Staff. When I turned him down, he got angry and started badmouthing me to Democratic officials in Los Angeles.

When the Prime Minister of Greece visited L.A., he wrote an email to him referring to me as the, "Idiot Greek president of USC."

It got so bad that a member of my staff reached out to Democratic members of Congress to see if they could convince him to stop behaving like that.

The response we received was basically, "If he's raising money, it will be difficult to do anything."

Then the 2016 election arrived and suddenly he became a big Trump supporter, raising money to support his election.

In 2021, he was sentenced to 12 years in federal prison for "falsifying records to conceal his work as a foreign agent while lobbying high-level U.S. government officials, evading the payment of millions of dollars in taxes, making illegal campaign contributions, and obstructing a federal investigation into the source of donations to a presidential inauguration committee," according to *The Daily Beast*.[20]

* * *

Very often I get the question: What was the secret of USC's fundraising success? First and foremost, it was a team effort by hundreds of people throughout the university.

I have to begin by giving credit to my wife, Niki. She worked tirelessly, hosting more than 26,000 people at the president's house over eight years. Nearly 5,000 of those guests were students who gathered with us on Thanksgiving Day or during the holiday parties in December.

She shook the hands of every single one of them as they arrived for dinners or afternoon receptions, both small and large. She was also in charge of coordinating the tea gatherings of the Trojan women organizations. For her it was always about building relationships and being grateful for the Trojan Family.

We never, ever solicited a single gift from anyone at the

president's house, and we never hosted a fundraising event at our home.

It was all about saying thank you. This is what makes USC different from other universities, especially public institutions.

* * *

When it comes to the achievements of the campaign, much credit goes to USC's deans, the talented faculty, and chairs of the medical school, along with the devoted directors of the school's research centers and institutes.

And, of course, I'm very grateful for the 460 development officers, some of whom were better than others, but they were all collectively the "soul of the battle."

USC alumnus Norman Schwarzkopf, the commander of the allied forces in the Gulf War, was asked, "What's the greatest lesson you've learned out of all this?"[21]

"I think that there is one really fundamental military truth," he said. "Unless the soldier on the ground, or the airman in the air, has the will to win, has the strength of character to go into battle, believes that his cause is just, and has the support of his country . . . all the rest of that stuff is irrelevant."[22]

Our development staff had the support of their president and their deans, believed they were making a difference, and worked very hard for their assignments. They are the unsung heroes of the campaign.

And I will always be very grateful to everyone who worked tirelessly to help us transform the future of USC and the lives of generations of Trojans.

PART FIVE

THE FUTURE OF HIGHER EDUCATION

CHAPTER 28

Enduring Harsh NCAA Penalties

«Νέοι γὰρ οἰακονόμοι κρατοῦσ' Ὀλύμπου
νεοχμοῖς δὲ δὴ νόμοις Ζεὺς
ἀθέτως κρατύνει
τὰ πρὶν δὲ πελώρια νῦν αἰστοῖ.»
ΑΪΣΧΎΛΟΥ ΠΡΟΜΗΘΕΎΣ ΔΕΣΜΏΤΗΣ, 148–150

"These are the new laws indeed
By which Zeus tyrannically rules;
And the great powers of the past he now destroys."[1]
AESCHYLUS, *PROMETHEUS BOUND*, LINES 148–150

When I became president-elect in 2010, I knew USC would soon be marking several milestones revolving around athletics. These included the 100th anniversary of the "Trojan" nickname and the 125th anniversary of the founding of USC's athletic program.[2,3]

USC's athletic director always reported directly to the president, so when I was provost, I didn't deal with many athletic issues. And yet, with the university's athletic history and tradition, I could see major storm clouds gathering on the horizon.

With the departure of Pete Carroll to the NFL and the possibility of being heavily penalized by the NCAA, there were potential problems arising for the reputation of the entire university.

After the initial hearing with the NCAA in Spring 2010, I received positive feedback from President Sample and those involved with the football and basketball programs.

Athletics was one of the most recognizable aspects of the university. If its reputation was at risk in the court of public opinion, I knew changes would have to be made in athletic compliance. But I didn't know how quickly they would have to happen.

⁂ ⁂ ⁂

Within weeks of my announcement as USC's next president, I reached out to Dave Roberts about the possibility of becoming vice president for athletic compliance.

We went for a long bike ride, from Torrance beach to Santa Monica and back. The ocean was a beautiful backdrop for our conversation throughout the 35-mile ride.

For many years, Dave had been a very successful attorney, who had three decades of experience in complex commercial litigation, had served as an arbitrator and mediator, and had argued cases before the California Supreme Court, the United States Court of Appeals for the Ninth Circuit, and the California Court of Appeals.[4, 5]

Although he wasn't a Trojan alumnus, he had played football at the University of California, Davis, and he loved USC football.

Ten years earlier, I had met him when he handled a case for the Integrated Media Systems Center, and I was very impressed by his legal mind and his leadership skills.

I explained to him what I had in mind. It was the first position of its kind in the nation, and I planned to elevate the importance of the position and commit the resources to build a strong office of compliance. It only took one more meeting to close the deal! He would start the same day I officially assumed the presidency: August 3, 2010.

⁂ ⁂ ⁂

Beyond creating a strong compliance office, we also needed to find out what we had to fix internally.

I consulted with several trustees, asking them to suggest the right person to do an internal investigation of USC's athletic department. Many recommended law firms, but one of our trustees gave me the best advice.

"Max, you need someone out of the box, but with experience in doing these investigations," he said. "How about the former FBI Director Louis Freeh? I can make the introduction, if you like."

Freeh and his team helped us assess the state of USC's athletic department and its processes. By the end of September, they provided us with a list of recommended changes to enhance all of the university's athletic operations.

They helped us design better athletic compliance protocols, especially for high-profile student-athletes, who were the most likely to be approached by agents and others who might not have their best interests in mind.

And the Freeh Group served as an advisor in helping us meet our goal of creating the best possible athletic department and athletic compliance office in the nation.

* * *

With all of this going on in the background, Mike Garrett still had to replace Pete Carroll, one of the most successful and popular coaches in recent history, who had left for the NFL in January 2010.

Mike always liked Lane Kiffin, USC's co-offensive coordinator under Pete Carroll. Kiffin left USC in 2007 after being hired as the head coach of the Oakland Raiders at 31, at the time making him the youngest head coach in modern NFL history.[6]

When Kiffin was fired by the Oakland Raiders one year later, it took him just over a month to land a college head coaching job at the University of Tennessee.

Mike Garrett was very negative about Steve Sarkisian, who also served as a co-offensive coordinator under Pete Carroll.

He thought Kiffin had an excellent football mind and that he was an outstanding recruiter of assistant coaches. Plus, with Lane Kiffin, Garrett saw the opportunity to recruit a whole collection of assistant coaches who were already on Kiffin's staff at Tennessee.

One morning when I was provost, President Sample asked me to join him and Mike Garrett for a phone interview with Lane Kiffin. I didn't say anything, I just listened to the conversation.

Clearly, Lane was very excited about the USC job and considered it a crowning achievement in his young career. It was clear that the call was merely a formality. And Lane Kiffin was officially announced as USC's head coach in January 2010.[7]

Steve Sample later shared with me his golden principle for dealing with athletics.

"The athletic director is responsible for the hiring and firing of coaches," Sample told me. "Nobody else interferes with that process, especially not trustees. Every trustee who loves football will have an opinion about who should be the next coach, and every member in the administration may have an opinion too. But this is a decision to be made by the athletic director and only the athletic director. The president can give advice, but nothing more than that. This is a decision fully owned by the athletic director."

It was wise advice and I adopted the same policy when I became president.

But soon the storm clouds that I had noticed earlier would begin growing darker by the day.

* * *

Only six months after Lane Kiffin took over as USC's head coach, the program was hit with severe sanctions.

It was the harshest penalty handed out by the NCAA since they delivered the "death penalty" to the SMU football team in 1987.[8] Not only football received sanctions. The NCAA report claimed that basketball player O. J. Mayo received improper benefits during the one year he played for USC.[9]

For many members of the Trojan Family, the NCAA's decision was considered drastic, and a large number of our alumni were deeply upset.

It looked like things couldn't get any worse. But I would soon be proven wrong again.

* * *

Just a few hours after the release of the NCAA's report, Athletic Director Mike Garrett spoke to a group of USC alumni at an event in San Francisco.

According to reports by ESPN and others, at one point in his remarks, Garrett apparently said, "As I read the decision by the NCAA, all I could get out of all of this was . . . I read between the lines and there was nothing but a lot of envy, and they wish they all were Trojans."[10]

The story noted that he received cheers from the pro-USC crowd, but, of course, that kind of comment is bound to create headlines for some and headaches for others.[11] Soon it was a firestorm that was raging out of control.

* * *

The tone of Steve Sample's first cabinet meeting after the sanctions were handed down was somber. It was one of his last cabinet meetings as president and he caught my attention when he said, "The next president will have to make the decision about what to do with our athletic director."

Of course, I was sitting there in that meeting as USC's president-elect. It was clear that Steve Sample understood that Mike Garrett would have to be replaced.

Unfortunately, he didn't want to be the one to tell him that he needed to step down.

* * *

I asked to meet with Mike Garrett, but he was nowhere to be found.

He wasn't returning any phone calls from senior administration. Finally, they tracked him down and asked him to come to a meeting.

I always respected Mike. He had won the 1965 Heisman Trophy as a running back for USC.[12] His track record of success during his tenure as athletic director is undeniable. As a leader, he was tough, but fair with his coaches. I always respected his values and he wasn't a cheater.

It wasn't an easy meeting. He was upset, accused the NCAA of racial discrimination, and he threatened litigation.

Because I respected him, I felt I was more than fair with his exit package.

On July 20, 2010, I sent out a message to the USC community, noting several changes in the athletic program.

After that announcement, two of USC's most prominent professors paid me a visit: Kevin Starr and Warren Bennis. Both academic titans, they were also huge fans of Trojan football. But they were there to express their frustration about how everything had happened.

"Steve should have never put you in the position to fire Mike Garrett," said Kevin Starr. "He should have done it."

"It would have been very easy to tell Mike Garrett, 'After 17 years, you go out with me and let Max pick a new athletic director,'" Warren added.

Sadly, given what I went through in the meeting with Mike, we have never spoken since.

❊ ❊ ❊

Now I had to find a new athletic director, and I had a surprising candidate in mind.

I got to know Pat Haden when he was a member of USC's Board of Trustees. When I was provost, I staffed the board's academic affairs committee, which Pat chaired at the time. I really liked him personally and respected his academic values and his deep love of USC's students.

He had made an incredible impact on and off the playing field. He was a Rhodes Scholar, who won with honor at USC and continued to win with honor in his professional career afterward. That is why he was so beloved by the Trojan Family.

But I would be asking him for something very unusual. He was already a university trustee and yet I was asking him to give that up—to have me as his boss—so that he could give back to our student-athletes.

However, I was certain that no one bled cardinal and gold like Pat Haden.

We met in my office for the full discussion. The first thing he said was, "I would like J. K. McKay to be with me as one of the associate athletic directors."

"Okay," I said.

Although he was going to become the highest paid athletic director in the nation, he reminded me that he would have to give up the Notre Dame football broadcasting job for NBC.

We shook hands and agreed to keep everything strictly confidential until the announcement went out. A week later, we had a follow-up breakfast meeting at the Cal Club, where we signed the contracts.

* * *

As soon as the announcement went out, we were surprised that the news was immediately a front-page story in the *Los Angeles Times*.

It turns out that one of the California Club employees was telling everyone that he'd witnessed Pat and I having that early breakfast meeting, and apparently someone tipped off the *Times*!

The reaction was swift and positive, drawing attention from national media and the sports community.

Bill Dwyre, the former sports editor and columnist at the *Los Angeles Times* wrote, "Credit to the new guy, president-elect Max Nikias. He either knew or listened to the right people. Either way, he got it right . . . Haden is a once-in-a-lifetime person who transcends fan loyalty and school bias. He's a class act."[13]

However, as we know, for even the most heralded of hires there is always a honeymoon period that, unfortunately, never lasts.

* * *

On the day of the announcement, I was in Charlottesville, Virginia, meeting with Gene Corrigan, the former athletic director at Notre Dame.

I'd consulted with him for help in hiring the athletic director, and he later stayed on as a consultant for USC's athletic department to help Pat Haden make the transition to the new role.

Before dinner, he took me for a walk in his neighborhood and we talked about the sanctions.

"To be fair," I said. "The sanctions are very severe, almost vindictive."

"I know, I know," he said. "Part of it was that they wanted to send a signal to other programs and chose to make an example of USC."

Then he added "My advice is to take Pat and your new

compliance person and go to Indianapolis. Meet with them and ask Pat to be a regular visitor, building relationships with the NCAA."

* * *

When the NCAA's sanctions were announced, the university was required to distance itself from Reggie Bush. This also included returning his Heisman Trophy. The only problem is that this had never happened before. No one knew what to do, or how to handle the entire process.

Before the announcement was made, Pat Haden and Dave Roberts urgently came to my office.

"We need to see you about Bush's Heisman Trophy," said Haden.

"You know, we're disassociating from Bush and removing his No. 5 jersey from the display in the Coliseum," said Roberts. "According to the penalties, the disassociation is forever."

There was a brief pause.

"But you don't have to return the Heisman," said Roberts.

"Yes, you don't have to return the trophy," said Haden.

"I consulted the executive committee of our Board of Trustees and all of them are in agreement. We can't keep the Heisman if we can't display it," I said. "So my decision is final. We will return it."

USC returned the Heisman Trophy on display in Heritage Hall. But Reggie Bush's trophy was a different story.

The entire process was a bit comic. The Heisman Trophy Trust had no process in place for how to get Bush to return the trophy, or for how to receive it when he did. Eventually, Reggie Bush did quietly return his Heisman, but his NFL career was already underway.

After the announcement was made, I received a call from a trustee who was a big football fan.

"Why did you return it? Why?" he screamed into the phone. "I wanted us to have seven trophies—the same as Notre Dame!"

No matter what you do, you can't make everyone happy.

⁂ ⁂ ⁂

During my first month as president of USC, with all of the other pressures of being the new leader of a university, I had my first meeting with the NCAA, along with Pat Haden and Dave Roberts.

For the trip, we were hosted by Jeff Smulyan, a USC trustee who lived in Indianapolis and had a lot of contacts at the NCAA.

In 2006, as soon as the story about Reggie Bush and possible impermissible benefits surfaced, he and Chairman Stanley Gold begged Steve Sample to get on a plane and visit the NCAA's offices. By having a conversation, they felt that the NCAA might allow self-imposed penalties.

But at the time, USC's football program was at its height and Steve Sample didn't want to hear about it.

For this trip, Jeff Smulyan told us that everyone at the NCAA was looking forward to seeing us and that they saw this visit as a new beginning.

The next morning Pat, Dave, and I had a series of meetings at the NCAA offices and we told them we planned to appeal the decision. Then Smulyan hosted a lunch for all of us and the NCAA leadership.

Clearly, everyone had great respect and admiration for Haden, and also admired Roberts as our new compliance chief.

⁂ ⁂ ⁂

In January 2011, I traveled along with our athletic leadership team and our legal consultants again to Indianapolis. The entire experience was new to me, and I felt out of my element in the snow and ice of Indianapolis.

When we got to the appeals hearing, the reception was as chilly as the weather outside.

It was clear that the infractions committee was not happy that USC had hired Lane Kiffin. It seemed like they didn't want to judge him under our new leadership and compliance programs, but rather that he had been part of Pete Carroll's program in the past.

As a group, we spent four hours and thirteen minutes presenting our case and making our appeal. It was difficult to read the responses of the committee members.

As we emerged from the appeals hearing, I addressed the reporters who had assembled outside by saying, "I want to thank the NCAA for giving us the opportunity before the committee for a good and fair hearing. We just have to wait for the ruling."

A decision was expected in four to eight weeks. We waited for nearly five months.

The NCAA's decision on USC's appeal came down on May 25, 2011, just a couple of weeks after commencement that year.

From the very beginning, we had known the entire process was an uphill battle, so it wasn't a complete shock when the Committee on Infractions denied our appeal. They wanted to make an example of USC and they didn't want to appear to soften their position.

It was disappointing to all of us, but it was our alumni that were really upset.

I'd had a long discussion with Haden and Roberts about whether USC should file a lawsuit against the NCAA. We even recruited an outside attorney to look into it. But in the end, we concluded that legally we didn't have a case. The bylaws that all universities sign essentially allow the NCAA to be the investigator, judge, and jury for any cases they choose to pursue. Without NCAA reforms, we didn't stand a chance in court.

But for our alumni, the case wasn't so much legal as it was emotional.

One morning, as I walked into my office, my chief of staff, ran in behind me and closed the door.

He looked shaken as he said, "The receptionist received a very upsetting phone call this morning from an alumnus who is very angry that you didn't file a lawsuit against the NCAA."

"Really, I'm not surprised," I said.

"He said that he, his father, and his grandfather are all Trojans," he continued. "And that from now on, you have no right to set foot in the L.A. Memorial Coliseum."

I shrugged, not knowing what else to say.

"And he said that if you do, he will kill you."

I didn't take it seriously, assuming it was just someone letting off steam.

But when I shared the story with the chairman of the board, his reaction was more serious.

He immediately issued an executive order as chairman of the board, stating that two DPS officers would always shadow me and Niki at all football games at the Coliseum.

* * *

Because our legal options were limited, we instead wanted to build an excellent working relationship with Indianapolis, which we did. In the long run, it helped USC when dealing with other potential infractions.

When Pat Haden or I spoke at events, the appeal inevitably came up. At one alumni event, after I finished my speech, an alumnus stood up and shouted, "Why didn't we file a lawsuit in the Reggie Bush case?"

"Giving the NCAA subpoena power by filing a lawsuit, we don't know what else they could find," I said.

* * *

In 2020, USC Football posted a message on Twitter, which read, "Welcome home, @ReggieBush."[14] After a decade, the disassociation with Bush had ended.

Finally, in April 2024, after 14 years, The Heisman Trust announced that the trophy would be returned to Bush along with a replica to USC.[15]

CHAPTER 29

Endless Adventures

«Τίς εὐδαίμων, ὁ τὸ μὲν σῶμα ὑγιής,
τὴν δὲ ψυχὴν εὔπορος, τὴν δὲ φύσιν εὐπαίδευτος.»
ΔΙΟΓΈΝΗΣ ΛΑΈΡΤΙΟΣ, ΒΊΟΙ ΦΙΛΟΣΌΦΩΝ, ΘΑΛΉΣ (1.33–1.37)

"Who is happy?" "He who has a healthy body,
a sound mind and a cultivated nature."[1]
DIOGENES LAËRTIUS, *LIVES AND OPINIONS OF EMINENT PHILOSOPHERS*, THALES (1.33–1.37)

Despite the sanctions, we did have two really outstanding years of Trojan football while I was president: the 2011 and the 2016 seasons.

Unfortunately, due to the NCAA ban, the 2011 team wasn't able to play in a bowl game. But that season had several highlights.

On November 19, 2011, the team traveled to play undefeated Oregon. Although everyone expected Oregon to win and play for the BCS Championship Game, USC was ahead at halftime 21-7.

At the half, Phil Knight appeared in our suite with Steve and Connie Ballmer. The Ballmers were USC parents, but Connie was a trustee and alumna of the University of Oregon. They were dressed up as Ducks!

"You're ahead because you've figured out our weaknesses on defense and you keep pounding on them," said Phil Knight.

As they were leaving, Steve Ballmer whispered, "Max, Max."

I turned to see him secretly giving the "Fight on!" signal, covering his hand with his green Ducks jacket.

Like practically all of the games Niki and I attended, this one went down to the final minutes, with Oregon missing a field goal attempt and USC winning 38–35.

After the game, USC wide receiver Robert Woods ran up, hugged me, and said, "President Nikias, SC is back!"

* * *

After the success of that season, in August 2012, preseason polls had USC ranked #1 in the nation.

As soon as I saw that, I called Dave Roberts and said, "Dave, I worry that agents will be going after our players again. Let's make sure we are even more vigilant in compliance."

He agreed to step up our efforts.

Despite several successes in previous years, the 2013 season did not go according to plan.

By the time USC played at Arizona State in late September, Pat Haden was on edge. He was so nervous about the game that he refused to watch it from the suite as he usually did. Instead, he stayed outside and followed the game on Twitter.

I thought it was strange and uncharacteristic of him, but apparently he was feeling the pressure of our alumni base, which is never satisfied no matter how well the Trojans play. Even when we were winning, there were constant complaints about Kiffin's play-calling!

At one point, Haden stopped by the suite and asked to talk to me.

"We're going to lose tonight—and probably badly," he said. "I already discussed it with my leadership team, and I've decided that we need to change the head coach. I'll fire Kiffin after the game."

I was very surprised. It came out of nowhere.

"Why don't you wait until the end of the season?" I asked.

"No, it needs to happen after the game," Haden said. "We already talked to Orgeron to take over as interim."

"Will you fire him tomorrow in your office?" I asked.

"No, I'll do it at the airport as soon as we arrive. The coaches have to go out for recruiting, I can't wait until 10:00 a.m. in my office."

"Pat, this is brutal," I said. "But it's your decision."

"I want to bring in Sarkisian as head coach," he said.

"Sarkisian? He doesn't have a good track record at Washington," I responded.

"He knows the recruiting market of Southern California," Haden insisted.

* * *

Haden's prediction for that night was correct. The game was a disaster. USC lost to Arizona State 62–41.[2]

Lane Kiffin was fired at 3:14 a.m.[3] Five years later, he described the incident as the low point of his career.

"I had no idea at all," Kiffin said in an interview with CBS Sports. "It totally caught me off guard. I got off the plane. I put my bag on the bus. I was going to sleep at the facility. Someone came and said, 'Pat wants to see you.' I left my briefcase on the bus."[4]

I understand that our fans and alumni are very passionate. But the Trojans were 3–2. And they finished 10–4, tied for second place in the Pac-12's South Division.[5] However, people weren't satisfied.

* * *

Pat Haden had chosen to move on from Lane Kiffin. There was only one problem. Ed Orgeron was popular among the players and he was gaining traction with the fans.

He wanted the job and expected to get it. He had a lot of

momentum going into the last game of the season against UCLA in the Coliseum. He even brought his wife and mother that day, but we lost to #22 UCLA 35–14.

After the game, Haden delivered the bad news. Orgeron wouldn't be USC's next head coach, but he was a great recruiter so there was a chance he could remain on staff.

Orgeron was very angry.

"You have to beat UCLA and Notre Dame," said Haden. "And you lost to both."

* * *

The Sunday after the UCLA game, Pat Haden, Mark Jackson, and J.K. McKay got on a private plane and flew to Boise to interview Chris Petersen. Previously, they had also interviewed Kevin Sumlin, the head coach of Texas A&M and former USC player and NFL coach Jack Del Rio.

Pat called me right after the interview.

"J. K., Mark Jackson, and I just finished interviewing Petersen," said Haden. "I'm not sure he'll be a good fit for us. We're off to Seattle to interview Sark."

Later in the evening he called me again and said, "Sark is my choice."

"Okay," I said. "Hiring and firing coaches is your responsibility. My job is to challenge your thinking. Petersen has a much better record than Sarkisian."

"He's not in the same league as Sark," said Haden. "And he doesn't know the Southern California recruiting landscape as well as Sark does."

In the end, it wasn't my decision to make. So USC announced the hiring of Steve Sarkisian on December 2, 2013.[6]

Almost immediately, we learned that Orgeron had resigned, even though he'd been offered a job as an assistant on Sarkisian's staff.[7]

I'm not saying that Orgeron should have been USC's next head coach. But you have to remember that he won six Pac-12 games during the 2013 season, which was more wins than Sarkisian had won in any of his five years at Washington.

Orgeron would later get a major college head coaching job, leading LSU to the 2019 national championship.

But the decision had been made. And USC needed a coach for the Las Vegas Bowl. Haden found that in assistant coach Clay Helton, who served as interim head coach for that game. Little did we know then that Helton would play a larger role in the future. Because the football program was about to make more headlines.

* * *

On the evening of August 22, 2015, Niki and I attended the annual Salute to Troy event, a major fundraiser for the athletic program that signaled the beginning of a new football season and a new academic year.

This was Steve Sarkisian's first big event as head coach. But soon he said several inappropriate things, including that Arizona State, Oregon, and Notre Dame all "suck," as well as shouting, "Get ready to f—n Fight On, baby!"[8]

It was embarrassing. And it turned out that he had been drinking too much.

There were 2,000 people attending the event, and Niki and I were hosting a table for major athletic donors. But it all happened so fast that none of us could believe it.

Apparently, Pat Haden and J. K. McKay were seen talking to Sarkisian backstage and determined that his assistants should finish the program.[9]

Sarkisian later claimed that it was an accident, telling reporters that, "The moral of the story is if you mix meds with alcohol, you say or do things you regret."[10]

Pat called me later that evening to update me on the situation.

"I made it clear to him with J.K that there will be zero tolerance," he said. "He heard me loud and clear."

"Pat, that's not good enough," I said with frustration. "It was an embarrassment, humiliating. I've already received phone calls from trustees who think he should be fired tonight. If we do that, it may cost us more than $30 million. You need to get a signed letter from him, stating that if it happens again, he is out instantly."

Pat agreed. The following week, at USC's annual coaches' compliance luncheon at the Galen Center, Sarkisian delivered the signed letter to Haden.

I thought that would be the end of it. Maybe it was just an unfortunate mistake. But less than two months later, there would be more headlines.

* * *

In September, USC lost its first Pac-12 game on the road at Stanford. A few weeks later, the Trojans lost a Thursday night game in the Coliseum to Washington, Sarkisian's former team coached by Chris Petersen.

On Sunday, October 12, I got a call from Pat Haden early in the morning. I was still in bed when the phone rang.

He told me that he'd learned Sarkisian didn't show up to practice. He placed Sark on a leave of absence, but after looking into what happened he later decided to fire him.

On Tuesday, Haden held a press conference in which he said "The decision I made didn't work out, and I own that. I own it. Have we gotten everything right? Clearly not . . . This happens. And I said I own it."[11]

Pat then made the decision to appoint Clay Helton as interim head coach.

Our student-athletes and Clay Helton had to pick up the

pieces of the mess that had been left behind. When Sarkisian was fired, USC's football team was only days away from traveling to South Bend to face Notre Dame.

The pressure was really on Pat Haden.

I released a statement, saying that the administration still supported him. Unfortunately, the alumni base was getting angry, and the sports media was very critical, believing Sark wasn't properly vetted before he had been hired.

That took a toll on Pat's health, which we would all witness the next Saturday in South Bend.

❋ ❋ ❋

The atmosphere in South Bend is always wild. On the way to the stadium, I noticed a sign outside Sacred Heart Catholic Church that read:

> GO IRISH.
> KICK USC'S ASS.
> LOVE JESUS

That Saturday I was on the sideline with John Mork, the chairman of USC's Board of Trustees at the time. All of a sudden, Pat collapsed.

The NBC broadcast even showed the video, Pat's face looking confused, his hand instinctively covering his heart.[12]

John Mork quickly rushed to his side and helped him walk back to the locker room. After getting checked out at a local hospital, John and Julie Mork offered to give Pat and his wife a ride back to Los Angeles on their private jet.

❋ ❋ ❋

As Niki and I rode on the team plane back to Los Angeles, I was thinking about the crises we were facing with athletics and USC's football program.

It was clear that changes needed to be made.

To his credit, with his health issues, it was Haden who decided to step down as athletic director. Once he had made that decision, I felt strongly that he shouldn't be the one picking the next football coach. I thought that decision should be left to the next athletic director.

Ultimately, J. K. McKay agreed with me. He helped convince Pat that Clay Helton should stay on as USC's head coach. It was only fair that we let the next athletic director assess the program's future.

* * *

In recruiting USC's next athletic director, I made it clear to everyone that this decision was the president's choice.

When talking to Pat, I used the analogy of the Catholic Church.

"The Pope gets to pick his Cardinals. But the outgoing Cardinal doesn't pick his successor," I said.

Later, in a radio interview, Pat repeated the metaphor when he was asked if he was involved with the search.

Unfortunately, throughout the process, I found myself being lobbied by some trustees about names suggested by Pat.

The search committee was only advisory and all candidates were to be vetted thoroughly. I was very impressed by Lynn Swann. I admired his values, his knowledge of football, and his business experience. As a former Trojan himself, he would also be an inspiration for many of our African American student-athletes.

Over the years, reporters from the *Los Angeles Times* have tried to claim that I hired Lynn because he was close friends with USC Life Trustee B. Wayne Hughes. But the truth is exactly what I told those reporters: "At no point was there any influence from any donor or member of the board. None whatsoever."

The night before the press conference to introduce Lynn as our new athletic director, I did give Wayne a courtesy call to let him know.

It was later revealed that Pat Haden wasn't informed of Lynn Swann's hiring until about five minutes before the announcement.

What people didn't know was that Lynn also had one request of me. He made it clear that he didn't want J.K. McKay as one of his associate athletic directors.

Again, unfortunately, when I asked J.K. to step down this did not sit well with Pat. That was my biggest disappointment. I was surprised by Pat's response and the two of us have barely spoken since that time.

* * *

During the first year of Lynn Swann's tenure, Clay Helton and the 2016 football team surprised us all.

The season started with a humiliating 52–6 loss to Alabama in Arlington, Texas. Then we lost to Stanford and Utah over the next three weeks.

But after Sam Darnold was named as the starting quarterback, everything started to change and we won our final eight games.[13]

Somehow we defeated #4 Washington in Seattle. Then we kept up the momentum, beating all of our top rivals, including Oregon, UCLA, and Notre Dame.

On Sunday morning, December 4, 2016, I received a call from Disney's Bob Iger.

"Max, I just learned from our ESPN reporters that the final CFP rankings will be released in one hour. USC is ranked #9 and slated to play at the Rose Bowl against #5 Penn State."

"This is great news! Thanks, Bob!" I said.

* * *

The Rose Bowl on January 1, 2017, was the biggest achievement for USC's football team since the Pete Carroll era.

It was a classic game. USC was trailing 49–35 in the fourth quarter and it looked like we would lose. But then we scored 17 straight points, winning 52–49 on a last-second field goal.[14]

After the game, Lynn Swann was asked if the victory was enough to return the Trojans to the pinnacle of college football.

"If we were back at the top of the national landscape, we'd be playing on Monday, January 9th," he said, referring to the College Football Playoff title game. "We're not there yet. It's a building process."[15]

* * *

In the background of the transformation happening in USC athletics, there was something happening that I would learn about later. More than six months after I stepped down as president, unbeknownst to me, the Varsity Blues cheating scandal was taking place.

When Varsity Blues hit the headlines, I first read the story like everyone else. I never met Rick Singer and I'd never even heard his name until I saw the news in March 2019.

For many years, USC encouraged its student-athletes to pursue the ideal of perfecting the mind and the body. Year after year, we watched the Graduation Success Rate of those exceptional student-athletes continue to climb.

The cheating that occurred during Varsity Blues is the exact opposite of everything USC athletics stands for. If I had known about what was happening, I would not have tolerated it.

* * *

During that time, in addition to elevating our athletic programs, it was clear that the infrastructure for Trojan athletics was falling apart.

As soon as I became president, our overarching strategy was to raise funds to renovate Heritage Hall, build the John McKay Center, and create the Uytengsu Aquatics Center. We also succeeded in getting a 99-year lease of the Coliseum with the State of California, and renovating it with a $315 million commitment from philanthropic giving.

* * *

Despite all of the challenges and successes during my years at USC, college athletics continues to evolve. So what does the future hold for college football and basketball?

Today it's all about the money! And I'm afraid that will only intensify in the years and decades ahead.

The "transfer portal" in college football, NIL deals, and the House vs. NCAA class action settlement—which allows up to 22 percent of annual revenues to be paid to athletes—have rapidly accelerated the transformation from student-athletes to simply athletes.[16, 17]

At the same time, a group of female student-athletes has objected to the $2.8 billion settlement, saying that it "vastly favors men."[18]

* * *

If nothing else, these changes have forever reduced the NCAA's authority over student-athletes. In the future, large corporations and wealthy donors who sponsor lucrative NIL deals will sway the top talent to a select few programs year after year.

Even the major conferences that have been the bedrock of

college competition for more than a century are realigning for lucrative television contracts.

In October 2022, USC and UCLA shocked some when they suddenly announced that they would be leaving the Pac-12 to join the Big-10.[19] This move followed an announcement in June 2022 that Texas and Oklahoma were leaving the Big-12 for the SEC.[20]

During my tenure at USC, we were always concerned about preserving the longstanding rivalries among the four California schools. We felt very strongly that these historic competitions should be protected in perpetuity.

With USC and UCLA joining the Big-10, those rivalries are finished.

* * *

While conference realignments may seem like sudden changes that happened overnight, they were driven by financial realities that became inevitabilities.

College football and basketball have really been serving as semi-professional sports, although few are willing to admit it. For the top stars, a major college program is just a brief detour on the journey to a highly-paid career in the NFL or NBA.

The intense competition for the best players and coaches has dramatically changed college sports. For the 2022 football season, USC hired Lincoln Riley from Oklahoma, with a compensation package that exceeded $110 million.[21]

He was given a 10-year guaranteed contract,[22] as well as his request for a new $200 million Football Operations and Performance Center and a second practice field.[23, 24]

At that price, few universities can afford to hire or fire coaches every few years.

College football is also no longer a three-year recruiting cycle. Because of the transfer portal, it's a one-year cycle. In Lincoln Riley's first year at USC, he recruited 40 new players in about two months, according to CBS Sports.[25] At Colorado, Coach Deion Sanders recruited 68 new players in his first season, and then added 50 new scholarship players, including 39 new transfers, the next season.[26]

For the top programs, there are no longer excuses for not winning immediately. You can recruit nearly an entire team in a matter of months, if you can generate enough interest or NIL funding.

* * *

To address the financial pressures, many universities have turned to television and streaming contracts to help balance their budgets.

Los Angeles is the second largest media market in the United States, after the New York/New Jersey area.[27]

It's no surprise that a market of that size has two NFL teams, two NBA franchises, two baseball teams, two hockey teams, and, yes, two major college football and basketball programs.

When I became president of USC, the Pac-10 was expanding to the Pac-12. The TV contract for the Pac-10 was $60 million per year. The Pac-12 commissioner at that time, Larry Scott, helped negotiate a $250 million television contract per year for the conference.[28] It surpassed everyone's expectations.

But when the Pac-12 network was created, the conference failed to get a contract with Direct TV, which limited the network's reach and influence in the long run.

In only five years, the Pac-12 went from having the highest television revenues of any conference to the lowest.[29] And that gap just kept growing.

In 2022, the Big-10 also announced a seven-year, $7 billion television contract with three networks—Fox, CBS, and NBC.[30]

With so much money at stake, college athletics will never be the same.

For the next few years, it will be the Wild West until some governing organization creates new rules.

❋ ❋ ❋

In the future, I predict that college football and basketball will consolidate into three super conferences. And when that happens that will be the beginning of the end of the NCAA.

Those major conferences will hold all of the power and money from the television contracts.

The expansion of the College Football Playoff will only accelerate the pace of change. For three years, I chaired the Board of Managers for the College Football Playoff. The original TV deal with ESPN was $500 million![31]

Over a 12-year period, each school in a major conference whether they made it to playoffs or not would get approximately $100 million total for that period.[32]

At one of the meetings, I told the new president of the University of Maryland that his school was going to be getting $100 million in extra funding over a 12-year period. He had no idea!

He immediately called his athletic director to let him know.

❋ ❋ ❋

From the very beginning, there were pressures to expand the CFP to include more teams. With only four teams qualifying, there were always schools that complained that they didn't reach the playoff.

For university presidents, the concern was always the academic calendar. December is a month of final exams and January starts a new semester or new term.

Finally, in September 2022, the official announcement was made that the playoff would increase to 12 teams in 2024.[33]

Sometimes I wonder if we'll all look back with nostalgia at a time when collegiate athletics was about training student-athletes to chase championships instead of everyone chasing the almighty dollar.

* * *

Despite all of the money involved in college football and men's basketball today, the great majority of athletic departments are facing financial deficits.

College athletic boosters are donating to NIL collectives instead of athletics departments,[34] severely reducing significant sources of revenue.

Although media contracts are large, so are the expenses, especially for teams that must now travel long distances practically every week.

If athletic departments have to allocate up to 22 percent of their total revenues to athletes—and this percentage will likely increase if athletes unionize—the current business model for college athletics is unsustainable.

This is why there are serious discussions about creating partnerships with private equity.[35] In May 2024, two major private equity firms launched an investment fund to provide loans to athletic departments—"in exchange for a share of additional revenue generated under their partnership," of course.[36]

Before we know it, non-profit and for-profit partnerships may be the future of college athletics. However, the move toward profits and paychecks has federal and state tax implications, both for athletes and for universities.[37]

* * *

While collegiate athletics is experiencing many changes, USC continues to make headlines.

In May 2023, USC Athletic Director Mike Bohn suddenly resigned.

The accusations that Bohn was not properly vetted broke just as USC was preparing to enter the Big 10.

Then, in July 2024, at the Big 10 media days, Lincoln Riley was quoted telling reporters: "We are playing catch up in facilities and NIL. We are playing catch up in resources within the program."[38]

This generated a big concern among the Trojan alumni base that their head coach was finding excuses, and that the team may not be formidable entering the Big-10 competition.

But in the rapidly changing world of college athletics it seems that some things never change.

CHAPTER 30

In the Spotlight

"All the world's a stage,
And all the men and women merely players:
They have their exits and their entrances;
And one man in his time plays many parts."[1]

SHAKESPEARE, *AS YOU LIKE IT*,
ACT II, SCENE VII, LINES 139–142

Athletics was not the only thing that drew attention to USC. When I was president-elect, I received an intriguing call from Hong Kong. It was trustee Ronnie Chan, who asked an interesting question.

"Max, have you decided which foreign country you're going to visit first?" he said. "It really sends a message which country you visit first."

"Ronnie, yes, I have decided without hesitation," I replied. "We'll visit India first and our trustee Ratan Tata will host the USC delegation."

Ronnie was very surprised. Perhaps he thought our first trip would be to China, especially considering that USC enrolled more students from there than any other foreign country. Or maybe he thought that his call would influence my decision.

But my mind had already been made up. And we began planning a trip to India in February 2011.

Over the next few years, in addition to India, our delegations would visit Israel; Brazil; Singapore and Indonesia; Mexico; Taiwan; and the United Kingdom. Every two years, we also held Global Conferences in Hong Kong, Shanghai, Tokyo, and Seoul.

The main reason for each of our trips was to establish educational partnerships and open USC offices, which were designed to promote the university, recruit students, and manage international parent and alumni relations.

We were building on decades of work that had helped the university establish relationships around the world. But we were entering a new era of USC's evolution.

❊ ❊ ❊

We were very fortunate to have USC trustee Ratan Tata to introduce us to several influential people, including the Prime Minister of India, Manmohan Singh.

For the meeting, Ratan and I went to his office in the Indian House of Parliament, an iconic circular building where the transfer of power once took place from the British government to the people of India.[2]

As we were walking towards the Prime Minister's office, from a distance I saw a man standing at the door waiting for us. I thought it was a guard in uniform, there for protection. As we got closer, I realized it was Prime Minister Singh himself!

He threw open his arms and hugged Ratan Tata, saying, "My dear Ratan, I was so looking forward to seeing you."

As soon as Ratan introduced me, he took both of my hands in his and I said, "Your excellency, it's a great honor to meet you. Thank you for seeing us."

"There are 100,000 students from India who pursue studies at American universities today," said Prime Minister Singh.

I nodded and then said, "Your excellency, I have 2 percent of that number at my university, which is the largest enrollment of Indian students at *any* American university."

Still holding my hands, he looked me straight in the eyes, smiled, and then said, "I want to thank you for educating and looking after my people."

At that moment, I felt a jolt in my body. It was a strong sense of obligation to look after the wellbeing of all of USC's students. As a foreign student myself, I identified with students from India—and other nations—who were going through the initial trials that come from being a stranger in a strange land.

Inside Prime Minister Singh's office, I was surprised by how small and humble it was. We sat in one corner, chatting about many things, including the challenges India faced with 23 different political parties.

"We don't seem to agree on anything," said Prime Minister Singh. "And many times I feel we are on the verge of falling off the cliff. Yet, God is looking after us as a nation."

Towards the end of the conversation, Prime Minister Singh asked me, "Which places are you visiting in India?"

"Mumbai, New Delhi, and Bangalore, where we are opening USC offices," I said.

He immediately raised his hands and smiled, saying, "But this is not India! You need to visit other places, the countryside, only then will you get a better feel of India."

After about 40 minutes, Ratan looked at me and said, "It's time to go."

We thanked Prime Minister Singh and he walked us to the door. As we were heading down the corridor towards the elevator, Ratan looked at me and said, "He never asks his visitors to leave."

"Never?" I asked.

"Not even his Chief of Staff is allowed to come in and say it's time for the next appointment. It is up to his guests to realize when it's time to go and none of us abuse that privilege!" said Ratan.

* * *

As we were leaving, I began to understand the popularity of

Ratan Tata.

As soon we stepped outside the House of Parliament, we were approached by a mob of reporters who wanted to know what we had discussed with the Prime Minister.

When Ratan told them that it was simply a courtesy visit because USC's delegation was in India, they didn't believe him!

Later, the headlines in *The Economic Times* read, "Tata Group Chairman Ratan Tata meets with PM."[3]

We were finally rescued by a member of the Indian parliament, who pushed us into his car, drove us around the building, and dropped us off at a garden far away from the media!

The moment was both frightening and fascinating. Ratan Tata was so well known—almost like a movie star—that everyone assumed that having a meeting with the Prime Minister must have some ulterior motive. But in reality, he was just kind enough to make the introduction because we were visiting India.

* * *

Beyond our many international trips, it was very important to promote USC to prominent people at the state and federal level.

I remember a story about California Governor Jerry Brown. After making changes to our admissions policies, we learned USC was about to lose a portion of the nearly $50 million per year in funds for Cal Grants. These were the California version of Pell Grants, and USC was one of the state's largest recipients of these funds.

"When I was Governor the first time back in the 1970s, I didn't know what I was doing. But now I do," he told me. "And I will step down with a budget, having a big reserve for the state of California. Period."

To do that, he had to find places to trim the budget, which included important money for our most vulnerable students attending private colleges in California.

We prepared a delegation to Sacramento that included a few USC trustees, along with four minority students who were receiving Cal Grants.

The day before our delegation left for Sacramento—very early in the morning—I was at home working out when my cell phone rang. It was Governor Brown, who was fuming.

"You are coming up here tomorrow to stage theatre with your students. If you have something you want from me, why don't you call me directly?" he shouted into the phone.

I reiterated how important the Cal Grant program had been for underprivileged California students.

"Why do you want to force all of the minority kids to have only the option to get a college degree from a UC System or a Cal State System school?" I asked. "Why not give them the option also for a private university education?"

I also gently reminded him that Cal Grants were put in place by his father, Pat Brown, when he was Governor of California.

It was a long discussion, and he clearly was under pressure to ensure a build-up of reserves in California's state budget, which, to his credit, he was able to do.

Eventually, we agreed to meet in his office, but he didn't want the students involved. He said he would meet with me and the chairman of our Board of Trustees, but that was it.

The first half hour of that meeting was spent talking about the Greek classics. He raised the topic of the three volumes of Werner Jaeger's *Paideia: The Ideals of Greek Culture*, and we had a good discussion.

We also spent a considerable amount of time discussing the anticipated evolution of online education. He was a strong proponent of online technology, especially as a way of cutting costs while still providing high-quality education.

Governor Brown was very concerned about the rising cost of tuition, and clearly wanted to keep it as low as possible at the UC system.

At the end of the meeting, Governor Brown showed me

pictures of his family, including a map of the ranch owned by his great-grandfather, who was a German immigrant and settled in California during the gold rush in 1852.

Then he looked at me and said, "Now do you see the difference between me, Deukmejian, and Schwarzenegger?"

"Yes, you're a fourth-generation Californian!" I replied.

"That's right!," he said. "And they were importers!"

At the end of our meeting, I had one small request. I begged him to meet with the USC students who had made the trip to Sacramento.

"Governor, it's so important for these kids to have the opportunity to shake your hand," I said.

He shook his head and kind of laughed. I'd worn him down.

Finally, he agreed to meet with them at 5:00 p.m. for a brief photo op. When we all arrived back at the Governor's suite that evening, he was standing there with his wife waiting for us.

He shook hands with all of the students and they got to take pictures with the Governor. It was a great moment and I really appreciated that he took the time to do that for our students.

* * *

Each year we also held an event in Washington, D.C., to interact with members of Congress and their staff that we often called "USC in D.C."

During those trips and on other occasions, I met with several prominent members of Congress. When Harry Reid was leader of the Senate, he was running late and we were waiting with a group of trustees.

Senator Reid rushed into the room and sat in his chair, holding a piece of paper that he kept reviewing. Then he looked me straight in the eyes and said, "I read here that USC is the most expensive university in the country."

"Senator, USC is an expensive university," I said. "But it also has the largest financial aid pool in the country—$330 million annually. More than 70 percent of our students receive some form of financial aid."

"Oh," Senator Reid said. "I didn't know that! I guess my young staffer here, who prepared this briefing for me, is a UCLA graduate!"

And he pointed out a young man in the corner, who was smiling!

* * *

During another visit, our group met with Mitch McConnell when he led the Senate. We were in his conference room and he gave us only 15 minutes.

We discussed the importance of university research, especially supporting the NIH. He was clearly very supportive of the NIH and promised that there was going to be an increase in the budget.

At the end, as was customary in each one of our meetings, I said, "Senator, thank you for your time, is there anything we can do to help you?"

He looked surprised and then said, "No, I don't need any help. Besides, if it weren't for your trustee Bruce Ramer here, I wouldn't have taken a meeting with anyone from California. And you can go back and tell your fellow liberal university presidents that Obama is not going to get what he wants!"

* * *

Sometimes the university found itself under political pressure from surprising sources. Take the case of the Dalai Lama, who in 2011 was invited by the students of USC to speak at the university for the first time.

But before the event, we had some issues. As soon as it was announced that the Dalai Lama was coming to campus, we were contacted by the Consul General of China in Los Angeles, who held the title of Ambassador.

He requested a meeting and came to my office with one of his aides. I was warned that he was going to file a formal protest on behalf of the Chinese government.

He was friendly, but very cold. And I'm sure he had a script in his mind that he had to deliver to me. As he talked, his face was very angry, visibly very upset.

"How dare you have this terrorist on your campus? Having him here is an insult to the Chinese people," he began.

He went on and on and on. I didn't interrupt him for 15 minutes. I just let him vent his frustrations.

When he finished, I said, "Mr. Ambassador, I understand your position and I understand that you are upset. However, I also have to tell you that on this university campus we protect the freedom of speech and freedom of expression."

He listened, but his face was still angry.

"I'm not the one who invited him," I said. "Actually, I don't invite very many speakers to campus. They're invited either by faculty or student organizations. In this case, he was invited by the students. And it doesn't mean that I agree or disagree with every speaker on this campus, or that our Board of Trustees agrees or disagrees with them. But my job, as president, is to protect freedom of expression."

It didn't seem to faze him, so I went on. But this time I leaned in closer so that I was right in his face.

"Besides, last year, I had President Obama, the President of the United States of America, come to this campus and give a speech. Do you have *any* idea how many letters and phone calls of complaint I received? I'm talking about the President of the United States."

As soon as I said that, the ice was broken. He couldn't help it. He started laughing out loud.

⁂

In 2017, our delegation visited Tokyo, Japan, where one of our most famous alumni was former Prime Minister Shinzo Abe.

Two years earlier, Abe visited USC because he had such fond memories of his time as a student.

One Saturday morning in 2015, Niki and I greeted him along with his wife, Akie Abe, the First Lady of Japan.

We met in the board room on the second floor of Bovard Administration Building. I surprised him with a USC letterman's jacket, which he loved and slipped on right away.

As he walked to the podium to say a few words to the small group assembled, his wife smiled and said, "Can you please tell us his grades when he was a student?"

Prime Minister Abe looked at me and said, "My grades are classified as top secret by the government of Japan."

The room erupted in laughter.

He was truly a great man and I thought about him a lot in 2022 after he was assassinated.[4]

⁂

I met President Barack Obama twice. In 2010, we had a private meeting before he spoke on the steps of Doheny Library to around 37,500 people.[5]

In 2014, I met him again when he was awarded the USC Shoah Foundation's Ambassador for Humanity Award, which was presented to him by Steven Spielberg.[6]

We sat at the same table during the dinner and at one point he leaned over and whispered in my ear.

"It is impressive how you got all these people affiliated with USC. You really got everybody," he said.

Later he mentioned that both of his daughters were considered attending USC. Immediately, I said, "I will be more than pleased to arrange a VIP tour of the campus for them."

He smiled. "Just a tour," he said. "Not the VIP one."

Eventually, the Obamas' younger daughter, Sasha, did graduate from USC.[7]

* * *

In 2014, former President George W. Bush and First Lady Laura Bush both came to USC to participate in the President's Distinguished Lecture Series.

About eight years earlier, I'd met him at a ceremony at the White House. Now here he was with his wife at my invitation. They arrived through the secure back door of my office and I saw President Bush from a distance. He was smiling broadly.

"Hey, buddy," he said. "How you doing?"

He was so friendly and down-to-earth that it was easy to forget that you were talking to the former leader of the free world.

Laura Bush sat on the couch with Niki. They got along so well that Laura ended up showing Niki pictures of her grandchildren.

We had a small dinner with a few trustees in the boardroom, and then we went downstairs to Bovard Auditorium for the event.

* * *

Even though it was six years after he'd left office, the event at USC was President Bush's first visit to a college campus, with the exception of when he went to Southern Methodist University in Dallas, Texas, for the opening of his presidential library.[8]

Bush's security detail was concerned that there might be opposition to his presence on campus, although that never materialized.

The one request they made was that there would be no

reporters at the event, which we ensured by making the event open only to students.

We didn't think about the fact that there might be a student reporter from *The Daily Trojan*, USC's student newspaper. At one point during the discussion the moderator asked President Bush his opinion of other world leaders and he said something like, "Putin is basically anti-American and, at his core, he believes that the demise of the Soviet Union is bad for the world."[9]

The next morning in *The Daily Trojan* there was a story about the event, which honestly was very positive. But the student reporter quoted President Bush's comment about Vladimir Putin.[10]

It wasn't long before the Russian ambassador to the United States filed a formal protest at the State Department, condemning President Bush's words about Putin.

I received a call from President Bush's staff wondering how that had happened when we'd agreed that no reporters would be present.

"There wasn't any media," I assured them. "It was a just a student who happened to work for *The Daily Trojan*. We had no way of knowing he was planning to write a story."

I did tell President Bush we had received one complaint from an African American student group.

"And what was that?" President Bush asked.

"Their complaint was that they were disappointed you didn't bring some of your paintings for an exhibit," I said.

He laughed.

"Oh, that's contrary to what I was expecting," he said.

* * *

I had one other encounter with a former U.S. President, which showed me that the stories we read about politicians are rarely the full account.

In 2014, former President Bill Clinton spoke at USC, again as part of the university's Presidential Lecture Series.[11] The event was held on a Friday night, which just happened to be Parents Weekend. Texas Governor Greg Abbott and his wife had a daughter attending USC at the time, so they were sitting in the front row.

In the green room, right before I stepped onto the stage to introduce President Clinton, I felt like I should tell him that Governor Abbott would be in the audience.

President Clinton immediately called over his Chief of Staff.

"I want to see him," said President Clinton. "I want you to bring him backstage after I'm done with the speech. I want to talk to the Governor."

When President Clinton began his remarks that night, the first thing he did was recognize the presence of Governor Abbott and thank him for being in the audience.

After the event, Governor Abbott and his wife were led backstage. Immediately, President Clinton gave him a warm welcome and the two began talking like old friends.

President Clinton's staff kept warning him that he had an event at Paramount Studios in only 40 minutes, but he kept ignoring them.

We often get the impression that the members of opposing political parties are never on speaking terms, but I watched them have one of the friendliest conversations you can have. It was like they'd known each other forever. And they went on for more than half an hour!

I heard President Clinton tell Governor Abbott, "You know, I follow the Congressional elections in Texas. Your candidates, they were much better than ours. They did a better job. That's why they got elected. And who do you think's gonna run for president from Texas next?"

"I'm gonna have so many former Governors running for president," said Abbott.

"All right, only for the nomination of the Republican Party," said President Clinton.

It was like they were two old pals, who were chit-chatting about politics. And I was very impressed by President Clinton's knowledge of local Texas politics.

Yes, 2014 was not as polarized as today. But if their conversation was any indication, maybe there's still hope for our political system in the future.

* * *

There is one last story I have to tell not because it's about someone I met internationally, but because he helped create connections among the Trojan Family around the world. It was a local story that went global.

In 2017, when we chose Will Ferrell to receive an honorary degree and give the commencement speech, we knew it would get a lot of attention.

I don't think any of us could have imagined that it would not only be hilarious, but also inspirational with so much heart.

More than six years after he delivered his memorable remarks, his speech has nearly 5 million views on YouTube and is considered one of the funniest commencement addresses ever delivered.[12] And it may be the only commencement speech that ends with a person singing a song.

I can tell you from experience that Will Ferrell is not just a great comedian, but also a great person who deeply loves the Trojan Family.

I'm sure his mind was already turning over ideas as soon as he was selected as the commencement speaker, but one day he called with a question.

"I just wanted to ask you—what should I talk about?" he asked.

Who am I to give Will Ferrell advice about how to entertain an audience? But I did my best to offer my opinion.

"Will, everybody knows you've been very successful. I think you're gonna impress the students most if you talk to them about your failures. You know, stories about how you didn't give up, or how you picked up the pieces and moved on."

"Okay, okay," he said.

And then he went off and worked his magic. It would be a memorable experience.

❊ ❊ ❊

On commencement morning, we had a small breakfast with Will and his wife, Mavis, and their five children. His mother, who was a teacher, was also there.

They were all so nice and it was wonderful to have a private moment before a public event that would soon make headlines around the world.

It was incredible to see how he commanded an audience of about 60,000 people that day.[13]

From the very moment he stepped to the podium, he was brilliant because he included the audience as he shared his own personal story.[14]

Soon it was the speech watched around the world. I got emails from all over Europe, Australia, and a phone call from the Governor of Texas, who was still laughing about it.

A few days later, Will was on *The Jimmy Kimmel Show* and they talked about his commencement speech. They even had a close-up of his hand-calligraphed USC honorary degree on national television.[15]

Jimmy asked him about the process of writing the speech. Will said he wrote the whole thing, but he said, "Dr. Max Nikias, the president of USC, who's a very wonderful gentleman, said 'Will you're going to be wonderful. You'll be great. Tell something about when you messed up, and you'll be great. So, I just talked about my failures. Who would have imagined you could get a doctorate talking about your failures?'"[16]

Will Ferrell is a world-class entertainer, but also a first-class human being.

When I stepped down as president of USC in 2018, one of the first texts I received was from him.

"I hope you are doing well," he wrote. "My mother wanted me to convey her best regards to you also."

He didn't have to send that text, but he did. And I will always remember that.

human being?

When I stopped [illegible] one of the [illegible] times I received [illegible] from him.

[illegible] wrote [illegible]

to come [illegible] you.

[illegible]

CHAPTER 31

Stormy Waters

«Εἰ δ' αὖ τις ῥαίῃσι θεῶν ἐνὶ οἴνοπι πόντῳ,
τλήσομαι ἐν στήθεσσιν ἔχων ταλαπενθέα θυμόν:
ἤδη γὰρ μάλα πολλὰ πάθον καὶ πολλὰ μόγησα
κύμασι καὶ πολέμῳ: μετὰ καὶ τόδε τοῖσι γενέσθω.»

ΌΜΗΡΟΥ ΌΔΥΣΣΕΙΑ, Ε 221–24

"And if a god will wreck me yet again on the wine-dark sea,
I can bear that too, with a spirit tempered to endure.
Much have I suffered, labored long and hard by now
in the waves and wars. Add this to the total—bring the trial on!"[1]

HOMER, *ODYSSEY*, BOOK 5, LINES 221–24

I also remember that the first time I ever heard the name of gynecologist Dr. George Tyndall was in December 2017.

In a short phone call, I was briefed on "HR" matters, including regarding Tyndall. During that short briefing, I was told Tyndall had engaged in harassing *comments* and that he was no longer at USC. In that conversation, there was no discussion of any concerns or complaints that Tyndall had physically assaulted, sexually assaulted, or sexually abused anyone.

At the time, it was like hearing the name of any other faculty or staff member I'd never met, who was no longer on campus.

To understand how many people's names I'd heard over three decades at USC, you have to understand that the university is the size of a small city. It's the largest private employer in the City of Los Angeles, with more than 25,000 people on the payroll and nearly 49,000 students. The medical enterprise owns a major hospital network, which has more than 1 million patient visits every year and more than 1,200 doctors. Other than large events, like major addresses to the medical school or the larger university, I'd probably never been in the same room as many of our 1,200 doctors.

At the time, Dr. George Tyndall was just another name.

* * *

I want to set the record straight about what I learned, when I learned it, and how I handled difficult challenges as they arose.

Given the size and complexity of USC, it is not really possible for the president to know every detail of what's happening throughout the university on any given day. Like any other large organization, the president relies on the management structure you have in place and the direct reports around you.

At any one time, I had approximately ten direct reports. Virtually every Tuesday, I held in-person meetings with those direct reports, who I informally called "my cabinet."

During those weekly meetings, cabinet members and other invited executives shared information on a variety of topics, discussing issues related to their areas of responsibility.

If there was a pressing matter, cabinet members didn't have to wait for the weekly meeting. I was always available for them.

This is not unusual. Even the best leaders across higher education and the Fortune 500 will admit they gain most of their information about daily operations from their direct reports.

There isn't any other way. You have to trust in the system and the people around you to bring the most pressing problems to your attention. Anyone who says otherwise has either never been the leader of a large and complex organization, or they're simply being disingenuous.

And yet, with a capable cabinet who knew the details of so many things happening across USC's two campuses, I never heard the name George Tyndall until December 2017.

* * *

On January 31, 2018, Tyndall's name came up again. He wrote a letter to me and several USC administrators claiming that he'd been mistreated during the university's investigation of complaints against him. He threatened to file a wrongful termination lawsuit, asking for $20 million in damages.

He was still a doctor I'd never met and had heard of only a month earlier, but now he was threatening to sue us.

So I asked for a briefing about his letter at the next cabinet meeting scheduled for February.

* * *

During the February 2018 cabinet meeting, Tyndall and his separation from the university was discussed.

Later, in my May 15, 2018, letter to the USC community, I also described what was laid out to the members of the cabinet, including myself, at that February meeting.[2]

Tyndall had been investigated by USC's the Office of Equity and Diversity (OED) in 2016, initially in response to complaints that he'd made discriminatory and sexually inappropriate comments.

During the course of the 2016 investigation, the university hired outside medical reviewers who concluded that the manner in which Dr. Tyndall performed physical exams "did not meet current practice standards."

In the February 2018 cabinet meeting, it was also laid out that Tyndall had been investigated by the OED in 2013, but they did not find conclusive evidence of a policy violation.

At the February 2018 cabinet meeting, again, there were no

reports or discussion about any concerns or complaints that Tyndall had physically assaulted, sexually assaulted, or sexually abused anyone.

At that point, I had no reason to believe that any members of my cabinet, or any of the people involved in the OED investigation, had any basis or reason to believe that Tyndall had physically assaulted, sexually assaulted, or sexually abused anyone.

During the February 2018 cabinet meeting, I also learned, for the first time, that when Dr. Tyndall's employment ended in June 2017, he stated that he was retiring from practicing medicine, and, as such, the university had not reported Tyndall to the Medical Board of California.

Prior to the February 2018 cabinet meeting I did not make or participate in any decision not to initially report Tyndall to the Medical Board. I'd never even heard Tyndall's name until December 2017. But when I learned at the February 2018 meeting that the university had not reported Tyndall to the Medical Board, I immediately directed that the university do so. This was based solely on the information I had learned in that meeting, namely that there were complaints that Tyndall made discriminatory and sexually inappropriate comments and what I had learned about the OED investigations. In my mind, that was enough to cause the university to report him to the Medical Board, which the university subsequently did.

During the February 2018 cabinet meeting, I also asked USC's Office of the General Counsel to give a report on Tyndall to the Executive Committee of the Board of Trustees at their March 7, 2018, meeting, and to the full Board of Trustees at their meeting on March 25, 2018.

At those meetings, the same facts that were conveyed at the February 2018 cabinet meeting were repeated.

Again, it was not reported nor was there any discussion at the March Executive Committee meeting or the March Board of Trustees meeting of any concerns or complaints that Dr. Tyndall had physically assaulted, sexually assaulted, or sexually abused anyone. And, based upon what had been communicated to me, I still had no reason or basis to believe that Tyndall had physically assaulted, sexually assaulted, or sexually abused anyone.

* * *

On the evening of Monday, May 7, 2018, everything changed.

A member of USC's communications department told me that the *Los Angeles Times* was still asking questions about Tyndall, but this time the inquiries were more serious.

Most concerning, and entirely new to me, were questions concerning allegations of sexual assault, which greatly concerned me. These new allegations sounded very different from those I understood to have been investigated by OED or that were ever communicated to me.

Suddenly, I felt a surge of fear and anger that I had experienced when any of USC's students had been placed in harm's way. That feeling animated me to take immediate action.

The next day, May 8, in a cabinet meeting, I stated that if the allegations were more serious than previously known, Tyndall should be reported to the Los Angeles District Attorney's office. The cabinet agreed that the communication USC received from the *Los Angeles Times* raised the possibility that additional information about Dr. Tyndall may exist of which the university was not previously aware.

On May 10, 2018, the university reported Tyndall to the Los Angeles County District Attorney's Office as I had directed. I was informed that the District Attorney's Office directed the university to report the matter to the Los Angeles Police Department, which it did.

In the May 8 cabinet meeting, I also determined that the university should go public with the allegations and set up a website and hotline to give Tyndall's former patients the opportunity to raise any complaints.

Given the concerning nature of the *Times'* questions, I requested that members of USC's communications department and the OED investigation team meet with *Times'* reporters, which they did on May 11, 2018.

I also called for an emergency telephonic meeting of the Executive Committee of the Board of Trustees that night and that the matter be reported to the Audit and Compliance Committee.

On the evening of May 8, I participated in the emergency meeting with the Executive Committee. In that meeting, I raised the issue of the need for an independent investigation into the Tyndall matter.

* * *

Given the severity of the new allegations, I also made the decision that we needed to tell the university community.

On May 15, 2018, I sent a message to more than 400,000 USC alumni worldwide and members of the USC community, informing the entire Trojan Family several hours *before* the first *Los Angeles Times* article was published.

It's important to note that as I soon as I learned of these new allegations, I took immediate action.

I also continued working closely with the Board of Trustees, to roll out a plan for new policies and procedures. We established the Office of Professionalism and Ethics and the USC Office of Ombuds Services, creating new structures to allow people throughout the university to bring issues to the attention of administrators, including the president.

* * *

On May 15, 2018, the *Times'* story was published. As I read the details, I was appalled.

The article contained detailed reports of sexual assault that I learned of for the first time from that story. To be clear: The first time I ever learned about any specific allegations of physical or sexual assault, or sexual abuse, by Tyndall was from that May 15 article.

It was also the first time I learned that any of Tyndall's conduct was not limited to a few students.

Dr. Tyndall had started at USC in 1989, two years before I arrived at the university as a professor of engineering. For nearly three decades, including under two previous administrations, Tyndall saw patients.

To this day, I remain very angry that he was allowed to engage in this repulsive behavior for almost 30 years. I share the anger and the disgust of many members of the Trojan Family, and I'm very proud of the young women who had the courage to come forward and tell their stories.

Unfortunately, I didn't know about their stories until I read the *Los Angeles Times* article on May 15.

Earlier, I suggested to the Executive Committee of the Board of Trustees that they conduct an independent investigation to find out exactly what had happened. The board retained the law firm of O'Melveny & Myers to do the independent investigation.

Despite the fact that I took immediate action at every step, unfortunately as president I was made the target by the media and a small group of the faculty throughout the summer of 2018. The total number of faculty (full-time, part-time, librarians and research) who signed petitions was no more than 688 out of 7,400, i.e. less than 10 perent to 14 percent of the faculty body depending how you want to count them.[3,4]

I was constantly attacked publicly by people who didn't know any of the internal details but were certain they knew the "true" story. This small group of faculty spent an inordinate amount of time and energy drafting ludicrous op-eds and circulating petitions, making it clear to me that emotions were running too high for reason to prevail. In an open letter to the USC community, former Chairman Stanley Gold called this group of faculty "know-nothing vigilantes."

Their allegations were false. And yet, unfounded allegations were directed against me personally, including the claim that I was "passing the buck" to other administrators.

The term "buck passing"[5] supposedly can be traced to poker games when a player chose not to deal, but rather pass the responsibility onto someone else. President Harry Truman, of course, made the phrase popular by placing a sign on his desk that read, "The buck stops here,"[6] meaning that the president ultimately makes a decision without passing it on to someone else.

And that's exactly what I did! Every time I learned new information, I took immediate action. I never engaged in, encouraged or promoted any cover-up, but attacked the situation directly with all the power I possessed.

There is a huge difference between taking action once you're made aware of a problem and refusing to take responsibility if you learned about the problem from the beginning.

* * *

Beyond this small faction of faculty, there were others who questioned if USC's challenges were the result of our ambitions to raise money or rise in the rankings. That's simply not true, of course.

There's a strange psychological effect when a scandal happens. People need someone or something to blame. And they lash out at the easiest (i.e., the most public) targets.

During my time as president of USC, I spent less than 20 percent of my time fundraising. More than 80 percent of my time was dedicated to projects that improved the university, especially for faculty and students.

And yet, despite the fact that I was facing the challenges head-on, there was this feverish desire to attack me personally.

⁂

I have always believed that being the president of a large, complex research university is so challenging that you have to love it. For many years, I truly did feel that way. But one day, I got up in the morning and realized, "I don't love this anymore." It was no longer fun being the president of USC.

I don't feel that I deserved the blame, even though I acted at every step along the way. But if the facts no longer matter, then why do it?

I understand that, in the summer of 2018, USC's Board of Trustees was briefed by O'Melveny & Myers on the results of their independent investigation. I was not permitted to attend that meeting. As such, I did not hear the results of the investigation. However, I do know that, after the meeting, there was a group of USC trustees who felt very strongly that I should not step down as president. I can only surmise that they learned the same facts about what I learned, when I learned it, and what I did as soon as I received new information that I described here.

In later newspaper interviews, according to USC trustees, the internal investigation of the Tyndall matter did not reveal a "moral failing in university leadership . . . it occurred because non-academic offices such as human resources did not advance with the rest of the university."[7]

As a result, the university honored all the terms of my contract. I do not believe the university would have done this if they didn't believe I'd done the right thing as soon as I learned new information.

But that was only one investigation.

Those same facts were also verified by an independent investigation by the Department of Education's Office of Civil Rights (OCR) in its report dated February 27, 2020. The OCR report states:

> Furthermore, in interviews with OCR, senior University

> administrators, including [President Nikias] . . . professed to have had little to no knowledge of [Dr. Tyndall's] matter, other than what the Office of General Counsel told them, and they were consistent in their statements to OCR that they were told by the Office of General Counsel that [Dr. Tyndall's] conduct involved harassing words and outdated medical practices, with no mention of the possibility of physical misconduct.[8]

As soon as I was made aware of the gynecologist situation, the report stated that "[President Nikias] had identified the matter to be of such significance that he directed the general counsel to brief the university's Board of Trustees" in March 2018.[9]

It's important to note that the OCR report did not implicate me or my predecessor, Steve Sample, in *any* wrongdoing.

Those are the facts from two independent investigations. But people will always believe what they want to believe.

* * *

I will tell you this. It's a frustrating and powerless feeling when the tide of public opinion begins turning against you. To watch as local media platforms assault your character, without any way to share your own story. When bad days arrive as they always do in leadership, I hope others are spared the anger and the accusations of the mindless mob who will rush to judgment without any apparent care or consideration for the truth.

To paraphrase from Shakespeare's King Lear, "*More dangerous than a poisonous tooth is the ingratitude of the benefited.*"[10] That's what it felt like.

But I want to make it clear that I was not terminated as USC's president. Instead, I suggested to the Executive Committee of the Board of Trustees that I should remove myself as a target, so that the university could have an orderly transition. I made this suggestion before I recommended Rick Caruso to be elected chairman.

By stepping down, I hoped to turn down the temperature and, again, do what was best for the university by going back to my tenured professor position. I was not a quitter. I was just sure that I couldn't win in an ocean of negativity and anger no matter how unfairly it was directed against me.

At the time, even Rick Caruso, then chairman of USC's Board of Trustees, wrote, "As he has always done, Max is taking this action in what he believes to be in the best interest of the university following controversies that have arisen from the unfortunate and unacceptable acts of others. From our investigations, which are not yet completed, we have found absolutely no wrongdoing on Max's part."

The independent investigation by O'Melveny & Myers was never published as Caruso promised me personally and the USC community.[11] I played no role in that decision. It lies solely within the province of the board.

If they do decide to release those findings, I have no objection to them doing so. I am confident they will provide further confirmation that I always acted in the best interests of the university.

❊ ❊ ❊

As time has passed, I have no regrets about how I handled the entire situation from the moment I first heard Dr. Tyndall's name.

I played no role in not reporting Tyndall to the police in 2016 because I'd never heard his name until December 2017.

In fact, in May 2018 when I first learned about the allegations of physical and sexual assault and sexual abuse against Tyndall—based on questions submitted to the university by the *Los Angeles Times*—I was the one who directed that Tyndall be reported to the District Attorney's Office.

❊ ❊ ❊

Am I disappointed in how it all turned out? Yes, of course. Was it painful for me, my wife, and my family to deal with the false allegations and mob-like assault in the summer of 2018? Yes, it was a betrayal. But am I bitter now? Of course not.

I still believe it was the right decision for me to suggest that I step down as president. That is what leadership is all about. As a leader, you need to know when to walk away. For me, the guiding principle has always been my heart. At that time, my heart was no longer singing—I no longer loved being a leader of the University of Southern California.

Although the summer of 2018 was difficult, I still believe in the American dream. I believe in the principles and the values of a great democratic society. I believe that students from all walks of life can succeed in this land of unparalleled opportunity.

And I still believe that, together, we made USC stronger and better, providing students with an excellent education that will open new doors of opportunities for the rest of their lives.

CHAPTER 32

Gradually, Then Suddenly

«Ἀλλ', ὅταν σπεύδῃ τις αὐτός, χὠ θεὸς συνάπτεται.
νῦν κακῶν ἔοικε πηγὴ πᾶσιν ηὑρῆσθαι φίλοις.»

ΑΪΣΧΎΛΟΥ ΠΈΡΣΑΙ, 742–743

"But when a man is of himself hurrying [to the doom appointed]
the gods too lend a helping hand.
A fountain of misfortune for all those dear to me
seems now to have been discovered."[1]

AESCHYLUS, *THE PERSIANS*, LINES 740–742

Looking back over my life, I wouldn't change anything. The challenges and the triumphs, the good days and the bad, they are all part of the great voyage that led me to where I am today.

However, the profession to which I have dedicated my career, has been undergoing dramatic changes. More than a decade ago, I began to see the cracks forming in the foundations of higher education.

In the quote above, Aeschylus implies that when people pursue their own destruction, often through their own actions and decisions, then the gods would rather aid in the acceleration of their downfall. This fall is followed by Nemesis, the goddess who personified divine retribution for hubris, punishment for excessive pride or ambition.[2]

In recent years, American higher education has been "hurrying to the doom appointed."

The academy is the descendant of the Renaissance and the

Enlightenment movements, inspiring humanity with the idea that knowledge could be expanded upon in order to improve society. The modern university became a place that preserved the most important ideas from the past, while also generating new research and innovations with the power to transform the future.

American universities accelerated the pace of progress by promoting freedom of inquiry, freedom of expression, and freedom of speech. They understood that the only way to advance knowledge in any intellectual endeavor is to engage a wide variety of voices and viewpoints in a rigorous and civilized debate to determine the best path forward.

And yet, despite the proclamations of universities as defenders of free speech, there have been some voices that have historically been muted or ignored. For much of the 20th century, many elite universities excluded or limited the number of Jewish students through "quotas" or other policies.[3]

In the 1960s and 1970s, many institutions revised their policies and officially discontinued these practices. [4] However, in the background, similar sentiments reemerged from time to time on the campuses of elite universities, but this time it was coming from another source.

In the early 2000s, campuses around the nation were confronted by activists affiliated with different movements, including one known as Boycott, Divestment and Sanctions (BDS).[5] "Modeled on the anti-Apartheid movement"[6] from the 1990s, its goal is essentially to force institutions to end any financial affiliation with Israel.

When I became president of USC in 2010, there were immediately groups pressuring the university to change its relationship with Israel which is the only true democracy in the larger Middle East region. Instead, two months into my presidency, I issued a statement noting that any divestment of organizations connected to Israel, or academic or cultural boycotts, would be "a betrayal of our values as a pluralistic university whose students, faculty, and alumni come from more than 110 countries, and who represent a diversity of political, cultural and religious beliefs."[7]

Our views on Israel were far more than mere words. In 2012, I led USC's first delegation of trustees, deans, and faculty to Israel, where we established collaborations with Yad Vashem and several top Israeli universities.

We also created a national strategy for recruiting more Jewish-American students, greatly expanding our efforts in the Northeast and Midwest, dramatically increasing the number of Jewish students enrolling at USC.

In addition to Israel, we also had groups who demonstrated on campus and demanded that we divest from fossil fuel companies. We informed them that the responsibility for those decisions rested with the Board of Trustees' investment committee, which always focused on the best financial interests of the university without the influence of outside activists.

* * *

Another example of outside activists and student protests we dealt with was an organization called the Student Coalition Against Labor Exploitation (SCALE) that wanted the university to pay dues to their union and also change our relationship with the apparel company JanSport.[8]

A large group of students, with the encouragement of social activist Tom Hayden, who showed up on campus one afternoon, stormed the administration building and held a "sit-in" to block the hallway leading to my office.[9]

The students were informed there were consequences to their actions. They could have been suspended, which meant they would have to vacate their residential college rooms that evening. If they were scholarship recipients, their financial aid would be terminated.[10] More importantly, we contacted the people they feared the most—their parents—and explained the consequences of suspension. The majority of parents were shocked and began calling their children.

In the end, there were no disruptive protests and none of the students who participated were suspended.[11]

Although USC held fast to its principles in dealing with the demands of protestors while I was president, I could sense that the atmosphere across higher education was beginning to change.

Instead of focusing on their historical mission of teaching, research, and innovation, universities started allowing activism to shape the conversation on campuses.

Presidents or Chancellors have incredibly complicated jobs just to keep their universities competitive and in the black. They can't respond to every request from constituents—from both inside and outside the university—who want them to personally comment and accept every demand they feel they have.

While university leaders were trying to keep up with the daily demands of increasingly complex organizations, a group of faculty and students, especially from the social sciences and humanities, became enchanted by ideas that were never part of the true mission of the university. They fell under the spell of activism, which abandoned the idea of creating and transmitting knowledge. Instead, they became self-created elites that felt "morally superior" and turned to attacking the institutions themselves.

With few exceptions, these professors spend more time on a daily basis branding themselves on social media platforms and promoting their activist agendas than focusing on serious academic scholarship.

It was at this moment that the modern university lost focus on its traditional mission, and lost control of the conversation.

More than 30 years ago, Roger Kimball noted how politics and "tenured radicals," especially in the humanities, were "corrupting" higher education. "The truth is that when the children of the Sixties received their professorships and deanships they did not abandon the dream of radical cultural transformation; they set out to implement it," Kimball wrote, "Now, instead of disrupting classes, they are teaching them; instead of attempting to destroy our educational institutions physically, they are subverting them from within."[12]

That transformation started gradually, gained momentum over the decades, and then reached a climax in recent years.

* * *

In an effort to avoid conflict and to appease a growing number of disgruntled constituents, university leaders found themselves trying to make concessions to certain groups just to get through the day without incident.

Although some praised the efforts with buzzwords such as "compromise," "transparency," and "shared governance," administrators were unknowingly ceding important ground in an ideological war over who would control the university itself.

Soon universities, which were once revered as places where people went willingly to face challenging ideas, were suddenly battlegrounds where some believed they should never be challenged by anything.

In short order, campuses were confronted with trigger warnings, safe spaces, the policing of microaggressions, the undermining of freedom of expression, the cancellation of invited speakers, and the mob mentality of social media.

In the end, outside agitators and their media platforms, activist faculty, and the impressionable students who fell under their influence were never interested in advancing knowledge of any kind. They were only intent on hijacking the intellectual power of the university to serve their own interests, all the while seeking to hide their increasingly questionable words and actions behind the protective cloak of "free speech."

Unfortunately, instead of recommitting to their historical mission, many universities surrendered their authority to the activist agenda, essentially allowing others to redefine the purpose of the very institutions they were supposed to be leading and guiding.

Around the nation, numerous speakers faced unexpected antagonism, often after being invited by student groups.[13] Prominent conservative authors like Heather MacDonald have had events protested and canceled.[14, 15] Dennis Ross, a former U.S. envoy to the Middle East, who has worked with both Democratic and Republican administrations, was disinvited to an event at MIT.[16]

At USC, I was always careful to balance the invitations to the President's Distinguished Lecture Series. That's why we hosted speakers such as Professor Victor Davis Hanson, Presidents Barack Obama, George W. and Laura Bush, Bill Clinton, former Secretary of Defense and Director of the CIA Robert Gates, and conservative British Prime Minister David Cameron. We wanted the university to interact with ideas from across the political spectrum, and we took this balance very seriously.

The day after Professor Hanson's talk, a *Daily Trojan* story quoted a student saying: "There's definitely a conservative bend to what he had to say. I definitely appreciate it even if I don't agree completely."[17]

On two different occasions, USC students also invited conservative activist David Horowitz to speak.[18] There were protests, but we went out of our way to have our Department of Public Safety ensure that there were no disruptions to the events.

* * *

By 2023, the fissures in the fault lines exploded into an earthquake that shook the foundations of academe, revealing ugly chasms of antisemitism on many U.S. campuses.

Following the October 7, 2023, attacks on Israel and in the Gaza Strip, universities across the nation were thrown into chaos with campus takeovers, violent protests, and pro-Palestinian encampments.

A *New York Times* opinion columnist noted that what happened on several campuses, "isn't free expression, nor is it civil disobedience. It's outright lawlessness."[19]

At Stanford, protestors reportedly broke into and occupied the president's office, "destroying property and injuring one person who was trying to clear the building."[20]

On campuses across the nation, the violence and destruction was compounded by the fact that many of the protestors tried to disguise their identities.[21] These were not the peaceful protestors of the 1960s, who gathered together for sit-ins and considered their arrests as a badge of honor. And this did not happen in the middle of a global pandemic in which masks were necessary to help prevent the spread of disease.[22]

Instead, the protestors' efforts to conceal their identities was closer to criminals who planned to engage in violence and destruction, and then get away without responsibility or repercussions.[23]

For those who came from outside campuses in order to stir up trouble, masks were simply a way to avoid being identified and arrested. But for students and faculty who joined in, hiding their identities was a way to participate in protests and also maintain anonymity.[24]

Many students and faculty were under the impression that they wouldn't suffer any consequences.

While numerous campuses tolerated protests with few, if any, penalties, it's not the same in corporate America. Google made headlines in the spring of 2024 when they abruptly fired 28 employees who protested a cloud-computing contract between the company and the Israeli government.[25] According to Google, the company has similar services for governments around the world, not just Israel.[26]

And yet some college students were surprised when they faced repercussions for actions that crossed the boundaries of free speech. At some institutions, students who have engaged in pro-Palestinian protests and encampments are having their diplomas withheldand some are even facing criminal charges.[27]

Some companies have even vowed not to hire students who participated in pro-Palestinian protests on college campuses.[28] According to a survey in May 2024, "Almost a third of employers are particularly worried about hiring recent graduates who have attended pro-Palestinian protests in the past six months, while 22 percent are reluctant to hire graduates who have participated in these demonstrations."[29]

As university presidents scrambled to keep the chaos from engulfing their campuses, their handling of the protests often created an even deeper divide between administrators and their many constituencies.

At USC, the decision not to allow its Muslim valedictorian to speak at commencement, and the removal of a pro-Palestinian encampment, followed by the cancelation of the university's traditional commencement ceremony, sparked fierce debate throughout the campus community.[30] In the end, USC's Academic Senate voted to censure both the provost and the president over the faculty's dissatisfaction over how "the events around commencement were handled."[31]

USC was criticized for not properly vetting its pool of potential valedictorian candidates.[32] As soon as the student speaker was announced, some, including USC's Chabad chapter, accused her of sharing "antisemitic and hate speech" on social media.[33]

By choosing her as the speaker and then later canceling the university-wide commencement, USC created its own media firestorm. It turned the campus into "ground zero" in the national story of protests and debates by pro-Palestinian and pro-Jewish organizations, as well as for complaints by parents and families of graduating students who were angered for many reasons by how the university handled the entire situation.

❊ ❊ ❊

Beyond USC, other university leaders were called before Congress to testify about their responses to the protests and to antisemitism on their campuses.[34, 35] In the first hearing with the presidents of MIT, Harvard, and the University of Pennsylvania, all three failed to express compassion for Jewish students by imagining the fear they must have felt at hearing slogans like "go back to Poland" or "from the river to the sea" being chanted by people who were members of their own campus communities.[36]

In other Congressional hearings, the president of Northwestern faced heavy criticism for negotiating a deal with pro-Palestinian protestors to get them to abandon their encampment on campus.[37]

The president of Columbia also testified, trying to refute allegations that she had allowed the university to become a "hotbed of antisemitism."[38]

Within 10 months of campus unrest, the presidents of four Ivy League universities—Harvard, Columbia, Cornell, and the University of Pennsylvania—had resigned.

⁂ ⁂ ⁂

Although university leaders made many missteps in their responses following October 7, it is important to trace how we arrived at this pivotal moment for higher education.

I am reminded of a passage from Ernest Hemingway's novel *The Sun Also Rises*, when one character asks another how he went bankrupt. The character replies: "Two ways. Gradually, then suddenly."[39]

It may seem like American universities became "morally bankrupt" in their responses all at once, but some claim that anti-Israeli and pro-Palestinian propaganda began appearing as far back as 25 years ago.[40] With funding from wealthy donors and sympathetic governments, the goal was to create activities, groups, and PR campaigns that supported the pro-Palestinian cause on U.S. campuses.[41]

After years of building these networks inside elite universities, prior to the October 7 attacks some media outlets reported that pro-Palestinian groups had been meeting and sharing ideas with student organizers for months to discuss strategies for large-scale protests.[42]

The National Students for Justice in Palestine posted visuals on the social media platform X, which "shared cartoons giving protesters ideas for 'non-violent' resistance, including throwing what appears to be a smoke bomb, jumping over barriers and lifting a garbage can, reminiscent of scenes at activist occupations of university buildings . . . "[43]

Others allegedly used websites such as CrimethInc.com to share ideas for ways to "use violence and break the law."[44]

It's important to note that while there were outbursts at numerous universities, most of them occurred on those considered "elite" institutions.[45]

Although there were protests at large, public universities such as the University of Nebraska-Lincoln and the University of Texas at Austin, some cities and states responded differently than others. The Governor of Texas acted decisively to end the encampment and issued a statement that the University of Texas would not divest from Israel. However, at George Washington University, they did not have the same support from the mayor of Washington, D.C. Although the university wanted to clear the encampment, the police response was delayed.[46]

In the end, UC Berkeley, USC,[47] UCLA, the Ivy League, and other highly-selective schools received criticism for their response to reports of antisemitism on their campuses.[48]

While the idea of "safe spaces" at universities has been rigorously debated, the current situation has created a truly unsafe environment for Jewish students. Around the nation, universities that are often among the top choices for attendance are reporting that students are actually afraid to say they are Jewish.[49] The only place where they feel they can speak openly about the antisemitism they are experiencing is at Hillel, the nation's largest Jewish student support organization. In other areas of campus, they feel that being Jewish may make them a target.[50]

This is not America. This is not what American university campuses are supposed to be. Students—no matter their personal or political beliefs—should never have to hide their identities or their beliefs in order to feel safe.

The problem is not just that their fellow students seem aligned against them, but members of the faculty are also involved. Without any regard for their Jewish students, some faculty are marching in lock step with pro-Palestinian protestors, chanting phrases and holding signs featuring clearly antisemitic sentiments.[51]

At Stanford, less than a week after the October 7 attacks, an instructor was removed from teaching after telling students that more people had been killed by colonizers than died during the Holocaust.[52] Then the instructor said, "Israel is a colonizer."[53]

An assistant professor at USC reportedly canceled finals, instead encouraging students to join the protests by posting a message online that read: "F*ck it. #FreePalestine."[54]

The professor's social media message, in part, read: "I'm canceling the Final Project. You don't have to do it. Everyone will get a good grade. I told you from the start I don't care about grades anyway."[55] It is not clear if she faced any disciplinary action.

Across the country, three Columbia University deans were put on leave and eventually resigned after exchanging "sarcastic and insensitive text messages during a campus panel on antisemitism."[56, 57]

This behavior is antithetical to the university's true mission of teaching, research, and innovation and cannot be tolerated.

The moment university leaders give in to the demands of activists who are pursuing anything other than the improvement of the university's mission of education and research, they have lost. The activists will never go away. They will only demand more and more. And leaders will continue to surrender more ground in the intellectual war over the true nature of the modern research university.

* * *

The responses to campus unrest have driven negative media stories and have shaken the confidence in higher education itself, especially at a time when inflation is high and tuition increases are also significant.

Universities are now facing pressures from alumni, donors and even venture capitalists, who invest in university endowments,[58, 59] to protect Jewish student populations and freedom of speech for opposing perspectives on their campuses.

Elite institutions are also facing a revolt from parents across the political spectrum, who are paying premium prices for their children to attend classes, and are now demanding tuition refunds and threatening to withhold future donations.[60]

Universities are also facing a flood of lawsuits from groups on all sides of the ongoing debates.[61] Some are being sued by pro-Palestinian protestors, who claim their First Amendment rights were violated, and others are facing legal action from Jewish students who say they were subject to antisemitic harassment.[62]

Although universities have long maintained they are welcome to all perspectives, that rhetoric has been exposed as a myth.

Despite claiming they are "champions of free speech," in recent years college campuses have experienced a dramatic increase in the number of speakers being disinvited.[63]

At campuses across the nation, many speakers have been canceled after they were invited by student groups, and then a small fraction of the campus community objected.[64]

The Foundation for Individual Rights and Expression (FIRE) keeps a list of de-platforming attempts, which they define as a "form of intolerance motivated by more than just mere disagreement with, or even protest of, some form of expression."

In recent years, there have been more than 1,500 deplatforming attempts, with 626 of those attempts being successful.[65]

The university, which traditionally protected the right to engage in free inquiry and expression, has somehow become an entity that polices the speech of anyone who doesn't align with a very vocal activist minority.

The problem is that no one—at a university or anywhere else—can go through life and not run across ideas with which they do not disagree. By not allowing the free flow of opinions across the ideological spectrum, universities are depriving campus communities of important conversations. It's only by confronting ideas that are challenging—even offensive to our own sensibilities—that we collectively determine what is "right and wrong." While this intellectual confrontation can be unsettling, the collision of ideas may force us to change our personal perspectives or the viewpoints of others.

In 2020, I met someone who had exactly that experience. At the annual Rancho Mirage Writers Festival, I interviewed Zachary R. Wood, who was an African American student at Williams College when he invited a speaker that had what many considered "white nationalist" leanings and beliefs.[66, 67] The president canceled the invitation, but Zachary disagreed, saying, "We should hear what he has to say, and take him to task for it. I wanted to understand his positions and refute them."[68]

It's these types of difficult dialogues that campuses are missing out on these days. In my opinion, universities are doing everyone a disservice by refusing to have these discussions at all.

* * *

This declining trust in higher education also comes at the worst possible moment. For many years, top administrators have been aware of an impending demographic decline in the number of college-age students. After 2025, the number of 17-year-olds in the United States will drop dramatically. In the next decade-and-a-half, this age group will decrease by 22 percent.[69] This will increase the competition for tuition-paying students at a tenuous time for colleges across the nation.[70]

At the same time, with all of the attention the campus protests of 2024 have received, it's inevitable that these incidents will lead to more Congressional oversight and more government regulation of American higher education, especially when it comes to protecting the freedom of expression for both liberal and conservative viewpoints on university campuses.

Elite institutions are already facing investigations from the Office for Civil Rights at the Department of Education.[71]

While it's not surprising that investigations, hearings, and talk of oversight are common reactions when tempers are high and as elections near, there are others who believe federal regulation should be a last resort.

Some believe that the best approach is overarching legislation such as the Antisemitism Awareness Act,[72] which passed in late October of 2023, and helps determine if actions were driven by antisemitism.[73]

But even some conservatives believe that limiting the freedom of individual institutions to set their own policies and procedures will simply be taking sides on cultural issues.[74]

With all of the turmoil on college campuses, the biggest question for the future of higher education is this: "Can universities be saved from themselves?" The challenge is so daunting that the expression "the remedy is worse than the disease,"[75] attributed to Francis Bacon, highlights the critical perspective when addressing this problem.

And if so, how can we ensure that universities reclaim and reimagine the vital role they have played for America and the world for more than a century?

CHAPTER 33

Is There Any Hope?

"Haudquaquam dictis violentia Turni
flectitur: exsuperat magis aegrescitque medendo."

P. VERGILIVS MARO, *AENEID*, XI. 45–46

"The fury of Turnus; it but mounts the more,
Grown worse with healing."[1]

VERGIL, *AENEID*, BOOK XI, LINES 45–46

Several changes need to be made to steer higher education clear of disaster. First, the job of the university president has to be refocused on its traditional role of advancing the mission of the institution. Administrators need to regain control of their campuses and universities need to ensure neutrality, not taking sides on political or social issues that don't directly impact the core mission of the institution.

To preserve academic quality, faculty hiring and promotion needs to be based on merit. Governing boards must step up and take responsibility by revisiting and revising the university's policies, and then strongly support the president's decisions. If universities don't take action on their own, they will inevitably face external pressure from Congress and federal courts, leading to a greater regulation of higher education. In addition to reducing institutional autonomy, this increased regulation will increase compliance costs and necessitate additional administrative staff and bureaucratic inefficiencies.

Because the role of the president has changed dramatically in recent years, leading a university is now more challenging than ever before. As a result, the tenure of presidents has been significantly shortened.

According to a 2023 survey by the American Council on Education, the average tenure of university presidents has dropped from 8.5 years in 2006 to only 5.9 years in 2022.[23] Shorter tenures can be very disruptive because they often focus the president and the institution on immediate issues instead of long-term strategies. Brief tenures also affect fundraising because potential donors require long-term cultivation.

More telling, perhaps, is this fact: "Over half—55 percent—of presidents planned to step down from their current positions within the next five years."[4]

Former Cornell President Frank H.T. Rhodes wrote, "The task of the college president, reduced to its essentials is to define and articulate the mission of the institution; develop meaningful goals; and then recruit the talent, build the consensus, create the climate, and provide the resources to achieve them. All else is peripheral."[5]

In other words, presidents must address a number of complex problems while constantly working to establish or nurture important relationships. There are the internal groups of faculty, staff, students, parents, and alumni who all have needs and ideas. And then there are a growing number of external constituents such as local, state, and federal representatives; real estate professionals for building projects; donors and potential donors; and many, many others.

Unfortunately, any president who followed Rhodes' prescription for success today would face rebellions from multiple internal and external constituencies, who would preoccupy them with all sorts of daily issues that are not part of the core mission of the university. With one crisis after another, even the most capable and talented leaders can quickly find themselves and their administration under attack.

Managing the demands of different ideological factions has become close to 90 percent of the job. With the rise of social media, any group can quickly organize, mobilize, and turn a small issue into a public relations inferno. Digital activists—who often act more like institutional anarchists—can use these tools to put pressure on individuals or universities. If you don't support their position or take up their cause, you can easily become a target.

Under the guise of holding leaders accountable, activist factions of faculty—in collaboration with outside organizations and media outlets—now find it fashionable to threaten no-confidence votes, stage demonstrations on campus, and organize "mob-like" assaults on social media whenever they are unhappy with how situations are handled, or if they simply don't get what they want.[6]

* * *

Another major problem is that there is no standard method for identifying potential leaders and no school of training for university presidents.

In higher education, it's rare when potential presidential candidates receive the mentoring and support they need.

When I served as dean and provost at USC, President Steve Sample asked me to carefully watch how he did things. Then I was no doubt tested with several difficult assignments as provost. Sample and I used to joke that we had the fastest and smoothest transition in American higher education. That's why I was able to immediately hit the ground running, announcing a fundraising campaign within a year and achieving all the successes we had. Our primary focus was to advance the mission of USC and raise its academic quality and financial well-being.

Another recent example of seamless leadership transition is Purdue University, where Mitch Daniels handed over the reins of leadership to Mung Chiang in January 2023. A lot of credit goes to Daniels, who worked closely with his Board of Trustees to ensure a quick and excellent transition to someone that he mentored internally.

⁂ ⁂ ⁂

The corporate world does a much better job of recognizing and mentoring those with leadership abilities. In higher education, leaders are often chosen based on some administrative experience within the academy, but without any mentoring or other traits deemed necessary for the individual institution. Few are trained in dealing with public attacks from inside or outside their universities, responding to widespread protests, or testifying before Congress.

In recent years, this is why there has been a trend toward finding university presidents from outside of academe, including politicians, military leaders, and other public officials who can spend most of their time managing crises and not focusing on the fundamental mission of a university.

⁂ ⁂ ⁂

Unfortunately, large groups of faculty, especially in the social sciences and the humanities, seem to exist only to promote their own political or other ideologies, allowing these agendas to influence their curricula and teaching. This politicization of teaching has a troubling impact not only on students, but also on the academic reputation of the university.

Each year the best and brightest students from around the world are welcomed to the campuses of elite universities. Of the nearly 4 million who graduate from American high schools each year, only about 300,000 have the credentials to attend the nation's top 65 universities. These students have unprecedented opportunities to receive an extraordinary education and make connections that will help them launch a successful career.

And yet, many of them are brainwashed to believe they are victims.[7]

Some see this victim mentality as the result of a cultural shift in which, instead of teaching children about resilience, we reward them for their unique gifts and talents.[8] Others, like author Heather MacDonald, believe it is "an ideological problem, not a psychological one."[9]

Because activism perpetuates ideologies that divide the world between the oppressed and an oppressor, it fosters a victim mentality that is disappointing and discouraging.

According to MacDonald, "You have minority students at Brown, for example, meeting with the provost and demanding that they be exonerated from any kind of academic expectations, such as showing up for class, because they have to protect their ability to exist on the Brown campus. This rhetoric has become standard. To be a minority on campus, in this view, is to be at actual risk of your life."[10]

We are doing these students—and our country—a disservice by allowing them to engage in this false narrative of victimhood, and not helping them understand that they have more abundance and opportunities than any generation in the history of the world.

* * *

Before universities can return their attention to improving the academic environment, they first have to regain control of their campuses.

After disruptive demonstrations, Columbia University is now considering a proposal to allow its security personnel to arrest protestors.[11] Many people may be under the impression that private universities' campus police already had this power, but that's not always the case.

In the early 2000s, USC was in a similar situation. Although the university had a Department of Public Safety, the officers didn't have the authority to make probable cause stops or arrests. They could detain a person, but then they had to call LAPD to make the actual arrest. If the LAPD's Southwest Division—one of the busiest in Los Angeles—was engaged in other activities, USC's DPS officers basically had to remove the handcuffs and let the person go.

This caused several problems. First of all, criminals had a lack of respect for the DPS officers because they knew they couldn't make arrests, and that even if they were caught in the act of a crime they might be let go. At the same time, it was demoralizing for the DPS officers to be placed in such a position when they were risking their lives each day to lower crime in the area.

After making a proposal to the Chief of LAPD when I was provost, a memorandum of understanding was signed that allowed USC officers to make arrests. With the help of many procedural and technological improvements such as security cameras—and making the uniforms of campus police officers similar to those of the LAPD—crime fell *dramatically*.

Despite all of the improvements, after I stepped down as president and during the Black Lives Matter Protests, some students and the USC Community Advisory Board wanted to abolish USC's Department of Public Safety. Fortunately, the effort failed.

* * *

There is a reason that private universities are currently revisiting policies for their campus police. Private universities in urban areas face much more complex challenges.

Municipal agencies are often reluctant to get involved in campus disruptions because private institutions have often allowed gatherings or protests.

Although, for example, the NYPD and LAPD are trained and equipped to deal with First Amendment protests, they are more prepared to handle them from a tactical and criminal perspective. If today's protestors engaged in non-violent protests like in the 1960s, they would simply be peacefully arrested. But in recent antisemitic and pro-Hamas demonstrations, which are often well-funded and highly-organized, some protestors have violently resisted arrests or engaged in other criminal activity.

Private universities will be more effective in dealing with demonstrations if their police officers have the power to make arrests. Empowering campus police will also give the university more options to choose when to engage with protestors, or to remove encampments, without having to wait for a response from municipal agencies, which are already dealing with their own funding and personnel challenges.

* * *

In response to the proliferation of faculty activism, an urgent and necessary step for academic leaders is to ensure the neutrality of university campuses. Institutions must choose not to make public statements that don't impact the "core function of the university."[12]

One Harvard professor, who belonged to a working group and reassessed the university's policies, said, "Harvard isn't a government. It shouldn't have a foreign policy or a domestic policy."[13]

And yet, for more than 15 years, universities across the nation have been issuing political statements that had nothing to do with the "core function" of their institutions.

As USC's president, I faced severe criticism from groups of activist faculty when I wouldn't take a stand against certain politicians or about certain issues. Although I would sometimes make statements about policies affecting higher-education, this wasn't enough for them. They were angry, and they turned on me publicly for not giving in to their demands.

Luckily, after facing backlash from alumni, donors and certain media outlets, universities are finally beginning to understand that they shouldn't be commenting on every issue, especially political ones. They are realizing that the only way forward is to refocus on their missions, reassess their policies, and ensure neutrality.

* * *

One policy area lawmakers, companies, and universities are revisiting is diversity, equity, and inclusion (DEI).

Lawmakers in more than 30 states have introduced legislation to adjust these programs. Texas, Florida, and Utah have completely banned diversity, equity, and inclusion efforts.[14]

While this legislation may seem purely political, it's important to note that Harvard and MIT recently ended the practice of requiring prospective faculty to agree to mandatory diversity, equity, and inclusion statements in order to be hired.[15, 16]

Universities are not the only organizations rethinking these policies. In July 2024, the Society for Human Resource Management (SHRM), the nation's largest advocacy group for human resource professionals, also decided to distance itself from the "equity plank."[17]

Beginning in January 2025, "Universities are suspending research projects, canceling conferences and closing offices in response to a volley of orders from President Trump banning 'diversity, equity and inclusion' across the U.S. government."[18]

Arizona State, Michigan State, and North Carolina State have discontinued DEI-related programs. Many other universities from coast to coast are re-examining their policies and projects, concerned they may lose federal funding.[19]

Although the origins of DEI policies can be traced back to the 1960s,[20] only in recent years have organizations really wrestled with their full implications. There is nothing wrong with "diversity" or "inclusion" as long as *meritocracy* is maintained.

In my 25 years of university leadership—from media center director, to dean, to provost, and then president—I embraced the entire Trojan Family because it was a "big tent" that was very diverse and inclusive.

At one point, USC welcomed students from all 50 states and more than 130 different countries,[21] as well as a wide range of religious and political beliefs.

However, from an academic standpoint, there is a problem with "equity." In certain programs, you may have student populations who aren't properly prepared to uphold the academic quality of the discipline and, therefore, the institution. If you lower standards or compromise on quality, the value of your institution's education and scholarship go to nothing.

As president, I refused to get rid of the SAT for admissions. Many can attest that all high school GPAs are not equal, and the SAT remains an important, independent indicator of quality. While some elite universities discontinued the SAT, including USC after I stepped down, more recently MIT, Johns Hopkins, and others are now reinstating standardized tests.[22, 23]

At USC, we also resisted significant pressure from some who claimed our student demographics should reflect the population of the L.A. basin or the state of California. We rejected that premise because USC is a private national and international university, so our student body reflected national averages without compromising quality. It's the job of the UC and Cal State Systems, which are public institutions, to represent local demographics.

* * *

Is there a way to maintain academic quality while also building a pipeline for underrepresented students, or students from challenging socioeconomic conditions? I believe that there is, and that the key is to invest your time and attention in underserved communities.

At USC, we went out of our way to identify and actively recruit qualified minority students from around the nation. We admitted more community college students, and thanks to a generous gift, we expanded USC's Neighborhood Academic Initiative (NAI) into East Los Angeles, growing its enrollment from 200 to 2,000 students.[24]

NAI works with students at K-12 schools near USC's two campuses. Every weekend students come to campus, accompanied by an adult in their household. The students receive greater academic attention from the moment they enter sixth grade until the moment they earn their high school diplomas, including special classes to prepare for the SAT. There are also classes for the adults—some of whom didn't attend high school—to teach them how to help their children prepare for college.

For more than 40 years, The USC Viterbi School of Engineering has also collaborated with local K-12 schools, teachers, and students, creating new avenues for students to learn about science, technology, engineering, and math (STEM) career options.[25]

I even had the chair of USC's Classics department teach Latin every week to NAI students. I felt very strongly that if these kids were going to college they should also have a basic education in Latin.

* * *

In 2017, I met with Frank Bruni, a reporter at the *New York Times*, to talk about the expansion of USC's NAI program and our other efforts to increase access to college.

In his story "Lifting Kids to College," Bruni highlighted our work at USC, writing: "But we also don't make enough disadvantaged kids eligible in the first place. We don't guide them through elementary, middle and high school so that they have the necessary grades, scores, skills and mind-sets. This is the problem that U.S.C. has been focusing on: University administrators figure that they can't just wait for public education to improve and should use some of their considerable resources to chip in themselves somehow."[26]

By September 2017, we also learned that Foshay Learning Center—right in the heart of South Los Angeles—was the source of more first-generation students at USC than any other high school.[27]

This is how you address "equity" in academia. By increasing the high school pipeline of qualified African American, Latino, and other minority students—without lowering academic standards.

* * *

In reclaiming their traditional role, universities also have to reassess their approach to "free speech" issues. Many point to the right of "peaceful assembly" as a reason to allow protests on campuses. But that does not mean protestors are free to do anything they want.

In 1941, the U.S. Supreme Court voted unanimously that there can be "reasonable time, place, and manner restrictions on speech for the public safety."[28] This applies to both public and private universities. Groups may decide to peacefully protest, but they are not free to do this at any time or place. They are also not free to yell and make noise to disrupt classes or any other university business.

A *Wall Street Journal* opinion columnist noted, "Just as we have an obligation to protect speech, we have an obligation to keep our students safe. Throwing fists, storming buildings, vandalizing property, spitting on cops and hijacking a university aren't speech."[29]

In 2023, at Stanford Law School, a U.S. Circuit Court judge was interrupted by student hecklers who disrupted a speech he was trying to deliver.[30] Although Stanford's own policy on academic freedom explicitly states that, "Protest is allowed, but disruption is not allowed,"[31] the school's associate dean for diversity, equity, and inclusion actually took the students' side, saying that the " judge's presence was painful for some students."[32] The associate dean left the school four months later,[33] but the students who disrupted the event received no discipline at all.[34]

❋ ❋ ❋

I believe universities must protect freedom of speech, but that means the rules must be the same for everyone across the political spectrum. The open exchange of ideas is not only the cornerstone of democracy; it is at the heart of all intellectual inquiry and discovery.

Some will express opinions or viewpoints with which we may disagree. It is not the duty of the university to protect students from hurtful ideas, but rather to protect their ability to live and learn in a community of scholars. We may personally find the views of some to be repugnant, but we are called to treat everyone with respect, even if we fervently oppose their ideas.

Protecting free speech does not mean protestors are free to take over campuses. Universities, especially private institutions, have a legal right to place restrictions on any protest. That can include confining protests to certain areas of campus, enforcing noise limits, and even restricting the number of demonstrators who can be in a single location and how long they can remain in that space.[35]

By allowing protestors to treat free speech as free reign to occupy whatever areas they choose, university leaders have surrendered control of their own campuses and, as a result, have lost their neutrality. Compounding the tragedy even further, the senseless murder of influential youth activist Charlie Kirk on a Utah college campus has sparked discussions about safety measures for university speakers.[36]

In August 2024, the American Association of University Professors, changed its policy on academic boycotts that has existed for nearly two decades. The group now claims that, "academic boycotts 'can be considered legitimate tactical responses to conditions that are fundamentally incompatible with the mission of higher education.'"[37] Although there is no mention of Israel in the policy change, it's clear that there is only one nation that certain groups are pressuring universities to boycott.[38] Moves like this will only increase the tension on campuses in the near future.

To try to maintain peace in these heightened times, institutions like Vanderbilt University and the University of Chicago have shown that it's possible to protect free assembly and also enforce strict policies for protestors.[39] At the University of Florida, if student protestors cross the line into violent actions they can be suspended from campus for up to three years,[40] a penalty that could derail an academic career or severely delay a professional one.

Universities should be looking for ways of preserving free speech and civil disobedience without handing over the entire campus to activists and protestors. They should be making their policies well-known, even requiring mandatory training on those policies for incoming students. However, unless they are fully enforced through severe punishment for violators, these policies will not be taken seriously.

There has to be no tolerance for lawlessness. Only strict discipline.

* * *

The most difficult challenge—and the one no one wants to talk about—is the problem of faculty who cancel exams, urge students to demonstrate, or do things like humiliate Jewish students in classes.[41, 42]

Universities have to revisit their faculty handbooks and revise their policies so that they have more "teeth." For faculty who violate those policies, there have to be real consequences. Regardless of their own political beliefs, faculty will have to respect other political views while teaching classes and being sensitive to Jewish students, or other student concerns.

* * *

To steer higher education in the right direction, the governing boards of American institutions must also step up and assume more responsibility for the state of their campuses. Board members should support university leaders who truly want to create neutral campus environments where all views are heard and debated in a civilized manner.

There are only two duties for being a good Board of Trustees member. The duty of loyalty and the duty of care. They must care about their academic community and the long-term mission of the university. And they must be loyal to the institution, not to a political agenda, personal ambition, or ideology.

Unfortunately, some board members may be less interested in serving their universities than serving themselves. These members weaken the institution because they are too busy trying to preserve their own image and promote their own agenda. In the case of public institutions, board members' first loyalty may be to the elected officials who appointed them.

If the president is constantly dealing with activist faculty, students, and the outside media that team up with them—and if the board members are not serving the best interests of the institution, or are very sympathetic to and supportive of activist faculty agendas—then there is no hope of fixing American higher education.

If universities are to be saved from themselves, it's vital for loyal and caring board members not to cave in to the pressures of radical activism. They have to change existing disciplinary policies for faculty, students and staff. They have to stand up to the pressure of activists who are determined to disrupt the mission of the university. They have to leave aside any personal loyalties to politicians or other groups, and stand up for the neutrality of their university, refocusing on its primary mission.

Maintaining neutrality in the face of activist pressure will require boards to carefully and explicitly outline what is "free speech" and what is simply unacceptable behavior. They will have to revise their faculty bylaws, enacting strict disciplinary actions for those who violate policies, especially activist faculty who encourage or participate in violent demonstrations.

Once stricter policies have been agreed upon, board members must rally behind the president in enforcing these rules that protect the reputation of the university and the lives of its students. Otherwise, they have virtually no chance of regaining control of their campuses.

Anytime something happens at their university—or half a world away—the romanticism of the 1960s will stimulate some faction of internal or external activists to take over campus, conduct no-confidence votes, and stir up dissent. When that happens, the president's job will soon be on the line, and make leading any university nearly impossible, as we have witnessed in recent years.

By focusing on the long-term goals of the institution and the policies that help fulfill that vision, board members can help universities return to the principles that have always been at the heart of higher education.

* * *

A major challenge in the near future will be the likelihood of greater federal regulation of higher education.

Congressional hearings have forced universities to revisit their policies, but the response has been too late and there have been too many unforced errors.

Sadly, without those hearings, the situation would likely have grown even worse. It's unfortunate, but true.

University boards also have to understand that their own actions will be monitored by regulators. Even the boards of private universities will not be immune to such scrutiny in the future. At Columbia, for example, Congress subpoenaed the board's minutes and communications in its investigation of antisemitism on campus.[43]

Universities receiving federal research funding (as all elite institutions do) or Medicare payments to their medical centers will be subject to serious regulation to ensure a more neutral environment on campus.

When necessary, the legal system will be used to enforce rulings to protect the rights and ensure the safety of Jewish students. Two rulings by federal judges against Harvard and UCLA signal a significant turning point. In Boston, a judge ruled that a lawsuit by Jewish students can go to trial over "accusations that Harvard was deliberately indifferent toward Jewish and Israeli students who said they feared for their safety after facing severe and pervasive harassment."[44] In California, a judge granted a preliminary injunction that will "force UCLA to maintain equal access to programs, activities or campus areas for Jewish and non-Jewish students alike."[45]

* * *

When President Donald J. Trump won reelection in 2024 and the Republicans secured majorities in both the U.S. House and the Senate, government regulation of universities accelerated beyond anyone's expectations.

In February 2025, the Department of Justice created the Federal Task Force to Combat Antisemitism, which announced an investigation into 10 elite universities, including USC and UCLA.[46] The Department of Education also announced civil rights investigations into more than 50 institutions around the nation.[47]

Harvard University became a primary target of the Trump administration's increased scrutiny. The administration froze $2.2 billion of Harvard's federal research funding,[48] threatened the university's tax-exempt status,[49] and announced it would revoke its ability to enroll international students. This announcement affects some 6,800 international students[50]—constituting about 27 percent of Harvard's student body[51]—possibly forcing them to leave the school or transfer to other universities.

Harvard filed two lawsuits, arguing that the administration's actions violated constitutional rights, including the First Amendment and due process protections.[52, 53]

Even if Harvard prevails in its legal challenges, the damage has likely already been done. The university's federal funding is unlikely to return to its former levels in the near future. The U.S. House of Representatives and the Senate also recently passed a bill that would increase the annual tax rate on university endowments, which will certainly be significantly higher than the historic rate of 1.4 percent

To deal with potential budget shortfalls, Harvard's president took a 25 percent salary cut and announced freezes in faculty hiring and merit-based raises,[54, 55] as well as the possibility of layoffs or staff reductions across the university.[56]

Harvard is not the only university tightening its belt to face financial uncertainties. Major universities from Columbia to MIT to Johns Hopkins to the University of Pennsylvania to USC have announced hiring freezes, staff reductions, or plans to reduce their budgets.[57]

❋ ❋ ❋

The chaos on campuses also poses a challenge for research universities trying to attract the best and brightest in STEM disciplines. American exceptionalism in science and technology and, as a result, the economic health of our entire country, depends upon universities being a magnet for top talent.

The U.S. leads the world in innovation in large part because the National Science Foundation, the National Institutes of Health, and the Department of War fund important university research. This funding ensures technological superiority in two ways: the education of the best minds (the transfer of knowledge) and research innovation (the creation of new knowledge).

For decades, the key driver of American innovation has been the powerful partnership between government and research universities. Virtually all of the scientific and technological advances that have improved and extended our lives since World War II can be traced to leading American universities or the talent educated by them.

To maintain our world-leading position in the sciences, engineering, medicine, and artificial intelligence, we need to always have the best minds focused on STEM disciplines. This is important not only for research, but also for the employment of graduate students, especially Ph.D. students, who are responsible for much of the nation's technological advances.

With some exceptions, when compared to the humanities and social sciences, STEM disciplines are perhaps less affected—although not entirely immune—to the forces of political activism and antisemitism that have led to the current breakdown on university campuses.

However, governments are now demanding greater accountability from universities about how government money is spent. For example, in February 2025, the National Institutes of Health (NIH) announced a new policy that caps "overhead recovery" (indirect costs for laboratories, facilities, utilities, and administrative research staff) at 15 percent on all new and existing research grants.[58] The National Science Foundation, Department of Energy and the Department of War followed with similar announcements. In the past, these reimbursement payments were sometimes between 55 and 80 percent.[59] Moving forward, research universities will lose the flexibility they had with the old overhead recovery system and will need to be very explicit that their indirect costs are legitimately being spent on facilities, equipment, and utilities for research laboratories.

Increased government scrutiny has also caused a rift among faculty members at some universities. At Columbia University, the freezing of federal research funds has created "a faculty civil war that pits medical doctors and engineers against political scientists and humanities scholars."[60] The situation became so intense that faculty from engineering, medicine, and business met with Columbia's president expressing frustration that their programs were essentially being "punished" although they were not involved in pro-Palestinian protests.[61]

One Columbia medical school faculty member said, "We're actually quite busy. We're actually doing our job . . . Medical doctors and scientific researchers are trying to save lives. We don't have the time to ruminate on all this."[62]

To repair the internal and external damage on their campuses, university presidents need to return their focus to advancing their universities' missions and academic quality, while also raising the resources and create the environment for STEM disciplines to educate talent and invent new technological innovations. In terms of laboratory infrastructure, these disciplines are very expensive to maintain, and require serious effort by universities to raise money through philanthropy.

The best strategy for preserving American technological exceptionalism is to improve the environments for researchers in STEM disciplines. There are no longer corporate research entities like the old Bell Labs, which conducted long-term fundamental research programs. Without university research programs, we are left with a disconnected system of large corporations and small start-ups that are primarily focused on short-term profits.[63] And the biggest threat to STEM disciplines, especially in the semiconductor industry, is the shortage of talent, i.e., the need for well-educated engineers and scientists with graduate degrees.[64] It is also important for the U.S. to remain a magnet attracting the best and the brightest with proper vetting and background checks from around the world.

As president, I used to say that corporations think in terms of the next several quarters, but universities think in terms of the next several decades. We must return to this long-term thinking and planning if we are to advance American exceptionalism in the future.

* * *

It will not be easy to turn the situation around, and there will be a lot of resistance to and anger at change. As Virgil implies in the quote at the beginning of this chapter, any remedy, "will grow worse with healing."

It's almost impossible to expect these changes—preserving public safety by empowering campus police, ensuring all ideas can be debated freely in a civilized manner, and admitting students and recruiting faculty based on merit— to happen quickly, if at all in an environment with tenured faculty.

The only hope, perhaps, assuming all the strategies discussed in this chapter are implemented and enforced, is to retain the quality and proper environment for engineering, medicine, and the sciences, as well as the entrepreneurial spirit of business schools. By doing so, universities help preserve American technological exceptionalism and thereby partially save themselves.

Epilogue

«Πατρὶς γάρ ἐστι πᾶσ' ἵν' ἂν πράττῃ τις εὖ.»

ΆΡΙΣΤΟΦΆΝΟΥΣ ΠΛΟΫΤΟΣ, 1151

"For one's native country is every land in which one prospers."[1]

ARISTOPHANES, *PLUTUS* (*WEALTH*), LINE 1151

When Niki and I arrived in California more than 30 years ago, we saw it as the Promised Land. In recent years, the Golden State has begun to lose its luster. The famous phrase "Go West, young man," which was coined just 15 years before the founding of USC, has been replaced by an exodus of people, businesses,[2] and intellectual capital from California, resulting in a loss of nearly $24 billion in 2022.[3]

We can see that our children and younger people are struggling to find affordable housing like we did 35 years ago.[4] A shrinking middle class, higher taxes, escalating housing prices and property taxes, rising gasoline and energy prices, aging infrastructure, poor transportation, increasing crime rates, restrictive regulations for businesses and housing development, and many other issues are causing people to pack up and move to other states.[5]

Currently, four out of 14 million California households are struggling to pay their utility bills because of the utopian push to achieve "carbon neutrality" by 2045.[6] This situation led Governor Newsom to shift approximately $880 million of taxpayer money to subsidize those who can't afford basic utilities.[7]

Nearly one-third of Californians live below or near the poverty line,[8] and it has the highest homeless population of any state, with more than one-third of the entire nation's individual homeless.[9] According to historian Victor Davis Hanson, "Twenty-seven percent of Californians were not born in the United States, a large minority of them residing in the United States illegally."[10]

Moreover, approximately 40 percent of the state's entire population—more than one in three Californians—is on Medi-Cal, the state's version of the Medicaid, practically doubling from the percentage of people enrolled in the program in 2012.[11, 12]

Urban downtowns have become unrecognizable, scarred by high crime rates and many homeless camps. Downtown Los Angeles, which many people worked so hard to develop and revitalize, is now creating a high-rise tower for those who are experiencing homelessness.[13] In San Francisco, major brands like Adidas, AT&T, J. Crew, Lucky Brand, Nordstrom, Old Navy, Walgreens,[14] Whole Foods, and many others have pulled out of downtown.[15]

These recent challenges culminated in January 2025 when a series of fires blazed across Southern California, ravaging neighborhoods from working-class Altadena to the glamorous ocean views of Pacific Palisades.

The fires destroyed more than 50,000 acres and over 15,000 homes and businesses, causing the displacement of 150,000 people and at least 29 deaths.[16, 17] Early estimates exceed $275 billion in total damages,[18] making it one of the most expensive natural disasters in American history.[19]

While no one may have been able to prevent all of the destruction, L.A. city leaders had forewarning. "The National Weather Service warned about its forecast for intense Santa Ana winds and significantly higher risk of wildfires two days before [Mayor Karen] Bass departed the city, and the day before her departure as well," according to *National Review*.[20]

However, Mayor Bass chose to attend the inauguration of the president of Ghana anyway, leaving the city without a leader on the ground to reassure citizens of the response.[21]

At one point, there was conflicting information about how the fires started, and even a false emergency evacuation alert that sent a wave of fear and confusion through 10 million residents of L.A. County.[22]

And then there is the water, which has been a contentious issue in Southern California since William Mulholland made a deal to pump it from the Owens Valley in the early 1900s.[23] To this day, nearly one-third of L.A.'s water supply comes from sources hundreds of miles away.[24]

In Pacific Palisades, firefighters lost water pressure, "impacting the ability to refill the three water tanks supplying the Palisades and a low percentage of hydrants in the area," according to the Los Angeles Department of Water and Power.[25]

Residents were infuriated when they learned that the 117-million-gallon Santa Ynez reservoir, which is located right next to the Palisades, was drained for some reason in 2024. As of early 2025, there is still no explanation from government officials for why they made that decision and chose not to refill the reservoir.[26]

In the meantime, President Trump ordered the U.S. Army Corps of Engineers to open two dams in Central California, releasing billions of gallons of water and criticizing state officials that they prioritize smelt fish over humans.[27,28]

For Southern California, the entire episode is a tremendous tragedy that will take years, possibly a decade, just to rebuild what was lost.[29] It's also a cautionary tale of the failure and incompetence of city and state government. And it could take even longer to heal the lack of trust in elected officials.

I'm reminded of what former Supreme Court Associate Justice Anthony Kennedy said to me over dinner at USC, where he confessed to me, "I worry about the future of our state. As citizens, we should be holding it in trust for future generations, not just for ourselves." All of this is happening in a state that, if it were a country, would rank fourth among all global economies,[30] producing more billionaires and more Fortune 500 companies than any state in the nation.[31, 32]

Maybe the late USC University Professor and California historian Kevin Starr was right when he wrote, "There has always been something slightly bipolar about California. It was either utopia or dystopia, a dream or a nightmare, a hope or a broken promise—and too infrequently anything in between."[33]

Despite all of its current challenges, including all of the turmoil that has damaged the reputation of American higher education, Southern California is a place of such brilliant beauty and magnificent Mediterranean splendor. I hope it regains its luster as a place of tremendous possibilities for the sake of our children and grandchildren.

Over the past few years, Niki and I have found ourselves in a new role: grandparents. I've always believed that education is about making the world a better place. When you have four grandchildren, it only increases your desire to improve the future for the next generation.

In many ways, my career has come full circle. When I arrived at USC in 1991, I had no idea I would pursue academic leadership. I could have enjoyed the laid-back life of a faculty member, engaging in research, teaching, and living in a beach community.

Today, among my many duties as a faculty member, I continue to expand opportunities for students from challenging socioeconomic backgrounds, especially students who transfer from community colleges to four-year degree colleges. Through the engineering school, I've set up programs for students across the L.A. basin.

I teach students courses on leadership through the classics, disruptive technologies, and engineering design ethics in artificial intelligence. I also enjoy writing books and setting up large interdisciplinary research projects between engineering and medicine. And I still receive regular invitations to give keynote speeches or moderate panels at several international conferences, delivering lectures on *Xenophon's* Cyropaedia*: The Art and Adventure of Leadership*; the promises of economic growth and the ethical dilemmas of artificial intelligence; cyber-securing democracy; the supply chain of semiconductor chips; and the future of American higher education.

❊ ❊ ❊

Niki and I are now both half a century and half a world from our early days in Cyprus. We now realize that all of our dreams have come true. Our parents' dreams that we would be the first in our families to get college degrees, and our dream of escaping the tragic situation in Cyprus and subsequently living the American Dream.

When I think of the course of my life, I am reminded of what Dante Alighieri wrote in the *Inferno*:

> Fear not; for our passage none can take from us:
> By Such has it been given to us.[34]

Becoming dean then provost and then the president of USC were each one stage of that voyage, though by far some of the most exciting.

I am very grateful much of that journey has been in the United States. There is no other country in the world that offers so many possibilities or opportunities. Although we live in times where the health of America's democracy and its place on the world stage are being questioned, given the polarization of our society, I am reminded that there has always been a sense of optimism here. In 1862, in the early years of the Civil War, Ralph Waldo Emerson, published his lecture "American Civilization" in which he proclaimed that, "America is another word for Opportunity."[35, 36]

Later President Ronald Reagan referred to America as a "shining city on a hill,"[37] a phrase taken from a sermon delivered by John Winthrop on board the Arbella as the Puritans made their way across the ocean to establish the Commonwealth of Massachusetts in 1630.[38, 39]

For the great voyage that brought us to this wonderful place—this shining city on a hill, this promised land of opportunity and prosperity—we have only appreciation and gratitude.

Acknowledgements

Books are written with words, but they are made possible through encouragement.

This one exists thanks to the inspiration of my family, including my wife, Niki; my daughters, Georgiana and Maria; and my sons-in-law, Brandon and Nick. For many years, they witnessed me rushing from event to event with little to time to slow down and reflect on the experiences of a lifetime. I'm eternally grateful for their belief and encouragement.

My gratitude also flows to Michael DeFelice, whose keen editorial eye and wise guidance helped polish the pages of this book.

To Elizabeth Bachmann, whose production expertise and steadfast commitment kept the entire production on track from beginning to end.

I am profoundly grateful to Roger Kimball, president and publisher of Encounter Books, who believed in this story enough to give it a home and bring it into the world.

And to Victor Davis Hanson, whose unwavering friendship over the past two and a half decades, encouragement to write about my experiences, and generous recommendation to Encounter Books were the catalysts that transformed years of thought and reflection into the book you now hold.

This book also would not have been possible without three former chairmen of USC's Board of Trustees—Stanley Gold, Ed Roski, and John Mork—as well as longtime trustees Bruce Ramer and Jeff Smulyan. They all felt that it was important for me to tell the story of the changing landscape of higher education as I experienced it, chronicling USC's dramatic ascent, and correcting the record when necessary. For their unwavering support, I am deeply appreciative.

I also want to thank my brilliant personal attorney Stacy Harrison, who read key sections of the manuscript to ensure that I preserved attorney-client privilege, and that I protected confidentiality for certain events described in the book.

Finally, I want to thank all of the incredibly talented people I have had the privilege and good fortune of working with throughout my career.

To Donnie Becker whose poetic words always bring stories to life in speeches and books.

To all of my Ph.D. students and postdoctoral fellows who made me look better over more than two decades of collaboration.

And to all of the leadership teams at USC, including those in the Integrated Media Systems Center (IMSC), the dean's office at the Viterbi School of Engineering, the Office of the Provost, and the Office of the President. It was always a team effort, and I am forever grateful for those who traveled alongside us, supported us, and worked closely with us to help make USC's remarkable ascent possible.

In the end, this book is simply a recollection of my experiences and how I felt about them as they occurred. The opinions and perspectives expressed are my own and do not reflect the University of Southern California or any of the people mentioned above or throughout this book.

Unless otherwise indicated, any resemblance to actual persons, living or dead, or to actual events is purely coincidental.

Awards and Honors

NATIONAL ACADEMIES

- Member of the National Academy of Engineering (NAE) (2008)
- Charter Fellow of the National Academy of Inventors (NAI) (2012)
- Fellow of the American Academy of Arts and Sciences (2013)
- Associate Member of the Academy of Athens (2016)
- Foreign Member of the Russian Academy of Sciences (2017)

AWARDS

- Fellow of the Institute of Electrical and Electronics Engineers (IEEE) (1991)
- Aristeio Medallion in the Letters, Arts, and Sciences of the Republic of Cyprus (2005)
- Thomas Kilgore Service Award of the USC Black Alumni Association (2007)
- Fellow of the American Association for the Advancement of Science (AAAS) (2007)
- IEEE Simon Ramo Medal (2008)
- Clifford C. Furnas Memorial Award, Alumni Association of the University at Buffalo (2008)
- Great Immigrants—Great Americans honoree by the Carnegie Corporation of New York (2011)
- Honorary Awards from the USC Alumni Association to Dr. and Mrs. Nikias (2011)

- Archon of the Ecumenical Patriarchate, the Order of Saint Andrew the Apostle of the Orthodox Christian Church (2012)
- Distinguished Alumni Award, Alumni Association of the University at Buffalo (2012)
- Los Angeles Police Department's Jack Webb Award (2014)
- Academic Leadership Award from Carnegie Corporation of New York (2015)
- Woodrow Wilson Award for Public Service (2015)
- Honored by the President of the Republic of Cyprus and the Federation of Cypriot American Organizations (2016)
- UNICEF Spirit of Compassion Award (2016)
- Ellis Island Medal of Honor (2016)
- Humanitarian Award of the Society for Brain Mapping and Therapeutics (2018)
- Excellence in Education Award, Armenian Education Foundation (2025)

HONORARY DEGREES

- University of Cyprus (2000)
- Hebrew Union College—Jewish Institute of Religion (2011)
- National Technical University of Athens (2015)
- University of Crete (2016)
- University of Piraeus (2016)
- University of Strathclyde (2017)

TECHNICAL AWARDS & RECOGNITIONS

- IEEE Signal Processing Best Paper Award (1988)
- Fred W. Ellersick Award of Outstanding Unclassified Paper at Military Communications (MILCOM) (1992)
- Formally commended by California Governor Gray Davis

for "helping California successfully meet the challenge of the new millennium through cutting-edge research" (January 2000)

- Honored by the California Legislative Assembly for exemplary record of technical leadership, member resolution #601 (2001)
- IEE A. H. Reeves Premium Best Paper Award (2002)

UNDERGRADUATE SCHOLARSHIP

- Greek State Scholarships Foundation (I.K.Y.) throughout undergraduate school at National Technical University of Athens (Έθνικό Μετσόβιον Πολυτεχνείο), Greece (1972–1977)

PRESIDENTIAL ACCOMPLISHMENTS (2009–2018)

- USC's popularity among students soared from 36,000 applicants to more than 64,000.
- The admissions rate dropped from 22 to 11 percent while university's six-year graduation rate rose from 88 to 93 percent.
- The number of academically qualified underrepresented minorities students increased from 22 to 27 percent reflecting national averages.
- The amount of unrestricted financial aid for undergraduate students increased from $180 million to $336 million.
- USC consistently ranked second or third among private colleges and universities in Pell Grant recipients.
- The Keck Medical Center's clinical revenues grew from $390 million to $1.8 billion. The number of Keck Doctors expanded from 512 to 1,200.
- The fundraising campaign inspired gifts from more than

400,000 donors, making it the most successful campaign in the history of higher education at the time, raising $7.16 billion in eight years. USC consistently ranked among the top five universities, along with Stanford and Harvard, in cash charitable donations.

- The university's endowment grew from $2.77 billion to $6.8 billion.
- In only eight years, the entire university infrastructure was physically transformed by adding 20 new buildings, constructing the massive USC Village, adding 1.3 million square-feet for eight student residential colleges, and increasing the total square footage of buildings on both campuses by 30 percent.
- The Los Angeles Memorial Coliseum and the adjacent BMO Soccer Stadium were transferred to USC under a 98-year master lease agreement with the State of California. USC completed a major upgrade of the Coliseum with $315 million funded solely from philanthropy.
- The academic improvements led to the *Wall Street Journal* ranking USC as the #15 university in the nation in 2017 for the first time. Only three universities west of Chicago were in the top 20: USC, Stanford, and Caltech.

About the Author

C. L. Max Nikias served as the 11th President of the University of Southern California, a position he held from August 3, 2010, to August 7, 2018. He is currently the President Emeritus and Life Trustee of the University and the holder of the Malcolm R. Currie Chair in Technology and the Humanities. He joined USC in 1991, and in addition to his work as a professor, he served as director of a media center, dean of engineering, provost, and president of the university. He is a member of the National Academy of Engineering, the American Academy of Arts and Sciences and the National Academy of Inventors. He is the recipient of the UNICEF Spirit of Compassion Award and the Academic Leadership Award of the Carnegie Corporation of New York. He is recognized internationally for his pioneering research in digital signal processing and digital media. The U.S. Department of War has adopted a number of his innovations and patents in sonar, radar, and communication systems.

Endnotes

CHAPTER 1

1 Euripides, *Helen*, trans. Arthur S. Way, Loeb Classical Library (London: William Heinmann, 1912), https://ia800301.us.archive.org/19/items/euripideswitheng01euri/euripideswitheng01euri.pdf..

2 J. Vitor Tossini, "The UK and Its 'Unsinkable Aircraft Carriers' -A Guide," *UK Defense Journal*, December 7, 2020, https://ukdefencejournal.org.uk/the-uk-and-its-unsinkable-aircraft-carriers-a-guide/.

3 Arthur J. Kerr, *A History of Cyprus*, History for the Confused, self-published, October 8, 2023.

4 Panayiotis Persianis, *Church and State in Cyprus Education: The Contribution of the Greek Orthodox Church of Cyprus to Cyprus Education During the British Administration (1878–1960)*, (Nicosia: Violaris Printing Works, 1978), 18.

5 Persianis, *Church and State in Cyprus Education*, 18.

6 William Mallinson, *Cyprus: A Historical Overview*, (Cyprus: Press and Information Office of the Republic of Cyprus, 2011), http://www.mfa.gov.cy/mfa/embassies/embassy_beijing.nsf/DMLcy_en/DMLcy_en?Opendocument.

7 Richard J. Aldrich and Ming-Yeh Rawnsley, eds., *The Clandestine Cold War in Asia, 1945–65: Western Intelligence, Propaganda and Special Operations*, (London: Frank Cass, 2013), 106.

8 "Cypriots on spot," *The Pittsburgh Press*, November 24, 1956, https://news.google.com/

newspapers?id=XqkvAAAAIBAJ&pg=4511,2773672&dq=sedition+3+years+in+prison+cyprus&hl=en&safe=active, 4.

9 David French, *Fighting EOKA: The British Counter-Insurgency Campaign on Cyprus, 1955–1959* (Oxford: Oxford University Press, 2015), 110.

10 French, *Fighting EOKA*, 142, 196, 220–222, 234, 304.

CHAPTER 2

1 *The Greeks and the Sea*, ed. Speros Vryonis, Jr., (New Rochelle, NY: Aristide D. Caratzas, 1993), 5, http://luna.cas.usf.edu/~murray/pdf/Vryonis-The%20Greeks%20and%20the%20Sea-.pdf.

2 "Famagusta," *Wikipedia*, accessed June 17, 2025, https://en.wikipedia.org/wiki/Famagusta.

3 "Bloody Christmas (1963)," Wikipedia, accessed June 17, 2025, https://en.wikipedia.org/wiki/Bloody_Christmas_(1963).

4 "Bloody Christmas (1963)," Wikipedia, accessed June 17, 2025, https://en.wikipedia.org/wiki/Bloody_Christmas_(1963).

5 Clement Dodd, *The History and Politics of the Cyprus Conflict*, (London: Palgrave Macmillan, 2010).

6 Alexis Papachelas, *The Dark Room 1967–1974*, (Athens, Greece: Metaixmio, October 14, 2021).

7 "The History of Varosha," Arkin Varosha Residences, accessed June 17, 2025, https://arkinvarosharesidences.com/en/the-history-of-varosha/.

CHAPTER 3

1 Sophocles, *Antigone* in *The Greek Plays: Sixteen Plays by Aeschylus, Sophocles, and Euripides*, ed. Mary Lefkowitz and James Romm, trans. Frank Nisetich, (New York, NY: Penguin Random House, 2016).

2 "Plaka the neighborhood of the Gods . . . Located at the base of the hill of Acropolis, Plaka is the oldest district in Athens." Bruce Hayllar, Tony Griffin, and Deborah Edwards, eds., *City Spaces-Tourist Places: Urban Tourism Precincts* (London, UK: Routledge, 2010), 31.

CHAPTER 4

1 Xenophon, *Cyropaedia*, trans. H. G. Dakyns (n.p.: Lighthouse Digital Publishing, 2012).

2 "Cyprus Detention Camps," Holocaust Encyclopedia, United States Holocaust Memorial Museum, accessed July 2, 2025, https://encyclopedia.ushmm.org/content/en/article/cyprus-detention-camps.

3 "Cyprus Detention Camps," Holocaust Encyclopedia.

4 "The Allies used supply chain management principles to move military supplies and armaments across the Pacific Ocean at strategic times. The U.S. shipped more than 17 million tons of cargo to the United Kingdom. Including 800,000 pints of blood plasma, 125 million maps, a replacement rail network, cigarettes, toothbrushes, and prefabricated harbors." David Kiger, "Is WW2 the greatest supply chain management in the World?," David Kiger's Blog, July 21, 2016, https://davidkigerinfo.wordpress.com/2016/07/21/is-ww2-the-greatest-supply-chain-management-in-the-world/.

CHAPTER 5

1 Euripides, *Children of Heracles* trans. David Kovacs, Loeb Classical Library 484 (Cambridge, MA: Harvard University Press, 1995).

2 Aristotle, *Poetics*, trans. S. H. Butcher (Arcadis: 2016), 10, Kindle.

3 "Athens Polytechnic Uprising," Wikipedia, accessed June 21, 2025, https://en.wikipedia.org/wiki/Athens_Polytechnic_uprising.

4 Henry Giniger, "Cyprus Fighting Goes on South of Turkish Sector," *New York Times*, August 19, 1974, https://www.nytimes.com/1974/08/19/archives/cyprus-fighting-goes-on-south-of-turkish-sector-clerides-government.html.

5 Steven V. Roberts, "Refugees in Cyprus Camp Wait Grimly to Go Home," *New York Times*, November 10, 1974, https://www.nytimes.com/1974/11/10/archives/refugees-in-cyprus-camp-wait-grimly-to-go-home-left-their-goods.html.

CHAPTER 6

1 C. P. Cavafy, *Collected Poems*, trans. Edmund Keeley and Philip Sheppard (Princeton: Princeton University Press, 1991).

CHAPTER 7

1 Plato, *Laches*, trans. W. R. M. Lamb, in *Plato in Twelve Volumes*, Vol. 2 (Cambridge: Harvard University Press: 1924), http://www.perseus.tufts.edu/hopper/text?doc=plat.+lach.+178a.

2 Kate Shea, Forgotten Crimes: Burglars Murder Fr. George C. Pantelis, Steal $10," *Buffalo News*, May 12, 2017, https://buffalonews.com/news/local/history/forgotten-crimes-burglars-murder-father-george-c-pantelis-steal-10/article_227941bd-3021-530f-8a89-6e3797eaac6b.html.

CHAPTER 8

1 Homer, *Odyssey*, trans. James E. Huddleston, available online at The Chicago Homer, https://homer.library.northwestern.edu/.

2 Peter Robinson, "'Tear Down This Wall': How Top Advisers Opposed Reagan's Challenge to Gorbachev—But Lost," *Prologue*

Magazine, Summer 2007, https://www.archives.gov/publications/prologue/2007/summer/berlin.html.

3 "Andrey Nikolayevich Kolmogorov," *Encyclopedia Britannica*, accessed June 21, 2025, https://www.britannica.com/biography/Andrey-Nikolayevich-Kolmogorov.

CHAPTER 9

1 "Immigration and Nationality Act," LBJ Presidential Library, accessed June 21, 2025, https://www.lbjlibrary.org/news-and-press/media-kits/immigration-and-nationality-act.

CHAPTER 10

1 Jonathon Lazear, *Meditations for Men Who Do Too Much* (New York: Simon & Schuster, 1992), 22.

2 "Origins," Information Sciences Institute, University of Southern California, accessed July 2, 2025, https://www.isi.edu/about/history/origins/.

CHAPTER 11

1 Niccolo Machiavelli, *The Prince*, trans. William. K. Marriott (n.p., Vizantia, 2017).

2 "IMSC Presents Landmark Internet concert event," Integrated Media Systems Center, University of Southern California, accessed July 2, 2025, https://infolab.usc.edu/imsc/news/symphony.html.

3 "IMSC Presents Landmark Internet concert event," Integrated Media Systems Center.

CHAPTER 12

1 Sophocles, *Oedipus Tyrannus*, trans. Hugh Lloyd-Jones, Loeb Classical Library (Cambridge, MA: Harvard University Press, 1997).

2 Thucydides, *History of the Peloponnesian War*, trans. Richard Crawley, (London: J. M. Dent & Sons, 1910), 122–3.

3 Donald K. Bandler, "September 11, 2001: Attack on America," (Remarks for Cyprus American Business Association Relief Dinner for September 11 Victims, Forum Hotel, December 11, 2001), https://avalon.law.yale.edu/sept11/bandler_001.asp.

CHAPTER 13

1 Xenophon, *Cyropaedia*, trans. H. G. Dakyns (n.p.: Lighthouse Digital Publishing, 2012).

2 Marc Ballon, "USC Viterbi Achieves Gender Parity in its Entering Class," Viturbi School of Engineering, University of Southern California, October 20, 2019, https://viterbischool.usc.edu/news/2019/10/usc-viterbi-achieves-gender-parity-in-its-entering-class/.

3 "According to the Society of Women Engineers, women and other minorities constituted approximately 16%–17% of engineering graduate students from 1990 to 2003. Furthermore, in 2003 approximately 20% (approximately 12,000) of new engineers were women, compared with about 80% of men (approximately 49,000)." "Women in engineering in the United States," Wikipedia, accessed July 2, 2025, https://en.wikipedia.org/wiki/Women_in_engineering_in_the_United_States.

4 C. L. Max Nikias, "Elevating a School," IEEE Signal Processing Magazine, March 2003, https://www.ese.wustl.edu/~nehorai/paper/nikias.pdf.

5 Lauren Clark, "John Mork: A Man of Energy," *Trojan Family Magazine*, December 5, 2012, 28–31, https://issuu.com/uscedu/

docs/tfm_2012_3_autumn; "USC Receives $110 Million Gift for Undergraduate Scholarships," Philosophy News Digest, Candid, April 28, 2011, https://philanthropynewsdigest.org/news/usc-receives-110-million-gift-for-undergraduate-scholarships.

6 Rob Asghar, *USC: Journey of Transformation* (Los Angeles, CA: University of Southern California, 2016), 44, https://bpb-us-w1.wpmucdn.com/sites.usc.edu/dist/3/919/files/2018/10/Transformation_Chapter-2_rs.pdf.

CHAPTER 14

1 Horace, *Odes* I.11, trans. John Conington (London: 1882), https://www.gutenberg.org/files/5432/5432.txt.

2 "Venture Capitalist Gives $22 Million to USC Engineering School," Philanthropy News Digest, Candid, November 12, 2004, https://philanthropynewsdigest.org/news/venture-capitalist-gives-22-million-to-usc-engineering-school.

3 C. L. Max Nikias, letter to USC community, May 8, 2012, https://bpb-us-w1.wpmucdn.com/sites.usc.edu/dist/3/919/files/2011/07/In-Memoriam_Kenneth-Leventhal.pdf; James Comtois, "Kenneth Leventhal, real estate accounting titan, dies at 91," *PERE*, May 10, 2012, https://www.perenews.com/kenneth-leventhal-real-estate-accounting-titan-dies-at-91/.

4 C. L. Max Nikias, letter to USC community, May 8, 2012, https://bpb-us-w1.wpmucdn.com/sites.usc.edu/dist/3/919/files/2011/07/In-Memoriam_Kenneth-Leventhal.pdf; James Comtois, "Kenneth Leventhal, real estate accounting titan, dies at 91," *PERE*, May 10, 2012, https://www.perenews.com/kenneth-leventhal-real-estate-accounting-titan-dies-at-91/.

5 Adam Smith, "The Viterbi Algorithm at 50," Virerbi School of Engineering, University of Southern California, March 16, 2017, https://viterbischool.usc.edu/news/2017/03/viterbi-algorithm-50/.

6 Smith, "The Viterbi Algorithm at 50."

7 "CREATE – The Nation's First Homeland Security Center," Center for Risk and Economic Analysis of Threats and Emergencies (CREATE), accessed July 2, 2025, https://create.usc.edu.

8 "Qualcomm Co-Founder, Wife Give $52 Million to USC Engineering School," Philanthropy News Digest, Candid, March 2, 2004, https://philanthropynewsdigest.org/news/qualcomm-co-founder-wife-give-52-million-to-usc-engineering-school.

9 "Home," USC Visions and Voices, University of Southern California, accessed July 2, 2025, https://visionsandvoices.usc.edu.

CHAPTER 15

1 Xenophon, *The Education of Cyrus*, trans., Wayne Ambler (Ithaca: Cornell University Press, 2001).

2 Ian Taylor, "Hurricane Katrina's Impact on Tulane's Teaching Hospitals," *Transactions of the American Clinical and Climatological Association* 118 (2007), 69–78, https://www.ncbi.nlm.nih.gov/pmc/articles/PMC1863583/.

3 Jordyn Holman, "Sig Ep Faces Ban for Up to Five Years," *Daily Trojan*, February 28, 2013, https://dailytrojan.com/2013/02/28/sig-ep-banned-from-the-row-for-five-years/.

CHAPTER 16

1 Homer, *Iliad*, trans. Robert Fagles (New York: Penguin Books, 1996).

2 "Collecting Testimonies," Shoah Foundation Institute, University of Southern California, accessed July 2, 2025, https://sfi.usc.edu/collecting.

CHAPTER 17

1 Homer, *Iliad*, trans. Robert Fagles (New York: Penguin Books, 1996).

CHAPTER 18

1 Charles E. Cerami, *Dinner at Mr. Jefferson's: Three Men, Five Great Wines, and the Evening That Changed America* (Hoboken, NJ: Wiley, 2008), 125.

CHAPTER 19

1 Xenophon, *Cyropaedia*, trans. Walter Miller, Loeb Classical Library (Cambridge, 1914).

2 "John R. Hubbard," University of Southern California, accessed July 3, 2025, https://www.usc.edu/profile/john-r-hubbard/.

3 "John R. Hubbard," University of Southern California.

CHAPTER 20

1 *The Greek Anthology*, Vol. 2, trans. William Roger Paton, Loeb Classical Library (Cambridge: 1916).

2 Larry Gordon and Eryn Brown, "USC steals 2 star brain researchers from UCLA," *Los Angeles Times*, May 10, 2013, https://www.latimes.com/health/la-xpm-2013-may-10-la-me-0510-usc-ucla-brain-research-20130510-story.html.

3 "The USC Roski Eye Institute is ranked #1 in the country for ophthalmology departments in National Institutes of Health (NIH) funding (Blue Ridge Institute for Medical Research)." "Training & Education," Keck School of Medicine, University of Southern California, accessed July 3, 2025, https://keck.usc.edu/ophthalmology/training-education/.

4 Sid Garcia, "LA hospital where RFK died honors his legacy," *ABC 7 News*, June 6, 2018, https://abc7.com/robert-f-kennedy-rfk-assassination-good-samaritan-hospital/3570647/.

5 "He graduated magna cum laude and put in the extra years to become an ophthalmologist, coinventing optical coherence tomography, a breakthrough technology that employed light

waves to take images of the retina." Paul Pringle, "Dr. Feelgood: 'Bad City' Exposes Secret Life of Scandalous USC Dean," *Los Angeles Magazine*, June 15, 2022, https://lamag.com/news-and-politics/dr-feelgood-the-secret-life-of-a-scandalous-usc-dean.

6 "Carmen Puliafito" Wikipedia, accessed on July 3, 2025, https://en.wikipedia.org/wiki/Carmen_Puliafito.

7 "Carmen Puliafito" Wikipedia.

8 Paul Pringle et al., "An overdose, a young companion, drug-fueled parties: The secret life of a USC med school dean," *Los Angeles Times*, July 17, 2017, https://www.latimes.com/local/california/la-me-usc-doctor-20170717-htmlstory.html.

CHAPTER 21

1 Virgil, Aeneid, trans. Robert Fagles (New York: Penguin Books, 2008).

2 Melissa Korn, "The Biggest Surprises in College Rankings," *Wall Street Journal*, September 27, 2016, https://www.wsj.com/articles/the-biggest-surprises-in-college-rankings-1475030103.

3 Melissa Korn, "The Biggest Surprises in College Rankings."

4 "Annual Address to the USC Faculty," President Emeritus C. L. Max Nikias, University of Southern California, February 9, 2011, https://clmaxnikias.usc.edu/2011/02/09/annual-address-to-the-usc-faculty-2011/.

5 Ron Mackovich-Rodriguez, "USC sees record number of applicants for fall 2018 admission," USC Today, University of Southern California, March 23, 2018, https://news.usc.edu/139338/usc-acceptance-rate-fall-2018-admission/.

6 Merrill Balassone, "Standout students abound in the Class of 2018," USC Today, University of Southern California, September 25, 2014, https://news.usc.edu/68982/standout-students-abound-in-the-class-of-2018/.

7 "USC announces fundraising campaign continuation as it reaches goal ahead of schedule," Grenzebach Glier and Associates, Huron Consulting Group, February 15, 2017, https://

www.grenzebachglier.com/news-events/usc-announces-fundraising-campaign-continuation-reaches-goal-ahead-schedule/.

8 Shauli Bar-on "The Bar-On Brief: Increased competition among universities will ease student debt," *Daily Trojan*, December 2, 2019, https://dailytrojan.com/2019/12/02/increased-competition-among-universities-will-ease-student-debt/.

9 "First-Generation College Students Transform the Face of USC," USC Today, University of Southern California, June 13, 2017, https://news.usc.edu/trojan-family/first-generation-students-transform-the-face-of-usc/.

10 "With nearly 24 percent of its undergraduates eligible for a Pell Grant, USC has a far greater share than at almost every other private, highly selective university." Eddie North-Hager, "High-achieving, low-income students connect with USC," USC Today, University of Southern California, January 19, 2016, https://today.usc.edu/at-usc-quality-equals-diversity/.

11 Eddie North-Hager, "High-achieving, low-income students connect with USC."

12 C. L. Max Nikias, "Why Elite Universities Should Admit More Community College Grads," *Washington Post*, October 23, 2014, https://www.washingtonpost.com/opinions/why-elite-universities-should-admit-more-community-college-grads/2014/10/23/b4dda968-4986-11e4-a046-120a8a855cca_story.html.

13 Douglas Belkin, "How USC Became a Leader in Recruiting Minorities," *Wall Street Journal*, May 30, 2016, https://www.wsj.com/articles/how-usc-became-a-leader-in-recruiting-minorities-1464660002.

14 Source: USC Admissions stats – Students enrolled in the arts – Fall 2011

15 "Annual gala honors USC veterans and ROTC students," President Emeritus C. L. Max Nikias, University of Southern California, April 1, 2016, https://clmaxnikias.usc.edu/2016/04/01/annual-gala-honors-usc-veterans-and-rotc-students/;

"Veterans Resource Center established for USC students," President Emeritus C. L. Max Nikias, University of Southern California, November 5, 2014, https://clmaxnikias.usc.edu/2014/11/05/veterans-resource-center-established-for-usc-students/; "Annual veterans dinner salutes service members," President Emeritus C. L. Max Nikias, University of Southern California, April 8, 2014, https://clmaxnikias.usc.edu/2014/04/08/annual-veterans-dinner-salutes-service-members/.

16 Peter Bergen, "How Petraeus changed the U.S. military," *CNN*, November 11, 2012, https://www.cnn.com/2012/11/10/opinion/bergen-petraeus-legacy/index.html.

CHAPTER 22

1 Sophocles, *Antigone*, trans. David Franklin and John Harrison (Cambridge: Cambridge University Press, 2003).

2 "Murders of Ming Qu and Ying Wu," Wikipedia, accessed July 3, 2025, https://en.wikipedia.org/wiki/Murders_of_Ming_Qu_and_Ying_Wu.

3 "Murders of Ming Qu and Ying Wu," Wikipedia.

4 "Man who killed two Chinese students in Los Angeles given multiple life terms," *The Guardian*, November 17, 2014, https://www.theguardian.com/us-news/2014/nov/17/killed-two-chinese-students-los-angeles-multiple-life-terms.

5 Greg Risling, "2 USC students from China fatally shot off campus," *Boston.com*, April 11, 2012, http://archive.boston.com/news/education/higher/articles/2012/04/11/2_usc_students_from_china_fatally_shot_off_campus/.

6 "Murders of Ming Qu and Ying Wu," Wikipedia, accessed July 3, 2025, https://en.wikipedia.org/wiki/Murders_of_Ming_Qu_and_Ying_Wu.

7 Dennis Romero, "Bryan Barnes, Javier Bolden Catch Possible Death Penalty Case in USC Murders," *LA Weekly*, May 22, 2012, https://www.laweekly.com/

bryan-barnes-javier-bolden-catch-possible-death-penalty-case-in-usc-murders/.

8 "Man who killed two Chinese students in Los Angeles given multiple life terms," *The Guardian*, November 17, 2014, https://www.theguardian.com/us-news/2014/nov/17/killed-two-chinese-students-los-angeles-multiple-life-terms.

9 Greg Risling, "2 USC students from China fatally shot off campus," *Boston.com*, April 11, 2012, http://archive.boston.com/news/education/higher/articles/2012/04/11/2_usc_students_from_china_fatally_shot_off_campus/.

10 "'They were showing off their wealth': Unsympathetic Chinese media says two USC students murdered in luxury BMW were killed because of their car," *Daily Mail*, April 12, 2012, https://www.dailymail.co.uk/news/article-2129081/They-showing-wealth-Chinese-media-says-USC-students-murdered-BMW-killed-make-car.html.

11 Wang Jun, "Memorial service held for slain students," *China Daily*, April 20, 2012, https://www.chinadaily.com.cn/world/2012-04/20/content_15094524.htm.

12 "Slain USC students honored at memorial," *Orange County Register*, April 19, 2012, https://www.ocregister.com/2012/04/19/slain-usc-students-honored-at-memorial/.

13 Wang Jun, "Memorial service held for slain students," *China Daily*, April 20, 2012, https://www.chinadaily.com.cn/world/2012-04/20/content_15094524.htm.

14 Tracy Bloom and Chris Wolfe, "USC Announces New Safety Measures After Fatal Beating of Grad Student," *KTLA5*, August 8, 2014, https://ktla.com/news/local-news/usc-announces-new-safety-measures-after-fatal-beating-of-grad-student/.

15 "USC Halloween Party Shooting Leaves Four Injured," *ABC News*, November 1, 2012, https://abcnews.go.com/US/usc-halloween-party-shooting-leaves-injured/story?id=17614878.

16 "LAPD detains two in campus shooting," *Daily Trojan*, November 1, 2012, https://dailytrojan.com/2012/11/01/lapd-detains-two-in-campus-shooting/.

17 "Man, 21, Sentenced To 40 Years To Life For 2012 Shooting Outside USC Halloween Party," *CBS News*, April 18, 2014, https://www.cbsnews.com/losangeles/news/man-21-sentenced-to-40-years-to-life-for-2012-shooting-outside-usc-halloween-party/.

18 "John Thomas Appointed UCLA Chief," Police Department, University of Southern California, March 11, 2024, https://adminvc.ucla.edu/news-views/winter-2024/john-thomas-appointed-ucla-chief-police.

19 Daniel Rothberg, "Nikias announces new campus security measures," *Daily Trojan*, November 7, 2012, https://dailytrojan.com/2012/11/07/nikias-announces-new-campus-security-measures/.

20 Adam Smith, "In memoriam: Xinran Ji, 24," USC Today, University of Southern California, August 1, 2014, https://news.usc.edu/66696/in-memoriam-xinran-ji-24/.

21 "Xinran Ji, 24," The Homicide Report, *Los Angeles Times*, July 24, 2014, https://homicide.latimes.com/post/xinran-ji/.

22 "Xinran Ji, 24," The Homicide Report, *Los Angeles Times*, July 24, 2014, https://homicide.latimes.com/post/xinran-ji/.

23 Kaidi Yuan, "Fourth and last defendant sentenced to life in prison in beating death of USC student," USC Annenberg Media, University of Southern California, March 10, 2019, https://www.uscannenbergmedia.com/2019/03/10/fourth-and-last-defendant-sentenced-to-life-in-prison-in-beating-death-of-usc-student/.

24 "Look up your college's numbers in the latest campus crime reports," Delmarva Now, https://data.delmarvanow.com/crimes-on-campus/criminal-offenses/us/00/2016/#csstable.

CHAPTER 23

1 Thucydides, *History of the Peloponnesian War* Vol. 1, trans. C. F. Smith, Loeb Classical Library 108 (Cambridge, MA: Harvard University Press, 1919).

2 Aristophanes, *Clouds*, trans. Ian Johnston, https://web.viu.ca/johnstoi/aristophanes/clouds.htm, lines 1005–1008.

3 "Jill and Frank Fertitta Hall, USC Marshall School of Business," Advanced Architectural Stone, accessed July 3, 2025, https://www.advancedarchitecturalstone.com/jill-and-frank-fertitta-hall-usc-marshall-school-of-business/.

4 "The Annenberg Foundation Commits $50 Million toward a New Building for the USC Annenberg School for Communication & Journalism," Annenberg Foundation, October 15, 2010, https://annenberg.org/news/annenberg-foundation-commits-50-million-toward-new-building-usc-annenberg-school/.

5 Abby Phillip and Charles Wells, "College Plans $1 Billion House Renovations," *Harvard Crimson*, April 11, 2008, https://www.thecrimson.com/article/2008/4/11/college-plans-1-billion-house-renovations/.

6 "UCLA: Freshmen Will Be Offered Four Years in Campus Residences," *NBC4 Los Angeles*, March 17, 2022, https://www.nbclosangeles.com/news/local/ucla-freshmen-will-be-offered-four-years-in-campus-residences/2850372/.

7 Carl Marziali, "USC Village approved by LA City Council," USC Today, University of Southern California, December 11, 2012, https://news.usc.edu/44892/usc-village-approved-by-la-city-council/.

8 Marziali, "USC Village approved by LA City Council."

9 Marziali, "USC Village approved by LA City Council."

10 Christopher Hawthorne, "Review: Disneyland meets Hogwarts at $700-million USC Village," *Los Angeles Times*, August 21, 2017, https://www.latimes.com/entertainment/arts/la-et-cm-usc-village-review-20170820-story.html.

11 "Facts About USC Village," USC Village, University of Southern California, accessed July 3, 2025, https://village.usc.edu/about/facts/.

12 Christian Camozzi, *Living and Learning: The Story of the USC Village* (Los Angeles: University of Southern California: 2018).

CHAPTER 24

1 Euripides, *Hecuba*, trans. Jay Kardan and Laura-Gray Street, https://www.didaskalia.net/issues/8/32/HecubaWorkingScript.pdf.

2 "Meet Hecuba, queen of Troy and centerpiece of USC Village's Central Piazza," USC Today, University of Southern California, August 17, 2017, https://news.usc.edu/126435/meet-hecuba-queen-of-troy-and-centerpiece-of-usc-villages-grand-piazza/.

3 "Christopher Slatoff," Christopherslatoff.com, accessed July 3, 2025, https://www.christopherslatoff.com/biography.

4 "Facts About USC Village," USC Village, University of Southern California, accessed July 3, 2025, https://village.usc.edu/about/facts/.

5 Arielle Yael Mokhtarzadeh, "Letter to the Editor: Statue of Hecuba represents the importance of female leadership," *Daily Trojan*, November 27, 2017, https://dailytrojan.com/2017/11/27/letter-editor-statue-hecuba-represents-importance-female-leadership/.

6 Mokhtarzadeh, "Letter to the Editor."

7 "History," Trojan Knights, accessed July 3, 2025, https://usctrojanknights.org/history.

8 Lauren Herstik, "U.S.C. Expands in a 'Neglected' Neighborhood, Promising Jobs and More," *New York Times*, August 15, 2017, https://www.nytimes.com/2017/08/15/realestate/commercial/usc-village-los-angeles-campus.html.

9 Herstik, "U.S.C. Expands."

10 Christopher Hawthorne, "Review: Disneyland meets Hogwarts at $700-million USC Village," *Los Angeles Times*, August 21, 2017, https://www.latimes.com/entertainment/arts/la-et-cm-usc-village-review-20170820-story.html.

11 Christian Camozzi, *Living and Learning: The Story of the USC Village* (Los Angeles: University of Southern California: 2018), 184, http://customsitesmedia.usc.edu/wp-content/uploads/sites/326/2018/10/17153943/Village_Chapter-6.pdf.

12 Camozzi, *Living and Learning*, 190, http://customsitesmedia.usc.edu/wp-content/uploads/sites/326/2018/10/17153943/Village_Chapter-6.pdf.

CHAPTER 25

1 Homer, *Iliad*, trans. Robert Fagles (New York: Viking Adult, 1990).

2 Eric Noland, "Rolling Out the Welcome Mat at the USC President's House," *Outlook San Marino*, July 30, 2014, https://customsitesmedia.usc.edu/wp-content/uploads/sites/326/2014/08/17160441/San-Marino-Outlook_Presidents-House.pdf.

3 Marissa Roy, "Nikias family hosts a USC Thanksgiving," *Daily Trojan*, November 29, 2010, https://dailytrojan.com/2010/11/29/nikias-family-hosts-a-usc-thanksgiving/.

4 Roy, "Nikias family hosts a USC Thanksgiving."

5 B. T. Jones, *The Seeley Mudd Estate: Its History, Furnishings, & First Families* (Los Angeles, CA: University of Southern California; 2010).

6 "Alson S. Clark," Wikipedia, accessed July 3, 2025, https://en.wikipedia.org/wiki/Alson_S._Clark.

7 "Antique amphitheater in the Ancient City of Salamis," *Cyprus Sun*, February 16, 2022, https://cyprussun-pro.com/blog/antique-amphitheater-in-the-ancient-city-of-salamis.html.

8 A. Stylianou and J. Stylianou, *The Painted Churches of Cyprus (Cyprus: Greek Communal Chamber, 1964): 155.*

9 B. T. Jones, *The Seeley Mudd Estate: Its History, Furnishings, & First Families* (Los Angeles, CA: University of Southern California; 2010), 7.

10 Jones, *The Seeley Mudd Estate,* 12

11 Eric Noland, "Rolling Out the Welcome Mat at the USC President's House," *Outlook San Marino*, July 30, 2014, https://customsitesmedia.usc.edu/wp-content/uploads/

sites/326/2014/08/17160441/San-Marino-Outlook_Presidents-House.pdf.

12 "Good Neighbors Campaign dinner salutes Trojans who support the community," USC University Relations, University of Southern California, September 15, 2017, https://communities.usc.edu/2017/09/15/good-neighbors-campaign-dinner-salutes-trojans-who-support-the-community/; "President honors Leadership Circle for life-changing generosity," USC University Relations, University of Southern California, September 29, 2017, https://communities.usc.edu/2015/09/29/president-honors-leadership-circle-for-life-changing-generosity/.

13 "The spirit of giving, 1.6 million times over," USC University Relations, University of Southern California, September 26, 2013, https://news.usc.edu/55575/the-spirit-of-giving-1-6-million-times-over/.

14 "The spirit of giving," University of Southern California.

15 Jack Flemming, "USC's presidential mansion sells for $25 million, a San Marino record," *Los Angeles Times*, July 7, 2021, https://www.latimes.com/business/real-estate/story/2021-07-07/uscs-presidential-mansion-sells-for-25-million-a-san-marino-record.

CHAPTER 26

1 Plato, *Laws*, in *Plato in Twelve Volumes*, Vol. 10 & 11, trans. R.G. Bury (Cambridge, MA: Harvard University Press: 1967), *https://www.perseus.tufts.edu/hopper/text?doc=Perseus%3Atext%3A1999.01.0166%3Abook%3D6%3Apage%3D753.*

2 C. L. Max Nikias, "President's Page," Trojan Family Magazine, Summer 2011, https://issuu.com/uscedu/docs/tfm_2011_2_summer1, 3.

3 Nikias, "President's Page," 3.

4 Charles Epting, *University Park, Los Angeles: A Brief History* (Charleston, SC: The History Press, 2013), 14.

5 Sarah Lifton and Annette Moore, *The University of Southern California: 1880–2005* (Los Angeles, CA: Figueroa Press, 2007), 31, https://news.usc.edu/18710/Birth-of-a-University/.

6 "There was quite a disagreement as to the price at which we should sell the lots," he wrote some years later. ". . . The general opinion was that the lots were not saleable at that price." So confident was Widney, however, that he offered to sell the first batch of lots, variously described as 26 or 30, to friends and business acquaintances for $200 each." Lifton and Moore, *The University of Southern California*, 31.

7 "Regional and State Unemployment — 2011 Annual Averages," Bureau of Labor Statistics, US Department of Labor, February 29, 2012, https://www.bls.gov/news.release/archives/srgune_02292012.pdf.

8 "Fas Regna Trojae," *Trojan Family Magazine*, January 6, 2012, 12-14, https://issuu.com/uscedu/docs/tfm_2011_3_autumn; "USC Announces $6 Billion Fundraising Campaign," *Philanthropy News Digest*, Candid, August 30, 2011, https://news.usc.edu/26529/usc-to-launch-largest-fundraising-campaign-in-higher-education-history/.

9 Emma Roller, "Stanford Campaign Brings In $6.2-Billion, a Record for Higher Education," *Chronicle of Higher Education*, February 8, 2012, https://www.chronicle.com/article/stanford-campaign-brings-in-6-2-billion-a-record-for-higher-education/.

10 Alvin Powell, "Harvard kicks off fundraising effort," Harvard Gazette, Harvard University, September 21, 2013, https://news.harvard.edu/gazette/story/2013/09/harvard-kicks-off-fundraising-effort/.

11 Larry Gordon, "USC to seek record-breaking donation total," *Los Angeles Times*, August 28, 2011, https://www.latimes.com/local/la-xpm-2011-aug-28-la-me-usc-funds-20110828-story.html.

12 Larry Gordon, "USC pursues aggressive fundraising effort despite hard times," *Los Angeles Times*, December 29, 2011, https://

www.latimes.com/health/la-xpm-2011-dec-29-la-me-adv-usc-giving-20111229-story.html.

13 Larry Gordon, "USC to seek record-breaking donation total," *Los Angeles Times*, August 28, 2011, https://www.latimes.com/local/la-xpm-2011-aug-28-la-me-usc-funds-20110828-story.html.

14 Holly Hall, "Can USC Really Raise $6-Billion?," *Philanthropy*, September 13, 2011, https://www.philanthropy.com/article/can-usc-really-raise-6-billion/.

15 "USC Ramps Up Campaign to Raise $6 Billion," Candid, January 2, 2012, https://philanthropynewsdigest.org/news/usc-ramps-up-campaign-to-raise-6-billion.

16 "James H. Zumberge," University of Southern California, accessed July 6, 2025, https://about.usc.edu/presidents/james-h-zumberge/.

17 "Driven by Dreams," Trojan Family Magazine, June 23, 2017, 41, https://issuu.com/uscedu/docs/tfm_sum17_issuu.

CHAPTER 27

1 Shakespeare, *Julius Caesar*, Act 4, lines 2217–18, https://internetshakespeare.uvic.ca/doc/JC_F1/scene/4.3/index.html.

2 Michael Wyland, "Duke University Sues Donor's Estate for $10 Million," *Nonprofit Quarterly*, August 24, 2016, https://nonprofitquarterly.org/duke-university-sues-donors-estate-for-10-million/.

3 "Alfred Mann," Trojan Family Magazine, June 23, 2016, 75, https://news.usc.edu/tributes/alfred-mann/.

4 "Alfred Mann," Trojan Family Magazine, 75.

5 "Alfred Mann," Trojan Family Magazine, 75.

6 Chinyere Cindy Amobi, "USC School of Pharmacy, Department of Biomedical Engineering announce naming gifts," USC Today, University of Southern California, November 17, 2022, https://news.usc.edu/203663/usc-pharmacy-biomedical-engineering-alfred-mann-foundation-gift/.

7 Amobi, "USC School of Pharmacy."

8 "$40 million gift from Alfred E. Mann Charities will boost CHLA research," HSC News, University of Southern California, April 6, 2023, https://hscnews.usc.edu/40-million-gift-from-alfred-e-mann-charities-will-boost-chla-research.

9 "About Sol Price and the Naming Gift," Sol Price School of Public Policy, University of Southern California, accessed July 6, 2025, https://priceschool.usc.edu/about/sol-price-naming-gift/.

10 "About Sol Price and the Naming Gift," Sol Price School of Public Policy.

11 "Schwarzenegger Commits to $20-Million for USC Institute," *Chronicle of Philanthropy*, August 2, 2012, https://www.philanthropy.com/article/schwarzenegger-commits-to-20-million-for-usc-institute/.

12 "Arnold Schwarzenegger," Sol Price School of Public Policy, University of Southern California, accessed July 6, 2025, https://priceschool.usc.edu/people/arnold-schwarzenegger/.

13 "$60 million gift names USC Suzanne Dworak-Peck School of Social Work," USC Today, University of Southern California, September 14, 2016, https://news.usc.edu/107250/60-million-gift-names-usc-suzanne-dworak-peck-school-of-social-work/.

14 Lynn Lipinski, "The Campaign for USC Hits $6 Billion and Keeps on Going," USC Today, University of Southern California, June 13, 2017, https://news.usc.edu/trojan-family/the-campaign-for-usc-hits-6-billion-and-keeps-on-going/.

15 Lipinski, "The Campaign for USC."

16 Alicia Di Rado, "Historic Campaign for USC Comes to a Close," USC Today, University of Southern California, https://news.usc.edu/trojan-family/campaign-for-usc-end/.

17 Lynn Lipinski, "The Campaign for USC Hits $6 Billion and Keeps on Going," USC Today, University of Southern California, June 13, 2017, https://news.usc.edu/trojan-family/the-campaign-for-usc-hits-6-billion-and-keeps-on-going/.

18 Masada Siegel, "Scandal Brings USC Into the Elite Ranks," *Wall Street Journal*, March 13, 2019, https://www.wsj.com/articles/scandal-brings-usc-into-the-elite-ranks-11552518553.

19 Masada Siegel, "Scandal Brings USC Into the Elite Ranks," *Wall Street Journal*, March 13, 2019, https://www.wsj.com/articles/scandal-brings-usc-into-the-elite-ranks-11552518553.

20 Erin Banco, "Feds Charge Trump Donor Imaad Zuberi With Hiding Work as Foreign Agent," *Daily Beast*, October 22, 2019, https://www.thedailybeast.com/imaad-zuberi-who-donated-dollar900000-to-trumps-inaugural-committee-indicted-by-feds.

21 John C. Maxwell, *Developing the Leaders Around You* (Nashville: Thomas Nelson, 1995).

22 Maxwell, *Developing the Leaders Around You*.

CHAPTER 28

1 Aeschylus, *Prometheus Bound*, trans. Philip Vellacott (London: Penguin Books, 1961).

2 "USC marks 100th anniversary of Trojans nickname," *Fox Sports*, February 23, 2012, https://www.foxsports.com/stories/other/usc-marks-100th-anniversary-of-trojans-nickname.

3 "USC to mark 125 years of award-winning athletics," USC Today, University of Southern California, https://usctrojans.com/news/2013/7/25/USC_To_Celebrate_125th_Anniversary_Of_Athletics_In_2013_14.

4 "NCAA Division I Committee on Infractions Roster," Infractions Process, NCAA, https://www.ncaa.org/sports/2018/3/20/ncaa-division-i-committee-on-infractions-roster.aspx.

5 C. L. Max Nikias, "USC Athletic Department" (memo), July 20, 2010, https://bpb-us-e1.wpmucdn.com/sites.usc.edu/dist/3/919/files/2011/07/Announcement.President.elect_.Nikias.pdf.

6 "Lane Kiffin," Wikipedia, accessed July 6, 2025, https://en.wikipedia.org/wiki/Lane_Kiffin.

7 "Lane Kiffin Named USC Head Football Coach," USC Trojans, January 12, 2010, https://usctrojans.com/news/2010/1/12/lane_kiffin_named_usc_head_football_coach.

8 Bill N., "USC Football: Trojans Sanction Appeal Is Rigged Like NCAA Sanctions," *Bleacher Report*, June 7, 2018, https://bleacherreport.com/articles/517524-usc-football-will-the-trojans-ncaa-sanction-appeal-help-or-hurt.

9 David Wharton and Baxter Holmes, "O.J. Mayo Scandal Leads to Heavy Sanctions for USC," *Los Angeles Times*, January 4, 2010, https://www.latimes.com/archives/la-xpm-2010-jan-04-la-sp-usc-basketball4-2010jan04-story.html.

10 Diamond Leung, "Mike Garrett: 'Nothing but a lot of envy,'" *ESPN*, June 11, 2010, https://www.espn.com/blog/pac12/post/_/id/10444/mike-garrett-nothing-but-a-lot-of-envy.

11 Leung, "Mike Garrett."

12 "Heisman Winner: Mike Garrett," Heisman, accessed on July 6, 2025, https://www.heisman.com/heisman-winners/mike-garrett/.

13 "The Renewal of the Trojan Empire," in Rob Asghar, *USC: A Journey of Transformation* (Los Angeles: University of Southern California, n.d.), 203, http://customsitesmedia.usc.edu/wp-content/uploads/sites/326/2018/10/17153950/Transformation_Chapter-10_rs.pdf.

14 USC Football (@uscfb), "Welcome home, @ReggieBush," X (formerly Twitter), 11:00 am, June 10, 2010, https://twitter.com/uscfb/status/1270732507412140032.

15 Pete Thamel, "After a decade, the disassociation with Bush had ended," *ESPN*, April 24, 2025, https://www.espn.com/college-football/story/_/id/40014492/reggie-bush-heisman-trophy-returned.

CHAPTER 29

1 Diogenes Laertius, *Lives of the Eminent Philosophers*, trans. Robert Drew Hicks, https://topostext.org/work/221.

2 "Arizona State 62-41 USC (Sep 28, 2013) Final Score," *ESPN*, accessed July 6, 2025, https://www.espn.com/college-football/game/_/gameId/332710009.

3 Aaron Torres, "Three years ago today Lane Kiffin was fired on an airport tarmac," *Fox Sports*, November 15, 2016, https://www.foxsports.com/stories/college-football/three-years-ago-today-lane-kiffin-was-fired-on-an-airport-tarmac.

4 Dennis Dodd, "Lane Kiffin: USC airport firing was the lowest point in my career," *CBS Sports*, January 9, 2016, https://www.cbssports.com/college-football/news/lane-kiffin-usc-airport-firing-was-the-lowest-point-in-my-career/.

5 "2013 USC Trojans Football Team," Wikipedia, accessed July 6, 2025, https://en.wikipedia.org/wiki/2013_USC_Trojans_football_team.

6 "USC Hires Steve Sarkisian as Coach," *ESPN*, December 2, 2013, https://www.espn.com/los-angeles/college-football/story/_/id/10068739/usc-trojans-hire-steve-sarkisian-washington-huskies-new-football-coach.

7 Kyle Kensing, "Ed Orgeron Resigns from USC: 5 Schools Who Should Hire Coach O," *Bleacher Report*, June 8, 2018, https://bleacherreport.com/articles/1873408-ed-orgeron-resigns-from-usc-5-schools-who-should-hire-coach-o.

8 Avinash Kunnath, "VIDEO: Steve Sarkisian reportedly drunk at USC donor event, drops F-bomb, pulled off stage, apologizes," *SBNation*, August 23, 2015, https://www.pacifictakes.com/usc-trojans/2015/8/23/9193283/usc-trojans-head-coach-sark-salute-to-troy-drunk-rumors-inebriated-turn-up.

9 Tyler Conway, "Steve Sarkisian Apologizes for Comments Made at 'Salute to Troy' Event," *Bleacher Report*, August 23, 2015, https://bleacherreport.com/articles/2553729-steve-sarkisian-apologizes-for-comments-made-at-salute-to-troy-event.

10 Tony Manfred, "USC football coach explains embarrassing drunken rant at kickoff event," *Business Insider*, August 25, 2015, https://www.businessinsider.com/steve-sarkisian-says-drunken-rant-the-result-of-alchol-meds-2015-8.

11 "USC AD Pat Haden: 'The decision I made didn't work out, and I own that,'" *ESPN*, October 13, 2015, https://www.espn.com/los-angeles/college-football/story/_/id/13880068/usc-athletic-director-pat-haden-says-decision-fire-steve-sarkisian-was-very-difficult.

12 Lindsey Thiry (@LindseyThiry), "Video of #USC AD Pat Haden on the sideline pregame from NBC," X (formerly Twitter), 7:44 p.m., October 17, 2015, https://x.com/LindseyThiry/status/655529846022365184.

13 "2016 USC Trojans Football Team," Wikipedia, accessed July 6, 2025, https://en.wikipedia.org/wiki/2016_USC_Trojans_football_team.

14 "2017 Rose Bowl," Wikipedia, accessed July 6, 2025, https://en.wikipedia.org/wiki/2017_Rose_Bowl.

15 Joey Kaufman, "Lynn Swann's demand for patience pays off for USC's football team," *Los Angeles Daily News*, September 5, 2017, https://www.dailynews.com/2017/01/04/lynn-swanns-demand-for-patience-pays-off-for-uscs-football-team/.

16 Becky Sullivan, "What we know and what we don't about a historic settlement to pay college athletes," *NPR*, May 24, 2024, https://www.npr.org/2024/05/24/nx-s1-4978680/house-ncaa-settlement-pay-college-athletes.

17 Michelle Brutlag Hosick, "Settlement Documents Filed in College Athletics Class-Action Lawsuits," NCAA, July 26, 2024, https://www.ncaa.org/news/2024/7/25/media-center-settlement-documents-filed-in-college-athletics-class-action-lawsuits.

18 Thy Vo, "Female Athletes Say $2.8B NCAA Deal 'Vastly Favors' Men," Law360, August 12, 2024, https://www.law360.com/employment-authority/articles/1868735/female-athletes-say-2-8b-ncaa-deal-vastly-favors-men.

19 Andrea Adelson, Kyle Bonagura and Adam Rittenberg, "Inside the stunning USC-UCLA move to the Big Ten -- and the chaos that followed," *ESPN*, July 11, 2022, https://www.espn.com/

college-football/story/_/id/34217498/inside-stunning-usc-ucla-move-big-ten-chaos-followed.

20 Heather Dinich, "Oklahoma, Texas agree to exit Big 12 Conference after 2023-24 season," *ESPN*, February 9, 2023, https://www.espn.com/college-sports/story/_/id/35625879/oklahoma-texas-exit-big-12-conference-2023-24-season.

21 James Dator, "Lincoln Riley's USC contract might be the greatest in sports history," *SB Nation*, November 30, 2021, https://www.sbnation.com/college-football/2021/11/30/22809357/lincoln-riley-usc-contract-breakdown.

22 "Lincoln Riley Net Worth, Salary and Contract," Sportskeeda, updated October 9, 2024, https://www.sportskeeda.com/college-football/lincoln-riley-salary-contract-and-net-worth.

23 "The State of Troy | Aug. 2: USC's Move To Big Ten, Paris Olympics, NIL Update and More," USC Trojans, University of Southern California, August 2, 2024, https://usctrojans.com/news/2024/8/2/The-State-of-Troy-August-2-USC-Move-To-Big-Ten-Paris-Olympics-NIL-Update.aspx.

24 Luca Evans, "USC's football camp kicks off on a new turf field, part of a planned $200 million facility," *Orange County Register*, August 2, 2024, https://www.ocregister.com/2024/08/02/uscs-football-camp-kicks-off-on-a-new-turf-field-part-of-a-planned-200-million-facility/.

25 Dennis Dodd, "How Lincoln Riley's success rebuilding USC through transfer portal offers peek at college football's future," *CBS Sports*, November 18, 2022, https://www.cbssports.com/college-football/news/how-lincoln-rileys-success-rebuilding-usc-through-transfer-portal-offers-peek-at-college-footballs-future/.

26 Brent Schrotenboer, "Will Deion Sanders' second roster flip at Colorado work this time? Here's why and why not," *USA Today*, August 29 2024, https://www.usatoday.com/story/sports/ncaaf/big12/2024/08/29/deion-sanders-colorado-football-season-opener-north-dakota-state/74966563007/.

27 "Los Angeles, CA is in the 2nd largest DMA in the United States, with a population of approximately 19 million and 5,838,090 television households, as reported by Nielsen Media." "Station Profile," Nexstar Media Group, accessed July 6, 2025, https://www.nexstar.tv/stations/ktla/.

28 "PAC-12 reaches media agreement with Fox & ESPN for $225-250 Million Dollars," *SB Nation*, May 3, 2011, https://www.californiagoldenblogs.com/2011/5/3/2151387/pac-12-reaches-media-agreement-with-fox-espn-for-225-250-million.

29 Jon Wilner, "San Jose Mercury News – Blogs: March 5, 2015 – The Pac-12's financial future: Comparing TV revenue to the SEC and Big Ten," College Hotline (blog), March 5, 2015, https://blogs.mercurynews.com/collegesports/2015/03/05/the-pac-12s-financial-future-comparing-tv-revenue-to-the-sec-and-big-ten/.

30 Adam Rittenberg, "Big Ten completes 7-year, $7 billion media rights agreement with Fox, CBS, NBC," *ESPN*, August 18, 2022, https://www.espn.com/college-football/story/_/id/34417911/big-ten-completes-7-year-7-billion-media-rights-agreement-fox-cbs-nbc.

31 "College bowl payouts surpass $500 million," *ESPN*, April 14, 2015, https://www.espn.com/college-football/story/_/id/12688517/college-bowl-game-payouts-surpass-500-million-first-year-college-football-playoff.

32 "College bowl payouts surpass $500 million," *ESPN*, April 14, 2015, https://www.espn.com/college-football/story/_/id/12688517/college-bowl-game-payouts-surpass-500-million-first-year-college-football-playoff.

33 "College Football Playoff Expands to 12 Teams Beginning in 2024," College Football Playoff, December 1, 2022, https://collegefootballplayoff.com/news/2022/12/1/cfp12-2425.aspx.

34 David A. Fahrenthold and Billy Witz, "How Rich Donors and Loose Rules Are Transforming College Sports," *New York Times*, October 21, 2023, updated October 22, 2023, https://

www.nytimes.com/2023/10/21/us/college-athletes-donor-collectives.html.

35 Bryan Shapiro, "Private Equity Takes Aim at the College Sports Industry," June 11, 2024, Duane Morris Sports Blog, Duane Morris, https://blogs.duanemorris.com/sportslaw/2024/06/11/private-equity-takes-aim-at-the-college-sports-industry/.

36 Shapiro, "Private Equity Takes Aim at the College Sports Industry."

37 Ron L. Brown, "Tax Implications When NCAA Student Athletes Make Money," Kiplinger, July 21, 2022, https://www.kiplinger.com/taxes/604955/tax-implications-when-ncaa-student-athletes-make-money.

38 Dennis Dodd, "Lincoln Riley finding his voice at USC, but meeting $100 million expectations is not coming as easily," *CBS Sports*, July 25, 2024, https://www.cbssports.com/college-football/news/lincoln-riley-finding-his-voice-at-usc-but-meeting-100-million-expectations-is-not-coming-as-easily/amp/.

CHAPTER 30

1 Shakespeare, *As You Like It*, ed. Jack R. Crawford (New Haven, CT: Yale University Press, 1919).

2 "It was the Central Chamber of the Council House where the official transfer of power took place in 1947 and Jawaharlal Nehru made his famous 'tryst with destiny' speech." Sidhartha Roy, "Parliament House: 144 pillars of pride," *Hindustan Times*, September 1, 2011, https://www.hindustantimes.com/delhi/parliament-house-144-pillars-of-pride/story-UBRQJ3tqmspQR34gkx1O2K.html.

3 "Tata Group Chairman Ratan Tata meets PM," *Economic Times*, February 23, 2011, https://economictimes.indiatimes.com/tata-group-chairman-ratan-tata-meets-pm/articleshow/7556753.cms.

4 "Assassination of Shinzo Abe," Wikipedia, accessed July 6, 2025, https://en.wikipedia.org/wiki/Assassination_of_Shinzo_Abe.

5 Martin Wisckol, "Obama draws 37,000 at USC rally," *Orange County Register*, October 22, 2010, https://www.ocregister.com/2010/10/22/obama-draws-37000-at-usc-rally-2/.

6 Josh Grossberg, "USC Shoah Foundation and Steven Spielberg Honor President Barack Obama with Ambassador for Humanity Award," USC Shoah Foundation, University of Southern California, May 7, 2014, https://sfi.usc.edu/news/2014/05/usc-shoah-foundation-and-steven-spielberg-honor-president-barack-obama-ambassador.

7 Cassie Hurwitz, "Sasha Obama Is Officially a College Graduate," *Oprah Daily*, May 16, 2023, https://www.oprahdaily.com/entertainment/a43906131/sasha-obama-graduates-college-usc/.

8 "George W. Bush Presidential Center Dedication Ceremony," George W. Bush Presidential Center, April 25, 2013, https://www.bushcenter.org/events-and-exhibits/george-w-bush-presidential-center-dedication-ceremony.

9 Nathaniel Haas, "USC hosts George W. Bush and Laura Bush," *Daily Trojan*, November 19, 2023, https://dailytrojan.com/2013/11/19/usc-hosts-george-w-bush-and-laura-bush/.

10 Haas, "USC hosts George W. Bush and Laura Bush."

11 Diane Krieger, "Bill Clinton speaks in Bovard Auditorium," USC Today, University of Southern California, November 8, 2014, https://news.usc.edu/70839/president-bill-clinton-speaks-in-bovard-auditorium/.

12 "Will Ferrell | USC Commencement Speech 2017," posted May 12, 2017 by USC, YouTube, 25 min., 43 sec., https://www.youtube.com/watch?v=mfjGmBVAL-o.

13 "Why Will Ferrell's USC Commencement Speech Was a Grand Slam," Duarte, May 2, 2019, https://www.duarte.com/presentation-skills-resources/will-ferrell-usc-commencement/.

14 "Why Will Ferrell's USC Commencement Speech Was a Grand Slam," Duarte, May 2, 2019, https://www.duarte.com/presentation-skills-resources/will-ferrell-usc-commencement/.

15 "Will Ferrell on His Viral Commencement Speech," posted June 8, 2017 by Jimmy Kimmel Live, YouTube, 3 min., 37 sec., https://www.youtube.com/watch?v=TUha9UsAtKE.

16 "Will Ferrell on His Viral Commencement Speech," posted June 8, 2017 by Jimmy Kimmel Live, YouTube, 3 min., 37 sec., https://www.youtube.com/watch?v=TUha9UsAtKE.

CHAPTER 31

1 Homer, *Odyssey*, trans. Robert Fagles (New York: Penguin Books, 1999).

2 C. L. Max Nikias, "Message from President Nikias," May 15, 2018, https://studenthealthresources.usc.edu/message-from-president-nikias-may-15-2018/.

3 "USC Faculty Letter to Board of Trustees," August 1, 2018, https://docs.google.com/document/u/2/d/1hxt-n9T2ZWh5nmNU7GOZhPuW-AoeyLY-EQM1qnqXlGxg/mobilebasic.

4 USC Academic Senate, "Faculty Composition: Who We Are & Who We Want to Be," May 2, 2019, https://academicsenate.usc.edu/faculty-composition-who-we-are-who-we-want-to-be/.

5 "Buck Passing," Wikipedia, accessed June 25, 2025, https://en.wikipedia.org/wiki/Buck_passing.

6 Harry S. Truman Presidential Library, "'The Buck Stops Here' Desk sign," accessed June 25, 2025, https://www.trumanlibrary.gov/education/trivia/buck-stops-here-sign.

7 "In an interview, Gold rejected the view that the Tyndall episode revealed moral failings in university leadership. He offered another position: that Tyndall and the previous scandal involving a former medical school dean occurred because non-academic offices such as human resources did not advance with the rest

of the university. 'We failed to look at keeping our infrastructure and systems apace with our growth,' Gold said." Harriet Ryan and Matt Hamilton, "Rocked by scandal, USC must heal its divisions and repair a broken culture," *Los Angeles Times*, December 23, 2018, https://www.latimes.com/local/lanow/la-me-usc-year-disruption-culture-20181223-story.html.

8 United States Department of Education Office for Civil Right, RE: OCR Docket No. 09-18-6901, https://www2.ed.gov/about/offices/list/ocr/docs/investigations/more/09186908-a.pdf, page 48.

9 Ibid., page 5.

10 Shakespeare, *King Lear*, Act One, Scene Four, lines 302–3, https://www.folger.edu/explore/shakespeares-works/king-lear/read/1/4/?q=tooth#line-1.4.288.

11 Austin Peay, "USC Promised Transparency, So Why Is It Acting 'Like The Kremlin'?," *LAist*, August 19, 2019, https://laist.com/news/usc-transparency.

CHAPTER 32

1 Aeschylus, *The Persians*, lines 740–742, trans. C. E. S. Headlam (London: George Bell and Sons, 1909), 23, http://ia601609.us.archive.org/20/items/persianstranslat00aescuoft/persianstranslat00aescuoft.pdf.

2 "Nemesis," Wikipedia, accessed July 7, 2025, https://en.wikipedia.org/wiki/Nemesis.

3 "Antisemitism and higher education in the United States," Wikipedia, accessed July 7, 2025, https://en.wikipedia.org/wiki/Antisemitism_and_higher_education_in_the_United_States.

4 "Antisemitism and higher education in the United States," Wikipedia.

5 "Boycott, Divestment, and Sanctions (BDS)," Wikipedia, accessed July 7, 2025, https://en.wikipedia.org/wiki/Boycott,_Divestment_and_Sanctions.

6 The Palestinian boycott, divestment and sanctions campaign (BDS) modeled on the anti-apartheid movement in South Africa." Amal Ghazal and Jens Hanssen, eds., *The Oxford Handbook of Contemporary Middle Eastern and North African History* (Oxford: Oxford University Press, 2021), 693.

7 "Statement by C. L. Max Nikias," President Emeritus C. L. Max Nikias, University of Southern California, July 13, 2011, https://clmaxnikias.usc.edu/2011/07/13/statement-by-c-l-max-nikias/.

8 Matt Lemas and Zoe Young, "SCALE holds sit-in outside Nikias' office," *Daily Trojan*, April 15, 2014, https://dailytrojan.com/2014/04/15/scale-holds-sit-in-outside-nikias-office/.

9 "Tom Hayden," Wikipedia, https://en.wikipedia.org/wiki/Tom_Hayden.

10 Matt Lemas and Zoe Young, "SCALE holds sit-in outside Nikias' office," *Daily Trojan*, April 15, 2014, https://dailytrojan.com/2014/04/15/scale-holds-sit-in-outside-nikias-office/.

11 Lemas and Young, "SCALE holds sit-in outside Nikias' office."

12 Roger Kimball, *Tenured Radicals: How Politics Has Corrupted Our Higher Education* (Chicago: Ivan R. Dee, 2008), 250

13 "Cancel Culture Database," *College Fix*, https://www.thecollegefix.com/cancel-culture-database/.

14 Jennifer Kabbany, "Black and Latino groups at Emory host 'safe space' in response to Heather Mac Donald speech," *College Fix*, January 29, 2020, https://www.thecollegefix.com/black-and-latino-groups-at-emory-host-safe-space-in-response-to-heather-mac-donald-speech/.

15 Jennifer Kabbany, "Blacklisting, vandalism, picket line: Outrage erupts at Bucknell ahead of Heather Mac Donald talk," *College Fix*, November 13, 2019, https://www.thecollegefix.com/blacklisting-vandalism-picket-line-outrage-erupts-at-bucknell-ahead-of-heather-mac-donald-talk/.

16 Jessica Costescu, "MIT Refused To Host Dennis Ross. It Invited a Hamas Apologist Instead," *Washington Free Beacon*, March 14, 2024, https://freebeacon.com/campus/mit-refused-to-host-dennis-ross-it-invited-a-hamas-apologist-instead/.

17 Camille Shooshani, "Visions and Voices hosts military lecture," *Daily Trojan*, January 27, 2014, https://dailytrojan.com/2014/01/27/visions-and-voices-hosts-military-lecture/.

18 Diana Kruzman, "Conservative writer David Horowitz visits campus," *Daily Trojan*, March 24, 2016, https://dailytrojan.com/2016/03/24/conservative-writer-david-horowitz-visits-campus/.

19 David French, "Colleges Have Gone off the Deep End. There Is a Way Out," *New York Times*, April 28, 2014, https://www.nytimes.com/2024/04/28/opinion/protests-college-free-speech.html.

20 Nanette Asimov and Rachel Swan, "Stanford says arrested protesters caused 'extensive damage' while occupying president's office," *San Francisco Chronicle*, June 5, 2024, https://www.sfchronicle.com/bayarea/article/stanford-palestine-protest-president-19496489.php.

21 Victor Davis Hanson, "The Disgrace and Fall of the American Elite Campus," *The Blade of Perseus* (blog), May 20, 2024, https://victorhanson.com/the-disgrace-and-fall-of-the-american-elite-campus/.

22 Hanson, "The Disgrace and Fall of the American Elite Campus."

23 Hanson, "The Disgrace and Fall of the American Elite Campus."

24 Hanson, "The Disgrace and Fall of the American Elite Campus."

25 Kate Gibson, "Google fires 28 employees after protest against contract with Israeli government," *CBS News*, May 13, 2024, https://www.cbsnews.com/news/google-fires-28-employees-after-protest-against-contract-with-israeli-government/.

26 Gibson, "Google fires 28 employees after protest against contract with Israeli government."

27 Michael Loria and Christopher Cann, "No diploma: Colleges withhold degrees from students after pro-Palestinian protests," *USA Today*, June 1, 2024, https://www.usatoday.com/story/news/nation/2024/06/01/college-degrees-withheld-after-israel-gaza-protests/73899493007/.

28 Matthew Impelli, "Business Owners Refuse to Hire Columbia Grads After Pro-Palestinian Protest," *Newsweek*, April 29,

2024, https://www.newsweek.com/pro-palestinian-protest-columbia-alumni-1895244.

29 Sawdah Bhaimiya, "Some employers are reluctant to hire college grads who attended pro-Palestinian protests, survey finds," *CNBC*, May 27, 2024, https://www.cnbc.com/2024/05/27/employers-avoiding-hiring-college-grads-over-palestinian-protests-survey.html.

30 Lexi Lonas Cochran, "USC cancels main commencement ceremony after nixing valedictorian's speech," *The Hill*, April 25, 2024, https://thehill.com/homenews/education/4622194-usc-commencement-valedictorian-speech-student-protests/.

31 Angie Orellana Hernandez, Matt Hamilton, and Jaweed Kaleem, "USC's faculty senate censures President Carol Folt and provost over commencement," *Los Angeles Times*, May 8, 2024, https://www.latimes.com/california/story/2024-05-08/usc-faculty-senate-vote-to-censure-president.

32 Andrew Lapin, "USC Shoah Foundation distances itself from pro-Palestinian valedictorian whose speech was canceled," *Cleveland Jewish News*, April 16, 2024, https://www.clevelandjewishnews.com/jta/usc-shoah-foundation-distances-itself-from-pro-palestinian-valedictorian-whose-speech-was-canceled/article_e6697a85-ab2d-5ad4-a443-adfdd6bb396a.html.

33 Josh Marcus, "USC valedictorian whose speech was canceled in Israel row shares redacted version," *Independent*, May 11, 2024, https://www.independent.co.uk/news/world/americas/usc-asna-tabassum-valedictorian-speech-b2543227.html.

34 Josh Moody, "Campus Leaders Stand Their Ground Before Congress," *Inside Higher Ed*, May 24, 2024, https://www.insidehighered.com/news/governance/executive-leadership/2024/05/24/campus-leaders-stand-their-ground-congress.

35 Annie Ma, "How the presidents of Harvard, Penn and MIT testified to Congress on antisemitism," *Associated Press*, updated December 12, 2023, https://apnews.com/article/

harvard-penn-mit-president-congress-intifada-193a1c81e9ebcc15c5dd68b71b4c6b71.

36 Ma, "How the presidents of Harvard, Penn and MIT testified to Congress on antisemitism."

37 Lisa Kurian Philip, "Northwestern president grilled by Republicans about deal with pro-Palestinian protesters," *NPR Illinois*, May 24, 2024, https://www.nprillinois.org/education-desk/2024-05-24/northwestern-president-grilled-by-republicans-about-deal-with-pro-palestinian-protesters.

38 Annie Ma and Collin Binkley, "Columbia's president rebuts claims she has allowed the university to become a hotbed of antisemitism," *Associated Press*, updated April 17, 2024, https://apnews.com/article/columbia-president-congress-israel-hamas-antisemitism-3255357b4443c1fb4bae8b8ea5774ee5.

39 Tim O'Reilly, "Gradually, then suddenly," *O'Reilly*, January 10, 2019, https://www.oreilly.com/radar/gradually-then-suddenly/.

40 Gary Wexler, "The Inside Story of How Palestinians Took Over the World," *Jewish Journal*, November 18, 2023, https://jewishjournal.com/commentary/columnist/365220/the-inside-story-of-how-palestinians-took-over-the-world/.

41 Wexler, "The Inside Story of How Palestinians Took Over the World."

42 Tawnell D. Hobbs, Valerie Bauerlein, and Dan Frosch, "Activist Groups Trained Students for Months Before Campus Protests," *Wall Street Journal*, May 3, 2024, https://www.wsj.com/us-news/education/student-campus-protests-veteran-activist-groups-17ccd094.

43 "Student protesters on US campuses trained for months with anti-Israel groups including SJP – report," *Times of Israel*, May 4, 2024, https://www.timesofisrael.com/liveblog_entry/student-protesters-on-us-campuses-trained-for-months-with-anti-israel-groups-including-sjp-report/.

44 "Rules for Campus Radicals, 2024," *Wall Street Journal*, editorial, May 2, 2024, https://www.wsj.com/opinion/campus-protests-crimethinc-reports-palestine-israel-f5a8054c.

45 Bret Stephens, "Should American Jews Abandon Elite Universities?," *New York Times*, June 25, 2024, https://www.nytimes.com/2024/06/25/opinion/jews-ivy-league-antisemitism.html.

46 Lauren Irwin, "Police clear GW protest, prompting House to cancel hearing on DC response," *The Hill*, May 8, 2024, https://thehill.com/homenews/education/4650874-police-clear-gw-protest-dc-mayor-house-testimony/.

47 Amir Vera, "US Department of Education opens investigation into USC after a student accused the school of allowing antisemitism on campus," *CNN*, July 27, 2022, https://www.cnn.com/2022/07/27/us/usc-antisemitism-complaint-us-education-department-reaj/index.html.

48 Bret Stephens, "Should American Jews Abandon Elite Universities?," *New York Times*, June 25, 2024, https://www.nytimes.com/2024/06/25/opinion/jews-ivy-league-antisemitism.html.

49 "Major Jewish Organizations Demand Removal of Northwestern University President and Board Chair Amid Racism Allegations," StandWithUs, May 30, 2024, https://www.standwithus.com/post/major-jewish-organizations-demand-removal-of-northwestern-university-president-and-board-chair-amid.

50 Bret Stephens, "Should American Jews Abandon Elite Universities?," *New York Times*, June 25, 2024, https://www.nytimes.com/2024/06/25/opinion/jews-ivy-league-antisemitism.html.

51 Nicole Narea, "What elite universities — and their critics — get wrong about campus antisemitism," *Vox*, December 15, 2023, https://www.vox.com/politics/2023/12/15/24001823/antisemitism-college-harvard-penn-mit-free-speech.

52 Taylor Romine, Kelly McCleary and Cheri Mossburg, "A Stanford University instructor has been removed from the classroom amid reports they called Jewish students colonizers and downplayed the Holocaust," *CNN*, October 13, 2023, https://www.cnn.com/2023/10/13/us/stanford-instructor-jewish-holocaust-comments-reaj/index.html.

53 Romine, McCleary and Mossburg, "A Stanford University instructor has been removed."

54 X message posted by Sarah Rebecca Kessler, https://www.instagram.com/amanda.markowitz/p/C6WvcPCJXtL/?img_index=1.

55 "USC professor cancels final, tells students to join Gaza Camp protest instead: 'F*ck it. Free Palestine,'" *Post Millennial*, April 28, 2024, https://thepostmillennial.com/usc-professor-cancels-final-tells-students-to-join-gaza-camp-protest-instead-f-ck-it-free-palestine.

56 Sharon Otterman, "3 Columbia University Deans Who Sent Insulting Texts Have Resigned," *New York Times*, August 8, 2024, https://www.nytimes.com/2024/08/08/nyregion/columbia-university-deans-resign-text-messages-antisemitism.html.

57 Susan Greenberg, "Columbia University Puts 3 Administrators on Leave," *Inside Higher Ed*, June 24, 2024, https://www.insidehighered.com/news/quick-takes/2024/06/24/columbia-university-puts-three-administrators-leave.

58 Juliet Chung and Berber Jin, "Harvard Is Trying to Smooth Things Over With Silicon Valley," *Wall Street Journal*, January 17, 2024, https://www.wsj.com/us-news/education/harvard-is-trying-to-smooth-things-over-with-silicon-valley-e4714765?mod=hp_lista_pos2.

59 Whizy Kim, "Who is Bill Ackman and why is he so mad?," *Vox*, January 13, 2024, https://www.vox.com/2024/1/13/24032176/bill-ackman-claudine-gay-harvard-plagiarism-business-insider-explained.

60 Clare Ansberry, Oyin Adedoyin, and Katherine Hamilton, "Colleges Have a New Source of Protest on Their Hands: Irate Parents," *Wall Street Journal*, May 3, 2024, https://www.wsj.com/us-news/education/college-protests-parents-angry-e93bb2ef.

61 Kathryn Palmer, "The Litigation After the Protest Storm," *Inside Higher Ed*, May 21, 2024, https://www.insidehighered.com/news/governance/executive-leadership/2024/05/21/litigation-after-protest-storm.

62 Palmer, "The Litigation After the Protest Storm."

63 Abby Jackson, "'Disinvitations' for college speakers are on the rise — here's a list of people turned away this year," *Business*

Insider, July 28, 2016, https://www.businessinsider.com/list-of-disinvited-speakers-at-colleges-2016-7.

64 Cleve Wootson, "She wanted to criticize Black Lives Matter in a college speech. A protest shut her down," *Washington Post*, April 10, 2017, https://www.washingtonpost.com/news/grade-point/wp/2017/04/10/she-wanted-to-criticize-black-lives-matter-in-a-college-speech-a-protest-shut-her-down/.

65 "Campus Deplatforming Database," Foundation for Individual Rights and Expression (FIRE), https://www.thefire.org/research-learn/campus-deplatforming-database.

66 Hank Reichman, "Free Speech is Fine, But the College President Knows Best," Academe Blog, the blog of Academe Magazine, February 19, 2016, https://academeblog.org/2016/02/19/free-speech-is-fine-but-the-college-president-knows-best/.

67 "John Derbyshire," Wikipedia, accessed July 8, 2025, https://en.wikipedia.org/wiki/John_Derbyshire.

68 Hank Reichman, "Free Speech is Fine, But the College President Knows Best," Academe Blog, the blog of Academe Magazine, February 19, 2016, https://academeblog.org/2016/02/19/free-speech-is-fine-but-the-college-president-knows-best/.

69 Dan Bauman, "Colleges Were Already Bracing for an 'Enrollment Cliff.' Now There Might Be a Second One," *Chronicle of Higher Education*, February 7, 2024, https://www.chronicle.com/article/colleges-were-already-bracing-for-an-enrollment-cliff-now-there-might-be-a-second-one.

70 Lydia Sidhom, "Why getting into a top U.S. college is about to get even more difficult," *San Francisco Chronicle*, July 15, 2024, https://www.sfchronicle.com/california/article/demographics-hardest-years-19563045.php.

71 "The investigation, led by the Education Department's Office for Civil Rights, follows a complaint that alleged Harvard failed to adequately respond to reports of antisemitic harassment on campus — one of a slew of complaints alleging skyrocketing antisemitism and Islamophobia on college campuses after Hamas' Oct. 7 attack on Israel." Miles J. Herszenhorn and Claire

Yuan, "U.S. Education Department Opens Investigation Into Harvard Following Antisemitism Complaint," *Harvard Crimson*, November 30, 2023, https://www.thecrimson.com/article/2023/11/30/ed-department-investigation-antisemitism/.

72 "H.R.6090 - 118th Congress (2023-2024): Antisemitism Awareness Act of 2023," Congress.gov, May 2, 2024, https://www.congress.gov/bill/118th-congress/house-bill/6090.

73 Neal McCluskey, "Feds Should Leave Campus Unrest to Others," *Cato at Liberty* (blog), Cato Institute, May 3, 2024, https://www.cato.org/blog/feds-should-leave-campus-unrest-others.

74 McCluskey, "Feds Should Leave Campus Unrest to Others."

75 Francis Bacon, *Of Seditions and Troubles*, in *Selected Writings of Francis Bacon* (New York: Modern Library, 1955), 44.

CHAPTER 33

1 Virgil, Aeneid, Book 11, lines 45–46, in *The Poems of Virgil*, trans. James Rhoades (London: Oxford University Press, 1921), 286, https://archive.org/details/poemsofvirgiloovirg/page/286/mode/2up.

2 Alia Wong, "Claudine Gay was just the start: US college presidents feel a chilling effect," *USA Today*, January 4, 2024, https://www.usatoday.com/story/news/education/2024/01/04/claudine-gay-college-presidents-chilling-effect/72101899007/.

3 Danielle Melidona, Benjamin Cecil, Alexander Cassell, and Hollie Chessman, "The American College President: 2023 Edition – Executive Summary" (Washington, DC: American Council on Education, 2023), https://www.acenet.edu/Documents/American-College-President-2023-Exec-Summary.pdf.

4 Melidona et al., "The American College President."

5 "In His Own Words: Quotes by Frank H.T. Rhodes," Cornell University, accessed July 2, 2025, https://www.cornell.edu/frank-rhodes/quotes/.

6 Danielle Douglas-Gabriel, "More college presidents face no-confidence votes over handling of protests," *Washington Post*,

May 10, 2024, updated May 11, 2024, https://www.washingtonpost.com/education/2024/05/10/faculty-no-confidence-leadership-college-protests/.

7 Mason McKie, "Victimhood culture has overtaken college campuses," *Washington Examiner*, May 10, 2018, https://www.washingtonexaminer.com/red-alert-politics/1400030/victimhood-culture-has-overtaken-college-campuses/.

8 Heather MacDonald and Frank Furedi, "The Campus Victim Cult," *City Journal*, March 11, 2018, https://www.city-journal.org/article/the-campus-victim-cult.

9 "Frank Furedi's book *What's Happened to the University?* is an astounding compendium of a cultural shift, with mind-boggling examples. However, I disagree, to a certain extent, with his diagnosis of the crisis on campuses. I think that it is fundamentally *an ideological problem, not a psychological one*." [Emphasis my own.] MacDonald and Furedi, "The Campus Victim Cult."

10 MacDonald and Furedi, "The Campus Victim Cult."

11 Douglas Belkin, "Columbia Looks to Give Campus Police Arresting Power After Protests," *Wall Street Journal*, August 5, 2024, https://www.wsj.com/us-news/education/columbia-looks-to-give-campus-police-arresting-power-after-protests-11d2b3bc.

12 Jessica McCann, "When should Harvard speak out?," *Harvard Gazette*, Harvard University, https://news.harvard.edu/gazette/story/2024/05/when-should-harvard-speak-out/.

13 McCann, "When should Harvard speak out?"

14 Char Adams and Nigel Chiwaya, "Map: See which states have introduced or passed anti-DEI bills," *NBC News*, March 2, 2024, https://www.nbcnews.com/data-graphics/anti-dei-bills-states-republican-lawmakers-map-rcna140756#.

15 Caroline Downey, "Harvard Faculty End Mandatory DEI Statements in Hiring," *National Review*, June 3, 2024, https://www.nationalreview.com/news/harvard-faculty-end-mandatory-dei-statements-in-hiring/.

16 Jeremy Peters, "Is This the End for Mandatory DEI Statements?," *New York Times*, June 6, 2024, https://www.nytimes.

com/2024/06/06/us/politics/dei-statements-harvard-massachusetts-institute-of-technology.html.

17 Ray Smith and Lynn Cook, "America's HR Lobby Scraps the 'E' From DEI," *Wall Street Journal*, July 12, 2025, https://www.wsj.com/business/the-nations-largest-human-resources-group-takes-the-e-out-of-dei-c84c62b6.

18 Nidhi Subbaraman, "Universities Close Offices, Halt Research in Response to Trump's Ban on DEI Moves intended to avert threats to vital federal funding," *Wall Street Journal*, January 31, 2025, https://www.wsj.com/us-news/education/trump-dei-ban-federal-funding-higher-education-8ae81c40.

19 Subbaraman, "Universities Close Offices, Halt Research in Response to Trump's Ban on DEI," *Wall Street Journal*, January 31, 2025. https://www.wsj.com/us-news/education/trump-dei-ban-federal-funding-higher-education-8ae81c40?gaa_at=eafs&gaa_n=AWEtsqdK-OG5G0Ns14MsLZk5ajEX0SXGIdQBcn5FYciddeOXM-Wc4H0-ClUxIny4HcUIw%3D&gaa_ts=6914e7fd&gaa_sig=A3Y-gCbKPm-_ggguk4-JdGjWtc-lJ1M_ilo_0FphxV5vXK8paAUxjIin-vfuGApvXTE8N3SN3iV5CtY4jCY1zstg%3D%3D.

20 Hellen Golden, "History of DEI: The Evolution of Diversity Training Programs," Notre Dame de Namur University, January 1, 2024, https://archive.vn/uAWrJ.

21 C. L. Max Nikias, "Annual Address to the USC Faculty," University of Southern California, February 13, 2013, https://clmaxnikias.usc.edu/2013/02/12/annual-address-to-the-usc-faculty-2013/.

22 Liam Knox, "Fresh Battle Lines in the Testing Wars," *Inside Higher Ed*, January 17, 2024, https://www.insidehighered.com/news/admissions/traditional-age/2024/01/17/reigniting-standardized-testing-debate.

23 Liam Knox, "Johns Hopkins Returns to Test Requirement," *Inside Higher Ed*, August 19, 2024, https://www.insidehighered.com/news/quick-takes/2024/08/19/johns-hopkins-reinstates-standardized-test-requirement.

24 University of Southern California, "Politico's John Harris interviews President Nikias," July 6, 2017, https://presidentemeritus.usc.edu/2017/06/06/alumni-reception-with-politico/.

25 USC Viterbi K-12 STEM Center, "About," accessed July 2, 2025, https://viterbik12.usc.edu/about/.

26 Frank Bruni, "Lifting Kids to College," *New York Times*, April 26,2017, https://www.nytimes.com/2017/04/26/opinion/usc-neighborhood-academic-initiative-lifting-kids-to-college.html.

27 Ron Mackovich-Rodriguez, "Foshay Learning Center provides more first-year USC students than any other high school," *USC News*, September 28, 2017, https://news.usc.edu/128499/foshay-learning-center-provides-more-first-year-usc-students-than-any-other-high-school/.

28 "Facts and Case Summary: Cox v. New Hampshire," United States Courts, accessed July 2, 2025, https://www.uscourts.gov/about-federal-courts/educational-resources/educational-activities/first-amendment-activities/cox-v-new-hampshire/facts-and-case-summary-cox-v-new-hampshire.

29 Ben Sasse, "The Adults are Still in Charge at the University of Florida," *Wall Street Journal*, May 3, 2024, https://www.wsj.com/articles/the-adults-are-still-in-charge-at-the-university-of-florida-israel-protests-tents-sasse-eca6389b.

30 Karen Sloan and Nate Raymond, "Stanford Law official who admonished judge during speech is on leave, dean says," *Reuters*, March 22, 2023, https://www.reuters.com/legal/legalindustry/stanford-law-official-who-admonished-judge-during-speech-is-leave-dean-says-2023-03-22/.

31 Jenny S. Martinez (Dean of Stanford Law School), letter to Stanford Law School community, March 22, 2023, https://law.stanford.edu/wp-content/uploads/2023/03/Next-Steps-on-Protests-and-Free-Speech.pdf.

32 Karen Sloan and Nate Raymond, "Stanford Law official who admonished judge during speech is on leave, dean says," *Reuters*, March 22, 2023, https://www.reuters.com/legal/legalindustry/

stanford-law-official-who-admonished-judge-during-speech-is-leave-dean-says-2023-03-22/.

33 Greta Reich, "DEI dean leaves Stanford Law School," *Stanford Daily*, August 23, 2023, https://stanforddaily.com/2023/08/23/dei-dean-leaves-stanford-law-school/.

34 Karen Sloan and Nate Raymond, "Stanford Law official who admonished judge during speech is on leave, dean says," *Reuters*, March 22, 2023, https://www.reuters.com/legal/legalindustry/stanford-law-official-who-admonished-judge-during-speech-is-leave-dean-says-2023-03-22/.

35 Kevin Francis O'Neill, "Time, Place and Manner Restrictions," Freedom of Speech Encyclopedia, Middle Tennessee State University, updated July 9, 2024, https://firstamendment.mtsu.edu/article/time-place-and-manner-restrictions/.

36 Douglas Belkin, "'It Will Scar This Generation.' Charlie Kirk's Death Ignites a Campus Reckoning," *Wall Street Journal*, September 14, 2025, https://www.wsj.com/us-news/education/charlie-kirk-shot-college-campuses-students-debate-a15ce232.

37 Michael B. Poliakoff and Steven McGuire, "AAUP Throws In With Campus Antisemites," *Wall Street Journal*, August 25, 2024, https://www.wsj.com/opinion/aaup-throws-in-with-campus-antisemites-academic-boycotts-israel-35f5b3b3.

38 Michael B. Poliakoff and Steven McGuire, "AAUP Throws In With Campus Antisemites," *Wall Street Journal*, August 25, 2024, https://www.wsj.com/opinion/aaup-throws-in-with-campus-antisemites-academic-boycotts-israel-35f5b3b3.

39 Ross Douthat, "Colleges Have Gone Off the Deep End. There Is a Way Out.," *New York Times*, April 28, 2024, https://www.nytimes.com/2024/04/28/opinion/protests-college-free-speech.html.

40 Ben Sasse, "The Adults Are Still in Charge at the University of Florida," *Wall Street Journal*, May 3, 2024, https://www.wsj.com/articles/the-adults-are-still-in-charge-at-the-university-of-florida-israel-protests-tents-sasse-eca6389b.

41 Taylor Romine, Kelly McCleary, and Cheri Mossburg, "A Stanford University Instructor Has Been Removed from the

Classroom Amid Reports They Called Jewish Students Colonizers and Downplayed the Holocaust," *CNN*, updated October 13, 2023, https://www.cnn.com/2023/10/13/us/stanford-instructor-jewish-holocaust-comments-reaj/index.html.

42 Carl Campanile, "Harvard Let Antisemitism Run Wild—as Jewish Students Face Slurs, Intimidation and Attacks, Suit Claims," *New York Post*, May 22, 2024, https://nypost.com/2024/05/22/us-news/harvard-condoned-antisemitism-against-jewish-students-lawsuit/.

43 Novi Zhukovsky, "New Blow To Columbia University as Congress Issues Searing Subpoena in Ongoing Antisemitism Investigation," *New York Sun*, August 21, 2024, https://www.nysun.com/article/new-blow-to-columbia-university-as-congress-issues-searing-subpoena-in-ongoing-antisemitism-investigation.

44 Jonathan Stempel, "Harvard University must face lawsuit over antisemitism on campus, judge rules," *Reuters*, August 7, 2024, https://www.reuters.com/legal/harvard-must-face-lawsuit-over-antisemitism-campus-us-judge-says-2024-08-06/.

45 Josh Christenson, "Fed Judge Smacks Down UCLA over Anti-Israel Encampment that Blocked Jewish Students from Campus," *New York Post*, August 14, 2024, https://nypost.com/2024/08/14/us-news/federal-judge-smacks-down-ucla-over-anti-israel-encampment-that-blocked-jewish-students-from-campus/.

46 U.S. Department of Justice, Office of Public Affairs, "Federal Task Force to Combat Antisemitism Announces Visits to 10 College Campuses that Experienced Incidents of Antisemitism" (press release), February 28, 2025, updated April 25, 2025, U.S. Department of Justice, https://www.justice.gov/opa/pr/federal-task-force-combat-antisemitism-announces-visits-10-college-campuses-experienced.

47 Natalie Schwartz, "Education Department Launches Probes into Over 50 Colleges after Anti-DEI Guidance," *Higher Ed Dive*, March 14, 2025, https://www.highereddive.com/news/

education-department-launches-probes-into-over-50-colleges-after-anti-dei-g/742619/.

48 Alvin Powell, "Trump administration freezes $2.2 billion in grants to Harvard," *Harvard T.H. Chan School of Public Health News*, April 15, 2025, updated April 22, 2025, https://hsph.harvard.edu/news/trump-administration-freezes-2-2-billion-in-grants-to-harvard/.

49 Melissa Quinn, "Trump says his administration is revoking Harvard's tax-exempt status," *CBS News*, May 2, 2025, https://www.cbsnews.com/news/trump-says-revoking-harvard-tax-exempt-status/.

50 "Is Trump Trying to Destroy Harvard?," *New York Times*, editorial, May 23, 2025, https://www.wsj.com/opinion/donald-trump-harvard-dhs-foreign-students-kristi-noem-b8ac80ed.

51 Michael S. Schmidt and Michael C. Bender, "Trump Administration Says It Is Halting Harvard's Ability to Enroll International Students," *New York Times*, May 22, 2025, https://www.nytimes.com/2025/05/22/us/politics/trump-harvard-international-students.html.

52 Matt Lavietes and Kimmy Yam, "Federal judge blocks the Trump administration from revoking Harvard's ability to enroll foreign students," *NBC News*, May 23, 2025, https://www.nbcnews.com/news/us-news/harvard-sues-trump-administration-move-block-foreign-student-enrollmen-rcna208723.

53 Alvin Powell, "Judge grants University's motion for temporary restraining order, blocking government's action," *Harvard Gazette*, May 23, 2025, https://news.harvard.edu/gazette/story/2025/05/university-sues-administration-over-move-to-bar-international-students-scholars/.

54 Alan Blinder and Stephanie Saul, "As Harvard Battles Trump, Its President Will Take a 25% Pay Cut," *New York Times*, May 14, 2025, https://www.nytimes.com/2025/05/14/us/harvard-garber-trump-pay.html.

55 Elise A. Spenner and Tanya J. Vidhun, "Harvard Pauses Merit-Based Wage Raises in Latest Austerity Measure," *Harvard Crimson*, April 29, 2025, https://www.thecrimson.com/article/2025/4/29/merit-raises-pause/.

56 Sara Randazzo, Douglas Belkin, and Emily Glazer, "Harvard Digs In for Battle, but Trump's Blows Are Landing," *Wall Street Journal*, May 24, 2025, https://www.wsj.com/us-news/education/harvard-trump-lawsuits-fight-d5f8ec8a.

57 Margaret Attridge and Elin Johnson, "These Colleges and Universities Are Cutting Costs Over Federal Funding Freezes," BestColleges, May 29, 2025, https://www.bestcolleges.com/news/colleges-university-cut-costs-federal-funding-freeze/.

58 David Clark and Lee Klump, "Legal Ruling on NIH Indirect Cost Reimbursement Policy," BDO, February 25, 2025, https://www.bdo.com/insights/industries/nonprofit-education/understanding-the-nih-s-new-indirect-cost-rate-policy-what-nonprofit-and-higher-education-cfos-need.

59 David Clark and Lee Klump, "Legal Ruling on NIH Indirect Cost Reimbursement Policy," BDO, February 25, 2025, https://www.bdo.com/insights/industries/nonprofit-education/understanding-the-nih-s-new-indirect-cost-rate-policy-what-nonprofit-and-higher-education-cfos-need.

60 Douglas Belkin, "Faculty-on-Faculty War Erupts at Columbia as Trump Targets Elite School," *Wall Street Journal*, March 11, 2025, https://www.wsj.com/us-news/education/columbia-university-trump-faculty-reaction-725a5e87.

61 Douglas Belkin, "Faculty-on-Faculty War Erupts at Columbia as Trump Targets Elite School," *Wall Street Journal*, March 11, 2025, https://www.wsj.com/us-news/education/columbia-university-trump-faculty-reaction-725a5e87.

62 Douglas Belkin, "Faculty-on-Faculty War Erupts at Columbia as Trump Targets Elite School," *Wall Street Journal*, March 11, 2025, https://www.wsj.com/us-news/education/columbia-university-trump-faculty-reaction-725a5e87.

63 Ben Southwood, "The rise and fall of the industrial R&D lab," *Works in Progress*, August 28, 2020, https://worksinprogress.co/issue/the-rise-and-fall-of-the-american-rd-lab/.

64 McKinsey and Company, "Reimagining labor to close the expanding US semiconductor talent gap," August 2, 2024, https://www.mckinsey.com/industries/semiconductors/our-insights/reimagining-labor-to-close-the-expanding-us-semiconductor-talent-gap.

EPILOGUE

1 Aristophanes, *Plutus*, trans. C. H. Richard (Cambridge: Pitt Press Series, 1912), 42.

2 Kary Grimes, "California Business Exodus For Friendlier States Continues," *California Global*, January 29, 2024, https://californiaglobe.com/fr/california-business-exodus-for-friendlier-states-continues/.

3 "The Blue-State Wealth Exodus Continues," *Wall Street Journal*, editorial, July 3, 2024, https://www.wsj.com/opinion/blue-state-exodus-irs-data-income-7c878e40.

4 Daniel Shoag, Issi Romem, anf David Garcia, "The First Step is the Hardest: California's Sliding Home Ownership Ladder," Terner Center for Housing Innovation, May 2023, https://ternercenter.berkeley.edu/wp-content/uploads/2023/05/Homeownership-Ladder-May-2023-Final.pdf.

5 Victor Davis Hanson, "America's First Third-World State," *National Review*, June 18, 2019, https://www.nationalreview.com/2019/06/california-third-world-state-corruption-crime-infrastructure/.

6 Joel Kotkin, "Climate Change Driving California's Golden Road to Decline," *American Greatness*, April 5, 2025, https://amgreatness.com/2025/04/05/climate-change-driving-californias-golden-road-to-decline/.

7 Imam Palm, "California wipes water debt for 4M residents," *KTLA5*, June 14, 2024, https://ktla.com/news/california/california-water-bill-relief/.

8 Sarah Bohn, Caroline Danielson, Sara Kimberlin, Patricia Malagon, and Christopher Wimer, "Poverty in California" (Fact Sheet), Public Policy Institute of California, October 2023, https://www.ppic.org/publication/poverty-in-california/.

9 "More than one of every three people in the United States experiencing homelessness as an individual was found in California (34%)." California Senate Housing Committee, "Fact Sheet: Homelessness in California," updated January 2024, https://shou.senate.ca.gov/sites/shou.senate.ca.gov/files/Homelessness%20in%20CA%202023%20Numbers%20-%201.2024.pdf.

10 Victor Davis Hanson, "America's First Third-World State," *National Review*, June 18, 2019, https://www.nationalreview.com/2019/06/california-third-world-state-corruption-crime-infrastructure/.

11 Stephen Moses, "Medi-Cal-amity: California's Reckless Expansion of Medicaid Long-Term Care to the Affluent," Paragon Health Institute, April 9, 2025, https://paragoninstitute.org/medicaid/medi-cal-amity-californias-reckless-expansion-of-medicaid-long-term-care-to-the-affluent/.

12 California Health Care Foundation, "Medi-Cal and the Federal Government — Policy at a Glance," January 22, 2025, https://www.chcf.org/resource/medi-cal-federal-government/#related-links-and-downloads.

13 Marissa Wenzke, "High-rise tower in downtown LA will house people experiencing homelessness," *CBS News*, June 19, 2024, https://www.cbsnews.com/losangeles/news/high-rise-tower-in-downtown-la-will-house-people-experiencing-homelessness/.

14 Sam Mauhay-Moore, "Walgreens to close another store in downtown San Francisco," *SFGate*, January 24, 2025, https://www.sfgate.com/local/article/downtown-sf-walgreens-closure-18625748.php.

15 Aaron Tolentino, "San Francisco Centre: Stores closing to begin 2024," *KRON4*, January 19, 2024, https://www.kron4.com/news/bay-area/san-francisco-centre-stores-closing-to-begin-2024/.

16 Roger Vincent, "Estimated cost of fire damage balloons to more than $250 billion," *Los Angeles Times*, January 24, 2025, https://www.latimes.com/business/story/2025-01-24/estimated-cost-of-fire-damage-balloons-to-more-than-250-billion.

17 Tim Stelloh, Marlene Lenthang, Rebecca Cohen and Phil Helsel, "California wildfires: What we know about L.A.-area fires, what caused them, who is affected and more," *NBC News*, January 17, 2025, https://www.nbcnews.com/news/us-news/california-wildfires-what-we-know-palisades-eaton-los-angeles-rcna188239.

18 Roger Vincent, "Estimated cost of fire damage balloons to more than $250 billion," *Los Angeles Times*, January 24, 2025, https://www.latimes.com/business/story/2025-01-24/estimated-cost-of-fire-damage-balloons-to-more-than-250-billion.

19 "By comparison, AccuWeather estimated the damage and economic losses caused by Hurricane Helene, which tore across six southeastern states last fall, at $225 billion to $250 billion." See "L.A. wildfires the costliest in American history? Here's what experts are saying," *Inc.*, January 11, 2025, https://www.inc.com/associated-press/l-a-wildfires-may-be-the-costliest-in-u-s-history-estimates-say/91106278.

20 Jim Geraghty, "A Timeline of Mayor Karen Bass's Disqualifying Conduct during the L.A. Fire Disaster," *National Review*, January 9, 2025, https://www.nationalreview.com/the-morning-jolt/a-timeline-of-mayor-karen-basss-disqualifying-conduct-during-the-l-a-fire-disaster/.

21 Soumya Karlamangla, Orlando Mayorquín and Tim Arango, "Mayor's Absence Is Considered a Sign L.A. Underestimated Fire Risks," *New York Times*, January 9, 2025, https://www.nytimes.com/2025/01/09/us/los-angeles-mayor-fire-response.html.

22 Jenny Jarvie, Grace Toohey and Terry Castleman, "Faulty evacuation alerts woke Angelenos in a panic. What's wrong with L.A.'s emergency system?," *Los Angeles Times*, January 9, 2025, https://www.latimes.com/california/story/2025-01-09/emergency-alert-text-message-los-angeles-fire.

23 Heal the Bay, "Exploring LA's Water Legacy in the Owens Valley," July 5, 2024, https://healthebay.org/exploring-las-water-legacy-in-the-owens-valley/.

24 Water Education Foundation, "Los Angeles Aqueduct and Owens Valley," accessed on June 27, 2025, https://www.watereducation.org/aquapedia/los-angeles-aqueduct-and-owens-valley.

25 Pacific Palisades Fire: Correcting Misinformation About LADWP's Water System – https://www.ladwpnews.com/pacific-palisades-fire-correcting-misinformation-about-ladwps-water-system/

26 "Outside investigations to examine LADWP's empty reservoir during Palisades Fire," *NBC4 Los Angeles*, January 28, 2025, https://www.nbclosangeles.com/investigations/outside-investigations-to-examine-ladwps-empty-reservoir-during-palisades-fire/3617569/.

27 Ian James and Jessica Garrison, "Acting on Trump's order, federal officials opened up two California dams," *Los Angeles Times*, January 31, 2025, https://www.latimes.com/environment/story/2025-01-31/trump-california-dams-opened-up.

28 White House, "Putting People over Fish: Stopping Radical Environmentalism to Provide Water to Southern California," January 20, 2025, https://www.whitehouse.gov/presidential-actions/2025/01/putting-people-over-fish-stopping-radical-environmentalism-to-provide-water-to-southern-california/.

29 Don Lee and Andrew Khouri, "L.A. fires hit family wealth. Daunting challenges await those trying to recover it," *Los Angeles Times*, February 3, 2025, https://www.latimes.com/business/story/2025-02-03/la-fires-altadena-homeowners-generational-wealth-insurance-rebuilding-costs.

30 Governor of California, "California's Strong Economic Week," https://www.gov.ca.gov/2024/04/19/californias-strong-economic-week/.

31 Abigail Tierney, "States with the largest population of billionaires in the United States in 2024," *Statistica*, June 27, 2025, https://www.statista.com/statistics/1125668/leading-states-billionaires-us/.

32 Tim Jones, "California has most Fortune 500 companies than any other state in US," *ABC7 News*, June 5, 2024, https://abc7news.com/post/california-fortune-500-companies-state-us-texas-new/14912475/.

33 Kevin Starr, *California: A History* (New York: Random House Publishing Group, 2007), 343.

34 Dante, *Inferno* VIII.104–105, trans. John A. Carlyle (London: 1867), https://books.google.com/books?id=3RS3JIs-lpH4C&printsec=frontcover&source=gbs_atb#v=onepage&q=our%20fate&f=false.

35 Ralph Waldo Emerson, "American Civilization," https://emersoncentral.com/texts/miscellanies/american-civilization/.

36 Annika Neklason, "Ralph Waldo Emerson's American Idea," *Atlantic*, November 28, 2019, https://www.theatlantic.com/ideas/archive/2019/11/the-atlantic-and-ralph-waldo-emersons-american-idea/602689/.

37 "It wasn't just Reagan who picked it up, either. After Miller, Winthrop's text has been quoted by almost every president to hold office: John F. Kennedy, Lyndon Johnson, Richard Nixon, Jimmy Carter, Ronald Reagan, George H. W. Bush, Bill Clinton, and Barack Obama." Abram Van Engen, "How America 'Became A City Upon a Hill,'" *Humanities* 40, no. 1 (Winter 2020): https://www.neh.gov/article/how-america-became-city-upon-hill.

38 Van Engen, "How America 'Became A City Upon a Hill.'"

39 "Arbella," *Wikipedia*, accessed June 27, 2025, https://en.wikipedia.org/wiki/Arbella.

Index

Abbott, Greg, 412
Abe, Akie, 409
Abe, Shinzo, 409
Aegina, island of, 60, 63
aerospace industry, 91, 123, 124, 126, 130, 358
Aeschylus, 335, 340, 429
Agnew, Spiro, 125
Agus, David, 270
Aisen, Paul, 271
Al Saud, Fahd bin Abdulaziz, 229
Allende, Isabel, 200
Altieri, Karen, 104, 106
Alvarez Marsal (A&M), 228
American Revolution, 118
Andrews, Mike, 144
Annenberg, Wallis, 305, 338
Antifonitis, Cyprus, 328
antisemitism, 3, 434, 436–37, 438–39, 440, 442, 449, 458, 460
Aristotle, 57
arithmetic, 13, 15, 16
Arizona State University, 386, 387, 389, 450
Arlington, TX, 393
Armstrong, Lloyd, 163, 183, 184, 187, 189
army training, 45–55
Association of American Universities (AAU), 188, 264
Assyrians, 8
Athens, Greece, 46, 48, 54–55, 57–58, 60–61, 64, 67, 69, 70, 71, 75, 77, 78, 100, 148
  Acropolis, 39, 59, 318
Leoforos Alexandras, 58, 62
  Metsovion Polytechnic, 40–41, 47, 54, 58, 59, 62, 68
  National Archaeological Museum, 59
  Plaka, 39
  University of Economics and Business, 58
athletics, 2, 194, 342, 349, 364, 371–83, 389, 392–93, 394–95, 397–400, 401
Austin, TX, 355
  University of Texas at, 438
avatars, digital, 140, 142
Ayia Marina, Greece, *see* Aegina, island of

Baizar, Tristan, 331
Ballmer, Connie, 385
Ballmer, Steve, 385
Bandler, Donald, 148–58
Bangalore, India, 403
Bardot, Brigitte, 30
Barkley, Matt, 263
Barnes, Bryan, 292
Basketball, 372, 375, 395, 396, 397, 398, 399
Bass, Karen, 464
Beatty, Warren, 268
Belgium, 115
Benning, Annette, 268
Bennis, Warren, 189–90, 356, 376
Bergen, Peter, 289
Berger, Mr (lawyer), 95–97
Berlin, Germany, 101
Bethesda, MD, 107
Bin Laden, Osama, 155
biological engineering, 145
biomedical signal analysis, 91
biotechnology, 145, 236
bispectrum, 102–104
Black Lives Matter protests, 448
blind equalization problem, 116
Bohn, Mike, 400
Bok, Derek, 285
Bolden, Javier, 292
Boston, MA, 100, 112–13, 115, 117, 118, 121–22, 186, 292, 458
Boston College, 215
Boston University, 226
Boy Scouts, 25–26
Bratton, Bill, 297
Brazil, 401
Breslauer, Jerry, 210
Broad, Eli, 211, 365
Brown, Jerry, 404–405
Brown, Pat, 405
Brown University, 282, 447
Bruni, Frank, 452
Brunold, Tim, 286
Buddy (dog), 331–33
Buffalo, NY, 79–80, 81, 82, 83, 85, 92, 95–96, 97–98, 100–101, 106, 325
General Hospital (BGH), 80, 84–85, 87, 89, 90
University of New York at, *see* SUNY Buffalo
Burton, Richard, 30
Bush, George H. W., 143
Bush, George W. 410–11, 434
Bush, Laura, 410, 434
Bush, Reggie, 217, 379–80, 382–83
Byzantines, 8

Cal Club, 214, 245, 263–64, 377
Calais, France, 78
Caltrans (California Department of Transportation), 167
Cameron, David, 434
cancer research, 221, 270
Caprio, Jim, 90, 91
carpentry, 10, 20, 25

Carroll, Pete, 171, 214–17, 257, 371, 373–74, 381, 394
Caruso, Rick, 333, 426–27
Catalina Island, 122
Chan, Ron, 401
Charlottesville, VA, 378
Checcio, Al, 345–46, 351
chemical engineering, 41–42, 166, 168, 174, 175, 178
Chiang, Mung, 445
Chicago, IL, 283, 366
  University of, 453
China Lake, CA, 104–105, 106, 108
Chobanian, Aram, 226
Christofias, Demetris, 257
citizenship, US, 116–18
Civil War, American, 117, 118, 467
Clark, Alson, 328
Clerides, Glafcos, 153–56, 158
Clinton, Bill, 143, 411–13, 434
Cold War, 91, 114, 124, 126
Columbia University, 132, 310, 311, 437, 439, 447, 458, 459, 461
communism, 118
Congress, US, 257, 367, 406, 437, 442, 443, 446, 458
Connecticut, University of (UConn), 97, 100–101, 104, 111, 112, 113
Cornell University, 307, 437, 444
Corrigan, Gene, 378
coup, Greek (1967), 30, 60, 64
Covid-19 pandemic, 203, 435
Crandall, Ed, 245
Crete, island of, 48–49, 53, 82
Crusaders, 8
Cunningham, William T., 143
Currie, Mal, 135–36
Cypriots, Greek, 9, 27, 48, 54, 55, 60, 67, 68, 75, 83, 149, 150, 151, 152, 153, 155, 156, 158
Cypriots, Turkish, 9, 13, 27, 28, 149, 150, 151, 152, 153, 154, 155, 156
Cyprus
  1974 coup, 61, 63–64
civil war, Cypriot, 55
early life in, 7–21, 23–33, 35–43, 45–55
'Golden Years', 30
  'green line', 149
  independence, 21
  religious division, 152
  Turkish invasion (1974), 55, 63–65, 66, 69, 81, 149
Cyprus, Church of, 9–10, 70
Cyprus, University of, 148
Cyprus National Guard, 47–48, 64

Dalai Lama, 407–408
Daley, Elizabeth, 133–34, 196–97, 198
Dallas, TX, 243, 355, 410
Daniels, Mitch, 445–46
Dante Alighieri, 467

DARPA (United States' Defense Advanced Research Projects Agency), 127
Day, Robert, 222, 266
DEI (diversity, equity, and inclusion), 450–51
Del Rio, Jack, 388
Delphi, Greece, 39
democracy, 39, 61, 63, 64, 65, 93, 118, 201, 232, 430, 454, 467
Democratic Party, 366–67
Denktas, Rauf, 151, 153, 155–56
Denver, CO, 177
Detroit, MI, 143
Deukmejian, George, 406
Diamesis, professor, 75
digital signal processing, 90–91, 97, 99, 101, 103–104, 105, 107, 111
Disney, 252, 393
diversity, 196, 318–20, 365, 431, 450, 454
Dornsife, Dana, 263, 338, 356
Dornsife, David, 263, 338, 344, 356
Dougherty, Dennis, 187–88, 195
Dover, England, 78
Drayton, Carey, 295
Dukakis, Michael, 149
Duke University, 251
Dworak-Peck, Suzanne, 360

Eastwood, Clint, 259
Eisenhower, Dwight D., 289
electrical engineering, 41–42, 59, 78, 79, 91, 94, 100, 111, 121–22, 169
Ellison, Larry, 270–71
Elytis, Odysseas, 38
Emerson, Ralph Waldo, 467
Engh, Michael, 305
enosis, 9, 27
EOKA (Ethniki Organosis Kyprion Agoniston), 10, 11, 12
Epidaurus, Greece, 39
Epstein, Dan, 176, 271–72
Epstein, Phyllis, 271

Famagusta, Cyprus, 10, 11, 14, 20, 23, 25, 26, 27, 28, 30–31, 33, 35, 36, 41, 43, 46, 53, 54, 57, 63, 64, 66, 67–68, 70, 156–57
FBI, 93, 277, 373
Ferrell, Will, 413–15
Ferry, Korn, 229, 240, 241
Fertitta, Frank, 304–305
Fertitta, Jill, 304
Fetter, Trevor, 243–44
Florida, University of, 450, 455
football, 81, 170–71, 177, 187, 198, 215, 217, 225, 229, 263, 303, 322, 323, 339, 358, 372, 374–75, 376, 377, 379–80, 382–83, 385, 389, 391–92, 393, 394, 395, 396, 397–98, 399

freedom of expression, 81, 93, 203, 408, 430, 433, 440, 454

Garrett, Mike, 215–16, 373–76
Gates, Robert, 434
gender diversity, 174–75
Germany, 65, 115
Gill, Indy, 268–69, 274
Glier, John, 343, 345
Gold, Stanley, 208, 212, 222, 228, 235, 243–44, 255, 346, 380, 424
Goldsmith, Rae, 341
Golomb, Sol, 184
Good Neighbors Campaign, 330–31
Great Recession (2008), 202, 213
Greek Independence Day, 47
Greenberg, Doug, 208
Grey, Brad, 270
Grossman, Marshall, 228
Gulf War, 368
gymnasiums (schools), 9, 32

Habeshi, Loizos, 13, 17–18
Habinek, Tom, 285
Haden, Pat, 377–82, 386–93
Hall, Randy, 167
Hamilton, Alexander, 245–46
Hamilton, Ontario, 94
Hanson, Victor Davis, 289, 434, 464
haptics, 140–41
Harrington, Katharine, 166, 196, 285, 293
Hartford, Connecticut, 95, 96, 97
Harvard University, 183, 275, 285, 307, 337, 341, 344, 362, 437, 449, 450, 458–59
Helton, Clay, 389, 390, 392, 393
Hemingway, Ernest, 437
Henderson, Brian, 219
Heraclitus, 146
Heraklion, Greece, 48–49, 52
Hermosa Beach, CA, 214–15
Higher-Order Spectral Analysis, 103–104, 111, 116, 119
Hollander, Dan, 211
Holman, Tom, 139
Hong Kong, 401
Horowitz, David, 434
Houston, TX, 355
Hsieh, Eva, 338
Hsieh, Ming, 338
Hubbard, Jack, 263, 349
Hughes, B. Wayne, 287, 392
Hwang, David Henry, 200

IBM, 137–38
IEEE (Institute of Electrical and Electronics Engineers), 103, 107, 116, 119
Iger, Bob, 252–53, 393
India, 170, 327, 356, 401–404
Indianapolis, IN, 379–82
Indonesia, 401

INS (Immigration and Naturalization Service), 117
Ioannides, Dimitris, 61
Iraq War, 289
Israel, state of, 46, 184, 270, 401, 430–31, 434, 435, 438, 439, 455

Jackiewicz, Tom, 267–69
Jackson, Mark, 267, 268, 279
Jaeger, Werner, 405
Jefferson, Thomas, 245
Johnson, Lyndon B., 67, 71
Johnson, Reginald, 333
Johnson, Suzanne Nora, 347

Kaprielian, Zohrab, 127–28, 357
Karaolos, Cyprus, 46, 47
Karavi family, 64–65
Karnad, Girish, 290
Karpas Peninsula, Cyprus, 8, 156
Kavafi, Constantine P., 38
Keck, Bill, 222, 266
Keck, Nicole, 222
Keck Foundation, 220–22, 266, 338
Kennedy, Anthony, 465
Kennedy, John F., 27, 117
Kennedy, Robert, 273
Kiffin, Lane, 216, 373–74, 383, 387
Kimball, Roger, 432–33
Kimmel, Jimmy, 414
King, Rodney, 124
Kirk, Charlie, 455
Kissinger, Henry, 67, 71
Klein, Herb, 125
Knight, Phil, 385
Kolmogorov, Andrey, 103
Komi Kebir, Cyprus, 8, 11, 23, 29, 154
Korea, 149, 327, 360
Korn, Melissa, 282
Kraft, Robert, 186
Kreditor, Alan, 180–81, 182, 185, 340, 350

Lainiotis, Dimitri, 91–92
Larnaca, Cyprus, 70
Las Vegas, NV, 298
Latin, 76, 290, 452
Lee, Spike, 200
Leventhal, Ken, 180, 184–85, 194, 205, 212, 223, 227, 235, 349–50
Liaison Committee on Medical Education (LCME), 229
Limassol, Cyprus, 154
Lipertis, Dimitris, 38
London, UK, 78–80, 81, 89, 100, 106, 292
  Imperial College, 79
  Queen Mary University of London, 78–79
Lord, Thomas, 357
Loren, Sophia, 30
Los Angeles, CA, 126, 131, 133, 183, 186, 212, 228, 232, 236,

292, 295, 306, 311–12, 314, 333, 346, 365, 366, 391, 397, 408, 417, 452, 464
Beverly Hills, 209
Children's Hospital, 359
City Council, 310–12
Foshay Learning Center, 453
Good Samaritan Hospital, 273, 364
Hollywood, 19, 126, 141, 144, 198, 199
LAPD, 277, 292, 294–96, 297–98, 300, 332, 421, 448, 449
LAX, 127
Los Angeles airport (Westchester), 106
Palisades fire, 464–65
Lucas, George, 139–40, 197–98, 199

MacArthur, Douglas, 216
MacDonald, Heather, 434, 447
MacLaine, Shirley, 268
Madison, James, 245
Makarios, Archbishop, 21, 61, 63–64, 77
Malibu, CA, 270
'Manhattan Project', 251
Mann, Alfred, 358–59
Mann, Claude, 358, 359
Marathon, Greece, 39
Marina Del Rey, CA, 182
Maryland, University of, 94, 398
Maryland Institute for Emergency Medical Services Systems (MIEMSS), 94
Massachusetts, 246, 467
mathematics, 16, 17, 31, 33, 36, 37, 38, 41, 42, 59, 75–76, 116, 175, 452
Mature, Victor, 19
Mayo, O. J., 375
Mazzocco, Lisa, 348
McConnell, Mitch, 407
McFadden, Dean, 112–13
McKay, J. K., 377, 388, 389–90, 392, 393
McMunn, Brent, 324
Mead, Jose Antonio, 282
meritocracy, 451
Miami, FL, 142
Michigan, State University of, 450
Michigan, University of, 361
microelectronics revolution, 99
Ming Qu, 291, 293
MIT (Massachusetts Institute of Technology), 40, 104, 437, 450, 451, 459
Molina, Gloria, 236–38
Monroe, Vicki, 106–107
Mork, John, 177–78, 338–39, 391
Mork, Julie, 177–78, 338–39, 391
movies, 18–19, 37, 38, 52, 81, 139–40, 270, 318, 366

Mudd, Seeley, 328, 329
Mulholland, William, 465
Multimedia University Academy, 143–44
Mumbai, India, 403
Munger, Charlie, 273, 361, 364
Mycenae, Greece, 39

nanotechnology, 168, 174
napalm, 27
National Bank of Greece, 68, 75
National Technological University (NTU) satellite system, 173
NATO, 81
Navy, US, 97, 104, 105, 107, 149
  Office of Naval Research (ONR), 113, 114
NCAA, 217, 371–83, 385, 395, 398
Nebraska-Lincoln, University of, 438
neutrality, 236, 443, 450, 454, 456–57, 458
New Delhi, India, 403
New Jersey, 18, 397
New London, CT, 101, 105, 107
New York City, NY, 39–40, 82, 92, 282, 310, 311, 348, 397
Newman, Paul, 31
Newport, RI, 107
Newsom, Gavin, 463
Nicosia, Cyprus, 14, 18, 27, 41, 43, 54, 64, 151
  US Embassy in, 149
Nikias, Chrysostomos, 12, 13–15, 24, 158 (grandfather of Max Nikias)
Nikias, Loizos (father of Max Nikias), 7, 10–11, 12, 13, 16, 20, 21, 23, 25, 27, 28, 29, 32, 40, 54, 66, 69, 70, 71, 80, 100, 133, 147
Nikias, Georgiana (daughter of Max Nikias), 107, 111, 113, 191, 326
Nikias, Georgoula (mother of Max Nikias), 12, 13, 14, 15, 20, 24, 26, 27–28, 31, 33, 147
Nikias, Maria (daughter of Max Nikias), 40, 117, 326
Nikias, Maroula (sister of Max Nikias), 12, 17, 20, 23, 147, 158
Nikias, Max
  assistant professor at Northeastern, 111–19
  Dean of USC School of Engineering, 163–91
  Director of IMSC, 135–46
  early life in Cyprus, 7–21, 23–33
  education, 35–43
  emigration to America, 75–88
  life in Athens, 57–71
  military service, 45–55
  professor at USC, 121–34

President of USC, 249–79, 281–315, 317–33, 335–51, 353–68, 371–83, 385–415
Provost of USC, 193–205, 207–47
researcher at SUNY Buffalo, 89–98
researcher at UConn, 99–108
resignation as President of USC, 417–28
visits to Cyprus, 147–59
Nikias, Niki (wife of Max Nikias), 37–38, 41, 42, 46, 51, 54, 55, 57, 58, 60, 62, 63–64, 65–66, 67, 68, 69, 70–71, 75, 81–82, 83, 86, 87–88, 89, 93, 98, 99, 100–101, 108, 111, 112, 116, 119, 122, 124, 157, 171, 182, 187, 198, 212, 254–55, 268, 290, 293, 298, 318, 324, 328, 332–33, 355, 358, 382, 385, 389, 391, 409, 410, 463, 466
emigration to America, 85
First Lady of USC, 256–57, 323, 325–26, 327, 329–30, 367
marriage to Max Nikias, 77–78
US citizenship, 117–18
visits to Cyprus, 113–14, 147–50, 158
Nixon, Richard, 67, 125
Northeastern University, 111, 112–13, 114, 115, 116, 186, 194
Northern Cyprus, Turkish Republic of, *see* Cypriots, Turkish
Northwestern University, 307
Notre Dame, IN, 170, 288, 377, 378, 380, 388, 389, 391, 393
NSF (National Science Foundation), 127, 130, 132, 133, 139, 140, 143–44
NYU, 307

Obama, Barack, 407, 408, 409–10, 434
Obama, Sasha, 410
Olympia, Greece, 39
Oppenheim, Alan, 103–104
Oregon, University of, 385–86, 389
Orgeron, Ed, 386, 387–88, 389
Ottoman Empire, 8, 47
Oxford University, 290

Panama City, FL, 107
Papandreou, Andreas, 118
Parks, Bernard, 312
Pasadena, CA, 197, 232, 247, 276, 292, 327, 339
Patton, George S., 216
Payden, Joan, 347–48
Pennsylvania, University of, 183, 225, 227, 269, 275, 307, 437, 459
Pennsylvania, State University of, 393
Pericles, 157–58

Perry, Jan, 312
Persians, 8
Petersen, Chris, 388, 390
Petraeus, David H., 289
philanthropy, 9, 224, 272, 296, 324, 335, 336–37, 338, 339, 343, 356, 359, 363, 395, 461
philately, 78
Phoenicians, 8
Pine, Janet, 275
Piraeus, Greece, 39
Plato, 146
Polydoros, Andreas, 79, 82, 262
power spectrum, 102
Price, Robert, 359
Price, Sol, 359
pro-Palestinian protests, 435–39, 440, 461
Psiloritis, Mount, Greece, 48, 52
Puliafito, Carmen, 241, 242–43, 275–79
Purdue University, 445
Putin, Vladimir, 411

quantum computing, 174

radar, 76, 90, 91, 99, 101, 105, 106, 107, 108, 113
Ramer, Bruce, 208, 209, 210, 258, 259, 407
Rancho Palos Verdes, CA, 232
Reagan, Ronald, 83, 91, 99, 101, 230, 467
Reed, Lorna, 256, 329
Reid, Harry, 406–407
Rhodes, Frank H. T., 444
Rhodes, island of, 39
Richard I, king of England, 8
ridesharing services, 297
Riley, Lincoln, 396, 400
Ritsos, Yannis, 66
Roberts, Dave, 372, 379, 380, 381, 386
Romans, 8
Roski, Ed, 214, 216, 254, 255, 256, 272, 287, 288, 338, 342
Roski, Gayle, 272
ROTC, 288

Sacramento, CA, 405, 406
Salamis, Cyprus, 8, 19, 328
Salonika, Greece, 39
Sample, Kathryn, 250, 327
Sample, Steven B., 98, 122, 133–34, 146, 163, 168, 171, 178, 183–84, 185, 186, 187, 188, 189–90, 193, 195–96, 197, 198–99, 200, 202, 204, 208, 211–13, 214, 215, 218, 222, 225, 230, 235–36, 239, 250, 252, 258, 327, 329, 342, 349, 350, 358, 359, 371, 374, 375–76, 380, 426, 445
San Diego, CA, 125, 176
San Francisco, CA, 348, 375, 464
San Marino, CA, 88, 325, 328–29, 333
Sanders, Deion, 397

Sarkisian, Steve, 216, 374, 387, 388–91
Saudi Arabia, 366
Savvopoulos, Dionysis, 61
Sawchuk, Sandy, 138
Schoen, Bill, 226
Schwarzenegger, Arnold, 304, 360, 406
Schwarzkopf, Norman, 368
Scott, Larry, 397
Scott, Peter, 79, 84–85, 91, 94, 262
Seferis, Giorgios, 38
Seoul, South Korea, 401
September 11 attacks, 157, 169
Shanghai, China, 202, 401
Shoah Foundation, 207–10, 222, 409
Shumway, Norman, 232
Siegel, John, 80, 85–87, 91, 94, 104, 113, 262
Silberstein, Lloyd, 302, 308, 314, 321
Silicon Valley, 129, 131–32, 179
Silverman, Dean, 145
Singapore, 402
Singer, Rick, 363, 394
Singh, Manmohan, 402–403
Skywalker Ranch, CA, 139–40, 198
Slatoff, Christopher, 318–21
Smith, Steve, 108
Smulyan, Jeff, 380
soccer, 13, 16, 24, 60
Solomos, Dionysios, 61
sonar, 76, 90–91, 97, 99, 101, 107, 114
Sophocles, 19, 200
South Bend, IN, 391
Spielberg, Steven, 198, 199, 207–208, 210, 259, 366, 409
Stallone, Sylvester, 81
Stanford University, 131, 165, 251–52, 232, 283, 286, 307, 337, 341, 344, 362, 364, 390, 393, 435, 439, 454
Starnes, Julie, 234
Starnes, Vaughn, 230–31, 233–34, 236, 245, 247
Starr, Kevin, 189, 288, 376, 466
STEM disciplines, 452, 460–62
Stevens, Mark, 131–32, 179–81, 269, 347
Stevens, Mary, 132, 269
Storrs, CT, 100, 101, 111
Strategic Defense Initiative (SDI), 99, 431
Student Coalition Against Labor Exploitation (SCALE), 431–32
submarines, 97, 101, 103, 107, 114–15
Sugar, Ron, 287
Sumlin, Kevin, 388
Sun Valley, ID, 268, 349, 360
SUNY Buffalo, 79, 91, 98, 100, 250, 262, 270
supermarkets, 83, 100
Swann, Lynn, 392–93, 394

Taiwan, 401
taksim, 27
Tata, Ratan, 401–402, 404
Taylor, Elizabeth, 30
Tenet Healthcare, 220–21, 223, 224, 226, 227–28, 235, 239–40, 243, 342
terrorism, 155, 408
Teucer, 8
Thanksgiving, 87–88, 122, 325–27, 367
theater, 19
Theodorakis, Mikis, 61
Thermopylae, Greece, 39
Thessaloniki, Greece, 48
Thomas, John, 295–96, 297, 298, 299, 300
Thomas, Tilson, 142
Thompson, Paul, 269
Thucydides, 157
Toga, Arthur, 269
Tokyo, Japan, 401, 409
Topping, Norman, 349
Torrance, CA, 254, 372
Troodos Mountains, Cyprus, 70
Truman, Harry, 424
Trump, Donald, 367, 450, 458–59, 465
TRW (aerospace company), 130
Tulane University, 203
Turkey, 27, 30, 55, 64, 65, 66, 81, 148, 155
Tutor, Ron, 167–68, 205, 287, 310
Twin Falls, ID, 311
Tyndall, George, 417–23, 425–27

UC Berkeley, 131, 144, 198, 263, 282, 300, 307, 438
UCLA, 127, 144, 229, 230–31, 233, 234, 247, 252, 269, 279, 282, 292, 296, 300, 307, 322, 323, 339, 343, 358, 364, 388, 393, 396, 407, 438, 458, 459
UCSD (University of California San Diego), 267, 271
Uncapher, Keith, 127–28, 174
USC (University of Southern California)
Annenberg School for Communication and Journalism, 196, 305
architecture, 301–15
Board of Trustees, 128, 135–36, 180, 199, 202, 207, 211–12, 214, 223, 226, 235, 237, 239, 245, 246, 251, 255, 256, 258, 278, 287, 303, 308, 309, 338, 345, 347, 349, 353, 358, 362, 377, 379, 391, 405, 408, 420, 422, 423, 425, 426–27, 431, 445, 456
branding, 266, 301, 302
Cardiovascular and Thoracic Institute (CVTI), 234

College of Letters, Arts and Sciences, 175, 191, 194, 263, 338, 356
Distance Education Network (DEN), 173
endowments, 198, 202, 224, 310, 335, 336, 341–42, 347, 348, 358–59, 360, 365
fraternities, 204
Hecuba statue, 317–19, 321–23
Industrial and Systems Engineering (ISE), 176
Institute for Creative Technologies (ICT), 144–45
Integrated Media Systems Center (IMSC), 116, 130, 136, 137, 138, 139–40, 142–44
Medical School (Keck School), 220–22, 231, 237, 242, 265–67, 269, 270, 271, 273, 275, 276, 279, 338
Office of Professionalism and Ethics (OPE), 278
School of Engineering (Viterbi School of Engineering), 123–24, 126–27, 131, 133, 146, 159, 163–67, 169–70, 172, 174, 175, 178, 180, 183, 185–86, 187, 452, 466
security, 284, 293–94, 297–99, 300, 308–309, 311
Seeley G. Mudd Estate, 327–28, 329, 333
Signal and Imaging Processing Institute (SIPI), 121
Tommy Trojan statue, 188, 218, 296, 317, 323, 363
Trojan Knights, 323
HSC (Health Sciences Campus), 202, 219, 223, 224, 226, 227, 228, 231, 234, 236, 238, 243, 246, 247, 274, 303, 329
Village, 303, 306, 308–314, 317, 321–22, 323–24, 361

Vail, CO, 104
Varsity Blues scandal, 363, 394
Venetians, 8
Vergina, Greece, 39
Villaraigosa, Antonio, 311–12
Virgil, 290, 462
visas, 80, 95, 96, 97
Viterbi, Andrew, 182, 183–85
Viterbi, Erna, 182

War, Department of, 116, 117, 460–61
Warminster, PA, 107
Washington, DC, 127, 140, 246, 289, 406, 438
Wayne, John, 19
Weiss, Karl, 115, 189
Weiss, Madeline, 115
Welch, Raquel, 30
Westchester, NY, 106
Whitaker Foundation, 113, 115
Widney, Robert Maclay, 335–36
Winthrop, John, 467
Wood, Zachary R., 441

Woods, Robert, 386
World War II, 18, 46, 50, 115, 460
World Wide Web, 130

Xenophon, 275, 466
Xinran Ji, 299–300

Yang, Debra, 278
Yaroslavsky, Zev, 236
Ying Wu, 291, 293
Yortsos, Yannis, 166, 167, 175, 176

Zemeckis, Robert, 259
Zumberge, James, 327, 350
Zumberge, Marilyn, 327